T0328994

Marx in the Anthropocene

Facing global climate crisis, Marx's ecological critique of capitalism more clearly demonstrates its importance than ever. *Marx in the Anthropocene* explains why Marx's ecology had to be marginalized, and even suppressed by Marxists after his death, throughout the 20th century. Marx's ecological critique of capitalism, however, revives in the Anthropocene against dominant productivism and monism. Investigating new materials published in the complete works of Marx and Engels (*Marx-Engels-Gesamtausgabe*), Kohei Saito offers a wholly novel idea of Marx's alternative to capitalism that should be adequately characterized as degrowth communism. This provocative interpretation of the late Marx sheds new light on recent debates on the relationship between society and nature and invites readers to envision a post-capitalist society without repeating the failure of the actually existing socialism of the 20th century.

Saito Kohei is an associate professor at the University of Tokyo. His book *Karl Marx's Ecosocialism: Capital, Nature and the Unfinished Critique of Political Economy* (2017) won the Deutscher Memorial Prize. His second book, *Hitoshinsei no Shihonron* [Capital in the Anthropocene] (2020), has sold over 500,000 copies in Japan and received the Asia Book Award, 2021.

Marx in the Anthropocene

Towards the Idea of
Degrowth Communism

Kohei Saito

CAMBRIDGE
UNIVERSITY PRESS

CAMBRIDGE
UNIVERSITY PRESS

University Printing House, Cambridge CB2 8BS, United Kingdom

One Liberty Plaza, 20th Floor, New York, NY 10006, USA

477 Williamstown Road, Port Melbourne, vic 3207, Australia

314 to 321, 3rd Floor, Plot No.3, Splendor Forum, Jasola District Centre, New Delhi 110025, India

103 Penang Road, #05–06/07, Visioncrest Commercial, Singapore 238467

Cambridge University Press is part of the University of Cambridge.

It furthers the University's mission by disseminating knowledge in the pursuit of education, learning and research at the highest international levels of excellence.

www.cambridge.org
Information on this title: www.cambridge.org/9781108844154

© Kohei Saito 2022

First published 2022

A catalogue record for this publication is available from the British Library

ISBN 978-1-108-84415-4 Hardback
ISBN 978-1-009-36618-2 Paperback

Cambridge University Press has no responsibility for the persistence or accuracy of URLs for external or third-party internet websites referred to in this publication, and does not guarantee that any content on such websites is, or will remain, accurate or appropriate.

For Teinosuke Otani

My teacher, devoted friend

Contents

Acknowledgements   ix

List of Abbreviations   xiii

Introduction   1

Part I   Marx's Ecological Critique of Capitalism and Its Oblivion

1. Marx's Theory of Metabolism in the Age of Global Ecological Crisis   13

2. The Intellectual Relationship between Marx and Engels Revisited
   from an Ecological Perspective   43

3. Lukács's Theory of Metabolism as the Foundation
   of Ecosocialist Realism   73

Part II   A Critique of Productive Forces in the Age of Global Ecological Crisis

4. Monism and the Non-identity of Nature   103

5. The Revival of Utopian Socialism and the Productive Forces of Capital   136

Part III   Towards Degrowth Communism

6. Marx as a Degrowth Communist: The *MEGA* and the
   Great Transformation after 1868   171

7. The Abundance of Wealth in Degrowth Communism   216

Conclusion   245

References   251
Index   268

Acknowledgements

While working towards the completion of this project since 2017, I have received generous assistance in various ways from scholars and friends all over the world. My approach to Marx's writings benefited immensely from my direct engagement with an ongoing project of new complete works of Marx and Engels, the *Marx-Engels-Gesamtausgabe*. I owe a great deal to my colleagues from the *Marx-Engels-Gesamtausgabe*, in particular Gerald Hubmann, Timm Graßmann, Regina Roth, Claudia Reichel, Jürgen Herres, Rolf Hecker and Carl-Erich Vollgraf in Berlin, Germany.

I also benefited from the JSPS Overseas Research Fellowship (2016–17), which enabled me to stay at the Department of Sociology at the University of California–Santa Barbara to conduct research with Kevin Anderson. His *Marx at the Margins* gave me indispensable inspiration for starting this book project. Ryuji Sasaki and Soichiro Sumida from Japan read and commented upon the entire manuscript. This time, again, they helped improve the logical consistency and clarity of the text. In addition, I have frequently discussed this project with my close colleagues Tomonaga Tairako, Makoto Itoh, Hideto Akashi, Kengo Nakamura and Midori Wakamori, who always provided me with immense encouragement and important suggestions. Patrick Eiden-Offe, Judith Dellheim and Terrell Carver also read and gave me invaluable comments on parts of the manuscript. Others offered comments in response to talks and papers presented at various conferences and lectures, especially Michael Heinrich, Frieder Otto Wolf, Christian Zeller, Bob Jessop, Babak Amini, Bini Adamczak, Kaan Kangal, Paula Rauhala, Joel Wainwright, Martin Wagner, Yibing Zhang, Ingo Stützle, Michael Löwy, Nick Srnicek, Michael Hardt, Paul Mason, Paul Burkett and John Bellamy Foster.

During the research, I had precious opportunities to attend various international conferences and seminars. Earlier versions of parts of this book have been presented at meetings of the Historical Materialism Conference (London), the Japan Society of Political Economy (Tokyo) and Marx-Collegium (Toronto). My deepest gratitude goes to Marcello Musto, who is a close collaborator on my important projects. I attended several key international conferences that he organized at York University (2017), ADRI in Patna, India (2018), and the University of Pisa (2019). Through these conferences, I had the opportunity to share my thoughts with other scholars and develop my ideas significantly. The publication of this book is an outcome of the support received from the Social Science and Humanities Research Council of Canada (SSHRC), Partnership Development Grant (890-2020-0091), 'The Global History of Karl Marx's *Capital*', which is also a collaborative project with Marcello Musto.

Vishwas Satgar and Michelle Williams at Witts University kindly invited me to Johannesburg for a week to give three lectures there in the summer of 2018. Leslie Esther and Alex Colas organized my visit to London to receive the Deutsche Memorial Prize awarded to my previous book *Karl Marx's Ecosocialism* (Monthly Review Press, 2017) and give other lectures and presentations in November 2018. I also want to thank Markus Gabriel and Sebastian Breu for organizing an international conference at the University of Bonn in June 2019, in which I presented the chapter on Georg Lukács. Sighard Neckel also invited me to an annual conference, 'Unsustainable Past – Sustainable Future?', at the University of Hamburg, which gave me an invaluable chance to discuss the relationship between Marxian economics and degrowth in the age of ecological crisis. In addition, the book is greatly indebted to Seongjing Jeong, who in 2018 kindly invited me to join a Korean research group for Social Science of Korea for 'Postcapitalism and the Innovation of Marxism' funded by the Ministry of Education of the Republic of Korea and the National Research Foundation of Korea (NRF-2021S1A3A2A02096299). International research with Korean scholars, including Sangwon Han, Seung-wook Baek, Hyun Kang Kim, Vladimir Tikhonov and Minzy Koh, helped widen the scope of the project. The research is also supported by the Japan Society for Promotion of Science (JSPS Kakenhi Grant Number JP20K13466).

Some of the main ideas were developed during the preparation of my previous book *Hitoshinsei no Shihonron* (*Capital in the Anthropocene*) (Tokyo: Shueisha, 2020), which turned out to be unexpectedly popular in Japan, selling half a million copies. I owe its great success to my editor Yuka Hattori, who devoted an enormous amount of time and energy to the book. Part of the current book can be regarded as a more rigorous and academic version of the Japanese book, and its clarity comes from her editorial assistance. Obviously, the current book is not a translation of the previous Japanese book. Rather, it builds on wholly new arguments with a more careful reading of materials and the reconstruction of key debates on Marxian ecology in recent years. Anwesha Rana from Cambridge

University Press patiently helped me in the preparation of the current book despite a significant delay in manuscript delivery due to the global pandemic in 2020–2022. I only hope the delay gave me more time to deepen my arguments. Special thanks go to Alexander Brown for his careful proofreading during the last stage of book production. Furthermore, Jacob Blumenfeld kindly helped me translate some German texts into English. All remaining errors are, however, my own.

I thank all publishers and editors for permission to draw on material from the following articles in the preparation of the indicated chapters. The content is significantly modified, enlarged and updated for the current book:

- Chapter 1, 'Marx's Theory of Metabolism in the Age of Global Ecological Crisis', *Historical Materialism* 28, no 2 (2020): 3–24.
- Chapter 2, 'Marx & Engels: The Intellectual Relationship Revisited from an Ecological Perspective', in *Marx's Capital after 150 Years Critique and Alternative to Capitalism*, ed. Marcello Musto (London: Routledge, 2020), 167–83.
- Chapter 7, 'Primitive Accumulation as the Cause of Economic and Ecological Disaster', in *Rethinking Alternatives with Marx*, ed. Marcello Musto (New York: Palgrave, 2021), 93–112.

Finally, it would have been impossible to complete the project without my family, Mao, Lichto and Lisa, who always supported and encouraged this project and gave me the passion to envision a better world in this dark time.

Abbreviations

Capital I	Karl Marx, *Capital*, vol. 1, trans. Ben Fowkes (London: Penguin, [1890] 1976).
Capital II	Karl Marx, *Capital*, vol. 2, trans. Ben Fowkes (London: Penguin, [1890] 1976).
Capital III	Karl Marx, *Capital*, vol. 3, trans. David Fernbach (London: Penguin, [1894] 1981).
Grundrisse	Karl Marx, *Grundrisse: Foundations of the Critique of Political Economy (Rough Draft)*, trans. Martin Nicolaus (London: Penguin, [1857–8] 1973).
IISG Sig B 91	Internationaale Instituut voor Sociale Geschiedenis, Karl Marx – Friedrich Engels Papers, Teil B Exzerpte von Karl Marx, Nr. 91.
MECW 12	Karl Marx and Frederich Engels, *Collected Works*, vol. 12 (New York: International Publishers, 1975–2004).
MEGA II/10	Karl Marx and Frederich Engels, *Marx-Engels-Gesamtausgabe*, section II, volume 10 (Berlin: Dietz Verlag, Akademie Verlag, De Gruyter, 1975–).
MEW 1	Karl Marx and Friedrich Engels, *Werke*, vol. 1 (Berlin: Dietz Verlag, 1956–68).

Introduction

The world is on fire. We are experiencing 'the end of the end of history' (Hochuli, Hoare and Cunliffe 2021). With the rapid deepening of the global ecological crisis in various forms such as climate change, oxidation of the ocean, disruption of the nitrogen cycle, desertification, soil erosion and loss of biodiversity, Francis Fukuyama's declaration of 'the end of history' after the collapse of the USSR (Union of Soviet Socialist Republics) (Fukuyama 1992) is approaching a totally unexpected dead end today, namely *the end of human history*. In fact, the triumph of neoliberal globalization only accelerated the rapid increase in environmental impacts upon the earth by human activities since the end of the Second World War – the so called 'Great Acceleration', the age in which all major socio-economic and Earth system trends record a hockey stick pattern of increase (McNeil and Engelke 2016) – and ultimately destabilized the foundation of human civilization. Pandemic, war and climate breakdown are all symptomatic of 'the end of history', putting democracy, capitalism and ecological systems into chronic crisis.

Many people are well aware of the fact that the current mode of living is heading towards catastrophe, but the capitalist system does not offer an alternative to the juggernaut of overproduction and overconsumption. Nor is there any compelling reason to believe that it will soon do so because capitalism's systemic compulsion continues to employ fossil fuel consumption *despite* consistent warnings, knowledge and opposition. Considering the fact that rapid, deep decarbonization that could meet the 1.5-degree-Celsius target of the Paris Agreement requires thorough transformative changes in virtually every sphere of society, more radical social movements embracing direct action have emerged, demanding to uproot the capitalist system

(Extinction Rebellion 2019). In this context, when Greta Thunberg denounced the 'fairy tales of eternal growth' in a speech, she made it explicit that the capitalist system that aims for infinite accumulation on a finite planet is the root cause of climate breakdown.

This represents a new historical situation, especially to Marxism that has been treated like 'a dead dog' after the collapse of actually existing socialism. As environmentalists learn to unequivocally problematize the irrationality of the current economic system, Marxism now has a chance of revival if it can contribute to enriching debates and social movements by providing not only a thorough critique of the capitalist mode of production but also a concrete vision of post-capitalist society. However, this revival has not taken place so far, and persistent doubts remain about the usefulness of having recourse to the Marxian legacy in the 21st century. Marx's political optimism most plainly expressed in *The Communist Manifesto* has been repeatedly cited as evidence of his notorious and unacceptable productivism and ethnocentrism.

It is surely too naïve to believe that the further development of productive forces in Western capitalism could function as an emancipatory driver of history in the face of the global ecological crisis. In fact, the situation today differs decisively compared with that of 1848: capitalism is no longer progressive. It rather destroys the general conditions of production and reproduction and even subjects human and non-human beings to serious existential threat. In short, Marx's view of historical progress appears hopelessly outdated. In this situation, if there is a slight hope of a revival of Marxism in this historical conjuncture, its essential precondition is the radical reformulation of its infamous grand scheme of 'historical materialism' that pivots around the contradiction between 'productive forces' and 'relations of production'. This constitutes the central topics of this book in order not to end (human) history but to envision another clear, bright future from a Marxian perspective without falling into pessimism and apocalypticism in the face of global ecological crisis.

Such a project cannot avoid the problem of 'nature'. This is all the more so because the end of the 'end of history' brought about the end of the 'end of nature'. Bill McKibben (1989) once warned that the idea of nature that the modern world presupposed for a long time is gone for good because global capitalism considerably modified the entire planet, leaving no pristine nature untouched.[1] This situation is now generally called *the Anthropocene,* in which humankind has become a 'major geological force' (Crutzen and Stroermer 2000: 18) with massive scientific and technological power capable of transforming the entire planet on an unprecedented scale.[2]

The reality of the Anthropocene is, however, far from realizing the modern dream of human emancipation through the domination of nature.

Climate change accompanied by sea-level rise, wildfires, heatwaves and change of precipitation patterns shows how the 'end of nature' dialectically turns into the 'return of nature' (Foster 2020); the earth and its limits are more and more tangible in such a way that humans can no longer control nature's power. It even subjugates them as an independent and alien force. In other words, the modern Baconian project is collapsing. Confronted with this increasing uncontrollability of nature, various critical theories of nature including eco-Marxism take up the urgent task of rethinking the relationship between humanity and nature (Rosa, Henning and Bueno 2021). However, the dominant narrative of the Anthropocene is a *monist* approach characterized by the hybridity of the social and the natural (Latour 2014; Moore 2015), which is *critical* of Marxism. In contrast, the current project aims to enrich the debate concerning the human–nature relationship by putting forward Marx's *dualist* methodology based on his theory of metabolism.

This theoretical task has important practical implications today. By comprehending Marx's method correctly, we can also recognize the unique contribution his work offers to recent debates on post-capitalism. And here is the third 'end' of post–Cold War values, that is, 'the end of capitalist realism'. Mark Fisher (2009) once lamented that 'capitalist realism' – the sense that 'it is easier … to imagine the end of the world than of capitalism' (Jameson 2016: 3) – severely constrains our political imagination, subjugating us to the regime of capital. The same tendency is discernible in environmentalism: 'It is easier to imagine a total catastrophe which ends all life on earth than it is to imagine a real change in capitalist relations' (Žižek 2008: 334). However, as the multi-stranded crises of economy, democracy, care and the environment deepen, the tendency of which was strengthened even more by the COVID-19 pandemic and the Russo-Ukrainian War, there are growing calls for radical 'system change'. Both Slavoj Žižek (2020a) and Andreas Malm (2020) argue for 'war communism', while John Bellamy Foster (2020) and Michael Löwy (2015) defend the idea of 'ecosocialism'.

In addition, there are intensive discussions on 'life after capitalism' (Jackson 2021) even among non-Marxist scholars. Thomas Piketty's (2021) dictum that it is 'time for socialism' is exemplary here, but a more ecological version of the same argument can be found in Naomi Klein's explicit endorsement of the idea of 'ecosocialism':

> Let's acknowledge this fact [that the Soviet Union and Venezuela are unecological], while also pointing out that countries with a strong democratic socialist tradition – like Denmark, Sweden, and Uruguay – have some of the most visionary environmental policies in the world. From this we can conclude that socialism isn't necessarily ecological, but

that a new form of *democratic eco-socialism*, with the humility to learn from Indigenous teachings about the duties to future generations and the interconnection of all of life, appears to be humanity's best shot at collective survival. (Klein 2019: 251; emphasis added)[3]

This is a remarkable shift, considering the fact that Klein is not a Marxist. Once Ellen Meiksins Wood (1995: 266) argued that 'the issues of peace and ecology are not very well suited to generating strong anti-capitalist forces. In a sense, the problem is their very universality. They do not constitute social forces because they simply have no specific social identity.' Today's situation concerning ecology looks quite different from Wood's time precisely because the planetary crisis provides a material basis for constituting a universal political subjectivity *against* capital. This is because capital is creating a globalized 'environmental proletariat' (Foster, York and Clark 2010: 47) whose living conditions are severely undermined by capital accumulation.

Inspired by these recent attempts to foster imagination and creativity for a more free, egalitarian and sustainable life, I draw upon Marx's theory in order to put forward a wholly new Marxian vision of post-scarcity society adequate to the Anthropocene. Such a revival of Marx's ecological vision of post-capitalism aims to enrich the discursive constellation around the Anthropocene, connecting this new geological concept to the contemporary issues of political economy, democracy and justice beyond the Earth sciences.

This new ecosocialist project for the Anthropocene is also supported by recent philological findings, thanks to materials published for the first time in the *Marx-Engels-Gesamtausgabe* (*MEGA*). The *MEGA* publishes in its fourth section Marx's notebooks on the natural sciences, and the scope of Marx's ecological interests proves to be much more extensive than previously assumed (Saito 2017). Although these notebooks were neglected even by researchers for quite a long time, recent studies demonstrate that through his research in geology, botany and agricultural chemistry, Marx intended to analyse various practices of robbery closely tied to climate change, the exhaustion of natural resources (soil nutrients, fossil fuel and woods) as well as the extinction of species due to the capitalist system of industrial production.

Consequently, ecological aspects of Marx's critique of political economy have become one of the central fields for revitalising the Marxian legacy in the Anthropocene. His concept of 'metabolic rift', in particular, has come to function as an indispensable conceptual tool for the ecological critique of contemporary capitalism (Foster, York and Clark 2010; Foster and Burkett 2016). This concept substantiates Marx's critique of the destructive side of capitalist production by demonstrating that it can be applied to contemporary ecological issues such as global warming, soil erosion, aquaculture, the livestock business and the disruption of the nitrogen cycle (B. Clark 2002; Clark and

York 2005; Longo, Clausen and Clark 2015; Holleman 2018).[4] Part I of the current book develops the metabolic rift approach further as the theoretical and methodological foundation of Marxian political ecology. In addition to Marx, Part I enriches Marxian ecology by dealing with Friedrich Engels, Rosa Luxemburg, Lukács György and István Mészáros, because their texts help comprehend the theoretical scope of the marginalized concept of 'metabolism' in Marxism.

However, this project is not simply about how to understand Marx's concept of metabolism more *correctly*. The task of developing Marxian ecology based on the concept of metabolic rift is worth carrying out as it has a practical relevance: different approaches to the ecological crisis will provide different solutions to it. In this context, it is noteworthy that 'post-Marxist' attempts to conceptualize the human–nature relationship in the Anthropocene *against* the concept of 'metabolic rift' have emerged. They are committed to philosophical monism. The proponents of the monist view problematize an 'ontological dualism' of Marxism (Castree 2013: 177) that they claim fails to adequately understand the ontological status of nature in the Anthropocene. Since capitalism thoroughly reconstructs the entire environment, nature as such does not exist, but is 'produced' through capitalist development. Monists, transcending ontological binarism, insist on replacing it with relational thinking: everything is a 'hybrid' of nature and society. Jason W. Moore (2015) in particular directs this critique against the concept of 'metabolic rift', claiming that it falls into the Cartesian dualism of 'Society' and 'Nature'. He instead puts forward a relational understanding of human–nature metabolism.

Yet monism once again revives a failed Prometheanism for the Anthropocene, justifying the ever-increasing intervention in nature. Such a 'geo-constructivist' approach maintains that there is already too much human intervention in nature in the Anthropocene (Neyrat 2019). Therefore, any attempt to stop the intervention in fear of environmental destruction is irresponsible and disastrous because the process is irreversible. According to the geo-constructivist approach, the only way forward is 'stewardship' of the earth by remaking the whole planet in order to secure human existence in the future, if not human emancipation. This revival of the Promethean project is sneaking into Marxist efforts to renew their vision of a post-capitalist future (Mason 2015; Srnicek and Williams 2016; Bastani 2019). In this context, Part II of this book offers a reply to various monist and Promethean currents in the Anthropocene through the lens of Marx's methodological dualism.

After critically examining the theoretical limitations of both monist and Promethean views, Part III elaborates on Marx's ecological vision of a post-capitalist society in a non-productivist manner. Using the new insights offered by the *MEGA*, it demonstrates that through interdisciplinary research in the natural sciences, humanities and social sciences, the late Marx experienced a theoretical breakthrough – *coupure épistémologique* in an Althusserian sense (Althusser 2005) – after 1868. His last vision of post-capitalism in the 1880s went *beyond* ecosocialism, and it can be more adequately characterized as *degrowth communism*. This previously unknown idea of degrowth communism begets useful insights to transcend persistent 'capitalist realism'. While there is growing interest in radical approaches today, it is not sufficient simply to develop an ecosocialist critique of contemporary capitalism. Only by going back to Marx's own texts is it possible to offer a positive vision of a future society for the Anthropocene. Such a radical transformation must be the new beginning of history as the age of degrowth communism.

However, if Marx really did propose degrowth communism, why has no one pointed it out in the past, and why did Marxism endorse productivist socialism? One simple reason is that Marx's ecology was ignored for a long time. It is thus first necessary to trace back the moment of its suppression. This genealogy of (suppressed) Marxian ecology starts with Marx himself. Referring to Marx's notebooks on the natural sciences that are published in the *MEGA*, Chapter 1 establishes Marx's concept of 'metabolic rift' by highlighting the three dimensions of the ecological rifts and their spatiotemporal 'shifts' mediated by technologies on a global scale. This original insight into capital's constant expropriation of nature as the root cause of the metabolic rift was deepened by Rosa Luxemburg in *The Accumulation of Capital*, which problematized the main 'contradiction' of capitalism due to its destructive impacts upon the people and environment in non-capitalist peripheries.

Although she employed the concept of 'metabolism', Luxemburg formulated it as a *critique* of Marx's narrow view of capital accumulation. Her critique implies that Marx's concept of metabolism was not properly understood even at that time. This misunderstanding was inevitable because many of Marx's writings were unpublished and unavailable to Luxemburg. Yet this problem also originates in Engels's attempt to establish 'Marxism' as a systematic worldview for the proletariat. In order to trace the original deformation of Marx's concept of metabolism, Chapter 2 reconstructs Engels's reception of Marx's theory of metabolism by carefully comparing Engels's editorial work on *Capital* with Marx's original economic manuscripts as well as their notebooks published in the *MEGA*. This investigation reveals subtle but decisive theoretical differences between Marx and Engels, especially in terms of their treatment of metabolism. These differences prevented Engels from adequately appreciating Marx's theory of metabolic rift, so the concept of metabolism came to be marginalized in Marxism.

This marginalization is clearly documented in the historical formation and development of Western Marxism in the 1920s, which further diverged from Marx's original insight into metabolism and his methodology. Here the problem of the intellectual relationship between Marx and Engels came to have a significant influence because it determined the entire paradigm of Western Marxism. Famously enough, Western Marxism highlighted the rigorous differentiation of Marx and Engels, accusing the latter's illegitimate extension of dialectics to the sphere of nature as a cause of Soviet Marxism's mechanistic social analysis. However, despite their harsh critique of Engels, Western Marxists shared the fundamental assumption with Soviet orthodox Marxism that Marx had little to say about nature, thereby neglecting the importance of his concept of metabolism and his ecological critique of capitalism.

As discussed in Chapter 3, the founder of Western Marxism, Lukács György, is an exceptional figure in that he clearly paid attention to this concept of metabolism. Although his critique of Engels's treatment of nature in *History and Class Consciousness* had an immense impact on Western Marxism, he actually had a different approach to the problem of nature that was formulated as part of his theory of metabolism in his unpublished manuscript of 1925–6 titled *Tailism and the Dialectic*. This manuscript was unknown for a long time, so Lukács's intention in *History and Class Consciousness* was not properly understood, and he was repeatedly criticized for various theoretical inconsistencies and ambivalences. However, looking at *Tailism and the Dialectic*, it becomes clear that his treatment of the relationship between humans and nature shows a continuity with Marx's own dualist methodology that analytically distinguished between the social and the natural. With this methodology, Lukács's theory of metabolism provides a way of developing Marx's 'non-Cartesian' dualism of *Form* and *Matter* as a critique of modern capitalist production. Nevertheless, his unique insight was suppressed by both orthodox Marxism and Western Marxism, leading to the marginalization of Marxian ecology throughout the 20th century.

Since Marx's dualist method is not correctly understood, the concept of metabolic rift continues to be exposed to various criticisms. Chapter 4 deals with Marxist versions of the monist view represented by Jason W. Moore's 'world ecology' as well as by Neil Smith's and Noel Castree's 'production of nature'. Despite their obvious theoretical differences, their monist understanding of capitalism shows how misunderstanding Marx's method generates problematic consequences that have practical relevancy.

As discussed in Chapter 5, the failure to understand Marx's method also results in the recent revival of the Promethean idea among Marxists. These utopian Marxists draw upon Marx's *Grundrisse* and argue that a third industrial revolution based on information technology (for example, artificial intelligence [AI], sharing economy and Internet of things [IoT]) combined with full automation could liberate humans from the drudgery of work and make the capitalist system of value obsolete. Despite their celebration of dream technologies of the future, the old Prometheanism remains. In order to decisively abandon Prometheanism, it is necessary to focus on Marx's concept of 'real subsumption' in the 1860s – that is, not in the *Grundrisse* written in the 1850s. Doing so reveals that Marx's critique of 'productive forces of capital' in *Capital* represents a major shift in his view of technological progress under capitalism. Marx came to realize that the capitalist development of technologies does *not* necessarily prepare a material foundation for post-capitalism.

However, his rejection of his earlier naïve endorsement of technological development posed a series of new difficulties for Marx. Once he started to question the progressive role of increasing productive forces under capitalism, he was inevitably compelled to challenge his own earlier progressive view of history. Chapter 6 reconstructs this process of self-critique in the late Marx. Only by paying attention to Marx's theoretical crisis does it become clear why he had to simultaneously study the natural sciences *and* pre-capitalist societies while attempting to complete the subsequent volume of *Capital*. By intensively studying these theoretical fields, Marx ultimately went through another paradigm shift after 1868. It is from this perspective that Marx's letter to Vera Zasulich sent in 1881 needs to be reinterpreted as the crystallization of his non-productivist and non-Eurocentric view of the future society, which should be characterized as degrowth communism.

This conclusion must be surprising to many. No one has previously proposed such a vision of Marx's post-capitalism. Furthermore, degrowth economics and Marxism have had an antagonistic relationship for a long time. However, if the late Marx accepted the idea of a steady-state economy for the sake of a radically equal and sustainable society, there will be a new space of dialogue between them. In order to start such a new dialogue in a fruitful manner, the final chapter will revisit *Capital* and other writings and reread various passages from the perspective of degrowth communism. In a word, Chapter 7 aims at the reinterpretation of *Capital* as an attempt to go beyond *Capital*. It will offer a fresh reading of some key passages which would otherwise turn into a naïve endorsement of productivism. Most notably, the radical abundance of 'communal/common wealth' (*genossenschaftlicher Reichtum*) in the *Critique of the Gotha Programme* signifies a non-consumerist way of life in a post-scarcity economy which realizes a safe and just society in the face of global ecological crisis in the Anthropocene.

NOTES

1   Bill McKibben does not necessarily deny that pristine nature did not exist even before the 1990s. He instead highlights that the 'idea' of nature as independent from human intervention can no longer be accepted as a valid conceptual tool due to the increasing human impacts upon nature. This situation has to do with the recent popularity of monist approaches, as discussed in Chapter 4, although McKibben does not participate in these debates.

2   Eugene F. Stoermer already used the term 'Anthropocene' in the 1980s, although he employed it in a different sense. A Russian geochemist, Vladimir I. Vernadsky developed the concept of 'biosphere' in the 1920s in order to highlight human impacts upon the biological life on a planetary scale, which has relevance to today's discussion of the Anthropocene (Vernadsky [1926] 1997; Steffen et al. 2011: 844).

3   Naomi Klein (2020) continues to argue for 'democratic socialism' in her more recent book too. Thomas Piketty (2020) also advocates for 'participatory socialism' not only for the sake of social equality but also for sustainability in the face of climate change. Their endorsement of 'socialism' represents a major shift in the general political tone towards the left.

4   Other recent literature on the metabolic rift approach includes Moore (2000, 2002), Mancus (2007), McMichael (2008), Gunderson (2011) and Weston (2014).

PART I

MARX'S ECOLOGICAL CRITIQUE OF CAPITALISM AND ITS OBLIVION

PART I

MARX'S SOCIOLOGICAL CRITIQUE OF
CAPITALISM AND ITS CRITICISM

1

Marx's Theory of Metabolism in the Age of Global Ecological Crisis*

For quite a long time, Marx's interest in ecological issues was neglected even among serious Marxist scholars. Marx's socialism was said to be characterized by a 'Promethean' (pro-technological, anti-ecological) advocacy for the domination of nature. Marxists, on the one hand, reinforced this impression by negatively reacting to environmentalism, which they believed to be inherently anti-working class and only functioning as an ideology of the upper middle class. On the other hand, the environmental catastrophe in the USSR – most notably represented by the ecological collapse of the Aral Sea and the Chernobyl disaster – reinforced the conviction among environmentalists that socialism cannot establish a sustainable society. As a consequence, there emerged a long-standing antagonism between the Red and the Green in the second half of the 20th century.

The situation is changing in the 21st century. No matter how devastating actually existing socialism was to the environment, its collapse and the triumph of capitalism has only contributed to further ecological degradation under neoliberal globalization in the last few decades. The ineffectiveness of conventional market-based solutions to ecological issues resulted in a renewed interest in more heterodox approaches including Marxian economics (Burkett 2006). At the same time, the collapse of the USSR and the declining influence

---

*This chapter draws on material from 'Marx's Theory of Metabolism in the Age of Global Ecological Crisis', *Historical Materialism* 28, no. 2 (2020): 3–24. Published with permission. The content is significantly modified, enlarged and updated for the current book.

of the past dogmas of orthodox Marxism 'open up an intellectual horizon and a field of reflection, where theoretical and conceptual issues could be discussed without being foreclosed by party-line polemics or divisive political loyalties' (Therborn 2009: 90). This situation both within and without Marxism led to the 'rediscovery' of Marx's ecology in the last two decades (I).

It was Istvan Mészáros's theory of 'social metabolism' that paved the solid path to this rediscovery. By investigating Mészáros's theory of metabolism, mainly developed in *Beyond Capital* and *The Necessity of Social Control*, Marx's ecological theory of 'metabolic rift' can be more firmly founded upon his critique of political economy (II). This clarification helps classify the three different dimensions of 'metabolic rift' in Marx's *Capital* (III). Correspondingly, there are three dimensions of *shifting* the ecological rift, which is why capital proves so elastic and resilient in the face of economic and ecological crises. However, these 'metabolic shifts' never solve the deep contradictions of capitalist accumulation. Rather, they only create new crises, intensifying the contradictions on a wider scale (IV). This is what Rosa Luxemburg problematized in *The Accumulation of Capital* (1913), in which she applied the Marxian concept of 'metabolism' to the analysis of global unequal exchange under capitalism. Despite her intention in introducing the concept to *criticize* Marx, her usage is actually compatible with Marx's understanding of the metabolic rift. Her critique is worth discussing here because it indicates that the problematic reception of Marx's theory of metabolism was already taking place in the beginning of the 20th century, leading to its subsequent neglect (V).

I
THE SUPPRESSION OF MARX'S IDEA OF ECOSOCIALISM

Since the 1970s, Marx was repeatedly accused of a naïve 'Promethean attitude' (Giddens 1981: 60): 'Marx's attitude toward the world always retained that Promethean thrust, glorifying the human conquest of nature' (Ferkiss 1993: 108). Even self-proclaimed Marxists admitted this flaw. For instance, Leszek Kołakowski (1978: 412) maintained that 'a typical feature of Marx's Prometheanism is his lack of interest in the natural'. According to critics, Marx's productivist view ignored the problem of natural limits and naively praised the free manipulation of nature: Marx was 'largely uncritical of the industrial system of technology and the project of human domination of nature' (J. Clark 1984: 27). They problematized Marx's optimistic assumption, inherent to his 'historical materialism', that the development of the productive forces under capitalism should be sufficient to provide a material basis for human emancipation. Due to the environmental degradation that occurred under actually existing socialism, environmentalists felt justified in denouncing that such 'a "productivist" "Promethean" view of history' as completely unacceptable (Benton 1989: 82).[1] The collapse of the USSR only multiplied critical voices against Marx's unecological view (Lipietz 2000).[2]

The image of Marx's productivism remains widespread even today. Fredric Jameson (2011: 150) points to 'Marx's own passionate commitment to a streamlined technological future'. While Jameson is rather affirmative of such a commitment, Axel Honneth (2017: 45) criticizes the limitation of Marxism in that one of the inherent ideas of Marxism is 'technological determinism' that supposes the linear progress of productive forces for the sake of 'domination of nature' (*Naturbeherrschung*). According to such a view, it is inevitable for Marxism that the question of ecology has been marginalized. As Nancy Fraser (2014: 56) maintains, '[Marx's thought] fails to reckon systematically with gender, ecology and political power as structuring principles and axes of inequality in capitalist societies – let alone as stakes and premises of social struggle.' Sven-Eric Liedman (2017: 480) concludes more explicitly that Marx was *not* an 'ecologically conscious person in the modern sense'.[3]

Fortunately, that is not the whole story. On the contrary, it is not an exaggeration to say that one of the most important developments in Marxian scholarship after the collapse of actually existing socialism in Eastern Europe is the 'rediscovery' of Marx's ecological critique of capitalism initiated by Paul Burkett (1999) and John Bellamy Foster (2000) in the *Monthly Review* as well as James O'Connor (1998), Joel Kovel (2007) and Michael Löwy (2015) in *Capitalism Nature Socialism*. Despite the tense relationship between the two journals due to theoretical differences that pivot around the concepts of 'metabolic rift' and the 'second contradiction of capitalism' respectively, they both demonstrated convincingly that a Marxian approach is useful to comprehend the ecological crisis as the manifestation of systemic contradictions of the capitalist mode of production.[4]

In particular, Foster and Burkett clearly show that Marx was an 'ecologically conscious person in the modern sense'. Carefully analysing Marx's research in the field of natural sciences – especially through a careful examination of Marx's reception of Justus von Liebig's theory of the robbery system of agriculture (*Raubbau*) in his *Agricultural Chemistry* (1862) – Foster and Burkett revealed the importance of Marx's theory of 'metabolism' (*Stoffwechsel*).[5] Based on this concept of metabolism, Foster (2000) explicates that Marx not only regarded the 'metabolic rifts' under capitalism as the inevitable consequence of the fatal distortion in the relationship between humans and nature but also highlighted the need for a qualitative transformation in social production in order to repair the deep chasm in the universal metabolism of nature. Since ecology proves to be an integral part of Marx's critique of political economy, his vision of post-capitalist society is reinterpreted as 'ecosocialism' (Pepper

2002; Brownhill et al. 2022). Soon the concept of 'metabolism' came to be regarded as a 'conceptual star' (Fischer-Kowalski 1997: 122) as it gave hope that this new idea of 'ecosocialism' might be possible to overcome the long-time antagonistic relationship between Red and Green.

Today, at least the existence of Marx's ecology – its usefulness and scientific validity put aside for now – retrospectively appears so obvious that one may wonder why it was neglected for such a long time. Here one can point to one reason.[6] The neglect of Marx's ecology has to do with the unfinished character of his critique of political economy. It is well known that Marx did not publish volumes II and III of *Capital* during his lifetime. After Marx's death, Engels edited and published them in 1885 and 1894, respectively, based on various manuscripts written at different times. Notwithstanding, Marxist scholars simply took Engels's edition of *Capital* to be the definitive version that truly reflected Marx's own views. It did not occur to them that Marx, especially in his later years, quite intensively studied the natural sciences and left behind a large number of notebooks consisting of various excerpts and comments related to environmental issues. Although Marx began this new research after the publication of volume I of *Capital*, he barely published after 1868 and could nowhere elaborate on the results of his new research. Inevitably, it was in these notebooks where Marx's ecological insights are documented, but until their recent publication they remained neglected in the archive and unpublished throughout the course of the 20th century (Saito 2017; *MEGA* IV/18).

In fact, few scholars were interested in studying these notebooks. David Riazanov, who was the founder of the Marx–Engels Institute in Moscow in the 1920s and the chief editor of the first *Marx-Engels-Gesamtausgabe* (*MEGA¹*), negatively commented on Marx's later engagement with the natural sciences, dismissing the importance of the notebooks for understanding his critique of political economy:

> If in 1881–82 he lost his ability for intensive, independent, intellectual creation, he nevertheless never lost the ability for research. Sometimes, in reconsidering these Notebooks, the question arises: Why did he waste so much time on this systematic, fundamental summary, or expend so much labour as he spent as late as the year 1881, on one basic book on geology, summarizing it chapter by chapter. In the 63rd year of his life – that is inexcusable pedantry. (Quoted in K. Anderson 2010: 249)

Such a dismissive attitude towards the late Marx only contributed to the widespread neglect of Marx's interest in ecological issues. Some leading ecosocialists thus argue that Marxian ecology 'extrapolates the ecological in Marx from brief and vague excursions in texts addressing subjects other than ecological dynamics' (Engel-Di Mauro 2014: 137).[7] However, the new complete works of Marx and Engels, the new *Marx-Engels-Gesamtausgabe* (*MEGA²*), have been publishing those new materials that document how Marx in his later years developed his ecological critique of capitalism.[8] The *MEGA* substantiates the claims made by a group of eco-Marxists, including myself, that Marx's theory of metabolism is the central pillar of his ecosocialist critique of capitalism.

II
THE REDISCOVERY OF MARXIAN ECOLOGY

Retrospectively, the Hungarian Marxist István Mészáros made a great contribution to properly comprehending Marx's concept of metabolism as the foundation of his political economy. It is no coincidence that Mészáros also discussed environmental issues under capitalism already in the 1970s. The foregrounding of Marx's ecology in *Beyond Capital* (Mészáros 1995) should be seen as the culmination of Mészáros's long-standing engagement with Marx's concept of metabolism.

In 1971, Mészáros began the first Deutscher Prize Memorial Lecture by referring to Isaac Deutscher's warning about the prospect of nuclear war that 'threatens our biological existence' (Deutscher 1967: 110). He went on to extend Deutscher's warning to another contemporary existential crisis for the 'whole of mankind' – that is, ecological destruction under capitalism. Mészáros's claim was provisional as it was made even before the publication of *The Limits to Growth* by the Club of Rome in 1972. He formulated the ecologically destructive nature of capitalist development as the 'basic contradiction' of capitalism as follows:

> [The] basic contradiction of the capitalist system of control is that it cannot separate 'advance' from destruction, nor 'progress' from waste – however catastrophic the results. The more it unlocks the powers of productivity, the more it must unleash the powers of destruction; and the more it extends the volume of production, the more it must bury everything under mountains of suffocating waste. (Mészáros [1972] 2014: 49–50)

Here Mészáros explicitly differentiated himself from the orthodox Marxism of his time, which was characterized by a naïve endorsement of the development of productive forces under capitalism as a progressive drive in human history. He warned that the wasteful and destructive system of production for the sake of endless capital accumulation would not bring about human emancipation but inevitably undermine the material conditions for the prosperity of society in the long run.

Since the earth is finite, it is obvious that there are absolute biophysical limits to capital accumulation.[9] Despite knowing this, capital is incapable of limiting itself. On the contrary, capital constantly attempts to overcome these limits only to increase its own destructiveness against society and nature. Hence arises the 'necessity of social control' to put an end to the wasteful and destructive tendency of capitalist development for the sake of human survival and preservation of the natural environment. Such social planning of production is, however, incompatible with the basic logic of capitalist production. Mészáros thus demanded a qualitatively different organization of social production by freely associated producers.

Fifteen years later, in *Philosophy, Ideology and Social Science* (1986), Mészáros formulated this issue of degradation and destruction of nature by capital with the concept of metabolism for the first time, highlighting its importance 'to all serious theory of ecology'. According to him, the ultimate problem lies in 'capital's *necessary* inability to make the real distinction between the safely transcendable and the absolute, since it must assert – irrespective of the consequences – its own, historically specific, requirements as absolute ones, following the blind dictates of self-expanding exchange-value' (Mészáros 1986: 195). Conflating its historical necessity with 'natural necessity', capital cannot recognize the true meaning of 'natural necessity', which consists of the *elementary* requirements of production confined by the universal metabolism of nature. It instead behaves as if even these absolute natural limits are transcendable – some might be actually transcendable with the aid of science and technology but obviously not all – and aims to subjugate them for the sake of its further valorization, leading to the 'degradation and ultimate destruction of nature' (Mészáros 1986: 183). Since capital cannot recognize absolute limits, a 'conscious *recognition* of the existing barriers' as the condition of the universal development of the individual is a revolutionary act. This anti-Promethean insight into the limit to growth marks an important step to the fusion of environmentalism and socialism.

Yet it is with *Beyond Capital* (1995) that Mészáros changed the whole discursive constellation around Marx's ecology by elaborating on this concept of metabolism much more systematically.[10] Mészáros focused on Marx's concept of 'social metabolism' in order to analyse the capitalist mode of production as a historically unique way of (re)organizing the transhistorical metabolic interaction between humans and nature on an unprecedented scale. He intentionally highlighted the concept as an anti-thesis to the narrow focus of traditional Marxism on the theory of surplus value as a disclosure of the exploitation of the working class by the capitalist. Instead Mészáros intended to expand the theoretical scope of a critique of capitalism *outside* factories. In fact, Marx characterized 'a process of social metabolism' as a flow of commodities and money through which the 'product of one kind of useful labour replaces that of another' (*Capital* I: 198). Mészáros, following this insight of Marx, advocated for a much more holistic and integral approach to the historical dynamics of social production and reproduction under capitalism.

Although its importance is still often underestimated, the concept of metabolism is essential for Marx's *Capital*. Marx defined 'labour', the most fundamental category of Marxism, in relation to the metabolism between humans and nature: 'Labour is, first of all, a process between man and nature, a process by which man, through his own actions, mediates, regulates and controls the metabolism between himself and nature' (*Capital* I: 283). This metabolic process is, first of all, a natural-ecological process, which is common to any historical stage, because humans cannot live without working upon nature through labour: 'It is the universal condition for the metabolism [*Stoffwechsel*] between man and nature, the everlasting nature-imposed condition of human existence, and it is therefore independent of every form of that existence, or rather it is common to all forms of society in which human beings live' (*Capital* I: 290). Humans can never escape from being a part of the 'universal metabolism of nature' (*MECW* 30: 63). This also means that humans cannot produce *ex nihilo* but always *ex materia*. Food, clothes, houses and even the most high-tech goods that 'dematerialize' the economy use energy and natural resources without exception. In this sense, human metabolism with nature is a 'natural necessity' that can never be suspended. This is why Marx wrote that labour works upon 'a material substratum' that exists without human intervention, and human labour 'can only change the form of the materials' (*Capital* I: 133).[11]

Furthermore, humans are dependent upon nature. Marx highlighted that both labour and nature play essential roles in the labour process: 'Labour is therefore not the only source of material wealth, i.e. of the use-values it produces. As William Petty says, labour is the father of material wealth, the earth is its mother' (*Capital* I: 134).[12] Humans can work upon, consume and discard nature, but their activities are constrained by natural laws and various biophysical processes of the universal metabolism of nature. According to Mészáros (1995: 138), this unceasing interaction constitutes the 'primary' level of the universal metabolic process between humans and nature, 'without which humanity could not possibly survive even in the most ideal form of society'.

On a more concrete level, the exact ways humans carry out their metabolism with the external environment differ significantly depending on the given objective natural condition such as climate, location, and availability and accessibility of resources and energy. These dimensions of the primary level of metabolism have to do with the natural substratum, which remains as a 'historical absolute' with its force: 'For no matter to what degree this natural substratum might (indeed must) be modified by ongoing human productive development, in the course the historical creation of "new needs" and the corresponding extension of the conditions of their satisfaction, ultimately it always remains firmly circumscribed by nature itself' (Mészáros 2012: 246). Similarly, Kate Soper (1995: 132) argues that 'those material structures and processes that are independent of human activity (in the sense that they are not a humanly created product), and whose forces and causal powers are the necessary conditions of every human practice, and determine the possible forms it can take'. The objective existence of nature independently of humans characterizes the basic insight of materialism.

Humans are, however, not simply confined by the given environment. They can reflect upon their own interaction with it. They can design tools to produce more efficiently, improve the quality of products, discover new materials and even invent totally new objects according to their needs. This is the unique character of human labour compared with other animals. As productive forces historically develop in this way, the objective conditions of production change greatly through human history. Notwithstanding this, the primary material condition remains throughout and cannot be abolished. The plasticity of nature does not negate its characteristic as a natural substratum of labour. If humans ignore the natural substratum, such violation of natural law causes multiple ecological contradictions such as pollution, resource scarcity and exhaustion.

At the same time, Marx cautioned that such a general description of the labour process can turn into a banal statement that humans are a part of nature and need to live with nature. While incessant metabolism is a transhistorical condition of survival that remains valid as long as humans live and work on the earth, Marx pointed out that this way of 'treating of the general preconditions of all production' is hammered out into 'flat tautologies', which 'indicate nothing more than the essential moments of all production' (*Grundrisse*: 86). The uniqueness of his economic analysis is rather his recognition that labour is always carried out under a certain set of social relations. Mészáros summarizes this point as the necessity of the social mediation of human metabolism with nature: 'There can be no escape from the imperative to establish fundamental structural relationships through which the vital functions of primary mediation can be carried on for as long as humankind is to survive' (Mészáros 1995: 139). Out of this imperative, a social structure emerges in the course of human history that is mediated by communication, cooperation, norms, institutions and law. Metabolism between humans and nature is, seen from this perspective, simultaneously a socio-historical process whose concrete forms significantly vary according to the structural relationships that exist in different times and places. They constitute what Mészáros calls the 'second order mediations of historically specific social reproductive systems' (Mészáros 1995: 139–40).[13]

The historical uniqueness of 'second-order mediations' under capitalism becomes immediately obvious when we compare them with those in non-capitalist societies. Marx contrasted modern capitalist production with that of ancient society:

> Wealth does not appear as the aim of production [in antiquity].... The question is always which mode of property creates the best citizens.... Thus the old view, in which the human being appears as the aim of production, regardless of his limited national, religious, political character, seems to be very lofty when contrasted to the modern world, where production appears as the aim of mankind and wealth as the aim of production. (*Grundrisse*: 487–8)

The primary goal of capitalist production is the valorization of capital above anything else. Capitalism is driven by the insatiable desire for profit-making and constantly increases the productive capacity. In contrast, in pre-capitalist societies production was conducted for the sake of satisfying concrete needs, and correspondingly the aim of production was use-values tied to the fulfilment of finite wants.

With the domination of this logic of capital for the sake of maximal valorization and the limitless expansion of capital, historically specific second-order mediation emerges by developing the world market, technologies, transportation and credit system, and artificial appetites. Capital wholly transforms and reorganizes the entire world as Mészáros argues:

> Every one of the primary forms [of metabolism between humans and nature] is altered almost beyond recognition, so as to suit the self-expansionary needs of a fetishistic and alienating system of social metabolic control which must subordinate absolutely everything to the imperative of capital-accumulation. (Mészáros 1995: 140)

Since there is no absolute limit in this process, capital is 'totalizing', continuously expanding and subordinating all aspects of the productive functions of both humans and nature to the imperative of capital accumulation. However, this 'capitalistically institutionalised second order mediation' as in the case of wage labour, commodity exchange and private property is 'alienated mediation'. Here one should note that it is characterized not only by the estrangement of labour but also by the 'alienation of nature' (Mészáros 1970: 110–11).[14]

Since his Deutscher Prize lecture in 1971, Mészáros remained convinced that capital's organization of social metabolism, with its second-order mediations, is incompatible with transhistorical material characteristics of metabolism between humans and nature on the primary level, leading to its degradation and ultimate destruction in the long run. To highlight this point, Mészáros used the expression 'absolute limit' of nature, which capital cannot overcome. It exists independently of capital, but capital cannot recognize the non-identity of nature and constantly aims to relativize the absolute in its attempt to become the absolute by totalizing the regime of capital. However, the subjugation of the natural cycle that exists prior to and independently of the formation of the capitalist cycle ultimately disrupts and destroys the universal metabolism of nature. In the moment of ecological crisis, a fundamental problem of capitalist second mediation manifests itself due to the asymmetrical relationship between society and nature – namely, nature as the material substratum can exist without humans, but not vice versa.

Today capital is no longer productive, but rather destructive and threatens human existence. This is the moment when the 'limits of capital' become discernible:

> Capital's limits can no longer be conceptualized as merely the material obstacles to a greater increase in productivity and social wealth, and thus as a brake on development, but as the direct challenge to the very survival of mankind. And in another sense, the limits of capital can turn against it as the overpowering controller of the social metabolism … when capital is no longer able to secure, by whatever means, the conditions of its destructive self-reproduction and thereby causes the breakdown of the overall social metabolism. (Mészáros 2014: 599)

As capital cannot stop expanding, it continues to increase its destructive power. Mészáros added that 'the capital system as a mode of social metabolic reproduction finds itself in its descending phase of historical development, and therefore is only capitalistically advanced but in no other sense at all, thereby capable of sustaining itself only in an ever more destructive and therefore ultimately also self-destructive way' (Mészáros 2012: 316). The development of capitalism no longer counts as 'development' because its inadequate mechanisms of social control ultimately threaten humanity's sheer survival. Mészáros differentiated himself from orthodox Marxists in explicitly acknowledging that the robbery inherent in the capitalist development of productive forces does not bring about progress leading to socialism.

Mészáros was presumably inspired by Lukács's theory of metabolism and his Hegelian discussion of the 'identity of identity and non-identity' (see Chapter 4). Both Lukács and Mészáros recognized that society is a part of the universal metabolism of nature as the latter encompasses everything and functions as a material foundation of all the kinds of human activity – humans cannot even think without brains – but society does bring about new socio-historical emergent properties and laws that do not exist without human beings. However, even those purely social properties are not entirely free from the rest of nature. This dialectical relationship between the social and the natural constitutes the complex dynamics of the social and natural metabolic processes that cannot be adequately grasped in the mechanical or social constructivist approaches.

III
THREE DIMENSIONS OF METABOLIC RIFT

Mészáros's legacy of the theory of metabolism was later taken up by John Bellamy Foster (2000) and Paul Burkett (1999), who have carefully examined Marx's own usage of the concept of metabolism in various texts and developed the key concept of 'metabolic rift'. Its basic thesis is relatively simple: the metabolic interaction of humans with the rest of nature constitutes the basis of living, but the capitalist way of organizing human interactions with their ecosystems inevitably creates a great chasm in these processes and threatens both human and non-human beings. Today, there are various attempts to analyse these rifts in terms of marine ecology (Stephano Longo), climate change (Naomi Klein, Brett Clark, Richard York, Del Weston), the disruption of the nitrogen cycle (Philip Mancus) and soil erosion (Hannah Holleman). These studies confirm the validity and fruitfulness of Marx's theory of metabolic rift.

Nevertheless, it is unfortunate that Marx did not elaborate on the concept of 'metabolic rift' in detail in *Capital*. Marx warned against an 'irreparable rift' in social and natural metabolism only in one passage (*Capital* III: 949). As a consequence, despite Foster's careful analysis of Marx's writings and the further application of this concept to various contemporary ecological issues by other scholars, critics feel justified in insisting that 'the implications of Foster's thesis for contemporary thought are vague and the conclusions atavistic' (Loftus 2012: 31). Others also object that the 'greening' of Marx's critique of capitalism is an excessive imposition of 'our' concerns upon the representative 19th century thinker, distorting and neglecting the existence of flaws and limitations in Marx's theory (Tanuro 2003; Kovel 2007). These criticisms are worth responding to here as they provide a good opportunity to clarify Marx's concept of metabolic rift and its systematic character at the beginning of this book. Even if the concept of rift may appear 'sporadic' in Marx's writings, his theory of metabolism is actually profound and solid. In fact, there are good reasons to assume that he would have elaborated on the concept of metabolic rift in more detail if Marx were able to finish *Capital* (Saito 2017).[15] I argue that there are three dimensions of metabolic rift in technological as well as spatiotemporal terms.

As elucidated in *Capital*, volume I, the transhistorical 'labour process' receives a new form as a 'valorization process' under capitalism, and its biophysical processes of metabolism between humans and nature are thoroughly transformed and reorganized for the sake of capital's valorization. This deep transformation pivots around a certain aspect of labour, namely 'abstract labour', as it possesses a uniquely capitalist function as the sole source of 'surplus-value'. Under the primacy of the logic of capital's valorization, not only the functioning of nature but also various aspects of concrete labour in the labour process are forcefully abstracted and subordinated to the primacy of (surplus-)value. Value as the objectification of abstract labour is nothing but the expenditure of human labour power in general. When value becomes the organizing principle of metabolism between humans and nature, it cannot fully reflect the complexity of the biophysical metabolic processes between them. It even utilizes concrete labour and natural environment as externalities in order to extract more value. Marx thus maintained that this transformation of the material world from the perspective of production of surplus-value has destructive consequences for both humans *and* nature: 'The same blind desire for profit that in the one case exhausted the soil had in the other case seized hold of the vital force of the nation at its roots' (*Capital* I: 348). Based on this theory of metabolism, Marx consistently problematized the capitalist squandering of two fundamental factors of production: 'labour power' (*Arbeitskraft*) and 'natural forces' (*Naturkräfte*). The alienation of labour and of nature are mutually constitutive of each other. In other words, capital not only exploits labour power but also subsumes the entire world, significantly affecting 'space (scale)' and 'time (rate)'. With its ever-expanding and accelerating scale of economy, capital brings about spatiotemporal transformations on an unprecedented level.

According to Marx, metabolic rift appears in three different levels and forms. First and most fundamentally, metabolic rift is the material disruption of cyclical processes in natural metabolism under the regime of capital. Marx's favourite example is the exhaustion of the soil by modern agriculture. Modern large-scale, industrial agriculture makes plants absorb soil nutrition as much as and as fast as possible so that they can be sold to customers in large cities even beyond national borders. It was Justus von Liebig's *Agricultural Chemistry* (1862) and his theory of metabolism that prompted Marx to integrate an analysis of the 'robbery' system of agriculture into *Capital* (Foster 2000; Saito 2017).

As the German chemist warned in his path-breaking book, inorganic substances such as phosphor and potash are essential to plant growth, but their availability to plants is limited in terms of their naturally occurring quantities in the soil because the weathering process that disperses these inorganic substances, through the actions of the atmosphere and rain water, takes quite a long time. Thus, Liebig highlighted the importance of respecting the 'law of replenishment' (*Gesetz des Ersatzes*) as the most fundamental principle of 'rational agriculture' that demands the return of a sufficient amount of the minerals absorbed by plants to the original soil, if farmers are to maintain soil fertility and secure long-term profitability. This necessity of replenishment counts as the 'primary mediation' in that *all* societies must respect it, wherever and whenever you are.

Liebig harshly criticized modern 'robbery agriculture' (*Raubbau*), which only aims at the maximization of short-term profit and lets plants absorb as many nutrients from the soil as possible without replenishing them. Market competition drives farmers to large-scale agriculture, intensifying land usage without sufficient management and care. As a consequence, modern capitalist agriculture created a dangerous disruption in the metabolic cycle of soil nutrients. In order to highlight its danger, Liebig even warned about the potential collapse of European civilization due to soil exhaustion. Impressed by *Agricultural Chemistry*, Marx in *Capital* praised Liebig's 'immortal merits' for revealing 'the negative, i.e. destructive side of modern agriculture', arguing:

> Capitalist production ... causes the urban population to achieve an ever-growing preponderance.... [As a result, it] disturbs the metabolic interaction between man and the earth, i.e. it prevents the return to the soil of the constituent elements consumed by man in the form of food and clothing; hence it hinders the operation of the eternal natural condition for the lasting fertility of the soil. Thus it destroys at the same time the physical health of the urban worker, and the intellectual life of the rural worker...; all progress in increasing the fertility of the soil for a given time is a progress towards ruining the more long-lasting sources of that fertility.... Capitalist production, therefore, only develops the techniques and the degree of combination of the social process of production by simultaneously undermining the original sources of all wealth – the soil and the worker. (*Capital* I: 637)

Here Marx formulated the problem of soil exhaustion as a contradiction created by capitalist production in the metabolism between humans and nature. Insofar as value cannot fully take the metabolism between humans and nature into account and capitalist production prioritizes the infinite accumulation of value, the realization of sustainable production within capitalism faces insurmountable barriers.

This fundamental level of metabolic rift in the form of the disruption of material flow cannot occur without being supplemented and reinforced by two further dimensions. The second dimension of metabolic rift is the *spatial rift*. Marx highly valued Liebig in *Capital* because his *Agricultural Chemistry* provided a scientific foundation for his earlier critical analysis of the social division of labour, which he conceptualized as the 'contradiction between town and country' in *The German Ideology* (*MECW* 5: 64).

Liebig lamented that those crops that are sold in modern large cities do not return to the original soil after they are consumed by the workers. Instead, they flow into the rivers as sewage via water closets, only strengthening the tendency towards soil exhaustion.

This antagonistic spatial relationship between town and country – it can be called 'spatial rift' – is founded upon a violent process of so-called primitive accumulation accompanied by depeasantization and massive urban growth of the working-class population concentrated in large cities. This not only necessitates the long-distance transport of products but also significantly increases the demand for agricultural products in large cities, leading to continuous cropping without fallowing under large-scale agriculture, which is intensified even more through market competition. In other words, robbery agriculture does not exist without the social division of labour unique to capitalist production, which is based upon the concentration of the working class in large cities and the corresponding necessity for the constant transport of their food from the countryside.

This spatial rift also means the concentration of wastes in the city, degrading its living conditions:

> Under the heading of production we have the waste products of industry and agriculture, under that of consumption we have both the excrement produced by man's natural metabolism and the form in which useful articles survive after use has been made of them…. The natural human waste products … are of the greatest importance for agriculture. But there is a colossal wastage in the capitalist economy in proportion to their actual use. (*Capital* III: 195)[16]

Excrement gave off a foul smell in the city of London at Marx's time, and cholera became prevalent. The problem of environmental degradation, in terms of both the living conditions of the working class in the city and soil exhaustion in the countryside accompanied by the misery of peasants, represents a typical consequence of the antagonistic spatial separation within a capitalist country. This continues to widen in the course of capitalist development and even creates an 'irreparable rift' in the metabolism between humans and nature on a global scale. Again, Marx problematized this contradiction, referring to Liebig:

> [In] this way [large-scale landownership] produces conditions that provoke an irreparable rift in the interdependent process between social metabolism and natural metabolism prescribed by the natural laws of the soil. The result of this is a squandering of the vitality of the soil, and trade carries this devastation far beyond the bounds of a single country. (Liebig.) (*MEGA* II/4.2: 752–3)

This spatial rift only worsens with the expansion of capitalism, even though the formation of the world market simultaneously creates a countertendency as discussed soon.

Andreas Malm's *Fossil Capital* (2016) provides another example of how capital profits from this antagonistic spatial organization. His work reconstructs the historical transition from water mills to steam engines fired by coal. River water is abundant and free. In short, water is a perfectly sustainable and free energy. This is an obvious but important fact, considering the prevailing 'Malthusian' explanation for the development of new technologies. According to this type of explanation, the increasing scarcity of resources and their corresponding increase in price in the race for economic growth leads to the discovery or invention of other, cheaper substituting materials. Malm rejects this myth, arguing that it does not apply to the eclipse of free and abundant water-power and its replacement by the steam engine dependent on the massive use of costly coal.

In order to explain this historical transition to fossil fuel, Malm argues, it is necessary to take into account the social dimension of the second-order mediation of 'capital'. As Malm explains, the use of fossil fuels did not start as a new substituent cheap energy resource but rather as fossil *capital*. The natural characteristics of coal, in contrast to water, as a transportable energy source that was suitable to monopoly ownership, proved to possess a unique social significance for the development of capitalist production. River water cannot be moved and waterpower requires communal management. Thanks to coal, capital was able to overcome these physical constraints, leaving the areas near the rivers where workers were more resistant, since labour power was relatively scarce. Coal enabled capital to build new factories in large cities where a larger number of workers were in dire need of jobs. This was basically how the power balance between capital and labour radically changed with the invention of the steam engine. Yet this change also intensified the antagonistic relationship between centre and the periphery, degrading both the living conditions of workers in the former and the natural environment in the latter.[17]

The third dimension of metabolic rift is the *temporal rift*. As is obvious from the slow formation of soil nutrients and fossil fuels and the accelerating circulation of capital, there emerges a rift between nature's time and capital's time. Capital constantly attempts to shorten its turnover time and maximize valorization in a given time – the shortening of turnover time is an effective way of increasing the quantity of profit in the face of the decreasing rate of profit (Saito 2018). This process is accompanied by increasing demands for floating capital in the form of cheap and abundant raw and auxiliary materials (*Capital* III: 200–5). Furthermore, capital constantly revolutionizes the production process, augmenting productive forces with an unprecedented speed compared with precapitalist societies. Productive forces can double or triple with the introduction of new machines, but nature cannot change its formation processes of phosphor or fossil fuel, so 'it was likely that productivity in the production of raw materials would tend not to increase as rapidly as productivity in general (and, accordingly, the growing requirements for raw materials)' (Lebowitz 2009: 138). This tendency can never be fully suspended because natural cycles exist independently of capital's demands. Capital cannot produce without nature, but it also wishes that nature would vanish.

When nature cannot catch up with the accelerating speed of capital, there arises a grave discrepancy between two kinds of time that are particular to nature and capital. Marx gives the following example of excessive deforestation under capitalism:

> The long production time (which includes a relatively slight amount of working time), and the consequent length of the turnover period, makes forest culture a line of business unsuited to private and hence to capitalist production, the latter being fundamentally a private operation, even when the associated capitalist takes the place of the individual. The development of civilization and industry in general has always shown itself so active in the destruction of forests that everything that has been done for their conservation and production is completely insignificant in comparison. (*Capital* II: 321–2)

The same problem can be found with the long time required for the natural formation of fossil fuels and capital's increasing demand for it. Long before peak oil became an issue for discussion, the possible exhaustion of British coal was a major social concern in Marx's time in its competition with the United States (US) economy (Jevons 1865).[18]

In reality, three dimensions of metabolic rift are interrelated and mutually reinforcing. Through technological media such as telecommunication, railways and airplanes, there occurs 'time–space compression' that aims to annihilate spatial and temporal distance by speeding up in favour of a shorter circuit of capital (Harvey 1990). The social construction of time and space by capital exerts great objective force, with which capital's second-order mediation radically transforms the relationship between humans and nature. Ultimately, this reorganization under the logic of capital intensifies the grave tension between social and natural metabolism. Marx was, however, not simply satisfied with acknowledging the static existence of such rifts but more interested in how they emerge in nature and how they are spatially and temporally (re)distributed in a disproportionate manner. This is the reason why Marx, in his later years, studied natural science intensively in order to comprehend the historical dynamics of capital accumulation and its ecological consequences.

IV
THREE DIMENSIONS OF METABOLIC SHIFT

The contradiction of capitalist accumulation is that increases in the social productivity are accompanied by a decrease in natural productivity due to robbery:

> It is possible for the increase in the social productivity of agriculture simply to compensate for a decline in natural productivity, or not even to do this much – and this compensation can only be effective for a certain period – so that despite the technical development, the product does not become cheaper but is simply prevented from becoming dearer. (*Capital* III: 901)

It is thus essential for capital to secure stable access to cheap resources, energy and food.[19] This is what drives capital to construct 'a system of general exploitation of the natural and human qualities' and 'a system of general utility' as Marx argued in the *Grundrisse*:

> Hence exploration of all of nature in order to discover new, useful qualities in things; universal exchange of the products of all alien climates and lands; new (artificial) preparation of natural objects, by which they are given new use values. The exploration of the earth in all directions, to discover new things of use as well as new useful qualities of the old; such as new qualities of them as raw materials etc. (*Grundrisse*: 409)

This is how capital strives to be a universal system, but this process is also accompanied by the universalization of its own contradiction.

The exploration of the earth and the invention of new technologies cannot repair the rift. The rift remains 'irreparable' in capitalism. This is because capital attempts to overcome rifts without recognizing its own absolute limits, which it cannot do. Instead, it simply attempts to relativize the absolute. This is what Marx meant when he wrote 'every limit appears a barrier to overcome' (*Grundrisse*: 408).[20] Capital constantly invents new technologies, develops means of transportation, discovers new use-values and expands markets to overcome natural limits. This is how it constantly 'shifts' the metabolic rift to other social groups living somewhere else, not only for the sake of buying time but also for minimizing the manifestation of negative effects in the centres through the hierarchical integration of the peripheries (Clark and York 2008). 'Metabolic shift' is a typical *reaction* of capital to the economic and ecological crisis it causes: 'For only the reactive and retroactive manipulation of symptoms and effects is compatible with the continuing rule of capital's *causa sui*' (Mészáros 2012: 87). Metabolic shift, however, cannot solve the problem as long as it cannot stop its insatiable process of accumulation.

This is why Marx declared that 'the *true barrier* to capitalist production is *capital itself*' (*Capital* III: 358; emphasis in original).

Corresponding to the three dimensions of metabolic rifts, there are also three ways of shifting them. First, there is *technological shift*. Although Liebig warned about the collapse of European civilization due to robbery agriculture in the 19th century, his prediction apparently did not come true. This is largely thanks to Fritz Haber and Carl Bosch, who invented the so-called Haber-Bosch process in 1906 that enabled the industrial mass production of ammonia (NH_3) by fixing nitrogen from the air, and thus of chemical fertilizer to maintain soil fertility. Historically speaking, the problem of soil exhaustion due to a lack of inorganic substances was largely resolved thanks to this invention. Nevertheless, the Haber-Bosch process did not heal the rift but only shifted, generating other problems on a larger scale.

The production of NH_3 uses a massive amount of natural gas as a source of hydrogen (H). In other words, it squanders another limited resource in order to produce ammonia as a remedy to soil exhaustion, but it is also quite energy intensive, producing a lot of carbon dioxide (CO_2) (responsible for 1 per cent of the total carbon emission in the world). Furthermore, excessive applications of chemical fertilizer leach into the environment, causing eutrophication and red tide, while nitrogen oxide pollutes water. Overdependence on chemical fertilizer disrupts soil ecology, so that it results in soil erosion, low water- and nutrient-holding capacity, and increased vulnerability to diseases and insects (Magdoff and van Es 2010). Consequently, more frequent irrigation, a larger amount of fertilizer and more powerful equipment become necessary, together with pesticides. This kind of industrial agriculture consumes not just water but large quantities of oil also, which makes agriculture a serious driver of climate change.[21] As Vandana Shiva points out, the robbery character of agriculture has not changed since Liebig's time: 'Contemporary societies across the world stand on the verge of collapse as soils are eroded, degraded, poisoned, buried under concrete and deprived of life' (Shiva 2015: 173).

While soil exhaustion due to robbery agriculture is limited to a piece of land, agrochemicals leak to the environment with water and disrupt the normal functioning of ecosystems. In short, metabolic shift creates externalities with the aid of new technologies. Soil fertility is artificially maintained and even strengthened, while capital does not pay for by-products. The creation of externalities is also an effective way to obscure the responsibility of companies for environmental problems due to the difficulty of proving the direct causation. Even if the responsibility is clarified and the relevant costs are internalized, the original conditions of the environment often never recover to their original state. At the same time, capital finds new business opportunities in these disruptions, taking the opportunity to sell more commodities such as chemical fertilizer and pesticide to the farmers. In other words, nature's biological systems are not mere obstacles or barriers for capital but their degradation creates new sources of profit. Capital utilizes nature as a 'vehicle for accumulation' (Kloppenburg 1988).

Following Kloppenburg's insight, Boyd, Prudham and Schurman (2001) extended Marx's concept of 'formal' and 'real subsumption under capital' to nature. According to Marx, 'formal subsumption' of labour under capital simply subjugates workers to the command of capital without changing the way they work (that is, the production of 'absolute surplus value'), while 'real subsumption' of labour reorganizes the entire produces of production in favour of capital accumulation through cooperation, division of labour and mechanization (that is, the production of 'relative surplus value'). Similarly, the 'formal subsumption' of nature is the simple exploitation of natural processes for the sake of commodity production in nature-based industries without capital's technological intervention in natural cycles and processes (for example, finding new sites of extraction, usage of machinery, developing preservation system). In contrast, 'real subsumption' of nature aims at manipulating biological processes with the aid of technologies so that nature is '(re)made to work harder, faster, and better' (Boyd, Prudham and Schurman 2001: 564). Real subsumption of nature fundamentally changes the natural metabolic cycle. Examples include growth hormones, synthetic fertilizers, pesticides as well as new biotechnologies, genetically modified organisms (GMOs) and biomedical implants. In this manner, capital creates opportunities for opening new markets in the midst of metabolic rift. Consequently, peasants and farmers become more and more dependent upon commodities such as seeds, fertilizers and pesticides provided by giant agribusiness companies. The real subsumption of nature deprives them of traditional knowledge as well as autonomy and independence in the production process. Furthermore, such commodification induces the concentration of capital in the sphere of agricultural production because the industrialization of operations and materials increases the minimum amount of capital to continue production on the level of socially average level (*Capital* III: 359).

After all, metabolic rift cannot be fully repaired unless the universal metabolism of nature is mediated in a *qualitatively* different manner by freely associated producers. Thus, there remains a constant need to shift the rift under capitalism, which continues to bring about new problems. This contradiction becomes more discernible in considering the second type of shifting the metabolic rift – that is, *spatial shift*, which expands the antagonism of the city and the countryside to a global scale in favour of the Global North. Spatial shift creates externality by a geographic displacement of ecological burdens to another social group living somewhere else. Again, Marx discussed this issue in relation to soil exhaustion in core capitalist countries in the 19th century. On the coast of Peru there were small islands consisting of the excrement of seabirds called *guano* that had accumulated over many years to form 'guano islands'. 'Guano' means agricultural fertilizer in the Andean Indigenous language Quechua, and the Indigenous people traditionally employed it as dung. In fact, guano is quite rich in minerals such as phosphate and nitrogen. It was Alexander von Humboldt who encountered the Indigenous usage of guano during a research trip to Peru in 1802. He investigated the effectiveness of guano and tested it on European soils. Guano turned out to be quite effective and its usage became quite popular as the best natural fertilizer across those areas of Europe and the United States (Cushman 2013).

This spatial shift helped a gradual decoupling of agricultural production from nutrient cycles within a given territory. Massive import of guano enabled exponential urbanization in capitalist centres. As natural conditions of production faded away from workers' everyday life, they came to share a perception of nature close to that of capitalists and landowners: the idea that nature is a depository of resources that can be freely exploited by humans. Marx wrote about this formation of a new common sense of the English people about moving the conditions of production to somewhere else in favour of their own affluence:

> Agriculture no longer finds the natural conditions of its own production within itself, naturally, arisen, spontaneous, and ready to hand, but these exist as an independent industry separate from it – and, with this separateness the whole complex set of interconnections in which this industry exists is drawn into the sphere of the conditions of agricultural production.... This pulling-away of the natural ground from the foundations of every industry, and this transfer of its conditions of production outside itself, into a general context – hence the transformation of what was previously superfluous into what is necessary, as a historically created necessity – is the tendency of capital. The general foundation of all industries comes to be general exchange itself, the world market, and hence the totality of the activities, intercourse, needs etc. of which it is made up. (*Grundrisse*: 527–8)

In the course of capitalist development, what used to be considered 'luxury' – something not 'naturally necessary' (*Grundrisse*: 527) – becomes 'necessary'. This change of appetite occurs to the working class too. By externalizing the material conditions of production, the working class in the Global North came to exploit others in the Global South, and in this way, new luxuries are adopted by the working class. This is how the 'imperial mode of living' of the capitalist centres spreads all over the society (Brand and Wissen 2021). By constantly shifting the ecological rifts and making them invisible to the capitalist centre, the current capitalist order of society appears attractive and comfortable for a wide range of social groups in the Global North. It thus facilitates a general social consensus, while its real costs are imposed upon other social groups in the Global South.

In the 19th century, guano became 'necessary' to sustain soil fertility in Europe. Millions of tons of guano were dug up and continuously exported to Europe, resulting in its rapid exhaustion. Extractivism was accompanied by the brutal oppression of Indigenous people and the severe exploitation of thousands of Chinese 'coolies' working under cruel conditions. Ultimately, the exhaustion of guano reserves provoked the Guano War (1865–6) and the Saltpetre War (1879–84) in the battle for the remaining guano reserves. As John Bellamy Foster and Brett Clark (2009) argue, such a solution in favour of the Global North resulted in 'ecological imperialism'. Although ecological imperialism shifts the rift to the peripheries and makes its imminent violence invisible in the centre, the metabolic rift only deepens on a global scale through long-distance trade, and the nutrient cycle becomes even more severely disrupted.

Ecological imperialism is accompanied by 'ecologically unequal exchange' of free energy and materials (Hornborg 2012). Its impacts are not fully represented in the unequal exchange of value, but it is essential to the process of capital accumulation. The centre accumulates more wealth and becomes more affluent, while the periphery remains underdeveloped or becomes even more impoverished. The negative consequences of the rift, such as exhaustion of resources, corporeal rift of slaves and environmental pollution, disproportionally emerge in those peripheries from which resources are constantly extracted and transported to the centre (Martinez-Alier 2002: 213).[22] This is representative of the spatial shift as a way of organizing the entire world that can be aptly called capitalist system.[23]

The third dimension of metabolic shift is the *temporal shift*. The discrepancy between nature's time and capital's time does not immediately bring about an ecological disaster because nature possesses 'elasticity'. Its limits are not static but modifiable to a great extent (Akashi 2016). Climate crisis is a representative case of this metabolic shift. Massive CO_2 emissions due to the excessive usage of fossil fuels is an apparent cause of climate change, but the emission of greenhouse gas does not immediately crystallize as climate breakdown. Capital exploits the opportunities opened up by this time lag to secure more profits from previous investments in drills and pipelines. Since capital reflects the voice of current shareholders, but not that of future generations, the costs are shifted onto the latter. As a result, future generations suffer from consequences for which they are not responsible. Marx characterized such an attitude inherent to capitalist development with the slogan 'Après moi le déluge!' (*Capital* I: 381).

This time lag generated by a temporal shift also induces a hope that it would be possible to invent new epoch-making technologies to combat against the ecological crisis in the future. In fact, one may think that it is better to continue economic growth which promotes technological development, rather than over-reducing carbon dioxide emissions and adversely affecting the economy (Nordhaus 1991). However, even if new negative emission technologies such as carbon capture and storage (CCS) are invented, it will take a long time for them to spread throughout society and replace the old ones. In the meantime, the environmental crisis will continue to worsen due to our current inaction. As a result, the expected effects of the new technology can be cancelled out. Barry Commoner already argued in the 1970s with regard to pesticides that 'in each case the new technology has worsened the environmental impact of the economic good' (Commoner 1971: 153). The same logic applies here. Furthermore, technological solutions sound attractive because they do not entail us changing our current lifestyle. In this case, the hope for new technologies functions as an ideology to legitimize the further usage of fossil fuels by temporally shifting the contradiction to the future. Mészáros thus warned against technocratic optimism: 'And finally, to say that "science and technology can solve all our problems in the long run" is much worse than believing in witchcraft' (Mészáros 2014: 29).

V
ROSA LUXEMBURG'S THEORY OF METABOLISM AND ITS OBLIVION

The elastic power of capital to shift the metabolic rift is quite astonishing as the history of capitalism demonstrates. Bill McKibben once formulated the historical dynamics of capitalism and ecological disaster in the following manner: 'The diminished availability of fossil fuel is not the only limit we face. In fact, it's not even the most important. Even before we run out of oil, we're running out of planet' (McKibben 2007: 18). This is not only because capital can constantly find new opportunities for a 'climate-change shock doctrine' (Klein 2019: 36) amidst the ecological crisis but also because it always shifts and externalizes the negative consequences to the sink in the Global South. In this way, the Global South suffers from doubly negative consequences. After suffering from the robbery of nature and labour power under ecological imperialism, it first faces the real impact of ecological crisis. As Stephan Lessenich (2018: 166) argues, the capitalist slogan 'After us, the deluge!' becomes 'Next to us, the deluge!' in an age of global ecological crisis when it is no longer possible to buy time before the deluge – be it heavy rain and flooding, or refugee flows and immigration waves. This is the essence of the 'externalization society' prevailing in the affluent Global North.

In the Marxist tradition, it was Rosa Luxemburg who attempted to develop the concept of 'metabolism' to conceptualize this unequal relationship between capitalist centres and non-capitalist peripheries as the essential condition for capital accumulation. In *The Accumulation of Capital*, Luxemburg criticized the destructive impact of capitalist development upon non-capitalist societies, even arguing that capitalism was borne fundamentally in a non-capitalist environment. In other words, capitalism is from the very beginning dependent on unequal exchange that provides not simply cheap but often *free* labour power of slaves as well as natural resources for the centre.

It is noteworthy that Luxemburg formulated her own thesis *against* Marx's theory of capital reproduction in volume II of *Capital* because in her view he treated English capitalism as if it were an independent and autarchic entity within which capital can reproduce itself without paying sufficient attention to its deep dependence on the extraction from non-capitalist societies:

> The Marxian schema of expanded reproduction thus does not correspond to the conditions of accumulation, as long as this is able to proceed; it cannot be conjured up out of the fixed, reciprocal relationships and dependencies between the two great departments of social production … as formulated by the schema. Accumulation is not merely an internal relation between the branches of the capitalist economy – it is above all a relation between capital and its noncapitalist milieu, in which each of the two great branches of production can partially go through the accumulation process under its own steam, independently of the other, although the movement of each intersects, and is intertwined, with the other at every turn. (Luxemburg [1913] 2015: 303)

Nevertheless, when she further described this process of unequal transportation of labour power and natural resources from the periphery to the centre, she took up Marx's concept of metabolism, clearly influenced by his usage of 'social metabolism' in *Capital*:

> While it is true that capitalism lives from noncapitalist formations, it is more precise to say that it lives from their ruin; in other words, while this noncapitalist milieu is indispensable for capitalist accumulation, providing its fertile soil, accumulation in fact proceeds at the expense of this milieu, and is constantly devouring it. Historically speaking, *the accumulation of capital is a process of metabolism occurring between capitalist and precapitalist modes of production.* The accumulation of capital cannot proceed without these precapitalist modes of production, and yet accumulation consists in this regard precisely in the latter being

gradually swallowed up and assimilated by capital. Accordingly, capital accumulation can no more exist without noncapitalist formations, than these are able to exist alongside it. It is only in the constant and progressive erosion of these noncapitalist formations that the very conditions of the existence of capital accumulation are given. (Luxemburg [1913] 2015: 302; emphasis added)

Her use of the term 'metabolism' indicates that she actually comprehended the emergence of serious metabolic rift on the international level. The problem of such a violent process of accumulation is not just about value transfer through unequal exchange of value nor severe exploitation of workers. It is fundamentally a process of expropriating labour power, energy and resources through ecologically unequal exchange (Moore 2000: 138). Here labour conducted by certain groups of humans such as slaves, the indigenous and women is exploited as 'free gift' to capital. Capital cannot stop such exploitation and expropriation from non-capitalist milieu but even reinforces them because this unequal transfer is constitutive of capitalist production: 'It becomes necessary for capital progressively to dispose ever more fully of the whole globe, to acquire an unlimited choice of means of production, with regard to both quality and quantity, so as to find productive employment for the surplus value it has realised' (Luxemburg [1913] 2015: 258).

Luxemburg found the absolute limit to capital in its dependence upon this kind of unequal exchange with the Global South. Capitalism strives to be a universal system, but it cannot be as long as it is essentially dependent on the non-capitalist system. When it becomes universal, it must break down because the exhaustion of externality is fatal for the externalization society:

> Capitalism is the first form of economy with propagandistic power; it is a form that tends to extend itself over the globe and to eradicate all other forms of economy – it tolerates no other alongside itself. However, it is also the first that is unable to exist alone, without other forms of economy as its milieu and its medium. Thus, as the same time as it tends to become the universal form, it is smashed to smithereens by its intrinsic inability to be a universal form of production. (Luxemburg [1913] 2015: 341)

Capital is destined to expand, so it cannot tolerate any intrusion of regulation that hinders this tendency, but this only increases its own contradiction in the long run.

In a sense, the Anthropocene represents a situation where the externality as the precondition for capital accumulation has been exhausted. The competition for robbery and externalization becomes more intensified with the rapid development of the BRICs. The problem is not simply that cheap nature is no longer available. As the space for externalization diminishes, the once-obscured metabolic rift becomes increasingly visible even in the Global North as climate crisis influences heatwaves, wildfires and super typhoons. Reflecting upon this situation, Immanuel Wallerstein (2013: 23) admitted that the 'normality of externalization is a distant memory'. He pointed out that the capitalist system is in terminal crisis now approaching the 'bifurcation' point of replacing the old system with a new one in which the 'issue of ecological degradation ... is a central locus of this debate' (Wallerstein 1999: 10).[24] It is increasingly visible today that the 'imperial mode of living' cannot be universalized, but this situation is fatal to capitalism. The contradiction of capitalism in the Anthropocene forces humans to rethink the legitimacy and effectiveness of capitalist social control as it comes to severely interfere with 'the elementary imperative of mere survival' (Mészáros 2012: 34).

Luxemburg intended to expand Marx's theory of primitive accumulation, but she formulated her theory of metabolism *against* Marx, who she thought focused solely on Western capitalism. Yet one passage in the chapter on primitive accumulation in volume I of *Capital* clearly refers to the destructive process in the periphery of capitalism as an essential component of the formation of capitalism:

> The discovery of gold and silver in America, the extirpation, enslavement and entombment in mines of the indigenous population of that continent, the beginnings of the conquest and plunder of India, and the conversion of Africa into a preserve for the commercial hunting of black-skins, are all things which characterize the dawn of the era of capitalist production. These idyllic proceedings are the chief moments of primitive accumulation. (*Capital* I: 915)

Of course, this is only a short passage, so Luxemburg criticized him despite her awareness of this passage: 'Yet we must bear in mind that all this is treated solely with a view to so-called primitive accumulation. For Marx, these processes are incidental, illustrating merely the genesis of capital, its first appearance in the world; they are, as it were, travails by which the capitalist mode of production emerges from a feudal society' (Luxemburg [1913] 2015: 345). In other words, Marx treated capitalism as a self-sufficient system once it is established as such. However, as discussed in Chapter 6 of this book, Marx *after the publication* of volume I of *Capital* in 1867 critically reflected upon this point, intensively studying pre-capitalist and non-Western societies. Consequently, Marx corrected his understanding of capitalism and learned to envision a path to communism in a fully different way after the 1870s.

However, Marx was not able to elaborate on his new ideas during his lifetime – except his brief reference to this problem in his co-authored preface to the Russian edition of *The Communist Manifesto*. In this sense, Luxemburg was certainly justified at the time to criticize Marx's theory of capital accumulation for its narrow focus on Western capitalism. Although her concept of metabolism could have developed and enriched theoretical possibilities already inherent in *Capital*, her criticism directed against Marx resulted in heated debates in the Second International, which hindered the development of Marx's theory of metabolism thereafter. However, there was a deeper theoretical reason for the marginalization of the concept of metabolism in the history of Marxism. The temptation to marginalize this concept – and correspondingly the question of Marx's ecological critique of capitalism – can be found *before* the Second International. Its origin can be traced back to Engels.[25] He must have known of Marx's serious engagement with the questions of natural science as well as non-Western societies, but he did not highlight this point. Here his understanding indicates some tension with Marx's theory of metabolism. It is thus necessary to reinvestigate the intellectual relationship between Marx and Engels from an ecological perspective in order to comprehend why Marx's concept of metabolism was marginalized for such a long time.

NOTES

1   Not all Marxists ignored environmental concerns in the 1960s and 1970s, when environmental degradation became a pressing issue. Referring to *The Limits to Growth*, Ernest Mandel expressed his concern in a lecture, for example:

> One has not necessarily to accept the predictions of unavoidable absolute scarcity of energy and raw materials of the Club of Rome type in order to understand that there is a collective responsibility for the present generation of humanity to transmit to future generations an environment and a stock of natural wealth that constitute the necessary precondition for the survival and flowering of human civilization. (Mandel 1995: 103–4)

Even if Mandel did not explicitly refer to Marx in this passage, a Marxian critique of capitalism also inspired ecological economists such as Karl William Kapp ([1963] 2000), Barry Commoner (1971) and Shigeto Tsuru (1976). The widespread anti-ecological characterization of Marxism turns out to be oblivious to this long tradition of classical Marxists. See Foster and Burkett (2016: 2) for a longer list of Marxian ecological economists.

2   Post-Marxism attempted to rescue some useful theoretical legacies of Marx's social philosophy, if not his political economy, but such attempts were understandably accompanied by the resolute rejection of Marxist economic

determinism, resulting in the shift of the theoretical focus from the economic basis to the 'autonomy of the political' (Laclau and Mouffe 1985; Rancière 1998). In this way, post-Marxism contributed to eliminating the problem of nature from the agenda of Marxism. This is understandable considering the fact that post-Marxism is a successor to Western Marxism. This problem will be discussed in the next chapter.

3   According to Liedman, this is because Marx 'imagined that the society that would replace capitalism could also restore the balance between humanity and nature in agriculture'. This critique does not make sense, and it makes a large part of today's environmental movements non-ecological 'in the modern sense' as long as they also attempt to 'restore' the balance between humans and nature. It is not clear what kind of environmental movement can be regarded as 'ecologically conscious' in light of Liedman's definition.

4   There are disputes between the *Monthly Review* and *Capitalism Nature Socialism*. While Foster and Burkett defend the validity of Marx's own ecological approach, Kovel (2007) maintains that Marx himself did not systematically elaborate on an ecological critique of capitalism. My own approach is closer to Foster and Burkett. However, I also draw inspiration from Japanese Marxists such as Shigeto Tsuru, Kenichi Miyamoto, Shigeru Iwasa, Tomonaga Tairako and Ryuji Sasaki.

5   The focus on Marx's reception took a different form in Japan, where ecological economics was pioneered by Marxian economists such as Shigeto Tsuru (1976) and Kenichi Miyamoto (1967) in the 1960s. The discussion of Marx's reception of Liebig's *Agricultural Chemistry* was also already present in the 1970s in works by Fumikazu Yoshida, Shigeaki Shiina and Masami Fukutomi. When Foster's work was translated into Japanese in 2004, his interpretation did not leave a strong impression among Japanese scholars because they were quite familiar with Marx's engagement with Liebig and its application to environmental issues. Consequently, while Foster's path-breaking formulation of the 'metabolic rift' spread quite effectively outside Japan, Japanese Marxists missed this great opportunity to prevent the decline of their theoretical and practical influence after 1991.

6   One may also wonder why some people so stubbornly refuse to acknowledge Marx's ecology. There is another reason related to the later reception of Marx's theory by Engels and by Western Marxism. This issue will be discussed in Chapter 2.

7   Obviously enough, this does not mean that Marx got everything right. I fully agree with Engel-Di Mauro's concern that today's critique of capitalism cannot be grounded upon the outdated science of the 19th century.

8   For example, Marx's notebooks on natural sciences are now available in the *MEGA* IV/18, 26 and 31.

9   One can think of American economist Kenneth E. Boulding's famous remark: 'Anyone who believes exponential growth can go on forever in a finite world is either a madman or an economist' (US Congress 1973: 248).

10   Among those ecosocialists who pay attention to Marx's concept of metabolism, Mészáros is the one who most adequately grasped the methodological core of Marx's argument based on Lukács's intellectual heritage, as discussed in Chapter 3. In Japan, Fumikazu Yoshida (1980) dealt with Marx's theory of metabolism in detail.

11   This point becomes more essential in Chapter 4 as those social constructivist advocators of the 'production of nature' erase the difference between 'first' and 'second nature', which is unable to provide an adequate treatment of the human–nature relationship. See also Napoletano et al. (2019).

12   This basic view expressed in *Capital* is consistent since *The German Ideology*, in which Marx made it clear that this materialist analysis needs to start from the problem of 'labour' as a unique human act of production:

> All historical writing must set out from these natural bases and their modification in the course of history through the action of men.... They themselves begin to distinguish themselves from animals as soon as they begin to produce their means of subsistence, a step which is conditioned by their physical organization. (*MECW* 5: 31)

13   Mészáros's method of focusing on the 'second-order mediation' is notably consistent with his earlier analysis of Marx's theory of alienation where he already employed this term. Although he did not use the expression 'metabolism' at the time, his characterization of 'a historically specific mediation of the ontologically fundamental self-mediation of man with nature' basically expresses the same thing (Mészáros 1970: 79).

14   It is not easy to distinguish between the first and the secondary mediations because these historical aspects of capitalism are 'inextricably intertwined with its transhistorical dimension' (Mészáros [1972] 2014: 73). It is necessary to recall here that Marx's critique of political economy is a critique of fetishism. It aims to reveal how these second-order mediations of human metabolism with nature constitute specific social dynamics and deepen multiple crises. Without adequately distinguishing these dimensions, an analysis easily falls into a fetish view to conflate the 'historical necessity' of capitalism as a 'natural necessity'. This critique of the fetish will play an important role in Chapter 4, which deals with the recent popularity of monist approaches in political ecology.

15   In Part III of the book, I argue however that there were reasons why Marx could not finish *Capital*. The reason has to do with the rapid deepening of his ecological thinking after 1868.

16   This passage was added by Engels. This is totally understandable considering the fact that his engagement with the deterioration of the working class in the city in his pioneering work of 1845 is one of his most significant achievements.

17   Furthermore, Timothy Mitchell (2013) points out that this separation was even reinforced by the pipeline of oil in the 20th century. While the extraction of coal requires a concentration of workers in the mine, which increases the

risk of their strong resistance, extraction and transportation of oil significantly reduce such risk.

18   Marx's engagement with Jevons will be discussed in Chapter 6.

19   This is what James O'Connor and more recently Jason W. Moore highlight as a grave contradiction of capitalist accumulation. This issue will be discussed in detail in Chapter 4.

20   Notably, in the *Grundrisse* Marx contrasted the 'real' and 'ideal' transcendence of the barriers.

> But from the fact that capital posits every such limit as a barrier and hence gets ideally beyond it, it does not by any means follow that it has really overcome it, and, since every such barrier contradicts its character, its production moves in contradictions which are constantly overcome but just as constantly posited. (*Grundrisse*: 410)

Ideal represents the side of capital, while the real the side of the material world. The limit cannot be overcome in the real world because it is not socially produced. Even if it is elastic, it is objectively there.

21   The food system is said to be responsible for one quarter of the world's greenhouse gas emissions.

22   This is the cause of the 'Netherlands fallacy', as if technological development alone solves the problem of environmental pollution (Ehrlich and Ehrlich 1990: 39). The fallacy is a product of ignoring the constant spatial externalization of negative impacts caused by the metabolic rift. At the same time, unequal exchange is characterized by the appropriation of space and time. By importing cotton, it is possible to save local space and times in the centre at the cost of time and space consumed elsewhere. Alf Hornborg (2006) calls this 'time–space appropriation'.

23   Ecologically unequal exchange persists in various forms under today's global capitalism. As a solution to climate crisis, solar panel and EVs are essential, but the associated battery technology is resource intensive, especially with regard to rare metals. The largest reserve of lithium is found in the Andean plateau, so Chile has become the second-largest lithium exporter. The Salar de Atacama salt flat is where all the lithium of Chile is extracted. Lithium only exists in dry places such as the large salt flats, as it is only gradually condensed in brine over a long period. Mining lithium is thus conducted by extracting this brine beneath the salt flats of Salar de Atacama and by letting the water evaporate so as to allow the further concentration of lithium. In this situation, it is quite obvious that excessive mining of brine makes the area even drier and also degrades the ecosystem. It endangers the Andean flamingo, which eats brine shrimp. Furthermore, it causes a lowering of the water table, reducing access to fresh water for Indigenous Antacameño communities (Aronoff et al. 2019: 148–9). The situation is exacerbated by copper mining that also extracts massive quantities of fresh water in the Salar. Ironically, the greening of the Global North is rather strengthening the robbery mining processes of lithium, cobalt, nickel and copper in the Global South (Arboleda 2020).

24   However, it is also true that Wallerstein's world-system theory did not pay sufficient attention to the ecological dimension, and Moore (2000) made an important contribution by synthesizing the world ecology into the theory of metabolic rift.

25   This critique does not negate the possibility of finding ecological concerns expressed by Engels, Kautsky and Liebknecht. My point is rather that they did not systematically elaborate on the ecological question with Marx's concept of metabolism, which is why their texts give an impression of Marx's 'sporadic' interests in the issue of environmental destruction.

2

The Intellectual Relationship between Marx and Engels Revisited from an Ecological Perspective*

As seen in the previous chapter, numerous critics have accused Marx of 'Prometheanism', and even self-proclaimed Marxists have concluded that his productivism is incompatible with environmentalism. However, with the deepening ecological crises under neoliberal globalization, the need to critically investigate capitalism's destructive influence upon the ecosystem has become much more pressing. Having rediscovered Marx's ecology in this context, various ecosocialists today employ the concept of 'metabolic rift' in order to analyse environmental degradation under capitalist production. Consequently, ecology has become one of the central fields for enriching the legacy of Marx's *Capital* in the 21st century. However, some Marxists still refuse to acknowledge the potentiality of Marx's ecology, dismissing it as 'apocalyptic' (Harvey 1996: 194). In particular, 'Western Marxism' broadly defined is often dismissive of Marx's ecosocialist project as an alternative to capitalism. For example, in an interview published in *Examined Life*, Slavoj Žižek ironically reformulates Marx's famous remark, maintaining that ecology is 'a new opium for the masses' (Žižek 2009: 158). Alain Badiou (2008: 139) repeats exactly the same judgement.

---

*This chapter draws on material from 'Marx and Engels: The Intellectual Relationship Revisited from an Ecological Perspective', in *Marx's Capital after 150 Years Critique and Alternative to Capitalism*, ed. Marcello Musto (London: Routledge, 2020), 167–83. Published with permission. The content is significantly modified, enlarged and updated for the current book.

One of the reasons for this denial of Marx's ecology can be traced back to an old problem that pivots around the 'intellectual relationship' between Marx and Engels (Carver 1983), that is, the identity and difference of these two founders of socialism. It is well known that Western Marxism as initiated by Lukács regarded natural science as Engels's domain of expertise, as in Adorno's comment that Marx's 'concept of "nature" in which productivity is consummated, also remains underdeveloped, as does the famous expression "metabolism with nature"' (Adorno 1974: 268). Since Western Marxism neglected Marx's extensive research in the natural sciences and marginalized his central concept of 'metabolism', it now faces a dilemma in the Anthropocene. It cannot develop a Marxist critique of ecological degradation unless it admits its earlier one-sided interpretation of Marx's social philosophy. Consequently, Western Marxists deny the possibility of Marx's ecology in order to defend their own theoretical consistency.

In contrast to Adorno, Žižek and Badiou, John Bellamy Foster (2000) and Paul Burkett (1999) adopted a more fruitful approach to the intellectual relationship between Marx and Engels. They not only pay attention to Marx's engagement with natural science but also effectively employ his methodological framework in order to analyse current environmental issues, demonstrating the relevance of Marx's ecology in today's world.

Foster and Burkett develop their ecological critique of capitalism by arguing that there exists *no* significant difference of opinion between Marx and Engels on ecology. Burkett argues, for example:

> As for substantial differences between Marx and Engels, I believe that this problem has often been overestimated – at times gravely so.... In the course of my work, I was *unable to find a single significant difference* in Marx's and Engels' respective materialist and class-relational discussions of natural conditions, and here that is the crucial issue. (Burkett 1999: 9; emphasis added)

It is undeniable that Foster and Burkett have quite convincingly shown the importance of Marx's (and Engels's) ecology founded on materialism as an integral part of his general critique of political economy and conducted meaningful dialogues with ecological economics in order to highlight the unique contribution of Marxian economics to political ecology (Burkett 2006). This great success notwithstanding, there remains the question of whether theoretical differences between Marx and Engels in terms of political economy, whose existence Foster and Burkett do not necessarily deny,[1] can also result in different views on the issue of ecology.

This chapter proposes a 'synthetic' approach to the earlier literature. By focusing on Marx's research in natural sciences ignored by Western Marxism, it aims at revealing the *differences* in terms of the ecological critique of capitalism between Marx and Engels that Foster and Burkett fail to acknowledge. Presupposing their obvious collaborations and common understandings, this chapter analyses *Capital* in relation to new materials published in the *Marx-Engels-Gesamtausgabe*, which were not considered in the earlier literature.[2] Section I will reveal the existence of a backstory behind the intellectual division of labour between Marx and Engels. By doing so, it becomes clear that both Marx and Engels had a strong interest in natural science, but for very different reasons. This is clear from Engels's critique of Liebig's theory of metabolism, which prevented him from fully appreciating Marx's own rapid methodological development in the 1860s that pivots around Liebig's concept of 'metabolism' (II). Consequently, Engels helped make Marx's ecology invisible by criticizing Liebig's concept of 'metabolism' (III). Seen from a genealogical perspective, Engels also contributed to marginalizing Marx's theory of metabolism through his influential project on the dialectics of nature. However, it is this suppressed method of Marx's political economy that indicates the theoretical direction for developing his unfinished project of *Capital* in the Anthropocene (IV).

I
INTELLECTUAL DIVISION OF LABOUR?

As seen in the previous chapter, Marx's ecology was ignored for quite a long time. One reason for neglecting Marx's legacy of ecology was the unfinished character of Marx's *Capital*. Until the recent publication of manuscripts and notebooks in the *Marx-Engels-Gesamtausgabe*, even scholars did not know of their existence, and they simply remained covered in dust in the two archives, the Russian State Archive of Socio-Political History (RGASPI) in Moscow and the International Institute of Social History (IISG) in Amsterdam. Yet there is another factor within the Marxist tradition that contributed to marginalizing Marx's ecological critique of capitalism in the 20th century. The reason for this neglect is that 'traditional Marxism' treated Marx's historical materialism as a closed dialectical system that would enable the working class to comprehend the truth of the universe, encompassing both human history and nature. The establishment of such a gigantic ideological apparatus was necessary for the mass mobilization of workers for Marxism against other socialist rivals such as Eugen Dühring and Ferdinand Lassalle. In other words, traditional Marxists likewise attempted to provide a proletarian 'worldview' (*Weltanschauung*) as a tool for the identification and mobilization of the socialist movement (Heinrich 2012: 24–5). However, such an attempt inevitably distorted Marx's original project in various ways.[3]

Traditional Marxists did not pay enough attention to Marx's economic manuscripts and even less to his notebooks because otherwise they were afraid to admit that these materials document the incomplete character of *Capital*. Instead, they simply focused on Engels's edition of *Capital* as the theoretical foundation of Marx's system of political economy that discloses exploitation of the working class and demonstrates the necessity of economic crisis as well as the inevitability of socialist revolution. Even though traditional Marxists admitted that Marx had almost nothing to say about the ontological status of nature in his published writings, they simply took recourse to Engels's *Dialectics of Nature* and *Anti-Dühring* in order to expand their materialist theory to the entire universe. The difference between Marx and Engels is erased in this assumption about their intellectual collaboration.

There are, however, obvious problems here. Traditional Marxists cannot deny that Marx did not produce any systematic account of the dialectics of nature. The universal system of Marx's dialectical materialism does not exist in Marx's original writings. Such a system must be carefully reconstructed by editing manuscripts, adding annotations to Marx's texts and even *omitting* what is inconvenient. They carefully chose what to publish and what not to because they were afraid that these unpublished writings might reveal the incomplete character of Marx's system or reveal new aspects that were not compatible with their own worldview.[4] What was incompatible was marginalized or even suppressed. However, Marx's economic manuscripts for *Capital* were finally fully published in 2012 in the *MEGA*.[5] Based on the *MEGA*, this chapter demonstrates the importance of the manuscripts and notebooks, especially Marx's notebooks on natural science.

Engels played an important role in this story as the founder of 'traditional Marxism' because he established Marxism as a worldview for the social and political movement of the working class. He highlighted the systematic and complete character of Marx's *Capital* as well as its superiority over Eugen Dühring's influential work in order to win hegemony within the Social Democratic Party during the period of Otto von Bismarck's antisocialist laws (Adamiak 1974).[6] It is well known that Engels edited Marx's manuscripts and published them as volumes II and III of *Capital*. He also republished various books, pamphlets and articles of Marx after his death. In doing so, he often added new prefaces and introductions, sometimes even adding and modifying original texts written by Marx. As Terrell Carver (1983: 119) points out, it was not Marx's *Capital* but Engels's *Socialism: Utopian and Scientific* that was the most read book on Marxism. It is no exaggeration to say that 'it was Engels who established the central tradition' (Lichtheim 1961:

235) and largely determined the course of Marxism in the 20th century. The leaders of the Second International as well as those who led the first successful seizure of the state power in the Russian Revolution were heavily influenced by Engels's views on history, the state and revolution. What these 'traditional Marxists' thought of as 'what everyone knows to be true about Marx' was actually nothing but 'a construct of the elderly Engels' (Carver 1983: 153). Despite the persistent claim in Marxism-Leninism that scientific socialism was a collaborative project of Marx and Engels and that Marx 'entirely shared Engels' conceptions' (Anguélov 1980: 132), Carver and supporters of his view determinedly reject the omnipotent worldview of traditional Marxist dialectical materialism (Paul Thomas 1976), even portraying their relationship as 'Marx contra Engels'; Marxists were deceived by 'Engelsism', which they ultimately hold responsible for the terror of Stalinism (Levine 1975: 241).

The most prominent example of stressing the difference between Marx and Engels is 'Western Marxism'. The category was originally employed by Maurice Merleau (1973: 59),[7] but its foundation goes back to the 1920s, in particular Lukács György's *History and Class Consciousness*.[8] Although Western Marxism is a broad category that encompasses great heterogeneity among those who are labelled as such, one of the key topics is this anti-Stalinist attempt to provide a more sophisticated *theory of society* without falling into a mechanistic worldview (Jacoby 1983: 583). Western Marxism, in a sense, attempted to save Marx's social philosophy by criticizing Engels's dialectics of nature and strictly limiting dialectics to society. In challenging the validity of traditional Marxism in reaction to Nikita Khrushchev's secret speech as well as the Russian invasion of Hungary in 1956, Western Marxists drew upon Hegel in order to counter the 'dialectical materialism' of Soviet Marxism. In this context, Western Marxism targeted Engels as the misleading founder of this problematic worldview based on economic determinism and scientism. If Engels were right about the independent and objective existence of dialectics in nature, it would be possible to conceptualize and formulate a dialectical method first through the investigations in natural science and then to apply it to the analysis of human society. However, such a procedure produces a mechanistic and positivist understanding of society that is incompatible with Marx's dialectical analysis of capitalism. Western Marxism thus regarded the realm of natural science as Engels's domain of expertise and completely separated it from Marx's dialectical philosophy of society.

This separation inevitably resulted in 'a basic shift in the whole centre of gravity of European Marxism towards philosophy' (P. Anderson 1976: 49). For example, Louis Althusser (2001: 35) criticized Engels's 'positivist theme' that erases philosophy. In his attempt to revive Marx's dialectic, Jean-Paul Sartre also denounced Engels's materialism as absurdity: 'I have always thought that such a fertile working hypothesis as historical materialism in no way required as a basis the absurdity of metaphysical materialism' (Sartre 2004: 51). Highlighting the intellectual division of labour between Marx and Engels, Lucio Colletti (1973: 132) even concluded that the views of Marx and Engels are characterized by 'two profoundly different ways of seeing things'. The central problem was the relationship between nature and dialectics. Alfred Schmidt in his treatment of Marx's concept of nature doubted 'whether dialectical determinations such as "totality", "contradiction", "productivity", "immanent negation" could in any sense be ascribed to nature' without falling into 'dogmatic metaphysics' (Schmidt [1971] 2014: 183–4, 51). In this manner, Western Marxists expelled Engels and his mechanistic dialectic of nature from their analysis, but at the same time they completely excluded the sphere of nature and natural science from Marx's social philosophy.

This decision was inevitable for Western Marxists in order to prevent Marx's social theory from descending into the crude materialism of Soviet Marxism, but in a sense, the 'divergence thesis' was 'motivated more by ideology than by evidence' (Blackledge 2020: 29). In fact, the price paid by Western Marxism was high. It became unable to integrate the problem of ecology into its analysis because it is the sphere where nature must play a central role. As a result, its heavily philosophical approach is unable to effectively respond to the ecological crisis in the Anthropocene.[9]

This is how both traditional Marxism and Western Marxism ended up neglecting the importance of Marx's serious research in the field of natural sciences throughout the 20th century. However, like Foster and Burkett, there are other classical Marxists who recognize Marx's strong interest in natural science and argue for the unity of Marx and Engels without falling into a positivist worldview.[10] They pointed out the following facts: Marx wrote a whole chapter of *Anti-Dühring* and revised Engels's manuscript, calling it 'very important' (Welty 1983: 183; *MECW* 45: 334); Marx himself used the term 'scientific socialism' (Stanley 2002: 43); and most decisively, Marx shared with Engels the dialectic of nature when he wrote in *Capital* about the transformation of quantity to quality (Foster 2020: 241). Thus, these Marxists conclude: 'To maintain anything more than that, however, makes Engels the scapegoat for Scientific Marxism; to differentiate him radically from Marx is … historically dubious and unjust' (Gouldner 1980: 251). Kaan Kangal (2020: 15, 185) argues that the existence of 'difference' that is natural for any collaborative project does not immediately mean 'break', concluding that Marx and Engels 'have a common worldview'.

Western Marxism, despite its claim to the authentic interpretation of Marx's philosophy, falls into nonsense when it denies his interest in natural science. Marx, following Hegel, described some natural phenomena as manifestations of an objective dialectic of nature. This is just one example of the many things upon which Marx and Engels agreed. To deny this fact would be absurd. Nevertheless, this does not immediately mean that they had pursued the same single project based upon a division of labour. Since they are ultimately two different people with different interests, it is natural to assume that there were important differences of opinion even if they shared many ideas. While it is unfair to scapegoat Engels 'as a convenient whipping boy' (Foster 2017: 48), one should not erase theoretical differences between Marx and Engels. Just as Marx's understanding of political economy cannot be equated with Engels's despite their long-standing collaboration (Otani 2016), the possibility of disagreement always remains, even when they simultaneously studied the same topic and *even when they believed that they shared the same interests*. In this context, the *MEGA* provides new materials with which to more rigorously re-examine their intellectual relationship and division of labour.

Ironically, it was Engels himself who emphasized this intellectual division of labour with Marx, giving credibility to the claim made by Western Marxism. According to his preface to the second edition of *Anti-Dühring* published after Marx's death, 'Marx was well versed in mathematics, but we could keep up with natural science only piecemeal, intermittently and sporadically'. Later, however, Engels reflected on this blind spot: 'When I retired from business and transferred my home to London, thus enabling myself to give the necessary time to it, I went through as complete as possible a "moulting", as Liebig calls it, in mathematics and the natural sciences' (*MECW* 25: 11). In fact, *Anti-Dühring* and *Dialectics of Nature* document Engels's serious study of developments in physics, chemistry and biology in his time. Consequently, his works greatly influenced the formation of the worldview of traditional Marxism. Because of Engels's authority as Marx's closest comrade, subsequent generations of Marxists could simply take for granted the existence of an intellectual division of labour between the two. This assumption makes it appear as if Marx did not have much to say about nature precisely because he had entrusted Engels with the further development of the dialectics of nature. Thus, Engels's *Dialectics of Nature* and *Anti-Dühring* became the key reference points in applying Marx's dialectical materialism to the sphere of nature. This was how 'Marxism' was 'invented' by Engels.

However, Engels in his preface to the second edition of *Anti-Dühring* (1885) hid some important information from his readers. At the time, this editor of *Capital* was occupied with sorting out Marx's manuscripts and notebooks, so he must have known that Marx also eagerly studied natural sciences, especially in his later years while writing the manuscripts of *Capital*. In fact, Marx and Engels often discussed various issues in natural sciences. Some of their close friends were experts in natural science, such as Carl Schorlemmer, Samuel Moore and Roland Daniels, and they also gave Marx and Engels intellectual stimulation to study chemistry, physiology and biology, forming a scientific community (Griese and Pawelzig 1995). However, Engels did not mention this fact and simply said that Marx 'only piecemeal, intermittently and sporadically' followed the rapid development of natural sciences.

While Marx and Engels surely shared an interest in natural science, Engels was more advanced in his research into natural science at first. Indeed, Marx in his letter to Engels dated 4 July 1864 wrote that he was inspired by Engels to read Carpenter's *Physiology* as well as Spurzheim's *Anatomy of the Brain and the Nervous System* and wrote: 'I invariably follow in your footsteps' (*MECW* 41: 546). However, after reading the seventh edition of Justus von Liebig's *Agricultural Chemistry* in 1865, Marx started to study natural sciences quite intensively (Foster 2000; Saito 2017). His reading list after 1868 expanded rapidly and came to include various fields of natural science such as chemistry, geology, mineralogy, physiology and botany. He rapidly caught up with Engels, though the latter also kept studying these topics. Loyal to his old habit of studying new materials, Marx, especially in his last years, left a large number of notebooks on natural science. In the last 15 years of his life, he filled one-third of his notebooks, half of which comprise excerpts from books on natural sciences.

On 19 December 1882, Engels acknowledged that Marx was more familiar with what can be considered today as the problem of increasing entropy with the consumption of fossil fuel:

> [The] working individual is not only a stabiliser *of present* but also, and to a far greater extent, a squanderer *of past*, solar heat. As to what we have done in the way of squandering our reserves of energy, our coal, ore, forests, etc., *you are better informed than I am*. (*MECW* 46: 411; emphasis added)

Engels's remark indicates how much Marx's ecological interest developed after 1865. Marx dealt directly with the 'squandering' of natural recourses by grounding his insights in geology and mineralogy (*MEGA* IV/31). Marx carefully read books by geologists such as James F. W. Johnston and Joseph Beete Jukes, but he also read newspapers and articles related to economy and ecology. He paid attention to the mechanization of coal mining, whose impact on workers as well as the environment must be carefully studied. In his letter to Jenny dated on 6 June 1881, Marx referred to the newly invented 'coal-cutting machine' in the United States and paid attention to how it would affect to the miners as well as threaten 'John Bull's industrial supremacy (*MECW* 46: 96). Even knowing all this, Engels did *not* mention this point in the preface to *Anti-Dühring* and instead simply claimed that his dialectics of nature was an application of the dialectical method 'founded and developed' by Marx (*MECW* 25: 9).

This is strange. Engels in the same preface emphatically maintained that the ideas developed in *Anti-Dühring* were fully compatible with Marx's, saying that he 'read the whole manuscript to him before it was printed' (*MECW* 25: 9), and Marx fully agreed with him. However, Engels' remark is not necessarily credible because this 'proof' was provided only *after* Marx's death (Carver 1983: 123). Moreover, Engels did not refer to Marx's serious engagement with natural science. This silence is quite remarkable because the existence of Marx's notebooks on natural sciences would provide even stronger 'evidence' for the dialectics of nature as their collaborative project was supported by Marx himself. Since Marx's notebooks had not been published at the time, Engels could have simply said that, inspired by his great theoretical endeavour, Marx was also greatly interested in investigating the dialectics of nature. But he did not mention the existence of these notebooks, so that they remained unpublished throughout the 20th century. Here one is tempted to symptomatically interpret Engels's unnatural silence: *he tacitly admitted that Marx's interest in natural sciences possessed a different character to his own.* Consequently, the honest Engels (unconsciously) avoided referring to Marx's serious engagement with natural science and instead simply emphasized their intellectual division of labour. If this is the case, what is the underlying difference between them?

II

Marx as Author and Engels as Editor of *Capital*

Since the publication of Marx's notebooks in the *MEGA* revealed that *both* Marx and Engels had studied natural science, Western Marxism's one-sided delimiting of the theoretical scope of Marx's dialectical analysis to the sphere of society is flawed. It is no longer credible to maintain that Marx's critique of political economy must be restricted to the analysis of society because he actively expanded it to analyse how the metabolic exchange between humans *and* nature is transformed and reorganized in favour of capital accumulation. In this sense, it is not possible to completely separate Marx and Engels. Nevertheless, this does not immediately mean that Marx and Engels shared the *same* interest in their research in natural science.[11] One needs to investigate the issue more carefully.[12]

The unfortunate problem is that, despite his serious engagement with natural sciences, Marx passed away in 1883 before completing *Capital*. Engels had to take up the task of editing volumes II and III of *Capital*. His effort was enormous, considering the fact that Marx left only a series of unfinished and fragmentary manuscripts, which were not at all suitable for publication in their original form. Volume II consists of eight manuscripts written between 1864 and 1881, which means that these manuscripts are not at the same level of theoretical maturity. The main body of the manuscript for volume III of *Capital* was written in 1864/65 (before the publication of volume I in 1867), so Marx was not able to integrate his later developments into the manuscript except for some fragmentary calculations on the rate of surplus value and profit (*MEGA* II/4.3 and II/14; Heinrich 2016).

Of course, Engels did his best, but it was impossible for Engels to perfectly understand Marx's intentions and objectives and to reflect them in his edition of *Capital*. As a result, differences inevitably emerged between Marx as the author and Engels as the editor of *Capital* (Roth 2002). According to Teinosuke Otani (2016), the first cause for misinterpretation of Marx's true intention in the manuscript was that the older Engels dictated the manuscript aloud to Oscar Eisengarten, who transcribed it. Engels used this transcribed text as the basis for his editorial work (*MEGA* II/12). Consequently, Engels overlooked the distinction Marx made in his manuscript as well as various mark-ups in it. Marx divided his manuscript into two parts, one for the main text of volume III and the other written as notes on relevant materials to be used mainly as footnotes. However, Engels mistakenly treated the latter as part of the main text too, so that the logical line of Marx's argument in the manuscript became partially invisible in the Engels edition. This would not have happened if Engels had directly looked at the original manuscript during his editorial work.

The second reason for misappropriation is that the only information available to Engels about chapter 5 of volume III[13] came from Marx's sporadic remarks in his private letters, so Engels inevitably had a strong prejudice about the object of Marx's analysis and its characteristics in chapter 5. Directly looking at the original manuscript (*MEGA* II/4.2), it is clear that the theme that chapter 5 as a whole deals with is interest-bearing capital, but Engels believed that the object of this chapter must be 'bank' and 'credit'. As a result, he made changes even in Marx's texts in order to reconcile the content of chapter 5 with his own understanding. Due to Engels's bias, the true shape of chapter 5 in Marx's manuscript became invisible in part 5 of the Engels edition.

Considering these differences in their respective understandings of political economy, there were probably noticeable differences in their ecology as well. In fact, when Engels neglected Marx's notebooks on natural sciences in the preface to *Anti-Dühring*, there existed a subtle disagreement between Marx and Engels concerning the concept of 'metabolism'. This problem is discernible in Engels's edition of volume III of *Capital*, in which Marx drew upon Liebig's critique of robbery agriculture in order to demonstrate the irrationality of capitalist production. Certainly, Engels recognized the importance of Liebig's critique of robbery agriculture as a foundation of Marx's ecological critique of capitalism. For example, in *The Housing Question*, he like Marx referred to Liebig, pointing to the 'antithesis of town and country'. He also argued for the reconstruction of 'an intimate connection between industrial and agricultural production' (*MECW* 23: 384). This is basically a continuation of what Marx and Engels demanded as the 'combination of agriculture with manufacturing industries' in the *Manifesto of the Communist Party* (*MECW* 6: 505). Also, in editing *Capital*, volume III, Engels supplemented Marx's description of robbery agriculture with concrete examples. He added the following passage, for example, in order to highlight Marx's intention of criticizing the wasteful loss of soil nutrients through the use of water-closets in large cities more clearly: 'In London, for example, they can do nothing better with the excrement produced by 4½ million people than pollute the Thames with it, at monstrous expense' (*Capital* III: 195). Here one can observe the intellectual *collaboration* between Marx and Engels based on Liebig's 'law of replenishment'.

However, things look rather different when the concept of 'metabolism' is at stake. Engels must have been aware that Marx discussed the problem of soil exhaustion with Liebig's theory of metabolism and its disruption due to the robbery system of modern agriculture. The hint is that Engels intentionally changed a particular passage related to the concept of metabolism in volume III of *Capital*. In his original manuscript, Marx wrote:

> [In] this way [large-scale landownership] produces conditions that provoke an irreparable rift in the interdependent process between social metabolism and natural metabolism prescribed by the natural laws of the soil. The result of this is a squandering of the vitality of the soil, and trade carries this devastation far beyond the bounds of a single country (Liebig). (*MEGA* II/4.2: 752–3)

Referring to Liebig, Marx highlighted the danger of a serious global disruption to the interdependent process between 'social metabolism' (capitalist production, circulation and consumption for the sake of profit) and the 'natural metabolism' prescribed by natural law (plant growth and soil ecology). This is the problem of the second-order mediation of the universal metabolism of nature that exists independently of human beings. The unique set of capital's metabolic organization aiming at its own infinite valorization with an ever-expanding scale is incompatible with the natural laws that exist prior to capital. The problem is aggravated by international trade because it increases the difficulty of fulfilling Liebig's law of replenishment. In this passage, Marx clearly formulated the tense relationship between the capitalist economic form determinations (*Formbestimmungen*) and the natural properties of the material world. This passage undoubtedly plays a central role in the conceptual and methodological framework of the metabolic rift approach (Foster 2000).

However, Engels modified the first sentence in his edition of volume III of *Capital* as follows: '… in this way it produces conditions that provoke an irreparable rift in the interdependent process of social metabolism, a metabolism prescribed by the natural laws of life itself' (*Capital* III: 949). Now the word 'natural metabolism' is omitted and 'soil' is changed to 'life'.[14] The omission of the term 'natural metabolism' is regrettable because the contrast between social and natural metabolism, which is key to Marx's method of distinguishing between the primary and the second-order mediation of metabolism, became obscure.[15] In this sense, the claim that 'Engels' and Marx's conceptions of the method of political economy are in accord' (Welty 1983: 294) needs to be questioned. Rather, this passage seems to imply a profound methodological difference between them. Certainly, there are a number of cases where Engels had to modify Marx's expressions whenever unclear, confusing or mistaken. However, in this passage, Marx's intention is not only clear but also this is a key passage for his theory of metabolic rift. What does Engels's editorial change signify?

Here it is first helpful to briefly overview Engels's 'dialectics of nature'. According to him, *Anti-Dühring* was written with the intention of grasping the laws of nature and history and especially to 'strip [them] of this [Hegelian] mystic form and to bring clearly before the mind in their complete simplicity and universality'. In contrast to Hegel's idealist objective dialectics, Engels claimed his dialectics of nature to be a *materialist* one that avoided Hegel's misconception of 'building the law of dialectics into nature'. For him, 'there could be no question of building the laws of dialectics into nature, but of discovering them in it and evolving them from it' (*MECW* 25: 11–13). In other words, his project sought to grasp the real laws of development of nature as they exist in nature 'objectively and independent' of human existence and activities (McLellan 1977: 73). It is an ontological investigation in that it dialectically develops movements, metamorphosis and evolution in nature through history (Jordan 1967: 167). Nevertheless, this ontological turn has become quite unpopular among those Marxists who wish to distinguish Marx's critique of political economy from Engels's scientism. Carver (1983: 107) argues that Engels's investigation, unlike Marx's, reflects the ontological dichotomy of 'matter' and 'consciousness' found in modern natural science. Similarly, Shlomo Avineri maintained that 'Engels's materialism, based on the mechanistic traditions of the eighteenth century, differed markedly from the main stream of Marx's thought' (Avineri 1970: 4).[16]

Although the laws of nature exist objectively, their comprehension has a great practical purpose for human beings.[17] In other words, Engels's dialectics of nature is tied to a practical demand for the realization of 'freedom' through the 'mastery' and 'control' of external nature. Accordingly, the construction of socialism as a free society means for Engels to become the 'real, conscious lord of nature', as he insisted:

> The extraneous objective forces that have hitherto governed history pass under the control of man himself. Only from that time will man himself, with full consciousness, make his own history – only from that time will the social causes set in movement by him have, in the main and in a constantly growing measure, the results intended by him. It is the humanity's leap from the realm of necessity to the realm of freedom. (*MECW* 25: 270)

He also wrote in *Dialectics of Nature* that

> our mastery of [nature] consists in the fact that we have the advantage over other being of being able to know and apply its laws. And in fact, with every day that passes we are learning to understand its laws more correctly ... we are more and more placed in a position where we can learn and even control the more remote natural consequences of our ordinary productive activities. (*MECW* 25: 461)

According to Engels, not only by abolishing the reified domination of capital independently of human consciousness and behaviour but also by fully appropriating the objective laws of nature can humans finally leap to 'the realm of freedom'.

Of course, Engels did not think that the recognition of the laws of nature would allow humans to arbitrarily manipulate nature. He was not naively advocating for the absolute domination over nature by maximizing the productive forces. In *Dialectics of Nature*, he even warned against the 'revenge' of nature:

> Let us not, however, flatter ourselves overmuch on account of our human victories over nature. For each such victory nature takes its revenge on us. Each victory, it is true, in the first place brings about the results we expected, but in the second and third places it has quite different, unforeseen effects which only too often cancel out the first.... Thus at every step we are reminded that we by no means rule over nature like a conqueror over a foreign people, like someone standing outside nature – but that we, with flesh, blood, and brain, belong to nature, and exist in its midst, and that all our mastery of it consists in the fact that we have the advantage over all other creatures of being able to learn its laws and apply them correctly. (*MECW* 25: 460–1)

This remark has often been cited as proof of Engels's ecological interest hidden in his otherwise highly abstract *Dialectics of Nature* (Salleh, Goodman and Hamed 2015: 102). He was particularly critical of capitalist production oriented towards short-term profit maximization that refuses to recognize natural limits: 'As the individual capitalists are engaged in production and exchange for the sake of the immediate profit, only the nearest, most immediate results must first be taken into account' (*MECW* 25: 463). If the laws of nature are continuously ignored, the project of dominating nature inevitably fails, which culminates in catastrophe: humans cease to be active, labouring agents but are obliged to behave passively at the mercy of nature's power, leading to the collapse of civilization. Thus, Foster concludes: '*For Engels, as for Marx, the key to socialism was the rational regulation of the metabolism of humanity and nature*, in such a way as to promote the fullest possible human potential, while safeguarding the needs of future generations' (Foster 2017: 50; emphasis added). Is this really so?

Engels was certainly an ecosocialist. Foster is right in this point. However, while Marx clearly demanded that 'the associated producers' 'govern the human metabolism with nature in a rational way' (*Capital* III: 959), Engels did *not* use the term 'metabolism' in demanding an ecosocialist future. Engels's ecology pivoted around nature's 'revenge', criticizing short-sighted profit maximization under capitalism. The key passage on 'metabolic rift' in *Capital* was also modified by Engels in accordance with this scheme of nature's revenge. Engels's edition of *Capital* emphasizes that the violation of natural laws of life would bring about a fatal consequence for human civilization, while the methodological approach unique to Marx's metabolic theory, which investigates how the law of value dominant in the social metabolism modifies the natural metabolism and causes an irreparable rift, has become rather unclear. Engels judged that readers would find Marx's original expression about the entanglement between economic form determinations – the 'second order mediation' – and the universal metabolism of nature hard to understand and changed the sentence into a more 'accessible' expression in accordance with his scheme of nature's revenge.[18]

Engels's modification of *Capital* may appear to be a subtle one. However, the significance of his editorial change becomes apparent when we notice the fact that, unlike Marx, he did *not* cherish Liebig's theory of metabolism. Indeed, in *Dialectics of Nature* he referred to Liebig's concept of metabolism *in the context of criticizing* him as a 'dilettante' in biology (*MECW* 25: 576). This expression clearly indicates that Engels was not entirely supportive of Liebig's view, except for his theory of robbery agriculture. Engels's dismissal of Liebig's theory of metabolism has to do with their different opinions concerning the origin of life. Liebig (wrongly) denied the possibility of the historical evolution of organic life from inorganic matter and accepted the hypothesis that 'eternal life' had been 'imported' to the planet from universal space (Liebig 1859: 291). Here it is possible to discern the influence of 19th-century vitalism that believed in certain inexplicable forces of life (Wendling 2009: 81). In opposition to this vitalist tradition, Engels correctly argued that life is the process of metabolism that historically emerged and evolved from inorganic non-life. 'Protein' confirms this point: 'Life is the mode of existence of protein bodies, the essential element of which consists in *continual metabolic interchange with the natural environment outside them*' (*MECW* 25: 578; emphasis added). Engels saw the origin of life in the chemical process of assimilation and excretion of protein bodies, and he pointed to the possibility of artificially creating a living organism by generating protein in a laboratory.[19]

Engels rejected Liebig's vitalism, with its separation of biology from chemistry and its inexplicable principles that are supposedly unique to living beings. According to Engels, inorganic bodies have metabolism as a chemical interchange with their environment, and once 'protein' historically evolved, metabolism came to exist as life. In this evolutionary process, there is no absolute rift between inorganic (inanimate) and organic (living) matters. Here Engels's concept of metabolism attains a unique theoretical importance in *Dialectics of Nature* to bridge chemistry and biology.

Since Engels's concept of metabolism emphasized the historical emergence of protein in opposition to Liebig, his ecology did not apply the concept of metabolism to environmental issues as Marx and Liebig had done. In doing so, however, he lost sight of the methodological role of Liebig's theory of metabolism in Marx's *Capital* as a way to analyse the relationality of humans and nature from both a transhistorical and socio-historical perspective and to reveal the particular contradictions of capital's second-order mediation. Engels limited the theoretical scope of metabolism to the process of the origin and evolution of life that proceeded *independently of* human beings and their social relations unfolded as the dialectics of nature. According to Engels's *Anti-Dühring*, the motor of dialectics characterized by 'negation of negation' is 'a law which ... holds good in the animal and plant kingdoms, in geology, in mathematics, in history and in philosophy' (*MECW* 25: 131). The main role he assigns to 'metabolism' is not as an ecological analysis of capitalism but as a demonstration that this objective law penetrates the whole of nature encompassing both inorganic and organic beings.[20]

Consequently, although Engels partially took up Liebig's views, he did not adopt the concept of metabolic rift in *Capital* but rather maintained the earlier scheme of the 'antagonism of town and country' already put forward in *The German Ideology*.[21] Here his personal interest in the dialectics of nature hindered his appreciation of the economic meaning of Marx's reception of

Liebig's theory of metabolism. In other words, Engels's modification implies that he could not entirely grasp the methodological foundation of Marx's critique of political economy that he developed in the 1850s and 1860s, which deals with how the metabolism between humans and nature is modified and reorganized through the formal and real subsumption of labour under capital. This is exactly how the differences between Marx and Engels in relation to political economy affects the sphere of ecology.

Certainly, Marx did not abandon his earlier insight about the 'antithesis of town and country' even in *Capital*, where he wrote:

> ... the foundation of every division of labour which has attained a certain degree of development, and has been brought about by the exchange of commodities, is the separation of town from country. One might well say that the whole economic history of society is summed up in the movement of this antithesis. (*Capital* I: 472)

This antagonism between town and country can be fruitfully reinterpreted as the antagonism between 'centre' and 'periphery' to analyse modern ecological imperialism in an ecological critique of capitalism (Clark and Foster 2009).[22] However, this should not relativize the theoretical significance of the fact that Marx started analysing the disturbance of metabolism between humans and the earth in accordance with his own method of political economy because this difference of method influences Marx's and Engels's visions of the future society.

III
DIALECTICS OF 'DOMINATION' AND 'REVENGE'

Both Marx and Engels regarded the conscious and teleological control of natural laws through labour as a unique human activity, which they often characterized as 'control' over nature. For example, Engels wrote in *Anti-Dühring*: 'Freedom therefore consists in the control over ourselves and over external nature, a control founded on knowledge of natural necessity' (*MECW* 25: 106). Such remarks are often taken by critics as a manifestation of his 'Baconian-Prometheanism' belief (Peter Thomas 2008: 42). A counterproof against such a criticism is Engels's warning against nature's 'revenge'. Engels held the necessity of correctly recognizing the laws of nature and applying them properly without necessarily advocating for the arbitrary manipulation of nature.

However, more recent criticisms have been directed against Marxism. For example, Jason W. Moore argues that Engels is too 'static' in arguing that if the law of nature continues to be ignored, nature will take revenge on humans *one day* (Moore 2015: 80). Neil Smith similarly rejected the revenge of nature as 'left apocalypticism' (N. Smith [1984] 2008: 247). In responding to Moore and Smith, one should note that Marx did not treat the disruption of the universal metabolism of nature under capitalism merely as revenge by nature but analysed the problem of metabolic rift from two more aspects. First, Marx repeatedly highlighted that capital does not simply accept the limits nature imposes. Capital is quite 'elastic' (*Capital* II: 433), constantly shifting the rift. In the *Grundrisse*, Marx also pointed out that this elasticity is a form of capitalist power based on the 'universal appropriation of nature' (*Grundrisse*: 409). The power of capital to buy time through metabolic shifts is astonishing, as history demonstrates. However, since capital's instrumentalist attitude cannot take sufficient account of the material aspects of the world, its incessant attempt to overcome natural limits only poses new ones. It is not therefore possible to know a priori whether capitals' elasticity can tame a given natural limit or not. An investigation into this *dynamic* relationship between capital and nature was the main topic for the later Marx. This is why his research shifted more and more to *empirical* topics in geology, agricultural chemistry and mineralogy in order to comprehend these dynamics, while Engels was more concerned with the transhistorical law of nature as a 'science' of the universe. Marx's purpose in studying natural science differs from that of Engels in that he aimed to comprehend the source of capital's astonishing elasticity in the interdependent historical process of social and natural metabolism.

Second, Marx's description of the disruption of the metabolism avoids the 'apocalyptic' tone of nature's revenge by emphasizing the *active* factor of resistance. The boundless extension of working hours as well as the intensification of labour result in the alienation of labour and physical and mental illness. This ultimately calls for the conscious regulation of reified power such as by establishing the normal working day or schools for vocational teaching founded by the state. A similar path can be envisioned with regard to nature. As the disruption of the universal metabolism of nature annihilates the possibilities for the co-evolution of humans and nature and even threatens human civilization, humans are obliged to establish more conscious social management of productive activities: 'But by destroying the circumstances surrounding that metabolism, which originated in a merely natural and spontaneous fashion, [the capitalist mode of production] compels its systematic restoration as a regulative law of social production, and in a form adequate to the full development of the human race' (*Capital* I: 637–8). All that capital cares about is whether its accumulation can be achieved, so it does not really matter even if most parts of the planet become unsuitable for humans and animals to live. Instead of waiting for the collapse of capitalism thanks to nature's revenge, it is indispensable that individuals confronting the global ecological crisis take active measures for the conscious control over the metabolism with their environment.[23]

As a vision for such a post-capitalist society in *Capital*, volume III, Marx famously wrote:

> The realm of freedom really begins only where labour determined by necessity and external expediency ends; it lies by its very nature beyond the sphere of material production proper. Just as the savage must wrestle with nature to satisfy his needs, to maintain and reproduce his life, so must civilized man, and he must do so in all forms of society and under all possible modes of production. This realm of natural necessity expands with his development, because his needs do too; but the productive forces to satisfy these expand at the same time. Freedom, in this sphere, can consist only in this, that socialized man, the associated producers, govern the human metabolism with nature in a rational way, bringing it under their collective control instead of being dominated by it as a blind power; accomplishing it with the least expenditure of energy and in conditions most worthy and appropriate for their human nature. But this always remains a realm of necessity. The true realm of freedom, the development of human powers as an end in itself, begins beyond it, though it can only flourish with this realm of necessity as its basis. (*Capital* III: 958–9)

This passage must be compared with Engels's view of the realm of freedom quoted previously because there is an important difference:

> The extraneous objective forces that have hitherto governed history pass under the control of man himself. Only from that time will man himself, with full consciousness, make his own history – only from that time will the social causes set in movement by him have, in the main and in a constantly growing measure, the results intended by him. It is the humanity's leap from the realm of necessity to the realm of freedom. (*MECW* 25: 270)

Engels argued for the necessity to consciously apply the law of nature, and his 'realm of freedom' consists precisely in this control over nature. According to Engels, the recognition and practical application of natural laws enable people to freely engage with nature to satisfy their own needs. That constitutes 'humanity's leap' to the realm of freedom.

In replying to the popular criticism that Engels unlike Marx was a 'necessitarian' (Peter Thomas 1998: 494) who thought that the transcendence of natural limits will be the condition for the realization of the sphere of freedom, John L. Stanley argued that both Marx and Engels recognized the natural basis for the realization of human freedom (Stanley 2002: 23). In fact,

Marx also thought of it as a necessary condition that producers confronted with the disruption of metabolism associate with each other and put a 'blind power' under their conscious control. Yet this does not mean that Stanley is correct in arguing that there is no difference between Marx and Engels. Alfred Schmidt ([1971] 2014: 135) problematizes the 'famous sudden leap' to the realm of freedom in Engels's vision of socialism – namely, mastery of natural laws *is* identified with the realization of the realm of freedom. Again, this has to do with his interest in natural science. Engels, who was primarily concerned with the dialectics of nature and modern science, placed great importance on human freedom based on recognizing the transhistorical law of nature. It is control over nature that *immediately* realizes the realm of freedom.

In contrast, Marx did not forget to add that 'this [mastery over nature] always remains a realm of necessity'. In other words, the new society based on the associated mode of production should realize the free development of individuality, but this takes place *beyond* freedom of labour. Labour is indispensable for human existence, and it needs to be meaningful and attractive for workers, but it is only one part of meaningful human activity. Freedom is not limited to the conscious regulation of the law of nature through natural science, and Marx's 'realm of freedom' rather includes creative activities such as art, the enrichment of love and friendship, caring for others, and hobbies like sport, playing music and reading books, which are essential for the all-round development of the individual. These activities realize the full development of individuality in communism. Compared to this vision, Engels's view of nature rather impoverishes the content of the realm of freedom by reducing it to the realm of necessity and put forward the Hegelian view of freedom as able to be realized by consciously obeying the necessity: 'Freedom is the insight into necessity' (*MECW* 25: 105).

IV
ENGELS'S NOTEBOOKS AND CRITIQUE OF POLITICAL ECONOMY

Marx's theory of metabolism also helps us understand the meaning of his extensive notebooks on natural sciences after 1868. Hints for imagining the unwritten part of *Capital* exist in these little-known notebooks. Their scope is wide-ranging and Marx's interest in natural science goes beyond the theory of ground rent in volume III of *Capital*. Even if the reason for his engagement with Liebig's *Agricultural Chemistry* in 1864–5 has to do with the theoretical question of ground rent, the meaning of Marx's reception of

Liebig's critique of modern agriculture cannot be contained in it, but it deals with broader ecological questions. Simply put, Marx aimed at comprehending how disharmonies in the material world emerge due to modifications of the universal metabolism of nature by the reified power of capital.

Marx's interest in ecological questions grew even further after 1868 because he was not fully satisfied with Liebig's critique of robbery agriculture. Instead, he gathered new materials including ones that were critical of Liebig's pessimistic and Malthusian view of agricultural development (*MEGA* IV/18; Saito 2017: 224). In this context, Marx's excerpts from Carl N. Fraas, a German agronomist in Munich, are of great importance not just for the sake of reconstructing Marx's ecological development but also for investigating the intellectual relationship between Marx and Engels. The pair shared various kinds of information, including on ecological questions. Marx wrote in his letter to Engels dated 25 March 1868 that he even found a 'socialist tendency' in Fraas's warning against excessive deforestation after making detailed notes from his book *Climate and Plant World over Time* (*MEGA* IV/18):

> Very interesting is the book by Fraas (1847): *Klima und Pflanzenwelt in der Zeit, eine Geschichte beider*, namely as proving that climate and flora change in historical times. He is a Darwinist before Darwin, and admits even the species developing in historical times. But he is at the same time agronomist. He claims that with cultivation – depending on its degree – the 'moisture' so beloved by the peasants gets lost (hence also the plants migrate from south to north), and finally steppe formation occurs. The first effect of cultivation is useful, but finally devastating through deforestation, etc. This man is both a thoroughly learned philologist (he has written books in Greek) and a chemist, agronomist, etc. The conclusion is that cultivation – when it proceeds in natural growth and is not consciously controlled (as a bourgeois he naturally does not reach this point) – leaves deserts behind it, Persia, Mesopotamia, etc., Greece. So once again an unconscious socialist tendency! (*MECW* 42: 558–9)

Prompted by Marx's high evaluation, Engels also later read the book by Fraas and made excerpts in his notebook of 1879–80 (*MEGA* IV/31). It is thus possible to compare Marx's and Engels's excerpts to see whether they really shared the same interests.

As indicated in Marx's latter to Engels, Fraas's book deals with climate change in ancient civilizations such as Mesopotamia, Egypt and Greece, due to excessive and irrational deforestation. Out of this similarity between Marx's engagement with Fraas and Engels's warning about nature's revenge in *Dialectics of Nature*, Stanley (2002: 18) points to the identity of their reception of Fraas's theory. Yet Stanley only superficially compares these two isolated remarks in Marx's letter and Engels's manuscript without looking at their notebooks. My detailed analysis of Marx's notebook on Fraas's work (Saito 2017) provides a foundation for its comparison with Engels's notebook on Fraas.

Although Engels's excerpts are short because Engels had already used Fraas's book in his *Dialectics of Nature*, they clearly document what he was most interested in. First, one immediately notices that the intellectual relationship between Marx and Engels in the field of natural science had been reversed compared to 1864, when Marx was still 'invariably follow[ing] in [Engels's] footsteps'. It is noteworthy that Engels's paraphrasing in his notebook on Fraas indicates that his view was influenced *by* Marx's high evaluation of the work. In other words, Engels now followed what Marx recommended to him.

In this letter, Marx highly valued Fraas's insight that 'cultivation – when it proceeds in natural growth and is not *consciously controlled* ...– leaves deserts behind it'. Marx carefully studied Fraas's explanation of how uncontrolled processes in ancient civilizations ultimately undermined the material foundations of their prosperity because excessive deforestation irreversibly changes the local climate in a manner unfavourable to indigenous plants. Engels wrote down the same opinion in his notebook: '*The development of people's agriculture leaves behind an enormous desert*' (*MEGA* IV/31: 515; emphasis in original). Engels summarized the significance of Fraas's work as a 'main proof that civilization in its conventional forms is an antagonistic process which exhausts the soil, devastates the forest, renders the soil infertile for its original products, and worsens the climate'. As an example, Engels noted that in Germany and Italy the average temperature increased '5 to 6 degrees (°Re)'[24] (*MEGA* IV/31: 512). This understanding that unconscious production results in 'deserts' is also reflected in his discussion on nature's revenge in *Dialectics of Nature*. In fact, Engels argued based on Fraas's argument that

> the people who, in Mesopotamia, Greece, Asia Minor and elsewhere, destroyed the forests to obtain cultivable land, never dreamed that by removing along with the forests the collecting centres and reservoirs of moisture they were laying the basis for the present forlorn state of those countries. (*MECW* 25: 461)

Here Engels was clearly influenced by Marx's evaluation of Fraas's work.

Second, Marx in the same letter characterized Fraas as a 'Darwinist before Darwin' (*MECW* 42: 558). Engels also documented in his notebook a passage from Fraas's *Climate and Plant World Over Time* that reminds him of Darwin's 'natural selection':

As said, oak is also quite sensitive to elements of natural climate (temperature and humidity), and when there is any subtle change in them, oak is left behind in the competition against more durable and less sensitive surrounding trees that strive together for natural growth and self-preservation. (*MEGA* IV/31: 515)

This passage is indicative because Engels added that he read Fraas's book in order to refute the 'belief in the stability of plant species based on a Darwinian argument' (*MEGA* IV/31: 515). In writing this comment, he must have thought that his own interests were surely identical to those of Marx.

However, a closer look at the notebooks reveals that Marx's interest in Fraas is not actually limited to nature's revenge and a Darwinian argument. In the beginning of 1868, Marx in addition to Fraas's work carefully read Georg Ludwig von Maurer's *Einleitung zur Geschichte der Mark-, Hof-, Dorf-, und Stadtverfassung und der offentlichen Gewalt*, in which the German historian of law dealt with the Germanic system of landed property. Actually, Marx placed Fraas and Maurer in the same context by characterizing them with the same 'socialist tendency' in his letter to Engels, and their relationship is much closer than that of Fraas and Darwin in Marx's notebook. However, at first glance, the reason Marx simultaneously studied Germanic society is not clear, as Fraas and Maurer appear to have no connection. Prompted by Marx's high evaluation of Maurer in the letter, Engels also read Maurer's book and integrated it into his own analysis. However, unlike Marx, there is no sign that Engels connected Fraas and Maurer.

A hint connecting Fraas and Maurer can be found in Fraas's work *Agrarian Crisis and Its Solutions* published in 1866, where Fraas quoted directly from Maurer's book and praised the sustainability of lands in Germanic communes:

If the Mark village did not allow sales except among village members of wood, straw, dung, and even livestock (pigs!) and also ordered that all the crops harvested within the village, and even wine, should be consumed within the village (out of this practice various socage rights [*Bannrechte*] were to emerge), the means must have been retained for the maintenance of land power, and furthermore, the use of additional nutrients from forests and pastures, and even the use of meadows manured by rivers served to increase the [soil's] power everywhere. (Fraas 1866: 210)

As is clear from this passage, Frass did not maintain that all pre-capitalist societies ignored the laws of nature and left deserts behind them. Rather, he highlighted that in Germanic society soil productivity increased under sustainable production through their communal regulation of the land and its products, in contrast to Greek and Roman societies where commodity production existed to some extent and the communal tie of members was somewhat dissolved.

In December 1867 or January 1868 Marx wrote down the title of Fraas's *Agrarian Crisis and Its Solutions* in his notebook (*MEGA* IV/18: 359). It is quite likely that after reading Fraas's book, Marx not only read further books by Fraas but was also interested in Maurer's analysis of Germanic communes. Upon reading their books, he found the 'socialist tendency' in Maurer's work too, so he came to pay more attention to different ways of organizing the metabolism between humans and nature in pre-capitalist societies.[25] This praise of the equal and sustainable production of pre-capitalist rural communes confirms that Marx did not overgeneralize nature's revenge due to ignorance of the laws of nature in pre-capitalist societies. Otherwise, he would have fallen into the reductionist view that all civilizations are bad for the environment.[26] Rather, he recognized that the particularities of pre-capitalist metabolism between humans and nature might be the source of vitality of certain rural communes. Compared to the metabolic rift created by capitalist production, these communes contain elements of economic superiority, even if equal and sustainable production was rather unconsciously accomplished by long-lasting tradition and customs, and not by recognising the laws of nature. This is why Marx found a 'socialist tendency' in Fraas's and Maurer's work. One should note that this evaluation is quite different from Engels's argument that pre-capitalist societies suffered from nature's revenge due to their ignorance of the natural laws and that their recognition and appropriation would realize the leap to the realm of freedom. It is possible to say that Engels continued to hold a unilateral view of historical development in this regard.

Furthermore, Marx's notebooks of 1878, which contain quite extensive geological excerpts from John Yeats and Joseph Beete Jukes, are noteworthy in that they expand his theory of metabolism. These long excerpts deal with various topics, and their meaning cannot be reduced to ecology. Nevertheless, it is clear that Marx studied geology for the sake of expanding his political economy. For example, Marx noted that an 'enormous sum of money is wasted in coal-mining alone due to ignorance' (*MEGA* IV/26: 478) and documented Jukes's comment on the 'great practical importance' of geology in his *Student Manual of Geology*, which is

> one of the chief points in the practical applications of geology in the British islands [both for the purpose of guarding against] a wasteful expenditure of money in rash enterprises, as well as [for] directing it where enterprise [may have a] chance of being successful. (*MEGA* IV/26: 642)

Furthermore, Marx paid attention to Jukes's description of how progress in geology improves methods of discovery and mining of raw and auxiliary materials such as coal and iron and increases productivity and how improvements in transportation influence the relationship between industry and agriculture (as well as extractive industry). What was unprofitable becomes profitable and what was infertile becomes fertile in the course of capitalist development. This brings about tremendous complications in the application of the law of the rate of profit to fall.

This does not mean that capital can be freed from geological conditions. By contrast, Marx eagerly documented in his notebook how geologic strata, as a natural condition that humans cannot modify, heavily influence the course of social development. Already in the 1850s Marx was interested in the relationship between human history and natural history. For example, Marx's intensive engagement with geology led him to adopt the concept of 'geological formation' from James F. W. Johnston in the *London Notebooks* in order to grasp the multiple layers of social formation; though that was a mere metaphor at the time. In the 1870s and 1880s, he went one step further to study the direct relationship between geological formation and social formation. He wrote down a passage from Jukes's book, for example:

> ... 'England is divided into two totally dissimilar parts, in which the form and aspect of the ground, and condition and employment of the people, [were] alike contrasted with each other'. Namely, the part to the north-west part of this life is 'chiefly Palaeozoic ground, often wild, barren and mountainous, but in many places full of mineral wealth.' The part to the south-east of it consists of 'Secondary and Tertiary ground, and generally soft and gentle in outline, with little or no wealth beneath the soil'. As a result, the 'mining and manufacturing populations' are to be found in the first district, and the 'working people of the latter' are mainly 'agricultural'. (*MEGA* IV/26: 641)

In *Capital*, Marx envisioned a 'new and higher synthesis, a union of agriculture and industry' beyond their antithesis (*Capital* I: 637). However, the unchangeable geologic characteristics that Jukes pointed out must be much more carefully treated when envisioning post-capitalism because they cannot be modified. In fact, Marx highlighted these passages in his notebooks so that he could come back to them later. If so, Leszek Kołakowski's critique that 'Marx can scarcely admit that man is limited either by his body or by geographical conditions' (Kołakowski 1978: 413) is completely refuted.[27]

In relation to Fraas and Darwin, Marx's excerpts from Jukes's book are also of interest because they also discussed how climate and precipitation effect the geological formation as well as flora and fauna. In the section titled

'Palaeontology', Jukes, referring directly to Darwin, pointed to great climate changes over time and argued that 'alternation of climates involves destruction of species' (*MEGA* IV/26: 219). In this vein, Marx also documented Jukes's remark that '*extinction of species* is still going on (*man himself* is the most active exterminator)' (*MEGA* IV/26: 233; emphasis in original). Marx studied climate change from a long-term geological perspective as well as its impact upon the environment, paying particular attention to human impacts, as Fraas did. A similar remark on climate change in North America due to excessive deforestation can be found in his excerpt from Yeats's *Natural History of the Raw Materials of Commerce*: '*The enormous clearings* have, on the other hand, *already sensibly modified the climate*' (*MEGA* IV/26: 36; emphasis in original). Here Marx's interest in Darwin is – unlike Engels's – not limited to encyclopaedic topics like the origin of life, natural selection and evolution that proceed independently of humans, but encompasses the empirical and historical ways of *human* metabolic interaction with nature and its negative impacts.

The key differences between Marx and Engels in their reception of the natural science can be summarized in the following way. Engels's focus was the scientific recognition of the transhistorical law of nature in order to realize the realm of freedom. Engels's dialectics of nature, founded on the philosophical dichotomy of consciousness/matter and idealism/materialism, advocated the ontological primacy of the latter. Despite Engels's interest in ecological issues under capitalist production, it is undeniably characterized by a philosophical and transhistorical scheme, as a result of which he ended up rejecting Liebig's concept of metabolism and remained satisfied with the 'antithesis of town and country' conceptualized in the 1840s. Furthermore, in Engels's discussion of the realm of freedom as well as of pre-capitalist societies, he held a more unilateral vision of historical development based on progressive recognition of natural laws with an aid of modern natural science.

In contrast, Marx never really adopted the project of materialist dialectics that Engels was pursuing, even if he 'may have given his friend moral support and encouragement to follow such wide-ranging scholarly inclinations' (O'Rourke 1974: 50). Marx, after 'breaking away from philosophy' (Sasaki 2021: 35) in *The German Ideology*, was not interested in such philosophical ontology. In fact, his engagement with natural science came to possess an increasingly empirical character after the 1860s. By enriching the concept of metabolism after the 1860s, Marx aimed at comprehending the physical and social transformation of the relationship between humans and nature from historical, economic and ecological perspectives. He also came to study different ways of organizing human metabolism with nature in pre-capitalist and non-Western societies and to recognize the source of their vitality for building a more egalitarian and sustainable society beyond capitalism. In other words, contrary to Stanley's assumption, Marx's engagement with natural science was not for the sake of establishing 'the universal science' (Stanley 2002: 37) as he had advocated in the *Economic and Philosophical Manuscripts* of 1844. Of course, this difference between the founders of Marxism need not be *over*estimated. Marx did not completely reject Engels's attempt to establish a materialist conception of nature.[28] At the same time, the difference must not be *under*estimated because it is relevant to understanding why Engels did not fully understand the scope of Marx's notebooks on natural science and modified the key passage on the metabolic rift in volume III of *Capital*. In fact, Engels's understanding determined the reception of Marx's theory in the successive generations.

Susan Buck-Morss once argued: 'Surely [Marx] shared the bourgeois belief in progress, and there was much in Marx's later writings to justify Engels's understanding of dialectics as a natural law of historical development' (Buck-Morss 1977: 62). This chapter demonstrates quite the contrary. It was precisely due to this difference between 'Marx's later writings' and 'Engels's understanding of dialectics' that the concept of metabolism and its ecological implication were marginalized throughout the 20th century. Marx's notebooks on natural science were also neglected by Engels after his death, and even talented Marxists in the following generations held onto the myth of the intellectual division of labour between Marx and Engels. While traditional Marxists failed to notice the importance of Marx's ecological concept of metabolism, even those Western Marxists who determinedly rejected Engels fell into the same one-sided understanding as traditional Marxists. This shows how strong Engels's influence was among Marxists in the 20th century. However, there was one exceptional Marxist who challenged this general trend and attempted to revive the Marxian legacy of metabolism. That was Lukács György.

NOTES

1   Foster and Burkett (2016: 10) write, for example:

> Engels's contributions were also of extraordinary brilliance, even if
> frequently overshadowed by those of Marx. Although the two thinkers
> were not identical, and must be distinguished from each other, attempts
> to separate them entirely, which have become common in some circles
> of Western Marxism in recent years, are, in our view, self-defeating and
> misguided. In relation to the ecological critique of capitalism, both were
> major contributors.

2 Foster and Burkett often refer to Marx's notebooks, but they do not pay attention to their chronology or their actual content. I will highlight the importance of the chronology because it reveals the development of Marx's theory.

3 As Michael Heinrich (2012: 24) argues, this attempt to establish Marxism as a proletarian worldview began with Engels in the face of the increasing influence of Eugen Dühring in Germany. In this sense, Engels surely had a political interest in emphasizing the systematic character of Marx's thought and in simplifying it so that working class people could comprehend it.

4 For example, the publication of the so-called *Economic and Philosophical Manuscripts of 1844* in 1932 as a part of *MEGA¹* led to a 'humanist' critique of Soviet Marxism. But it is also noteworthy that the Russians wanted to treat this bundle of text as 'manuscripts' and bestow a systematic character upon the general structure of the text, even though Marx did not have any actual plan to publish it. As Jürgen Rojahn (2002) shows, the text was rather a spontaneous product of Marx's process of studying political economy.

5 However, except for a few Marxists (for example, Heinrich [2013]; Otani [2013]), Marxian scholars do not pay attention to the economic manuscripts of *Capital* even today. In a sense, their position remains close to that of traditional Marxists. English translation of Marx's manuscript of 1864–5, which is the main manuscript for volume III of *Capital*, was published in 2015 (Marx 2015). However, in its introduction, Fred Mosely (2015: 41) argues that there is no significant difference between the manuscript and Engels's edition of *Capital* except for a few points. This is the dominant attitude of Marxian scholars in the English-speaking world, which basically underestimates the importance of the *MEGA*.

6 Ironically, *Dialectics of Nature* also remained incomplete, but the debate proceeded as if Engels's philosophy were complete. Kaan Kangal (2020) challenges this widely shared assumption of the more or less complete character and attempts a more nuanced reconstruction and evaluation of Engels's philosophy.

7 As Merleau-Ponty points out, the expression itself, however, originally comes from *Karl Korsch's Marxismus und Philosophie* (Korsch 1966: 63). The relevant paragraph in Korsch was not translated into English, and this is probably why Merleau-Ponty became the reference point in the English-speaking world.

8 See Chapter 3 for a more detailed discussion of the so-called Lukács problem (Foster, York and Clark 2010: 224).

9 Ironically, due to its rejection of the evolutionary–ecological aspect of nature, Western Marxism shares with Soviet Marxism the assumption that the sphere of nature is the realm of mechanism and positivism.

10 Throughout this book, I distinguish between 'traditional Marxism' and 'classical Marxism'. The two schools both maintain the general validity of the Marxian approach elaborated in *Capital*. The former is close to the Soviet worldview of dialectical materialism, while the latter endorses Marx's basic concepts such

as labour theory of value, reification, class and socialism without falling into determinism and reductionism.

11   This does not negate the contribution of Engels to the issue of ecology, especially in relation to the issue of entropy and the second law of thermodynamics (Foster and Burkett 2016; Foster 2020; Royle 2020). The aim of this chapter is rather to understand the differences between Marx and Engels.

12   Of course, not all Western Marxists deserve the same degree of criticism. Although Lukács at first reproached the application of dialectic to nature, he also admitted that Marx did not completely separate the relationship between 'society' and 'nature' but comprehended both in their integrity (Foster 2013). As discussed in the next chapter, in *Tailism and the Dialectic* Lukács (2002) recognized that the concept of 'metabolism' expresses this unity, even by acknowledging the existence of dialectics of nature. Also, Herbert Marcuse wrote: 'History is also grounded in nature. And Marxist theory has the least justification to ignore the metabolism between the human being and nature' (Marcuse 1978: 16), leading him to a much more active engagement with the ecological crisis in his last years (Marcuse 1992). This is not a coincidence because, as seen in the previous chapter, the concept of metabolism is the key term for the Marxian ecological critique of capitalism. This marks a clear contrast to Alfred Schmidt ([1971] 2014), who can only integrate ecological critique by criticizing Marx and having recourse to the romanticism of Ludwig Feuerbach (Saito 2017: 85). Yet there is also a possibility of developing a critical theory of nature based on Adorno's philosophy of non-identity (Cassegård 2021). I return to this issue in Chapter 4.

13   Chapter 5 corresponds to part 5 (chapters 21–36) of the current edition edited by Engels.

14   The second modification might be due to Marx's bad handwriting because *Boden* and *Leben* look similar in his original handwriting.

15   Considering the importance of this passage, it is very unfortunate that the recent English translation from Marx's manuscript for volume III of *Capital* (Marx 2015) is heavily dependent on Ben Fowkes's earlier translation of the Engels edition published by Penguin. It often ignores Marx's original text, which basically ruins the basic meaning of this translation project. Unfortunately, this key passage quoted here is one of those examples. Fred Mosely, who wrote the introduction to this translation, does not consider these changes. If one does not pay attention to these 'minor' changes, it is not necessary to read the manuscript from the beginning, but one can simply continue reading Engels's edition. However, without a careful reading of these changes, one inevitably ends up concluding that there is no important difference between the Engels edition and Marx's original manuscript. For a further critique of this translation, see Sasaki (2018).

16   To be fair, Engels did not simply separate objective natural laws and human consciousness. The famous discussion on the role of labour in the transition from ape to human cannot be reduced to a mechanistic explanation. Furthermore,

his interest in Darwin's theory of evolution as well as thermodynamics clearly rejected the mechanistic worldview. Rather, in contrast to Engels's alleged positivism (Peter Thomas 1988), his dialectics is an investigation of the interconnected universality of nature, which is characterized by continuous integration of qualitatively new emergent properties (Foster 2020).

17 Here again, Engels is not a mechanically materialist thinker.

18 This has to do with the fact that Engels's economic understanding of capitalism is also tied to the so-called breakdown theory. He did not appreciate Marx's concept of 'productive forces of capital' and the 'real subsumption of labour under capital', which will be discussed in Chapter 5.

19 Of course, Liebig was also not entirely a naïve vitalist. In the 1840s, Liebig conceived the processes of absorption, assimilation and excretion of nutrients as 'metabolism' and tried to explain this life activity as a chemical process. One of his great achievements as a chemist at the time was the discovery of the organic compound of hippuric acid, demonstrating the possibility of overcoming the 'two kinds of kingdom', that is, the spheres of plants and animals (Goodman 1972). Animals were supposed to consume what plants provide, but Liebig found that horses (and, of course, other animals) also produce organic compounds in the course of their metabolism. Liebig's theory of metabolism is actually quite critical of the dominant vitalist dualism of Jean-Baptiste André Dumas and Jean Baptiste Boussignault. Notwithstanding, Liebig could not fully abandon the idea of vital forces either (Brock 1997: 313).

20 Lukács (2002) started with a similar dialectics of nature independent of humans, but he also used the concept of metabolism to trace the further development of dialectics in the sphere of the social. See the discussion in Chapter 3.

21 Using this scheme, Engels predicted that the technological development and planned economy in socialism would render concentration in large cities unnecessary and thus overcome the antagonism:

> Abolition of the antithesis between town and country is not merely possible. It has become a direct necessity of industrial production itself, just as it has become a necessity of agricultural production and, besides, of public health.... It is true that in the huge towns civilisation has bequeathed us a heritage which it will take much time and trouble to get rid of. It must and will be got rid of, however protracted a process it may be. (*MECW* 25: 282)

22 One should also recall Engels's deep interest in environmental destruction under colonial rule:

> What cared the Spanish planters in Cuba, who burned down forests on the slopes of mountains and obtained from the ashes sufficient fertilizer for one generation of very profitable coffee trees – what cared they that the heavy tropical rain afterwards washed away the unprotected upper stratum of the soil, leaving behind only bare rock! In relation to nature, as to society, the present mode of production is predominantly

concerned only with the immediate, the most tangible result; and then surprise is expressed that the often remote effects of actions to this end turn out to be quite different, are mostly quite the opposite in character. (*MECW* 25: 463)

23 Obviously enough, Engels was also interested in revolutionary movements without falling into pessimism.

24 '5 to 6 degrees (°Re)' (that is, in Réaumur scale) is equivalent to 6.25–7.5 degrees Celsius.

25 The question is discussed more closely in Chapter 6.

26 Marx also avoided the romantic view that all pre-capitalist societies were sustainable, and that capitalism is responsible for all evils.

27 Marx in the 1850s held such a view influenced by Liebig's optimism, but both of them clearly distanced themselves from it later (Saito 2017).

28 In fact, there are passages in *Capital* where Marx was influenced by Engels (see *Capital* I: 338).

3

Lukács's Theory of Metabolism as the Foundation of Ecosocialist Realism

Today, there are robust discussions on the ecological crisis that pivot around the Anthropocene as a new geological age. Since the entire surface of our planet is now covered by traces of human economic activities, there apparently exists no pristine 'nature' that remains untouched by humans. Bill McKibben's claim about the 'end of nature' (McKibben 1989) has become quite compelling 30 years after it was first pronounced, but the full-blown impact of climate change beyond any human control signifies the ultimate failure of the modern Promethean dream of absolute domination over nature. The catastrophic situation created by this failure recalls Engels's warning about the 'revenge' of nature as well as Max Horkheimer's discussion of the 'revolt of nature' in *Eclipse of Reason* (Horkheimer [1947] 2005: 86).

The 'revenge' and 'revolt' of nature seem to redistribute the agency, creating a new ontological situation, in which the passive 'things' in nature appear to acquire agency *against* humans. This appearance of the total remaking of nature as well as the new agency of things is the reason why both Noel Castree's 'production of nature' and Bruno Latour's 'actor–network theory' (ANT) are gaining increasing popularity in recent debates over political ecology. While Castree (2005) denies the existence of a nature independent of human beings, Latour (1993) rejects the modern dualist conception of subject and object, redistributing agency to things as 'actants'. Their ideas are certainly quite different, but they share a common belief in the superiority of ontological monism over dualism in the face of the *hybridity* of the social and the natural that they think of as characteristic of the Anthropocene.

In this context, the Marxian concept of 'metabolism' (*Stoffwechsel*) as the theoretical foundation for Marxian ecology has been the target of harsh criticism. Especially, its central concept of 'metabolic rift' has been accused of 'epistemic rift' (Schneider and McMichael 2010: 467) due to its 'Cartesian dualism' of 'Nature' and 'Society' as two fully separate and independent entities. There are accordingly various attempts even among Marxists – particularly by Jason W. Moore (2015) – to replace this dualist treatment of capitalist development with a post-Cartesian one for a better understanding of the current ecological crisis. It is unfortunate that Marx never systematically elaborated on the ontological status of nature in his critique of political economy – it was not the task of his critique of political economy to elaborate on such an issue. However, not every Marxist ignored its theoretical relevance. This chapter makes recourse to Lukács György and his *History and Class Consciousness* in order to reply to recent critics in defence of Marx's theory of metabolic rift.

This approach might sound contradictory, as Chapter 2 criticized the unjust neglect of nature in the tradition of Western Marxism. In fact, as the foundational work of Western Marxism Lukács's *History and Class Consciousness* can be regarded precisely as an attempt to exclude the sphere of nature from Marx's dialectical analysis. Furthermore, *History and Class Consciousness* has been criticized for its inconsequent 'ontological dualism' (Vogel 1996). However, the lack of clarity in Lukács's *History and Class Consciousness* comes not only from his 'premature' thinking but also from the difficulties he faced in attempting to criticize Orthodox Marxism in the 1920s. For political reasons, he was often compelled to hide or obscure his real intentions, which led to various critiques against his ambivalences and inconsistencies. These criticisms continue to constrain our understanding of his work until today.

In replying to these critics, I will argue that by looking at Lukács's theory of metabolism more carefully, as it is developed especially in his self-defence of *History and Class Consciousness,* published much later under the title *Tailism and the Dialectic*, the position he elaborated in *History and Class Consciousness* is *not* incoherent. Furthermore, Lukács's theory of metabolism is also relevant to today's debates as it is superior to that of his critics in its avoidance of both Cartesian dualism and Latourian monism. In order to demonstrate this point, this chapter first reconstructs the alleged inconsistency of Lukács's 'methodological' and 'ontological dualism' (I). It then defends the theoretical consistency of *History and Class Consciousness* in the face of criticism of his grave inconsistencies, by looking at Lukács's unpublished *Tailism and the Dialectic*. However, despite the discovery of this manuscript, criticisms of Lukács remain. The main challenge comes from Paul Burkett's critique of Lukács's 'scientific dualism' that he thinks is incompatible with

Marx's materialism (II). Against such a critique, I will show that Lukács correctly adopted Marx's own method as well as his theory of metabolism. On the one hand, he argued for 'ontological monism' based on Marx's theory of metabolism. However, Lukács also advocated for 'methodological dualism' with his concept of 'identity of identity and non-identity', which he took over from the young Hegel's conception of the absolute (III). Developing the Marxist treatment of the problem of nature, Lukács contributed to establishing an ecosocialist realism for a critical analysis of the global ecological crisis in the Anthropocene (IV).[1]

I

'AMBIVALENCES' IN *HISTORY AND CLASS CONSCIOUSNESS*

History and Class Consciousness is fundamentally a work of disputes, challenging the dogmas of Orthodox Marxism and attempting to explore the true legacy of Marx's philosophy. Such an ambitious project inevitably triggered a lot of criticisms in the 1920s. Even those who are sympathetic to Lukács's good intention, almost without exception point to the theoretical contradictions and to the difficulties that emerged because he was still trapped in the paradigm of Orthodox Marxism (Fracchia 2013: 87). One of the main problems arises in his treatment of society and nature. This is of great interest here as it has to do with the intellectual relation between Marx and Engels that was discussed in the previous chapter.

In a famous footnote in *History and Class Consciousness*, Lukács limited the applicability of Marx's dialectical method only to society while reproaching Engels's unjustified expansion of the dialectical method to nature:

> It is of the first importance to realize that the method is limited here to the realms of history and society [*historisch-soziale Wirklichkeit*]. The misunderstandings that arise from Engels's account of dialectics can in the main be put down to the fact that Engels – following Hegel's mistaken lead – extended the method to apply also to knowledge of nature. However, the crucial determinants of dialectics – the interaction of subject and object, the unity of theory and practice, the historical changes in the reality underlying the categories as the root cause of changes in thought, etc. – are absent from our knowledge of nature. (Lukács 1971: 24)

It is this claim, though hidden in a footnote, that made him one of the 'real originators of the whole pattern of Western Marxism' (P. Anderson 1976: 29), whose main characteristic is the dismissal of Engels's dialectics of nature by highlighting its fundamental difference from Marx's social philosophy.[2] According to Lukács, two methods, one for natural science and the other for social analysis, must be strictly separated and must not be confused. Otherwise, the method of natural science will intrude into Marxist social analysis so that the Soviet mechanistic understanding of social development would emerge, as was the case in Nikolai Bukharin's positivist dialectic. According to the standard interpretation, Lukács intended to save Marxism from Engels's scientism, which is incompatible with Marx's original dialectical method. Lukács's criticism became quite influential, determining the general direction of Western Marxism.

However, as seen in Chapter 2, such a rigorous separation of Marx and Engels as well as of social science and natural science met with a negative response. Allen Wood, for example, argues that the interpretation put forward by Lukács 'has no basis whatever in Marx's texts' as he more than once explicitly asserts that dialectical principles are 'verified equally in history and natural science' (A. Wood 1981: 223). This was a common reaction already in the 1920s. Antonio Gramsci, another original founder of Western Marxism, questioned Lukács's claim in the following manner in his *Prison Notebooks*:

> [Lukács] seems to contend that we can deal with dialectics only about the human history but not about nature.... If his claim presupposes a dualism between nature and humans it is wrong.... How can we disconnect dialectics from nature if we should grasp the history of humans as the history of nature as well (besides, through the history of sciences)? (Gramsci 1971: 448)

Today's general evaluation of Lukács's provocative claim is that, though his intention was correct, he 'erred in the opposite direction by separating them too categorically' (Jay 1984: 116).

In this context, Steven Vogel in his *Against Nature* characterizes Lukács's distinction of society and nature as 'methodological dualism', which prohibits the misapplication of two methods. This distinction between social analysis and natural science assumes that there is a real border that must not be violated. Thus, Vogel points out that this methodological dualism is necessarily accompanied by '*ontological* dualism' of nature and society (Vogel 1996: 18; emphasis in original). In short, the particularities of each realm that require different methods stem from the differences of properties unique to the respective realms.

However, Vogel finds this implicit presupposition of ontological dualism in Lukács's discussion problematic because this ontological distinction runs counter to Marx's fundamental materialist claim about the continuity of nature and humanity. According to Vogel (1996: 41), Marx's concept of metabolism expresses the ontological situation where 'the natural and the social are woven together in an inextricable connection'. In other words, Lukács's 'ontological dualism' is not compatible with Marxian materialism as 'ontological monism'. According to Vogel, Lukács as a talented Marxist was actually aware of this incompatibility, but he could not fully give up ontological dualism. As a consequence, Lukács ended up suffering from various inconsistencies and contradictions in *History and Class Consciousness*.

Vogel maintains that one of Lukács's ambivalences manifests in his attitude towards the progress of modern natural science. On the one hand, Lukács seems to believe that the application of the method of natural science in the realms of nature produces *more objective* and *less problematical* – that is, less ideological – knowledge than social science: 'When the ideal of scientific knowledge is applied to nature *it simply furthers the progress of science*. But *when it is applied to society* it turns out to be ideological weapon of the bourgeoisie' (Lukács 1971: 10; emphasis added). In this passage, Lukács appears to simply problematize the misapplication of the method of natural science to society as a tool of bourgeois domination, but not its correct application within natural science.

On the other hand, Lukács's *History and Class Consciousness* – especially in its most prominent essay 'Reification and the Consciousness of the Proletariat' – criticized modern science by revealing the problems that arise from its 'contemplative attitude'. Vogel (1996: 21) summarizes Lukács's critique of natural science in four points. The first principle of natural science is *immediacy*. Nature appears as given and can be objectively known as 'pure facts': 'the immediately given form of the objects, the fact of their existing here and now and in this particular way appears to be primary, real and objective' (Lukács 1971: 154). Second, this creation of 'pure facts' is carried out through the *total quantification* of the world. Modern science aims at quantifying everything in a mechanistic fashion so that its objects of study can be comprehended with regular, universal and predictable laws, which allows humans to manipulate them. The third principle is *simplicity*. For the sake of calculability, the complicated appearance of natural phenomena must first be broken down to simple elements, and then they can be combined to explain more complicated phenomena. The fourth principle is *ahistoricity*. The mechanistic law of nature is supposed to be eternal and unchanging over time.

Lukács rejected these naïve presuppositions of modern science by arguing that this kind of 'formalism' reflects the world of 'reification' created by capital – that is, the world of quantified things that appear as an alien force to humans. This reified worldview in Lukács's view results in various theoretical difficulties in natural science because it has to forcefully abstract from the complexity of the real world. First, the objectivism inherent in the idea of immediacy is unable to erase all subjective aspects from its analysis. Second, quantification for the sake of calculability neglects various concrete and qualitative aspects of the world that resist quantification. Third, the reductionistic method based on simplicity suffers from the loss of totality and consists only of isolated facts, so it is unable to deal with holistic and relational properties of the world. Finally, an ahistorical understanding of nature cannot explain historical and evolutionary changes, so they must be dismissed as mere contingency. In short, the formalism of modern science finds the concreteness and qualitative diversity of the real material world 'beyond its grasp' (Lukács 1971: 105). Natural science presents itself as a neutral and objective science that can explain everything in the universe, but in reality, insisted Lukács, its neutrality and objectivity are secured only by violently dismissing the unquantifiable and temporal aspects of the material world.

According to Lukács, this method of natural science became dominant because it worked in favour of the capitalist production, whose rationalization of the production process is directed by the drive to maximize profit. With this background, natural science even functions as a 'bourgeois ideology': its application contributes to the radical transformation and reorganization of the entire process of production in favour of capital's valorization by strengthening its domination over workers. Simultaneously, naturalism obscures this capitalist function of science that is hostile to workers by presenting itself as an objective and neutral method of investigating unchanging 'pure facts'. It mystifies the underlying social relations of capitalism behind those facts and compels everyone to accept them as given:

> As the products of historical evolution they are involved in continuous change. But in addition they are also precisely in their objective structure the products of a definite historical epoch, namely capitalism. Thus when 'science' maintains that the manner in which data immediately present themselves is an adequate foundation of scientific conceptualisation and that the actual form of these data is the appropriate starting-point for the formation of scientific concepts, it thereby takes its stand simply and dogmatically on the basis of capitalist society. It uncritically accepts the nature of the object as it is given and the laws of that society as the unalterable foundation of 'science'. (Lukács 1971: 7)

Human lives are subsumed into the quantified world of science – especially in the labour process, where the fruits of natural science are actively applied as technologies in order to increase the productive forces of capital. Consequently, a naturalistic and objectivistic rationalization ultimately creates the 'reified' world in which humans are subjugated to the alien forces of non-human objects. In fact, the uniquely capitalist element of commodity production modifies the labour process into abstract, fragmented and repetitive activities under the system of mechanical rationalization. The production process is increasingly quantified through a breakdown of organic activities of labour into partial activities that exclude any arbitrary, contingent and subjective factors, and workers can only participate in the automated process with the same 'contemplative attitude'. Based on the principle of calculability, capital aims 'to abandon empiricism, tradition and material dependence', so that human activities are reified only to acquire a thing-like character. This is how the realm of society becomes 'second nature'. The sphere of the social and that of the natural get closer to each other than ever in modern capitalism.

Ontological dualism starts to collapse here. This is exactly why, in Vogel's view, Lukács's critique of natural science is *not* consistent. If the knowledge of nature is thoroughly mediated by social relations under capitalism, there is no longer any essential superiority of natural science over social science. If Lukács's critique of modern science is right, the neutrality of natural science turns out to be 'bourgeois ideology'. This conclusion apparently contradicts Lukács's own earlier statement about the neutrality of natural science. Furthermore, Lukács criticized the presupposition of the immediacy of nature. Nature is not simply given without any historical change but is thoroughly mediated by social relations. What appears to be ahistorical turns out to be always already mediated and modified by a certain set of social relations. Lukács even proclaimed that 'nature is a social category' (Lukács 1971: 130). This is also problematic in Vogel's view. If nature is really a social category, then it becomes a social construct. It is no longer possible to maintain ontological dualism between the social and the natural because both are *social constructs*. However, if ontological dualism breaks down, methodological dualism collapses as well, and Lukács, despite his alleged loyalty to Marx's materialism, falls into an 'idealist' social constructivism of nature.[3]

In this vein, Steven Vogel attempts to save Lukács's legacy. His radical solution, however, is to push Lukács's remark that 'nature is a social category' much further by maintaining that nature is '*literally* socially constructed': 'the "natural" world and the social one are not distinguishable' (Vogel 1996: 7; emphasis in original).[4] According to Vogel, Lukács's critique of false immediacy in *History and Class Consciousness* should have led him to both 'methodological' and 'ontological *monism*'. Vogel laments that although Lukács hinted this possibility, he was not able to pursue this radical path of social construction of nature because, for classical Marxists like Lukács, the claim that nature is 'built' was 'too close to the sort of idealist' (Vogel 1996: 40).

Vogel's idea of the social construction of nature might remind us of Marx's own critique of Ludwig Feuerbach in *The German Ideology*: 'He does not see that the sensuous world around him is not a thing given direct from all eternity, [… but] a historical product, the result of the activity of a whole succession of generations, each standing on the shoulders of the preceding one' (*MECW* 5: 39). Marx wrote already in 1844 that humankind as a 'species being' would be able to 'see himself in a world that he has created' (*MECW* 3: 277) once capitalist alienation is transcended in communism. In fact, the idea of 'production of nature' may seem a perfect description of the ontological situation of the Anthropocene, where nature as such no longer exists due to planetary human intervention. While Marx could still count as a perfect prophet of the Anthropocene, Lukács's ontological dualism, on the contrary, appears totally outdated.

II
LUKÁCS'S DIALECTICS OF NATURE AND SCIENTIFIC DUALISM

Lukács's 'ambiguities' and 'inconsistencies' can be summed up in two points. First, his 'methodological dualism' assumes that the method of natural science can produce a neutral and objective knowledge, while the method of social science reveals the historicity and class character of the bourgeois categories. However, Lukács's critique of modern science reveals the ideological and historical character of natural science under capitalism. Thus, the first ambiguity is related to 'scientific dualism'. Second, Lukács's 'ontological dualism' presupposes that there is an undialectical nature that exists prior to and independently of society. At the same time, he also emphasizes that 'nature is a social category'. This is the second ambiguity concerning 'ontological dualism', especially with regard to the ontological status of nature.

However, considering Lukács's undoubted philosophical talents, it is odd that he made such obvious mistakes because these two ambiguities are too clear to be overlooked:

1. If he so thoroughly criticized the presupposition of immediacy in natural science, it would not make sense to simultaneously argue, based on 'scientific dualism', that natural science is neutral and ideology-free.

2. If he explicitly said that nature is a 'social category', it would obviously be contradictory to suppose the 'ontological dualism' of Society and Nature at the same time.

It is therefore necessary to be more cautious in dealing with Lukács's argument and to suspect that Vogel and others may have missed something.

One needs to re-examine if there really is no alternative interpretation of *History and Class Consciousness* that can be more consistent, compelling and productive.

It is not unreasonable to suspect that Lukács's remark in a footnote was exaggerated by later generations. Western Marxism used Lukács's footnote to justify its own decision to focus on the sphere of society.[5] This decision was accompanied by scapegoating Engels as a figure who founded a positivist methodology that led to Stalinism. In other words, the footnote was rather *politically* utilized in order to clearly differentiate those authors in Western Europe from Soviet Marxism and thereby to save Marx. By excluding the sphere of nature, Western Marxism restricted Marx's conclusions to society, and their discussions came to pivot around the concept of 'reification' as a normative foundation for a critique of capitalism (Honneth 2008). It is probable that Lukács's alleged 'ambiguities' emerged precisely because Western Marxism too easily avoided the problem of nature in his *History and Class Consciousness* based on a single footnote as a justification for its own exclusive focus on the realm of society. However, such an interpretation not only turns out to be incompatible with Lukács's own view but also significantly narrows his theoretical scope of 'reification', which has serious consequences today. By its omission of the problem of nature from Marxism, Western Marxism is unable to deal adequately with the ecological crisis.

One may respond in the following manner. Lukács's later self-criticism of *History and Class Consciousness* might be taken as a reason to deny any possibility of defending its theoretical consistency. When he finally gave permission to reprint *History and Class Consciousness* in 1967, Lukács added a long, self-critical preface. In this preface, he explicitly regretted the fact that his treatment of nature as a 'social category' strengthened 'the tendency to view Marxism exclusively as a theory of society, as social philosophy, and hence to ignore or repudiate it as a theory of nature' (Lukács 1971: xvi). This was, Lukács wrote, due to the fact that the central Marxist concept of 'labour' was missing in *History and Class Consciousness*, even though it is the fundamental activity mediating the metabolic exchange between society and nature: '... the purview of economics is narrowed down because its basic Marxist category, labor as the mediator of the metabolism between society and nature, is missing' (Lukács 1971: xvi). In the 1960s, Lukács apparently abandoned his original claim from the 1920s and gave credibility to the Western Marxist interpretation of his work, even if he now distanced himself from it.

However, Lukács hid an important fact in this preface. Although widely ignored even today, the discovery of Lukács's manuscript *Tailism and the Dialectic*,[6] written between 1925 and 1926, and its subsequent publication in 1996 challenges his claim made in 1967. The existence of the manuscript was totally unknown for a long time as he made no reference to it during his lifetime, and it was only later discovered in the joint archive of the Comintern and the Central Party Archive of the Communist Party of the Soviet Union (CPSU). This early manuscript, which Vogel and others do not take into account, is of great significance for the current investigation because Lukács attempted to respond to criticisms raised against *History and Class Consciousness* and still passionately defended his own claims, especially with regard to the problem of nature.[7] His key concept here is 'metabolism' (*Stoffwechsel*).

Lukács's *Tailism and the Dialectic* fundamentally differs from the preface of 1967 in that he drew upon Marx's concept of 'metabolism' between humans and nature in order to *defend* the central thesis about the problem of nature developed in *History and Class Consciousness*. As quoted earlier, he utilised the same concept for the opposite reason in the preface of 1967. In other words, when he later used the lack of this concept as proof of his inadequate treatment of nature in *History of Class Consciousness*, Lukács distorted the history of his personal intellectual development. It is true that the concept of 'metabolism' does not play a central role in *History and Class Consciousness*. However, in 1925–6, Lukács insisted that the concept of 'metabolism' is indispensable to correctly understand the key theme in *History and Class Consciousness*, namely, to avoid the ontological dualism of Nature and Society and the one-sided focus on society. This one-sidedness is exactly the consequence into which Western Marxism fell by ignoring Marx's concept of 'metabolism'. Lukács was already well aware of this risk at the time, and this is why he came to highlight the importance of the concept of 'metabolism' in the unpublished manuscript.

Knowing the existence of the manuscript, it becomes more interesting to reread the preface of 1967 because even there Lukács tacitly said that '*contrary to the subjective intentions of its author*, objectively it falls in with a tendency in the history of Marxism' to 'view Marxism exclusively as a theory of society' (Lukács 1971: xvi; emphasis added). The 'objective' consequence of this is clearly discernible in various critiques raised against him and the aftermath of Western Marxism. By contrast, it is worth examining what Lukács's own 'subjective intentions' actually were because no one has properly investigated this issue. One can find hints in *Tailism and the Dialectic*.

In this unpublished manuscript, Lukács attempted to reply to his critics such as Abram Deborin, the Russian Marxist, and Ladislaus Rudas, who was an influential Marxist–Leninist philosopher in the Hungarian Communist Party. These orthodox Marxists actually picked up the footnote about the 'methodological dualism', arguing that Lukács's rigid separation of society and nature inevitably made him fall into 'ontological dualism', which is incompatible with Marxism because materialism should be founded on ontological monism. Rudas wrote, for example:

> If the dialectic is restricted to society, then two worlds exist, with two quite different sets of laws: nature and society. In nature phenomena are undialectical, in society they are dialectical. Fine. All the great philosophers may have been monists, but that does not mean that they were right. According to L. the world is dualist. (Rudas 1924: 502)[8]

Rudas also argued that Lukács's view is contaminated by idealist 'subjectivism' whose social constructivist idea in the social realm ignores the objective, material preconditions for the formation of class consciousness and socialist revolution. Due to the footnote, Lukács in the 1920s was already criticized for his dualism and idealism. This is why it is worth taking a closer look at his counterargument in *Tailism and the Dialectic*.

What is most important in the current context, however, is Rudas's use of the concept *Stoffwechsel* in his article 'Oxthodoxer Marxismus?'. It is with this concept that he criticized the separation of society and nature in Lukács's *History and Class Consciousness* and defended Engels's dialectics of nature with reference to Marx's *Capital*: 'For in this sense industry is an eternal natural process between humans and nature in which humans mediate their metabolism with nature (Marx. Kapital. I. 140)' (Rudas 1924: 515).[9] According to Rudas, since the concept of metabolism is missing, laws of nature suddenly disappear in Lukács's analysis of capitalist society as if society could exist independently of them. Deborin (1924: 617) agreed with Rudas's critique of dualism, adding that it is precisely in the labour process in which the identity of subject and object is realized, unlike in Lukács's 'idealist' approach to this problem based on his Hegelian speculative idealism.

Notwithstanding this, it may seem strange that Lukács responded so seriously to 'second-rate authors' like Rudas and Deborin in *Tailism and the Dialectic*. Michael Löwy (2013: 66–7) regards this, together with the absence of the concept of 'reification', as one of the 'serious shortcomings' of *Tailism and the Dialectic*. He maintains that Lukács did not publish it because he had 'doubts' and 'finally changed his mind and did not agree anymore with its political and philosophical orientation'. This need not to be the case. Lukács utilised the critiques raised by Rudas and Deborin as an important opportunity to elaborate on his own 'subjective intention'. Rudas's reference to the concept of 'metabolism' in *Capital*, to which Lukács did not pay sufficient attention in *History and Class Consciousness*, prompted him to reflect upon his inappropriate and inaccurate expression in the footnote. Even if he decided not to publish *Tailism and the Dialectic* – which can be equally well explained from the political situation surrounding him – the concept of metabolism remained central to Lukács's philosophical project even in his last unfinished manuscript *Ontology of Social Being* (*Zur Ontologie des gesellschaftlichen Seins*). This fact indicates how important the debate with Rudas and Deborin was to the development of some of his key life-long ideas.

First, in *Tailism and the Dialectic* Lukács reflected upon his formulation of the controversial footnote. He clarified his 'subjective intention' in the footnote in *History and Class Consciousness* by stating that he talked 'always (on two occasions!) only of *knowledge of nature* and not nature itself' (Lukács 2002: 97; emphasis in original). According to Lukács, it is simply wrong to say that his critique of Engels's dialectics of nature would lead to the idealist construction of nature because he was only talking about 'knowledge of nature'. In other words, Lukács's position differs from Steven Vogel's social constructivist approach to nature, even when he said 'nature is a social category'. He meant that knowledge of nature is conditioned by social relations. This is an epistemological argument. In fact, after claiming that nature is 'a social category', Lukács actually continued to argue in *History and Class Consciousness*: 'That is to say, what *passes for nature* … [is] all socially conditioned' (Lukács 1971: 234; emphasis added). Here he did not talk about the ontological status of nature at all (Feenberg 2017: 130).

In fact, Lukács explicitly recognized the objective existence of nature prior to human beings: 'Self-evidently society arose from nature. Self-evidently nature and its laws existed before society (that is to say before humans)' (Lukács 2002: 102). Notably, this remark also points to the fundamental *continuity* of society and nature as society 'arose' from nature. His intention to distance himself from Cartesian dualism is clear. In other words, he held with neither social constructivism of nature nor ontological dualism. Lukács also had no intention of denying the existence of an objective dialectics of nature, which 'exist prior to people and function independently of them' (Lukács 2002: 103): 'Self-evidently the dialectic *could* not possibly be effective as an *objective principle of development* of society, if it were not already effective as a principle of development of nature before society, if it did not already *objectively exist*' (Lukács 2002: 102; emphasis in original). Dialectics of society exist objectively only because dialectics of nature existed prior to the formation of society and because society arose from nature. This remark constitutes a complete negation of Western Marxism, which argues that 'the idea (later espoused by Engels) that nature exists independently of, and prior to, man's efforts to transform it is utterly foreign to Marx's humanism' (Ball 1979: 471). After all, his point in the footnote of *History and Class Consciousness* is *not* that dialectics of nature do not exist. He rather argued that it cannot be directly applied to the analysis of society because society does not simply consist of natural laws independent of humans. The sphere of society contains uniquely social dimensions consisting of interrelations of the subject and the object. This is why 'methodological dualism' is necessary *despite* Lukács's endorsement of 'ontological monism' in the spirit of Marxist materialism.

Lukács's claim is understandable in the face of the tendency within Soviet Marxism that emerged from Engels's usage of dialectics through the generalization of the objective dialectics of nature over the whole society. What Lukács problematized is Engels's explanation of how 'dialectical' knowledge can be acquired through scientific experiment. For example, Engels maintained that even Kant's 'thing in itself' can be known thanks to the development of natural science through industry and experiments in the laboratory. However, according to Lukács:

> But Engels' deepest misunderstanding consists in his belief that the behaviour of industry and scientific experiment constitutes praxis in the dialectical, philosophical sense. In fact, scientific experiment is contemplation at its purest. The experimenter creates an artificial, abstract milieu in order to be able to observe undisturbed the untrammelled workings of the laws under examination.... (Lukács 1971: 132)

The problem is obvious: if a laboratory experiment is understood as the dialectical practice, as Engels seems to believe, its application to society would lead to a mechanistic understanding of the objective law of history. Especially in capitalism, because the thing-like character of human relations appears as 'second nature', the method of natural science can be easily expanded to include the social realm, producing the positivist view of society. Even if Engels cautioned against the overgeneralization of this type of dialectics, this misleading type of dialectics predominated more and more as a method for analysing society and history within Orthodox Marxism. This is why Lukács rejected Engels's dialectics of nature as a tool for critical social analysis.

Lukács's defence of the existence of dialectics of nature in *Tailism and the Dialectic* must be disappointing to Western Marxists. Yet nor is Lukács's critique of Engels pleasant to those who want to defend the usefulness of Engels's dialectics of nature. Paul Burkett thus argues that Lukács continued to assume 'scientific dualism', which highlights the neutrality and objectivity of modern natural science, while degrading the epistemological status of social science: 'Lukács slides into the view that natural science itself is "more objective", and therefore less *internally problematical* than social science' (Burkett [2001] 2013: 8; emphasis in original). There are, according to Burkett, still paradoxical remarks in *Tailism and the Dialectic* that only make sense if we do not assume Lukács accepted scientific dualism.

As seen earlier, Lukács did have a critique of the ideological character of modern natural science, even when he acknowledged the objective character of natural laws. Is this ambiguous? For Vogel and Burkett, the answer is 'yes'. However, there is one key concept in *Tailism and the Dialectic* to which they do not pay attention, namely 'metabolism'. Strangely enough, Burkett, despite his usual inspiring focus on the concept of 'metabolism' in his careful treatment of Marx's ecology (Burkett 1999), hardly pays attention to Lukács's concept of 'metabolism'. However, one should recall the fact that Lukács's 'subjective intention' was not correctly understood in *History and Class Consciousness* at the time, and this is why he felt the need to go back to Marx's *Capital* and to introduce this concept of 'metabolism' in *Tailism and the Dialectic* in order to more clearly express his intentions. It is unfair to attribute 'scientific dualism' to Lukács without discussing his key concept of 'metabolism'.

III
LUKÁCS'S THEORY OF METABOLISM AND ONTOLOGICAL MONISM

The general assessment of Lukács's theory of 'metabolism' is not necessarily high. Other important eco-Marxists such as Brett Clark and John Bellamy Foster, for example, write that 'in the 1920s, Lukacs emphasized the "metabolic interaction with nature" through labor as a key to Marx's dialectic of nature and society. He did not, however, go any further' (Clark and Foster 2010: 124). This statement is misleading as Lukács did go further. In fact, the concept of metabolism continued to play a central role in his work right up until his last unpublished manuscript from the 1960s, *Ontology of Social Being*.[10]

As discussed in Chapter 1, the concept of metabolism originates in Marx's *Capital*. Humans can only live on this planet through their incessant metabolic interaction with nature mediated by labour. Obviously, this is a transhistorical, general condition for human survival (as it is, of course, for other animals), but even this abstract comprehension of human metabolism already highlights two things. First, there is something peculiar about the human labour process. Certainly, humans are part of nature, and consciousness is a product of biological evolution, but Marx argued that the conscious and teleological activities of human labour indicate an essential difference from other animals whose metabolism with nature is largely predetermined by instinct and a given natural environment. Only humans can relate to extra-human nature by reflecting upon their objective conditions as well as their subjective desires, which brings about much more dynamic transformations of production in the long run.

This leads to the second unique quality of human metabolism with nature. According to Lukács, this transhistorical process is modified by the increasing 'predominance of the social element' (Lukács 2002: 99). This is because labour is not only a transhistorical physiological activity but also a *social* activity. The concrete ways of carrying out labour are conditioned not only by natural conditions, whose laws cannot be arbitrarily modified by humans, but also by social relations. It is this 'double determination' of the labour process that Marx highlighted: 'From the specific form of material production arises in the first place a specific structure of society, in the second place a specific relation of men to nature' (Lukács 2002: 100; *MECW* 31: 182). With the development of productive forces, natural-ecological processes of metabolism between humans and nature are more and more mediated in a socio-historical manner by means of the social division of labour, cooperation, communication and various social norms, laws and institutions.

In this context, Lukács argued that human knowledge is subsequently conditioned by metabolic interaction with nature: 'Since human life is based on a metabolism with nature, it goes without saying that certain truths which we acquire in the process of carrying out this metabolism have a general validity – for example the truths of mathematics, geometry, physics, and so on' (Lukács 1975: 43). Knowledge of nature is indispensable in order to successfully realize the teleological activity of labour. Especially, in the earlier stages of human history, when human metabolism was still heavily determined by given natural conditions, human knowledge was largely prescribed by the need to satisfy basic needs. In this sense, the content of scientific discoveries are also social products of human metabolism with nature. In other words, knowledge of nature is not only materially but also socially and historically mediated in the process of human metabolism with nature, even if the objective dialectics of nature exist independently of and prior to humans on an ontological level: 'Our knowledge of nature is socially mediated, because its material foundation is socially mediated' (Lukács 2002: 106). This is what Lukács meant in the footnote in *History and Class Consciousness* when he claimed that *our knowledge of nature is not independent of but inevitably belongs to the* 'realms of history and society' (*historisch-soziale Wirklichkeit*), so they must be objects of the dialectics of society. This is also why 'nature is a social category'.

In fact, Lukács already wrote in *History and Class Consciousness*:

> From this we deduce the necessity of separating the *merely* objective dialectics of nature from those of society. For in the dialectics of society the subject is included in the reciprocal relation in which theory and practice become dialectical with reference to one another. (It goes without saying that the growth of *knowledge* about nature is a social

phenomenon and therefore to be included in the second dialectical type.)
(Lukács 1971: 207; emphasis added)

Even if the dialectics of nature exist prior to humans, their knowledge about nature cannot be treated as if it could exist independently of human praxis. In this sense, there is no 'scientific dualism' between social and natural science. It is possible to investigate the underlying social relations of modern natural science without discarding its objectivity. It is this type of social dialectical knowledge of nature that must be distinguished from Engels's objective dialectics of nature, which he often describes as a process independent of humans. Engels's project is 'merely' descriptive of that which exists independently of human metabolism with nature and of social factors. In Lukács's opinion, Engels's lack of a theory of metabolism meant he did not sufficiently integrate the social aspects into the dialectical development of the knowledge of nature. This is what Lukács wanted to say in his controversial footnote and he clarified the point in *Tailism and the Dialectic*: 'Our consciousness of nature, in other words our knowledge of nature, is determined by our social being. This is what I have said in the few observations that I have devoted to this question; nothing less, but nothing more' (Lukács 2002: 100).[11]

Such emphasis on sociality and historicity of human metabolism with nature also marks a clear contrast with the self-understanding of modern natural science characterized by the 'contemplative attitude'. Of course, Lukács did not deny the possibility of obtaining objective and universally valid knowledge of nature through the method of modern natural science.[12] Nevertheless, the 'contemplative attitude' conceals the fact that knowledge of nature is mediated by social metabolism with nature; in other words, it forgets its own social foundation in the 'capitalist society, whose metabolism with nature forms the material basis of modern natural science' (Lukács 2002: 114). Due to this reification, that is, forgetfulness, of social relations, humans come to treat nature simply as an independent existence that is immediately accessible and manipulable through natural science, turning it into a bourgeois ideology.

In Lukács's opinion, it is the modern scientific worldview that falls into the 'dualism' of nature and history: in the modern scientific worldview, anything related to society is deprived of the true objectivity, while only ahistorical objects in nature that exist independently of society are considered to be objective.[13] This is exactly what Lukács attempted to overcome through his critique of the false immediacy of pure 'facts', which are an abstraction from the real historical metabolic process between humans and nature. What is abstracted here is significant because it constitutes the interplay of the subject and the object, as well as theory and practice in history: 'Categories that appear today as "eternal", as categories directly taken from nature, e.g. work in physics, are actually historical, determined by the specific metabolism between capitalist society and nature' (Lukács 2002: 131).[14] This statement might give the impression that Lukács is advocating for a social constructivist treatment of knowledge of nature. It is true that Lukács argues that the knowledge of nature must be analysed as a historical product in relation to the socio-historical process of metabolism with nature. However, Lukács distances himself from relativism, as he explicitly states: 'The fact that modern natural science is a product of capitalist society takes nothing away from its objectivity' (Lukács 2002: 115). Truth is historical,[15] but its content is objective:

> However – in as far as it pertains to the objective reality of social being and the nature mediated through this – it is objective truth, absolute truth, which only changes its position, its theoretical explanation, etc., because of the knowledge that 'overcomes' it, and which is more comprehensive and more correct. (Lukács 2002: 105)

To sum up, Lukács did not argue for 'scientific dualism'. By contrast, he consistently highlighted that the transformation of our knowledge of nature is tightly linked to the transformation in the constellation of the social beings, which always changes with the socio-historical development of metabolism with nature. As Feenberg (2017: 132) puts it, 'Knowledge of nature, like social knowledge, is dialectical.' By highlighting this point, Lukács was arguing for the establishment of a new dialectical conception beyond the division of social science and natural science. This would require a critical analysis of the categories and methods of natural sciences in relation to concrete human metabolism with nature, which is mediated not only by material conditions but also by social relations such as class, gender and race. This is exactly what Burkett demands by transcending scientific dualism.

However, this is not the end of the story. What is more, Lukács's concept of metabolism is also essential to avoid the 'ontological dualism' that Rudas and Vogel ascribe to Lukács. Ontological dualism is founded upon the absolute separation between Society and Nature – so-called Cartesian dualism. Yet the Marxian concept of 'metabolism' emphasizes their incessant interchange mediated by human labour. Humans are without doubt a part of nature. To put it differently, they are a part of the incessant flow and flux of the universal metabolism of nature. This view is incompatible with Cartesian dualism. As Kate Soper points out, Cartesian dualism confronts a difficulty in terms of explaining how the two fully separated substances – 'mind' and 'body' in Descartes, and now 'the social' and 'the natural' – interact with each other: 'To accept the Cartesian picture is simply to accept that there exist two utterly different kinds of substance…, and that they miraculously but inexplicably operate continuously upon each other' (Soper 1995: 43–4). Vogel's monist alternative is compelling only when we assume that Lukács embraced the Cartesian dualism of Nature and Society. Yet the basic insight of Lukács's theory of metabolism is an ontological monism that recognizes the continuity of humans and extra-human nature in the biophysical processes of the universal metabolism of nature. Humans and non-human nature are mediated by labour and intertwined. There is no absolute separation, so the accusation of Cartesian dualism directed against Marxism is a strawman argument.

On the other hand, Vogel's idea of social constructivism of nature is counterintuitive. The fact that nature is affected by the social does not mean that nature is socially constructed. For example, even if X is affected by social practice, this fact alone does not make X a social construct. Likewise, nature undergoes constant changes through labour, so there is no 'pure' pristine nature. However, this obvious fact alone does not turn nature into a social construct. There still exists a natural substance, upon which the social works. Similarly, nature cannot be simply resolved into a social category by the single fact that nature is affected by labour or that the knowledge of natural science is discovered through a set of social practices in the laboratory. As Mauricio Ferraris points out, such a discussion confuses the ontological and epistemological dimension (Ferraris 2014: 33). After all, nature is not produced in the same way as a watch is produced through labour. Ironically, it is the advocates of post-Cartesian monism that presuppose Cartesian dualism. They tacitly separate the two entities in a dualist manner, so that humans touching it would immediately make nature a social construct.

Since Lukács rejected Cartesian dualism, he did not argue for a flat ontology either. While he insisted on the unity of the social and the natural in the constant process of metabolism between society and nature, Lukács did not forget to add that there are 'new, equally objective forms of movements' (Lukács 2002: 102) that exist *only* in certain social conditions – so-called social beings. In other words, he emphasized the *qualitative* difference of the purely social that emerges in the metabolic process of the entanglement of society and nature without negating their continuity. This historical interrelation and entanglement in the process of metabolism is the fundamental insight of Lukács's 'historical materialism'. Historical materialism makes it clear that there is a fundamental unity in the natural, ecological process of metabolic interchange between humans and nature ('materialism'), whose actual processes and appearances are, however, always already socio-historically mediated and evolve accordingly ('historical').[16]

In fact, in another unpublished manuscript, *Ontology of Social Being*, the late Lukács claimed that there is a qualitative 'leap' (*Sprung*) between the realm of nature and the realm of society (Lukács 1984: 169). Although society 'arises' from nature, there are new, qualitatively different properties in the realm of the social emerging from social relations mediated by human language, social labour and other activities. These emergent properties bring about radically new dimensions in the process of human metabolism with nature. Thus, it is necessary to carefully investigate these qualitatively different 'social forms' in order to reveal the historical uniqueness of social beings under capitalism. For example, the 'value' of a desk as a commodity is a 'purely social' property that attains a universal form only in capitalism, but it is as objective as its brown colour, even if you cannot touch or see value as a sensible property of the desk (*Capital* I: 139). Indeed, what is produced through social relations attains objective social power and the appearance of agency, even confronting humans as an alien force: 'The direct forms of appearance of social beings are not, however, subjective fantasies of the brain, but moments of the real forms of existence' (Lukács 2002: 79).

In short, *both* 'continuity' and 'break' (*Bruch*) exist in the course of the historical development of human metabolism with nature. In order to express this complex relationship between society and nature, Lukács borrowed an expression from Hegel, calling this differentiated unity of society and nature in their incessant metabolism the 'identity of identity and non-identity' (Lukács 1984: 395): humans are a part of nature and embedded in the universal metabolism of nature ('identity') but at the same time distinguished due to new qualitatively distinct emergent properties of society that do not exist in extra-human nature ('non-identity'). These two aspects exist together in reality as 'identity' or 'unity-in-separation'.[17] This 'identity of identity and non-identity' is the key to differentiate Lukács's view from those of both flat ontology and social constructivism.[18] With the 'identity of identity and non-identity' between nature and society in mind, one can argue that a scientism that privileges the neutral objectivity of natural science places too much emphasis on the *discontinuity* (non-identity) between nature and society, thus falling into Cartesian and scientific dualism. Social constructivism, on the other hand, depends too much on the sameness and *continuity* (identity) between society and nature, missing new, purely social qualities, so it is unable to reveal the uniqueness of the capitalist way of organizing human metabolism with their environment. This insight into Lukács's methodology is necessary to understand his theory of 'crisis'.

IV

TOWARDS LUKÁCS'S THEORY OF CRISIS AS A CRITIQUE OF ECOLOGICAL CRISIS

In contrast to today's dominant monist flat ontology that tends to erase the distinction between society and nature, Lukács consistently argued for analysing the 'double determination' of metabolism between humans and nature which is socio-historical as well as natural-ecological. He adopted a more nuanced description of the metabolic relationship of society and nature based on unity-in-separation by suggesting we 'consider this metabolism with nature in its double determination, as much as an interaction with nature – which exists independently from humans – as well as simultaneously determined by the economic structure of society at any one time' (Lukács 2002: 113).

Lukács's point is that the natural and the social are obviously entangled in reality, but this does not mean that they need not be distinguished. On the contrary, it is all the more essential to distinguish them and to analyse their unique determinations by the capitalist economic structure. This is the only way the historically unique character of capitalist production becomes comprehensible. It is in this particular sense of paying attention to the dimension of purely social forms that Lukács's *analytical* distinction of nature and society plays an essential role. However, this methodological dualism is radically different from the one that Steven Vogel characterizes as Lukács's dualist method because Lukács does not presuppose ontological dualism of Society and Nature.[19]

Lukács's 'methodological dualism' is close to Alf Hornborg's analytical separation of the natural and the social. Hornborg argues for a dualist methodology precisely because nature is subsumed into the social in the Anthropocene:

> But does this mean the categories of Nature and Culture, or Nature and Society, are obsolete and should be discarded? On the contrary, never has it been more imperative to maintain an *analytical* distinction between the symbolic and the pre-symbolic, while acknowledging their complex interfusion in the real world. Only by keeping Society and Nature *analytically* apart can we hope to progress in the demystification of that hybrid web in which we are all suspended. (Hornborg 2012: 34)

In contrast to Vogel, who ends up arguing for both methodological and ontological monism, Hornborg maintains that an 'analytical dualism' is all the more important for critical theory in the age of hybridity. Andreas Malm (2018: 53) makes a similar distinction between 'substance monism' – equivalent to 'ontological monism' – and 'property dualism'. Even though the social and the natural belong to the same ontological level and share the same substance, their properties are different like 'mind' and 'body', so it is necessary to analyse them separately. Only based on this separation can one reject the fetish view that accepts the appearance of hybridity as given.

While the analytical separation of society and nature gains a critical function in the Anthropocene,[20] it is not sufficient for Lukács. In Lukács's Hegelian terminology, he advocated taking the dimension of the 'totality' into account. In fact, the 'identity of identity and non-identity' is nothing but young Hegel's expression for the absolute. While emphasizing the double determination of the natural and the social, Lukács claimed that the natural and the social must not remain separated all the time, as they never exist separately in reality, but only in the 'identity of identity and non-identity'. In fact, Marx also argued that social forms cannot exist without a material 'bearer' (*Träger*): 'Value is independent of the particular use-value by which it is borne, but a use-value of some kind has to act as its bearer' (*Capital* I: 295). A prominent example in *Capital* is money. Its function as the 'general equivalent form' is something purely social, but it requires gold as its bearer. As a result, gold as money is a classic example of the hybridity of the social and the natural in capitalism, resulting in fetish. In order to avoid the fetish confusion of the social and the natural, it is first analytically necessary to comprehend the logic of 'value-form'. In the reified world, however, the purely social power of 'commodity', 'money' and 'capital' subsume their material bearers and transform the entire world according to the logic of capital's valorization. Only through comprehending this tension of 'unity-in-separation' (Holloway and Picciotto 1978: 3) or 'unity-in-opposition of nature and society' (Napoletano et al. 2019: 8) is it possible to treat the natural and the social in their relation to the dynamic process of the historical development of the capitalist mode of production.

After comprehending the importance of this analytical separation *and* combination of the social and the natural, one can understand Lukács's true intention in his critique of the 'immediacy' that is characteristic of the modern 'contemplative attitude'. As seen earlier, Lukács pointed to the need to analyse the mediated character of natural science, but this mediatedness also needs to be understood as a double determination. Vogel only pays attention to one of these aspects, falling into a social constructivism of nature.

On the one hand, *the natural is mediated by the social*. Behind the development of natural sciences, there exist social relations that constitute a historically particular way of organizing the metabolism between humans and nature. Under the capitalist mode of production, this metabolism is obviously driven by capital's infinite drive for valorization. Accordingly, this process of subsumption of nature under capital brings about the 'rationalization' of the production process based on quantification and mechanization and later of the entire social sphere, so even human beings are treated like things. This reversal of the subject and the object is what Marx criticized as 'reification' (*Versachlichung*). On the other hand, *the social is mediated by the natural.* Lukács sees the second problem of reification in the fact that such a process of quantification of the world forgets the mediation by 'matter' (*Materie*).[21] In other words, the dimension of the 'material' always persists despite its historical modifications under certain social relations because social 'forms' always require their 'bearers'. They cannot be simply reduced to pure social constructions and total quantification. Nature persists. What is more, the relationship between economic form and matter is asymmetrical: the latter can exist without the former, but *not vice versa.* This is exactly why the formalism of modern capitalism that tendentially erases the non-identity of nature as capital's bearers ultimately results in serious contradictions.

Now it becomes clear that Lukács did not simply praise the modern natural sciences as more objective and neutral than the social sciences. By contrast, he consistently problematized the formalism of reified natural science because its contemplative attitude cannot fully take into account the non-identity of nature due to its 'indifference of form towards content' (Lukács 1971: 126). This has an important ecological implication.[22]

As the totalizing tendency of capital strengthens itself with the development of capitalism, its contradiction crystalizes as 'crisis'. Everything, including human and non-human nature, is commodified, through which the value-form is uniformly imposed upon the various products of labour. Total quantification through the value-form is representative of identity-thinking, which suppresses non-identity of material world by reducing the differences of various use-values and imposing an abstract measure of value. Under the totalizing logic of commodification, nature is reduced to a mere vehicle for capital's valorization without acknowledgement of its own independent purposiveness. Erasing the distinction between the social and the natural is 'a recipe for hubris' (Henning 2020: 306) that leads to techno-optimist interventions in the natural environment. As long as the formal and reductionist approach characterized by identity-thinking persists in the reified world, the material is increasingly marginalized:

> This rational objectification conceals above all the immediate qualitative and material-character of things as things. When use-values appear universally as commodities they acquire a new objectivity, a new substantiality which they did not possess in an age of episodic exchange and which destroys their original and authentic substantiality. (Lukács 1971: 92)[23]

When non-identity is reduced to identity in the course of the instrumentalization of non-human nature, the process of quantification becomes more and more violent. However, the non-identity of nature persists in reality. The natural world exceeds our full grasp, and it cannot be fully controlled, often resulting in unforeseen hazards precisely due to our intentional actions.[24] This contradiction ultimately manifests itself as 'crisis', which Lukács formulated in the following way:

> This rationalisation of the world appears to be complete, it seems to penetrate the very depths of man's physical and psychic nature. It is limited, however, by its own formalism. That is to say, the rationalisation of isolated aspects of life results in the creation of-formal-laws. All these things do join together into what seems to the superficial observer to constitute a unified system of general 'laws'. But the disregard of the concrete aspects of the subject matter of these laws, upon which disregard their authority as laws is based, makes itself felt in the incoherence of the system in fact. This incoherence becomes particularly egregious in periods of crisis. At such times we can see how the immediate continuity between two partial systems is disrupted and their independence from and adventitious connection with each other is suddenly forced into the consciousness of everyone. (Lukács 1971: 101)

Since modern rationalization driven by natural science inevitably creates tension with the material dimension of the world as its bearer, the rationality of formal laws adds up to the 'relative irrationality of the total process' (Lukács 1971: 102). In the moment of crisis, the interdependence of each factor within the totality of the system becomes manifest in a way that formalism can neither adequately anticipate nor handle. No matter how much productive forces and technologies develop, warned Lukács, it is impossible to continue suppressing the qualitative side of the natural world. Its non-identity explodes in periods of crisis. This ultimately poses a serious threat to human prosperity. After all, human beings are natural beings, and the 'biological basis of life remains the same even in society' (Lukács 1986: 91). Ecological crisis as a metabolic rift is the 'crisis' in Lukács's sense.

Lukács's realist account of historical materialism combined both dimensions of the social and the natural by bringing them into unity, without falling into dualism. In doing so, he called for establishing a new dialectical science that takes into account both dimensions for the sake of establishing a more sustainable society beyond capitalism. However, this 'subjective intention' of the early Lukács was poorly understood at the time and later neglected. Revisiting Lukács's dualist method and his theory of crisis is more important than ever today. However, there is currently a general popularity of monist views that accept the hybridity of the natural and the social. It is worth re-examining the validity and the superiority of monism from a Marxist perspective. Upon closer examination, it becomes clear that Marx's methodological dualism provides a more powerful tool not only to analyse the ecological crisis but also to envision a post-capitalist future beyond the crisis of the Anthropocene.

NOTES

1   In this way, István Mészáros, who was Lukács's colleague, was able to integrate Marx's theory of metabolic rift into his own theory at a very early stage by recognizing the need for a critique of capital's 'ultimately uncontrollable mode of social metabolic control' (Mészáros 1995: 41).

2   Another fundamental characteristic of Western Marxism is its recourse to Hegel's philosophy. This also plays an important role in the second half of this chapter.

3   Vogel is not alone here. In the face of these theoretical ambiguities, Andrew Arato and Paul Breines conclude that Lukács's extension of his sociological critique of reification to all sciences is 'less convincing, given his difficulties with "nature"' (Arato and Breines 1979: 121). Andrew Feenberg (1981: 204) also judges that 'Lukács does not have a fully coherent theory of either nature or natural science'.

4   See Vogel (2015: 44–5):

> The environment is socially constructed; society is environmentally constructed. Humanity and the environment cannot be separated from each other – a conclusion that does *not* mean that we are masters of the world, or that it masters us either, but rather that 'world' and 'we' are so deeply interconnected that there is no way to tell where one leaves off and the other begins.

5   This tendency continues today. Axel Honneth (2008) typically reduces the entire theoretical relevancy of Lukács's theory of reification to the problem of mutual recognition and its forgetfulness.

6   The German title *Chvostismus* originates from a Russian term that Lenin employed in *What Is to Be Done?* (Löwy 2013: 69). Lukács aimed to criticize those Marxists who passively follow – 'tail-ending' – the objective course of history that proceeds independently of human consciousness.

7   This fact alone is quite interesting when compared with previous literature. Arato and Breines (1979: 190) maintained that Lukács already in 1924–6 went through a 'substantial shift' with regard to his earlier position made in *History and Class Consciousness*. However, this is not the case, and he still defended his earlier view at the time.

8   For the relationship between Rudas and Lukács, see Congdon (2007). The English translation of Rudas's work is based upon Lukács (2002).

9   Rudas wrote: 'Denn in diesem Sinne ist die Industrie ein ewiger Naturprozeß zwischen Mensch und Natur, in dem der Mensch seinen Stoffwechsel mit der Natur vermittelt. (Marx. Kapital. I. 140).'

10   This last work of Lukács was neglected and even 'despised' for quite a long time because even 'Lukács's students fought to boycott the project because they preferred *History and Class Consciousness*' (Infranca and Vedda 2020: 16). Foster is also aware that Lukács kept employing the concept until the 1960s, making his dismissal appear rather strange.

11   Lukács repeated the same point in another passage in *Tailism and the Dialectic*:

> That objective dialectics are in reality independent of humans and were there before the emergence of the people, is precisely what was asserted in this passage; but that for thinking the dialectic, for the dialectic as knowledge (and that and that alone was addressed in the remark), thinking people are necessary. (Lukács 2002: 107)

12   It is absurd to characterize *History and Class Consciousness* as 'the first major irruption of the romantic anti-scientific tradition' into Marxism (Jones 1971: 44).

13   Rudas is actually the one who fell into Cartesian dualism, when he criticized Lukács's footnote that the absolute separation of society and nature actually results in dualism and subjectivism. He only regarded 'subject = human (society)' and 'object = nature', so any product of 'the socio-historical process of development' becomes 'subjective', while only those things that are independent from the 'historical process of the social development' can be seen as possessing 'true objectivity'. Consequently, all social forms are treated as merely subjective under Rudas' methodology. This inflexible separation is responsible for a mechanistic understanding of nature that supposes the eternal objectivity of nature.

14   It was Herbert Marcuse who correctly grasped Lukács's point without knowing *Tailism and the Dialectic* and linked the *historische Wirklichkeit* and *Stoffwechsel* when he wrote:

> If the Marxian dialectic is in its conceptual structure a dialectic of the historical reality, then it includes nature in so far as the latter is itself part of the historical reality [*historische Wirklichkeit*] (in the metabolic interaction [*Stoffwechsel*] between man and nature, the domination and exploitation of nature, nature as ideology, etc.). But precisely in so far as nature is investigated in abstraction from these historical relations, as in the natural sciences, it seems to lie outside the realm of dialectic. (Marcuse 1958: 143–4)

15   Lukács's favourite example is the affinity between Darwin's theory of natural selection and the endless atomistic competition in the modern market society,

an example which is borrowed from Marx's own remark in his letter to Engels dated 18 June 1862:

> I'm amused that Darwin, at whom I've been taking another look, should say that he also applies the 'Malthusian' theory to plants and animals, as though in Mr. Malthus's case the whole thing didn't lie in its not being applied to plants and animals, but only – with its geometric progression – to humans as against plants and animals. It is remarkable how Darwin rediscovers, among the beasts and plants, the society of England with its division of labour, competition, opening up of new markets, 'inventions' and Malthusian 'struggle for existence'. It is Hobbes' *bellum omnium contra omnes* and is reminiscent of Hegel's Phenomenology, in which civil society figures as an 'intellectual animal kingdom', whereas, in Darwin, the animal kingdom figures as civil society. (*MECW* 41: 381)

16　This is different from Jacob Moleschott's understanding of the (vulgar) materialist theory of metabolism, which reduces everything to the eternal cycle of matter (*Stoff*) and thus deprives materialism of any *historical* dimension (Saito 2017: 84).

17　The term was originally used for analysing the relationship between the economic and the political in the state debate (Holloway and Picciotto 1978: 3). This conception adequately grasps the unique methodology of Marx's critique of political economy.

18　Honneth's critique of Lukács's 'idealism' that 'mind and world coincide with one another' (Honneth 2008: 27) misses this point.

19　Andrew Feenberg (2017: 121) adequately argues: 'The problem he addressed with the contrast between natural scientific study of nature and society is a methodological one. It was not intended to institute a dualism of nature and society generally but only to preclude the application of natural scientific methods to the social world.' Feenberg (2015: 234) also cautions that critics, confounding the nature appropriated in the labour process with the nature of natural science, render 'Lukacs's methodological distinction of nature and society far more substantive than Lukacs himself intended', turning it into an ontological one. Here Feenberg apparently changed his earlier view that Lukács had a 'real contradiction' due to this 'methodological split between history and nature'. He had previously argued that as long as such a split exists, Lukács's idealist goal of 'a "heroic rationalism" that accepts no boundaries' can never be achieved (Feenberg 1981: 210–11). Such a reconstruction of the German idealist tradition, as if Hegel attempted to dissolve the entire world into the spirit, sounds absurd, and it is also nonsense to assume that Lukács followed such a path.

20　This issue will be discussed in the next chapter.

21　Marx himself distinguished between two aspects of the English term 'reification'. He actually used two terms *Versachlichung* and *Verdinglichung*. *Versachlichung* expresses the inversion of the subject and the object, while *Verdinglichung* is the fusion of the economic form and its material bearer. The latter can thus be translated as 'thingification'.

22 *History and Class Consciousness* is marked by the Hegelian positive view of the totality, according to which the proletariat is assumed to realize the absolute unity of the subject and the object. In such a theoretical scheme, even the unity and reconciliation of society and nature can be established beyond the modern alienation from nature. It is problematic to assume such a romantic reconciliation of society and nature, and this is why Theodor W. Adorno ([1966] 1990) correctly emphasized the 'non-identity' of the subject and the object, as well as of society and nature. The late Lukács increasingly distanced himself from his earlier position in *History and Class Consciousness* and came to emphasize the irreducible non-identity of nature.

23 In *Tailism and the Dialectic*, Lukács repeated the same point: 'But [the impartial attitude towards nature by natural scientists] does make it impossible for them to interpret the contradictions that arise in concrete material as dialectical contradictions…, in their connection to the totality, as moments of a unified historical process' (Lukács 2002: 118).

24 Ecomodernism is another example of eliminating the non-identity of nature, as discussed in Chapter 5.

PART II

A CRITIQUE OF PRODUCTIVE FORCES IN THE AGE OF GLOBAL ECOLOGICAL CRISIS

4

Monism and the Non-identity of Nature

As discussed in Part I, the concept of metabolism is crucial for a Marxian analysis of the global ecological crisis in the Anthropocene. However, persistent criticisms are directed against those eco-Marxists who seek to develop the concept of metabolic rift. The criticisms have been reinforced recently as those political ecologists who problematize the concept of the Anthropocene as an anthropocentric and Eurocentric narrative also maintain that eco-Marxists are not only productivist but also dualist. According to critics, the dualist notions of nature's 'revenge' and 'metabolic rift' are unable to properly grasp the historical dynamics of ecological crises caused by capitalist accumulation.

This chapter, following Marx's ecological analysis and method, defends his ecosocialist realism in a non-Cartesian manner against monist conceptions of the world. While many critiques of the Anthropocene narrative are valid, they do not immediately justify the claim that monism is superior to dualism in conceptualizing the current ecological crisis (I). The problem of monism becomes particularly visible when investigating influential discourses in current environmental geography. Prominent critiques of Cartesian dualism of Society and Nature in the Marxist tradition come from Neil Smith's 'production of nature' and Jason W. Moore's 'world-ecology'. Although their reconceptualization of the human–nature relationship looks quite radical at first glance, a series of theoretical difficulties in these monist approaches become discernible upon closer examination.

There are obviously significant differences between Smith and Moore. David Harvey's critique of neo-Malthusianism in the 1970s heavily influenced

Smith's 'production of nature' approach. Their fear of Malthusianism, however, made them dissolve real natural limits into a social construction, so both Harvey and Smith were hesitant to recognize the necessity of integrating environmentalism into the Marxian critique of capitalism. In fact, the 'production of nature' approach is haunted by an illegitimate kind of anthropocentrism, which undermines nature's independence and autonomy as non-identical with society. Consequently, they ended up underestimating the impact of the global ecological crisis under capitalism (II).

In contrast, Moore's treatment of the ecological crisis is characterized by a determined negation of anthropocentrism. Through his monist concept of *oikeios*, he denounces advocates of 'metabolic rift' for falling into a 'Cartesian dualism' of Society and Nature. He maintains that his theory of 'world-ecology' offers a more fertile way to combine Marx's ecology with his political economy than does the Metabolic Rift School that is characterized by dualism (III). In defence of the Marxian concept of 'metabolic rift', this chapter clarifies Marx's intention to strictly distinguish society and nature in *Capital*, even though Moore claims that his own post-Cartesian view is more loyal to Marx's philosophical framework. However, Moore's treatment of the key passage of *Capital* is too hasty. He incorrectly identifies Marx's expressions of 'rift' and 'separation' with Cartesian dualism and suppresses them. This omission indicates Moore's failure to fully appreciate Marx's dualist methodology implied in his discussion of 'irreparable rift' (IV).

Since Moore abandons the concept of 'rift', his theory of capitalist crisis narrowly focuses on the *economic* crisis of capital's valorization due to the 'end of Cheap Nature', a concept akin to James O'Connor's 'second contradiction of capitalism'. In contrast, Marx was concerned with the issue of the *ecological* crisis from an 'anthropocentric' perspective because he consistently recognized the 'non-identity' of nature (V). Finally, it is not accidental that the monist understanding of the society–nature relationship underestimates the ecological crisis precisely because it marginalizes this non-identity of nature. Consequently, it risks falling into an ecomodernist vision of geo-constructivism to create the 'good Anthropocene' by justifying further technological intervention in the name of stewardship of the Earth system (VI).

I
ANTHROPOCENE, CAPITALOCENE OR TECHNOCENE?

The concept of the Anthropocene has become popular in the last decade, but it has inevitably been subject to various criticisms. Andreas Malm and

Alf Hornborg (2014), for example, point to the possible fallacy of 'fetishism' in the Anthropocene narrative. According to them, there is a tendency in Anthropocene narratives to identify the ultimate cause of today's environmental catastrophe in ancient causes like the 'use of fire' (Raupach and Canadell 2010: 211). In this framework, the ecological crisis was set in train once our ancestors started to use fire to dominate nature. Such a discourse attributes the origin of today's ecological crisis to a certain 'essential' trait of human beings. It abstracts from the social relations that largely determine how humans relate to nature and who are most responsible in this process. Consequently, such an essentialist view prevents us from investigating the ecological crises in relation to the modern social system of capitalism and its specific relations of power, capital, hegemony and technology.[1]

Sighard Neckel (2021: 138) also criticizes the way the term 'Anthropocene' treats human species as the single subject of planetary transformation and conceals economic inequality under capitalism. The *Anthropos* that is responsible for the ecological crisis is an abstract concept, which is actually nothing but an idealist fiction. Geographical, economic and political inequalities in the emission of greenhouse gas clearly indicate that humans as such are by no means responsible for the global climate change. In reality, those who are most responsible for the current situation are people with a high income living in the Global North. The negative consequences of climate change are unevenly distributed to the poor and marginalized in the Global South who lack the financial and technological means to adjust to it. In short, the current changes in the climate are tightly linked to power relations under the hegemony of global neoliberal capitalism, and reflecting upon climate justice requires us to take hierarchies consisting of class, race and gender into account. Nevertheless, such an approach is, according to Neckel, absent in the dominant Anthropocene narrative that subsumes everyone under the unified entity of human species. Consequently, this master narrative of the Anthropocene obscures the constitution of the current status quo through the violence, oppression and exploitation of capitalism.

For example, Dipesh Chakrabarty, a prominent historian of the Anthropocene, avoids a critique of capital by arguing that it 'is not sufficient for addressing questions relating to human history once the crisis of climate change has been acknowledged and the Anthropocene has begun to loom on the horizon of our present' (Chakrabarty 2009: 212). It is plain enough that this insufficiency does not legitimate his avoidance of a 'critique of capital'. This kind of Anthropocene narrative 'denaturalizes' the current ecological crisis by emphasizing human impacts but ultimately only 'renaturalizes' it, such that it cannot critically examine the social relations constituted by capitalism (Malm and Hornborg 2014: 65).

Without consciously questioning the existing capitalist mode of production and its hierarchies, proponents of the Anthropocene often end up aspiring to further technological development and 'domination over nature' as the only solution to the coming ecological catastrophe, all the more because this approach is compatible with capital's drive to further economic growth. They demand the 'management' of the Earth system for human survival amid the deepening ecological crisis. For example, Paul Crutzen, the inventor of the Anthropocene concept, proposes geo-engineering as a solution to climate change. This technology involves disseminating aerosol sulphate into the atmosphere to reduce sunlight and cool down the planet (Crutzen 2006: 212). Yet scientific discussions concerning terraforming the earth, no matter how robust they may be on the level of computer calculation, raise ethical questions. It is questionable whether elites in developed countries should be allowed to make a political decision that will nevertheless have enormous impacts upon the entire planet, while people who are more likely to experience their negative consequences are excluded from that decision-making process. Without a democratic process of decision-making, technocratic countermeasures against the ecological crisis from above are likely to reinforce existing inequalities and the social divide, leading to 'ecofacism' (Gorz 1980: 77) or 'technofascism' (Illich 1977: 14). This is why the Anthropocene narrative is criticized as 'a grand narrative seeking legitimation for the installation of a global, pilotable, management machine' (Neyrat 2019: 9).

Against this productivist myth of the Anthropocene, Stefania Barca (2020) determinedly rejects the Anthropocene narrative. Drawing upon the ecofeminist tradition, Barca criticizes the master narrative of the Anthropocene from the perspective of 'forces of reproduction'. In contrast to the instrumental logic of capitalist modernization, 'forces of reproduction' such as domestic work, nursing, subsistence farming and fishing are characterized by the act of *caring* based on the recognition of interdependency with other human and non-human life. Based on this concept, Barca argues that capitalist development and its incessant economic growth are founded on its exploitative dependence on the unpaid reproductive labour of women, peasants, slaves and indigenous people. The essential contribution of women, non-Europeans, indigenous peoples and non-human creatures remain devalued and marginalized today. The concept of the Anthropocene does not change this situation. The master narrative reproduces and reinforces the existing relations of domination and subordination due to its tacit acceptance of hierarchical *dualism* such as 'human and nature (non-human)', 'civilization and barbarism', and 'man and woman' (Plumwood 2002). This is because these dualisms inherent to the Anthropocene help obscure the white, male and heterosexual subjectivity of Western rationality.[2]

Opposing the master narrative of the Anthropocene, Malm, Hornborg, Neckel and Barca rightly emphasize the importance of examining the historical specificity of capitalist production and its appropriation of economic, political, gender, racial and geographical inequalities. In this vein, they propose alternative geological epochs such as the 'Capitalocene' (Moore 2016; Malm 2016), 'Technocene' (Hornborg 2015) and 'Plantationocene' (Haraway 2015). With the term 'Capitalocene', Malm, for example, aims to highlight the 'geology not of mankind, but of capital accumulation.... [C]apitalist time, biochemical time, meteorological times, geological times are being articulated in a novel whole, determined in the last instance by the age of capital' (Malm 2016: 391). The surface of the entire planet is covered by capital's footprints, so the logic of capital needs to be analysed as the organizing principle of the planetary metabolism.[3]

II
MONISM AND THE PRODUCTION OF NATURE

Since capitalism essentially relies on a series of dualistic hierarchies, a critique of the Anthropocene demands that we reflect upon the prejudices arising from modern binarism. Considering the fact that even those who are critical of capitalism have often been trapped into the productivist myth of domination over nature as well as the marginalization of reproductive work, it is no coincidence that monist views have become dominant in recent critical environmental thought and even in Marxian ecology. However, even if the old dualist schemes surely need revision, it does not immediately follow that monism is always superior to dualism. In fact, as mentioned in the last chapter, Malm and Hornborg distance themselves from Latourian monism and defend a non-Cartesian kind of dualism despite their critique of the Anthropocene concept.

One of the main monist approaches in the Marxist tradition is the social 'production of nature' as a kind of social constructivism. According to its proponents, although eco-centric approaches lament the destruction of 'first nature', that is, pristine nature external to society and untouched by humans, such a naïve society–nature separation fails to grasp the actual dynamics of the social formation of nature in capitalism. Nature as such does not exist anymore as Neil Smith declares that 'nature is nothing if it is not social' (N. Smith [1984] 2008: 47). The Anthropocene seems favourable to such a bold claim, giving credibility to the account that 'the social and the natural are seen to intertwine in ways that make their separation – in either thought or practice – impossible' (Castree 2001: 3). Noel Castree (2013: 6) even suggests treating 'nature' as 'a particularly powerful fiction: it's something made, and no less influential for being an artefact'.

However, there are various problems with this kind of social constructivist approach to nature. First, it is necessary to distinguish between its epistemological and ontological dimensions, as discussed in the previous chapter. Our 'knowledge of nature' is discursively mediated by scientific praxes, and 'making sense of nature' is inevitably constrained by social power relations. As long as human access to nature is conditioned by language, there is no full transparent and direct access to external nature as such. This does not mean, however, that external nature independent of humans does not exist as if nature itself were ontologically constructed. In this warming world, temperatures will continue to increase, ice will melt and sea levels will rise, even if there is no language and no human beings. These phenomena are objective and count as obvious facts that exist independently of human consciousness. Nature is socially *affected* and *modified* by humans, so natural events like droughts and wildfires are affected by climate change due to CO_2 emission from human economic activities fuelled by the burning of coal and oil. In this sense, societies are physically reconstituting nature in such a way that they suffer from unintentional manufacturing 'risks' as a by-product of capitalist development (Beck 1992). Nevertheless, we cannot conclude from this social influence and reconstitution that nature is 'built' as a social construct.

In short, the social production of nature confuses 'modification' and 'construction' (Malm 2018: 37). For its advocates, touching is building. However, even if we touch a tree, it does not mean that we have 'built' the tree. The tree retains its independent existence. While we can build a house, it is not possible to build nature by sowing, cutting trees or mining coal. Rather, all economic activities are dependent on trees and coal, whose processes of formation are *independent* of humans. Nature is an objective presupposition of production. Vogel's constructivist critique of nature welcomes Bill McKibben's 'end of nature' in a literal sense, but the end of nature is simply not the case. Even today human labour is extremely dependent upon what is produced by nature without any human intervention, namely fossil fuel.[4] If there were really no longer any nature left, there would no longer be anything for capital to extract. Capitalism and our economic activities require nature at least as a form of natural resource that exists prior to its extraction and exploitation.

Marx clearly recognized the objective and independent existence of nature, highlighting this point with the expression 'substratum' in *Capital*: 'This substratum is furnished by nature without human intervention. When man engages in production, he can only proceed as nature does herself: i.e. he can only change the form of the materials' (*Capital* I: 133). Marx's theory of metabolism negates the idea that nature is built by labour. Labour 'only changes' its forms. In arguing that touching immediately turns nature into built nature, Vogel and Smith presume the absolute separation of Society and Nature that exists prior to global capitalism. Only then is it possible for them to argue that when society touches nature, the latter immediately disappears. Since such a presupposition of Cartesian dualism is obviously problematic, Vogel's conclusion that we should treat nature as something akin to a 'shopping mall' (Vogel 2015) is dubious as well.

In order to avoid falling into Cartesian dualism, whose negation only leads to an extreme form of social constructivism of nature, the concept of 'societal relationship with nature' (*gesellschaftliche Naturverhältnisse*) put forward by Christoph Görg is a useful point of reference as it allows a more nuanced treatment of the society–nature relationship. Görg (2011: 49) acknowledges that nature is *materially* modified by economic and technical practices and *symbolically* constructed through cultural and scientific discourses, but unlike Smith, Castree and Vogel, he does not argue that nature is socially produced. Following the tradition of Adorno's negative dialectic, Görg instead refers to the 'non-identity of nature' and the 'preponderance of the object' (*Vorrang des Objekts*), which is reminiscent of Lukács's discussion of the 'identity of identity and non-identity'.

According to Adorno, the preponderance of the object is what characterizes materialism: 'It is by passing to the object's preponderance that dialectics is rendered materialistic' (Adorno [1966] 1990: 192).[5] There is always an aspect of objects that cannot be reduced to thought. Matter signifies non-identity with concepts, and this non-identity signifies that nature is more than human. In this sense, Adorno's critical theory maintains a realist view that 'something' outside exists (Görg 2011: 51). There exist apparent affinities between nature and society because society is also a part of nature, so society cannot fully dissociate itself from nature because of its constitutive preponderance.[6] Society remains founded upon nature: 'society itself is determined by the things of which it is composed and ... therefore necessarily contains a non-social dimension' (Adorno 2006: 122). Nature is a precondition through which mediating social activities become possible, and nature and society are not separate and independent entities, but they are the two interrelated poles that encompass an array of impact potentials and contexts that are socially malleable, but which always escape comprehensive organization and control. It is not coincidental that nature is experienced as an independent and autonomous entity despite our daily conviction that humans belong to it. Contact between nature and society does not represent the 'end' of nature but an essential character in the eternal process of social organization of human metabolic interaction with the environment.

In this context, Thomas Jahn and Peter Wehling, who likewise adopt the standpoint of a 'societal relationship with nature', argue that nature and society are interdependent and mediated in a processual interaction on both symbolic and material levels, but it is these two dimensions that must be separated 'analytically' (Jahn and Wehling 1998: 84). Analytical separation is essential not only because nature ontologically retains its independence separate from society but also because by erasing the essential difference between the two realms, it becomes impossible to comprehend *how* each historical stage of society organizes its unique metabolic interchange with nature. This historical and social investigation is, as Jahn and Wehling observe, possible only based on the analytical distinction between society and nature.

In addition, the 'societal relationship with nature' approach reveals another important problem of the 'production of nature' – that is, its 'anthropocentric' character (Castree 2001: 204). Constructivism of nature is characterized by its one-sided focus on how society *works upon* nature. This risks falling into a Promethean approach to nature, especially due to its insufficient attention to the non-identity and the preponderance of nature. From Adorno's standpoint, the social constructivist approach is problematic because the meaning of nature is reduced to only that which exists to humans. This approach thus tends to reinforce an instrumentalist attitude towards nature. In fact, nature can easily appear as a passive medium of human agency, as if it could be modified and manipulated at will. The social constructivist approach does not challenge the dominant narrative of the further technological intervention and modification of the natural environment for the sake of stewardship of the earth. It is rather compatible with a productivist version of the Anthropocene narrative, but this is exactly why environmentalist criticisms of productivism directly apply to the scheme of production of nature.

Even if such a productivist vision is not so explicit and the production of nature claims to be concerned with ecological issues (Castree 2002), the risk is always there. Marxism is traditionally sympathetic to technological progress. Even today's most prominent Marxist geographer, David Harvey, shows a surprisingly negative reaction to the ecological turn in Marxism. Harvey wrote against John Bellamy Foster, claiming that his view of the ecological crisis is too 'apocalyptic':

> Against this [postulation of a planetary ecological crisis] it is crucial to understand that it is materially impossible for us to destroy the planet earth, that the worst we can do is to engage in material transformations of our environment so as to make life less rather than more comfortable for our own species being, while recognizing that what we do also does have ramifications (both positive and negative) for other living species.... Politically, the millenarian and apocalyptic proclamation that ecocide is

imminent has had a dubious history. It is not a good basis for left politics and it is very vulnerable to the arguments … that conditions of life (as measured, for example, by life expectancy) are better now than they have ever been and that the doomsday scenario of the environmentalists is far-fetched and improbable. (Harvey 1996: 194)

Harvey is hesitant to incorporate 'pessimistic' ecological ideas into Marxism, claiming that 'a socialist politics that rests on the view that environmental catastrophe is imminent is a sign of weakness' (Harvey 1998: 19). Furthermore, Harvey (1998: 19–20) stated that 'the invocation of "limits" and "ecoscarcity" as a means to focus our attention upon environmental issues makes me as politically nervous as it makes me theoretically suspicious'. Here Harvey agrees with Neil Smith ([1984] 2008: 247), who had criticized 'left apocalypticism' for its recognition of natural limits because environmentalism falls into Malthusianism: 'But the Malthusian scenario has never as yet really grabbed hold' (Harvey 2011: 94).[7] He rather stresses capital's ability to convert any 'limits' to mere 'barriers' (Harvey 2011: 90). Here a 'socialist hesitation before environmentalism' (Foster 1998: 56) is undeniable. Harvey's scepticism towards environmentalism ends up drawing upon journalists like Greg Easterbrook and Julian Simon. Famously enough, Easterbrook, in *A Moment on the Earth*, argues that humans can 'terraform' Mars in order to have two biospheres as a solution to overpopulation.

Neil Smith shows the same hesitation before environmentalism. In the afterword to the third edition of his *Uneven Development*, he expresses a 'skeptic's' attitude to the ways that global climate change is discussed in the public sphere. This scepticism arises from his fear of what he calls 'nature-washing': '… nature-washing reconstructs the apparently unassailable power of natural agency over and above the social' (N. Smith [1984] 2008: 246). Such a view of natural agency, says Smith, only leads to 'apocalypticism' because it acknowledges the existence of forces of nature that humans cannot change. He cannot accept it because it contradicts Smith's basic standpoint on the production of nature that is characterized by his ungrounded optimism that social power is always able to overcome the power of natural agency. Similarly, Noel Castree is concerned about the 'over-confidence' of the Intergovernmental Panel on Climate Change (IPCC) in its denunciation of climate 'denialists' and recommends that discussions in the mass media should be more 'balanced' (Castree 2013: 242, 258). According to Castree, the exclusion of denialist voices from public discourse is undemocratic, and the IPCC represents a new form of neo-Malthusianism, even if many environmentalists often problematize the conservative estimation of the IPCC reports. Castree's remark sounds anti-scientific, considering the fact that the most recent IPCC report (AR6) now considers human impact as the cause of climate change to be 'unequivocal'.

In any case, these three prominent geographers are surprisingly reluctant to recognize natural limits even in the face of the ecological crisis. The reason is their 'fear of Malthusianism', which has to do with Harvey's early intellectual career. His contribution to the problem of nature originates from his prominent article 'Population, Resources, and the Ideology of Science', published in the 1970s, which deals with the population explosion and the scarcity of natural resources and denounces neo-Malthusianism as an *ideology* (Harvey 1974). At that time, the Club of Rome's report *Limits to Growth* and Paul R. Ehrich and Anne H. Ehrich's *Population Explosion* were causing great anxiety about overpopulation and resource scarcity shortage. There were various criticisms of their pessimistic tone, but in Harvey's view even the critics of *Limits to Growth* shared the neo-Malthusian paradigm that he thinks overemphasized the existence of objective natural limits.

Against the grain, Harvey points out that natural limits are not absolute. Resource scarcity does not exist a priori without any reference to society but can be determined only under a certain set of social relations. In other words, overpopulation and resource scarcity do not exist independently of capitalistically constituted relations of production but are relational concepts whose meaning requires the specification of what and how society produces. By presupposing these historical relations as given and by fixing the purpose of social production and the manner of technical appraisals of nature as unchangeable, the size of populations becomes the only variable that can be modified in the face of resource scarcity, inevitably falling into Malthusianism (Harvey 1974: 270). Harvey warns that environmentalism often makes this kind of error despite its appeal to scientific facts. Here science plays an ideological function that masks or even justifies the existing social constellation of power and domination in Western capitalism.

Harvey's critique of the ideology of science is founded upon Marx's concept of 'relative surplus population' as a critique of Malthus's theory of absolute surplus population. In the face of neo-Malthusianism, Harvey revives this Marxian approach to the issue of overpopulation and resource scarcity. Although Harvey as a 'materialist' nowhere negates the existence of physical nature, this critique of neo-Malthusianism has made him reluctant to recognize *any* natural limits because he too hastily identifies their recognition as guilty of 'Malthusianism'.[8] When Malthusianism becomes such a broad framework, there is no room for environmentalism. As quoted earlier, he even maintains that 'it is materially impossible for us to destroy the planet earth', but the Anthropocene demonstrates that it is utterly possible for humans to destroy the planet Earth to the extent that it will become unhabitable for humans (and many other living beings).

Harvey's hesitation explains why these Marxian geographers who advocate the production of nature thesis turn out to be quite reactionary in the sphere of ecology despite their self-claimed radical reconceptualization of the society–nature relationship. Again, it is helpful to refer to Adorno and Horkheimer's *Dialectic of Enlightenment*. The modern project of instrumental reason is characterized by a 'lack of reflection' (Horkheimer and Adorno [1944] 2002: 158) that ignores the non-identity of nature and reduces it to a mere tool to be controlled and exploited for the sake of exchange value in capitalism (Cook 2011). 'Reification' is the 'forgetfulness' of society's embeddedness in nature as well as nature's otherness. This neglect results in 'imperialism' against nature (Horkheimer [1947] 2016: 76). The danger of monism in the 'production of nature' derives from its obscuring of the difference between the social and the natural that undermines the reflexibility over the non-identity of nature. According to Adorno, nature can be useful for humans in various ways, but non-human nature has its own purposiveness that is indifferent and irrelevant to humans. Under the identity thinking of capital, nature is damaged even more.[9]

It is important to highlight that the recognition of objective natural limits is *not* equal to Malthusianism. As Harvey rightly points out, Malthus's theory of overpopulation is founded on an 'ideology of nature' in that it obscures the historical and social character of subsistence (what people need), natural resources (what they can use) and scarcity (how much they can use) under capitalist relations. The problem of overpopulation arises not because the world is not rich enough to feed everyone but because its wealth is quite unevenly distributed in favour of the rich in the Global North – hence, Harvey's call to radically transform the capitalist relation of production for a fairer and more just share for everyone. Harvey is certainly correct, but this kind of critique in no way needs to eliminate the objective biophysical limits of the Earth. No matter how hard capital attempts to discover new frontiers of nature and new markets, there is no infinite space on the earth after all. Technological progress can push limits back *to some extent*, but entropy increases, available energy decreases and natural resources get exhausted. These are objective facts that are independent of social relations and human will. It is inadequate to call the recognition of these objective limits 'weakness' and decry their 'apocalyptic vision of a planetary ecological crisis'. If this recognition counts as Malthusianism, then the only way to avoid the Malthusian trap would be the dogmatic denial of natural limits as such. Combined with Marxian Prometheanism, this easily turns into the problematic endorsement of further technological intervention in the form of genetic engineering, geo-engineering and nuclear fusion.

III

FROM THE ANTHROPOCENE TO THE CAPITALOCENE

Despite his problematic conclusion, Castree (2001: 204) at least recognized the problem of anthropocentrism inherent to the 'production of nature' and argued for investigating 'how produced nature affects capitalism'. In this context, Jason W. Moore's discussion on the 'Capitalocene' marks a theoretical advance compared with the 'production of nature', as he clearly integrates the recent fruits of various critical discussions that pivot around the Anthropocene and overcomes the shortcomings of Smith and Castree.

What is noteworthy here is Moore's criticism of Engels's 'revenge of nature'. According to Moore, Engels's theoretical limitation is apparent in his 'static' and 'ahistorical' treatment of nature. Agreeing with Smith and Harvey, Moore claims that Engels's conceptualization suffers from the 'fetishization of natural limits' (Moore 2015: 80). This inevitably leads to the 'consequentialist bias of Green Thought' (Moore 2015: 171) because Engels's ecological critique is trapped in a 'Cartesian dualism' of 'Society' and 'Nature', two fully independent entities. His analysis can only confirm the predictable 'consequence' that capitalism destroys nature. Engels's conclusions may be correct – his claim that nature stops being a passive medium but attains agency rather matches Moore's own view – but at the same time everyone already knows that capitalism is bad for the environment. Thus, Moore puts forward another grandiose project of 'world-ecology'. It aims to analyse the world-historical *process* of how humans and nature incessantly 'co-produce' each other through the web of life, culminating in the ecological crisis.

Moore claims that his view is founded on Marx's own, even though he criticizes Engels. As discussed in Chapter 2, it is not unreasonable to distinguish Marx and Engels, but Moore's critique does not end with simply rejecting Engels's treatment of the human–nature relationship. Moore's main opponent is John Bellamy Foster and his colleagues, who employ the concept of 'metabolic rift'. This rejection is surprising, considering the concept's growing popularity among Marxists as well as the fact that Moore himself used to employ it in order to grasp the tense relationship between humans and nature under the capitalist world-system (Moore 2000, 2002).

All the same, in *Capitalism in the Web of Life*, Moore significantly altered his attitude towards the concept of metabolic rift, now denouncing it as 'Cartesian dualism'. Cartesian dualism assumes that Society works *upon* Nature, but Moore argues that such a static division of Society and Nature cannot adequately analyse the dynamic historical process of capitalist development 'through' nature – that is, the dialectical 'co-production' of society and nature in the singular web of life. 'Nature is co-produced. Capitalism is co-produced. Limits are co-produced' (Moore 2015: 232). Without being able to adequately deal with natural limits, the 'metabolic fetish', and its manifold resource- and energy-determinisms' represent the highest stage of this 'Green Arithmetic' (Moore 2015: 180): Society plus Nature equals Crisis. This is apparently too static like Engels's 'revenge of nature'. Today's ecological crisis is, according to Moore, a crisis of 'modern-in-nature' – that is, not the result of an 'irreparable rift' between Society and Nature but of the constant (re)configuration of flux and flow in the entire web of life under capitalism.

Moore criticizes Engels and Foster, but *not* Marx himself. On the contrary, he defends his own interpretation as the true and more productive successor of Marx's 'theory of value' and 'philosophy of internal relations' (Moore 2015: 22). He claims that only by combining his critique of political economy with his ecological analysis can the potential of Marx's value theory be fully realized. Foster's interpretation, on the contrary, falls into an 'epistemic rift' between 'political economy' based on the 'theory of monopoly capital' (Paul Sweezy and Paul A. Baran) and 'ecology' based on the 'theory of metabolism' (Lukács and Mészáros). The debate over whether 'Marx's ecology' exists has been affirmatively decided. The current controversy in Marxian political ecology centres on the search for an adequate method to conceptualize the relationship between humans and nature under capitalism and its contradictions in the Anthropocene.

Moore's method of world-ecology softens the binary of society and nature. In order to avoid falling into the static and apocalyptic conception of the metabolic rift, as Moore believes Foster does, he argues that it is necessary first to abandon the epistemological framework that Society works *upon* Nature and destroys it. This is why Moore highlights that nature and human 'co-produce' together. Nature is in no sense a passive medium. In fact, the development of capitalism is always conditioned by nature. In this sense, nature possesses a certain form of agency as an 'actant' (Moore 2015: 196).[10] For example, Moore describes that coal formation in England was a key actant for British capitalism to take off. Compared to Smith's and Castree's production of nature approach, Moore focuses not simply on how capitalism produces nature but also how capitalism is produced through nature. He thus replaces the dualist conception of 'Nature *plus* Society' with 'society-*in*-nature or nature-*in*-society', and the idea that 'capitalism acts *upon* nature' is substituted by the monist scheme that capitalism 'develops *through*' the web of life because what is constructed is an intricate networked assemblage consisting of social and natural arrangements of actants. In this way, his monist ontology attempts to avoid anthropocentrism, which allows him to elaborate on a more suitable framework of the Capitalocene – at least at first glance.

Moore's monist terminology is influenced by a popular discourse within political ecology that is characterized by a 'hybrid' understanding of the human–nature relationship. This kind of monism challenges the modern view of the subject–object relationship that attributes agency exclusively to humans. As Bruno Latour (1993) argues, agency must be redistributed to 'things'. Such a new theoretical framework is quite critical of Marxism (Latour and Lépinay 2009), demanding a rethinking of its labour theory of value, especially because of its 'anthropocentric' character. It is thus understandable that Moore also proposes its revision when he claims that capitalism puts nature to 'work' in order to produce value:

> How is nature's work/energy transformed into value? ... The question shifts our thinking away from too much of one thing (humans, or capitalism) and too little of another thing (Nature), and towards the *longue durée* relations and strategies that have allowed capitalism-in-nature to survive. And capitalism has survived not by destroying nature (whatever this might mean), but through projects that compel nature-as-*oikeios* to work harder and harder – for free, or at a very low cost. (Moore 2015: 13)

According to Moore, nature's 'work' does not directly produce value – that would be a negation of Marx's labour theory of value – but the expropriation of the unpaid work of nature essentially contributes to capital's valorization.[11] In this sense, nature is exploited, and Moore (2019: 53) even calls it 'biotariat'.

This extended conception of 'work' to include non-human work is common among those who criticize the anthropocentrism of the Anthropocene discourse. Stefania Barca (2020: 19) argues that 'capitalism adopted this [anthropocentric] model of rationality in reshaping the notion of modernity as the capacity to extract value from both human and non-human work'. The critique of the master narrative of the Anthropocene 'allows to see that the key commonality between all non-master Others is a broadly defined but still cogent notion of *labour*: from different positions, and in different forms, women, slaves, proletarians and animals and non-human nature are all made to work for the master' (Barca 2020: 6; emphasis in original).

This treatment of 'work', which redistributes agency to nature and blurs the distinct roles of humans and nature in the production process, shows how Bruno Latour's actor–network theory (ANT) is intruding into political ecology. Latour argues for 'blurring the distinction between nature and society *durably*, so that we shall never have to go back to two distinct sets' (Latour 2004: 36). According to his hybridism, it is no longer possible to distinguish between social and natural phenomena. Latour, referring to ozone depletion and wildfires, argued already in the early 1990s that the issue of environmental destruction cannot be neatly categorized into the sphere of humans and the sphere of nature. Natural phenomena such as ozone holes and climate change are deeply entangled with social phenomena (production of Freon gas and emission of carbon dioxide from car and airplanes): 'All of culture and all of nature get churned up again every day' (Latour 1993: 2). As everything seems to have become hybrid of society and nature in the Anthropocene, Latour's hybridism has become a popular way to describe the Anthropocene in which things possess the active agency in uncontrollable wildfires and gigantic typhoons.

In short, according to Latourian monists, the Anthropocene is the age of post-natural post-humanism, in which the hierarchical divide between humans and non-human is dissolved into the world of 'actants' (Purdy 2015: 271–2). This kind of understanding can be found among those who take a Marxist approach. For example, Christoph Bonneuil and Jean-Baptiste Fressoz refer positively to Latour and ask about how to overcome the dualism of human and nature: 'How then are we to overcome the dualism between nature and society'? Then, they answer this question by emphasizing the importance of comprehending a 'double relation of internality' consisting of 'natures pervaded by social' and 'societies pervaded by nature' (Bonneuil and Fressoz 2016: 41). It is in this context that Bonneuil and Fressoz speak highly of the 'ecologized Marxism of Jason Moore' and argue that the metabolisms have 'political agency' too (Bonneuil and Fressoz 2016: 35–7).

Even Slavoj Žižek is influenced by Latour's monist approach. Žižek, who had rejected ecology as 'a new opium for the masses', recently changed his opinion after the global pandemic and now recognizes the seriousness of the ecological crisis as a contradiction of capitalism. However, in advocating for 'a radical philosophical change' adequate to the Anthropocene, he also points to the insufficiency of the Marxian dualist concept of 'metabolism':

> To confront the forthcoming ecological crisis, a radical philosophical change is thus needed, much more radical than the usual platitude of emphasizing how we, humans, are part of nature, just one of the natural species on Earth, i.e., of how our productive processes (our metabolism with nature, as Marx put it) is part of the metabolism within nature itself. (Žižek 2020a: 115)

Here Žižek supports Latour's 'assemblage' by criticizing Foster's concept of metabolic rift, which he thinks is not radical enough for the sake of adequately handling the current entanglement of the social and the natural.[12] This is how Moore's self-proclaimed 'loyalty' to Marx's philosophy is effectively gaining more influence. Nevertheless, if Moore is right, the concept of 'metabolic rift' is no longer tenable. Before abandoning the concept, it is necessary to look at his claims a little more carefully.[13]

Moore's project of 'world-ecology' is an expansion of Immanuel Wallerstein's world-system analysis.[14] In order for the capitalist centres to attain greater profits, they exploit cheap labour from the peripheries by creating a 'semi-proletariat' whose costs of reproduction for capital is artificially low because they have other means of subsistence. This 'unequal exchange' based on the exploitation of cheap labour results simultaneously in 'overdevelopment' in the Global North and 'underdevelopment' in the Global South. In Wallerstein's theoretical scheme, the object of exploitation was human labour power, but that only deals with one side of the actual process of unequal exchange because it misses nature, the other essential component of production. There also exists 'ecologically unequal exchange' (Hornborg and Martinez-Alier 2016). Thus, it is not only labour power in the periphery that is exposed to capitalist robbery but also the non-human environment such as resource, food and energy. In other words, capitalism, which treats human beings as a mere tool for capital accumulation, inevitably regards nature simply as an object to be squandered. Extending Wallerstein's argument, it is possible to say that the capitalist centres expropriate nature and externalize the costs and burdens that lie behind economic development to the peripheries.

Moore argues that capitalism's lifeline is an abundant and cheap supply of what he calls the 'Four Cheaps', consisting of labour-power, food, energy and raw materials: 'The law of value in capitalism is a law of Cheap Nature' (Moore 2015: 53). It is noteworthy that Moore includes 'labour-power' within 'Cheap Nature'. 'Cheap Nature' consists of a large number of humans such as the poor, women, people of colour and slaves. Capital not only expropriates natural resources but also constitutes and thoroughly utilizes gender hierarchy, violent colonial rule and technological domination over humans and nature to secure profitability and to globally expand the capitalist mode of production. Moore argues that capitalism did not simply develop through the 'exploitation' of (male and white) workers in industrialized capitalist centres. Rather, it is essentially dependent on the 'expropriation' of the 'unpaid work' of the Four Cheaps. Through such a constant 'thingification' (Césaire [1955] 2000: 42) of the world, capitalism reassembles networks of humans and nature and makes them 'work' harder for the sake of profit making.[15]

Upon this background, Moore attacks Foster's metabolic rift as 'Cartesian dualism', arguing that his own post-Cartesian approach is a more productive interpretation of Marx's own ecological critique of capitalism: The 'dialectical thrust of Marx's philosophy is to see humanity/nature as a flow of flows' (Moore 2015: 22). Moore proposes to analyse constant metabolic 'shifts' in the 'singular metabolism' of co-produced society and nature.[16]

Moore's treatment of Marx's text is dubious, however. When he criticizes the metabolic rift between social and natural metabolism and replaces it with 'metabolic shift' in the singular metabolism, it is strange that he does not mention Marx's own usage of 'rift'. He writes: 'Rather than ford the Cartesian divide, [Foster's] metabolism approaches have reinforced it. Marx's "interdependent process of social metabolism" became the "metabolism of nature and society". Metabolism as "rift" became a metaphor of separation, premised on material flows between Nature and Society' (Moore 2015: 76). While 'interdependent process of social metabolism' is taken from *Capital*, volume III, 'metabolism of nature and society' is Foster's formulation (Foster 2013), so that it sounds as if he produced a dualist understanding of metabolism in favour of the concept of metabolic 'rift', distorting Marx's original and post-Cartesian insight.

However, the passage to which Moore refers shows that Marx himself employed the concept of 'rift', as he wrote that capitalist production 'provoke[s] an irreparable rift in the interdependent process of social metabolism and natural metabolism'. Moore arbitrarily cherry-picks from Marx's original passage in favour of his own monist understanding of capitalism in the web of life. It is 'arbitrary' because Marx clearly distinguished and contrasted two kinds of metabolism – one social and the other natural – warning against the formation of rupture in their perpetual interaction under capitalism. Did Marx also fall into the 'Cartesian divide' by mistake? Or, is it an intentional expression that is consistent with his method?

IV
NON-CARTESIAN DUALISM OF 'FORM' AND 'MATERIAL'

First, Moore too hastily borrows an existing concept of Cartesian dualism without sufficiently considering its applicability to the Marxian concept of 'metabolic rift'. The accusation of falling into Cartesian dualism of Society and Nature makes sense only if Society remains fully outside Nature without any interaction like 'mind' and 'body' do in Descartes's philosophy (Soper 1995). Seen from this perspective, the Marxian concept of metabolism is anti-Cartesian from the very beginning because neither Marx nor Foster assumes such an absolute separation of society and nature. The basic insight of Marx's theory of metabolism is, on the contrary, that humans always produce as a part of nature and that their activities are entangled with extra-human nature more and more in the course of capitalist development. Thus, the question needs to be reformulated in the following way: why did Marx intentionally draw upon a dualist distinction of social and natural metabolism, *even though* he held a monist understanding of the universal metabolism of nature?[17]

As discussed in the last chapter, there is actually nothing wrong with separating the social from the natural *and* insisting at the same time that humans are also a part of it. As Foster says:

> There is no contradiction in seeing society as both separate from and irreducible to the Earth system as a whole, and simultaneously as a fundamental part of it. To call that approach 'dualist' is comparable to denying that your heart is both an integral part of your body and a distinct organ with unique features and functions. (Foster and Angus 2016)

It is possible to add that the difference between society and nature is even greater than that between heart and body. It is rather analogous to the relationship between mind and body. Mind has a property that cannot be reduced to the materiality of the body, even though mind is connected to the materiality of the brain. The reduction of mind to activities of the brain would be crude materialism (Gabriel 2019), which is another extreme form of identity thinking opposed to social constructivism. Similarly, society does not exist without nature, but social relations produce their own unique *emergent properties* that do not exist in nature without humans, even if the emergent properties of society cannot be fully separated from their material basis and bearer. Capital is parasitic to its bearers and is thoroughly dependent on them, but capital remains blind to them until their degradation appears as an obstacle to valorization. This paradoxical character of capital is exactly why Marx's critique of political economy puts emphasis on the distinction *and* interconnectedness of the 'purely social' forms and their material 'bearers' and analyses their tension due to their non-identity.[18]

Thus, the rejection of Cartesian dualism does not automatically lead Marx to a flat ontology without any distinction between the social and the natural, something for which Hegel (1977: 9) once ridiculed Schelling as equivalent to 'the night in which ... all cows are black'. Instead, Marx emphasized the uniqueness of human metabolism with nature compared with that of other animals. This is not necessarily outdated anthropocentrism. Since Marx insists that only human labour under certain social relations produces *value*, the category of value in Marxian economics is inevitably anthropocentric. Due to this anthropocentric labour theory of value, critics often emphasize the essential contribution of nature to production by recognizing its power to produce value. However, here again, the question needs to be formulated the other way around. Marx's theory of metabolism clearly recognized the essential contribution of nature to production. If so, it is necessary to ask why Marx nevertheless formulated his labour theory of value without redistributing agency to nature and refused to attribute nature's 'work' to an agency that produces value.

Here the purely social dimension of 'value' is of importance because it is what gives human labour – more precisely abstract labour – a privileged role *in capitalism* compared to non-human nature. Marx's labour theory of value is anthropocentric, but he also added that not all human labour produces value, distinguishing productive from unproductive labour. Depending on social relations and material conditions, the same concrete labour can be productive or unproductive of value. Where does this difference come from?

The production of value is tied to commodity production, and Marx argued that 'private labour' as a unique form of social division of labour necessitates the category of value: 'As a general rule, articles of utility become commodities, only because they are products of the labour of private individuals or groups of individuals who carry on their work independently of each other' (*MECW* 35: 83). Private labour designate a situation where labour is carried out without any previous social coordination among the members of a society. When private producers without any shared interest and personal ties meet in the market in order to obtain products that others have, commodity exchange takes place. In this sense, the social relation between private producers is based on a relation between their products. In seeking to exchange their own products at an appropriate rate, private producers compare the 'worth' of their products. In doing so, use-value cannot be the standard for exchange as use-values of products are all different and incomparable. Private producers instead recognize a common social power of products, which Marx calls *value* as the objectification of the abstract labour that is common to all products of human labour. As Sasaki (2021: 67) argues, '... the only way for their labour products to come into that relation [of exchange] is for the products to be treated as things of value'. *Only private labour produces value* and provides the products of labour with an economic form determined as the commodity.

Here private producers are compelled to unconsciously treat their products as things of value. They create this purely social category of value. Nevertheless, it is not an imaginary fiction but has an enormous objective power. Thus, Marx investigated how the purely social form of value that contains 'not an atom of matter' dominates the metabolic processes of nature. The capitalist mode of production subsumes the entire society under the formal logic of value mediated by human agency as the personification of commodities, money and capital. Compared to non-capitalist societies, value brings about an historically specific dynamic of social and natural metabolism.

The purely social power of value contains no atoms of matter, but it is deeply entangled with the material conditions of the universal metabolism of nature because humans are part of nature. Precisely because nature exists independently of and prior to those social categories and continues to retain non-identity with the logic of value, the primacy of profit maximalization results in a series of disharmonies within natural metabolism. 'Rift' is not a 'metaphor' as Moore argues. Rift exists between the social metabolism of commodities and money and the universal metabolism of nature. Moore believes the concept of rift automatically implies a dualism, so he intentionally ignores Marx's own usage of it. In contrast, Marx's metabolic rift is consistently deduced from his labour theory of value. In Marx's view, it is essential to separate the unique form of value-producing labour as the organizing principle of the modern bourgeois society. Otherwise, it is not possible to comprehend how the actual process of capitalist accumulation develops 'through nature'. The logic of value determines what counts as Cheap Nature and how certain humans and non-humans are used as free gifts of nature. Value must be comprehended based on private labour as a unique way of organizing social division of labour. This is why labour power cannot be reduced to a form of Cheap Nature because such a conception only obscures the logic of how and why the particular and central form of labour under commodity production necessitates the category of value.[19]

Moore undermines the central role of labour in Marx's political economy in favour of monism. Therefore, he dismisses 'metabolic rift' as a mere metaphor that does not exist in the actual web of life. The cost of reducing the rift to a metaphor is high, however. Andreas Malm points out that the allegedly radical view of Moore's world-ecology is not radical enough because it occurs only on the level of 'language' (Malm 2018: 181). Indeed, Moore's phraseology, which is filled with newly invented vocabularies and hyphenations such as 'capitalism-*in*-nature' and 'develop *through* the oikeios', reminds us of Marx's famous eleventh thesis: 'The philosophers have only interpreted the world, in various ways; the point is to change it' (*MECW* 5: 5). Thereby Marx rejected Feuerbach's 'philosophy of essence' (*Wesensphilosophie*) that aimed at enlightening the masses by pointing out the 'truth' that God, an alienated omnipotent being, is in reality nothing but a projection of humans' own infinite and universal essence as 'species-being'. Marx criticized Feuerbach that it is not sufficient to reveal the essence of Christianity and posed the question in a 'materialist manner' (*Capital* I: 494), namely, 'why' and 'how' people accept such an illusion and it actually dominates people's life (Sasaki 2021: 36). Even if Feuerbach is right in pointing out that God is a product of the human imagination, it is necessary to ask how a certain set of social behaviour constantly produces and reproduces the alien power of God over human beings. Unless these social praxes are radically modified in reality, calls for the correct recognition of the true essence are unable to overcome alienation.

Similarly, it is not enough to replace the dualism of Society and Nature with monist expressions in language of hyphenation because a certain form of dualism *does* possess an objective force to shape reality, even if Moore with his 'philosophical lens' wishes to 'interpret' the world in a monist way. In other words, when Marx described the problem of 'rift' between social and natural metabolism in a dualist manner – as well as other issues such as 'productive' and 'unproductive' labour – it is not because he mistakenly fell into the Cartesian dualism. He did so consciously because the uniquely social relations of capitalism do exert an alien power in reality. A critical analysis of this social power inevitably requires separating the social and the natural respectively as independent realms of investigation and analysing their entanglement thereafter. This is also what Lukács advocated. If the reality is dualist, re-describing it in a monist manner may end up mystifying the particular arrangements and functioning of existing social forces characteristic of capitalism. In short, despite Moore's critical intention, his theory can fall into the 'ideology of science'.

Take an example of the 'planetary boundaries'. The increasing emission of CO_2 in the great acceleration is a social phenomenon tied to a certain way of organizing social production based on fossil fuels. Beyond a certain tipping point, it is probable that irreversible, rapid and unexpected changes will be triggered through positive feedback effects. Due to the melting of the Antarctic ice sheet because of climate change, methane gas contained in the ice will be released, accelerating climate change. Ocean acidification and deforestation causes the decrease or extinction of certain species, which disturbs the food chain, leading to the decrease of other species too. These chain reactions are not directly caused by human activities, and nor can humans change them. This is why they are considered 'irreversible'. The fact that ice melts beyond 0 degrees or that shells need calcium carbonate ($CaCO_3$) but that the absorption of CO_2 decreases carbonate ion (CO_3^{2-}) and increases bicarbonate ion (HCO_3^-) in the ocean is not something humans can determine nor modify according to will, no matter how hard they try. These phenomena are determined by natural processes that exist independently of and prior to human intervention. Although capitalist development affects nature through the commodification of fossil fuels, this fact does not make the natural process social either. The environmental problem emerges precisely because natural laws exist objectively and independently of social ones, and because a particular way of organizing social metabolism based on the massive consumption of fossil fuels greatly diverges – that is, creates a 'rift' – from the conditions of sustainable production prescribed by nature's biophysical processes.

This is why Andreas Malm (2018: 85) demands to focus on social causes of ecological crises based on *human* 'agency', which must be strictly distinguished from causal chains in nature. The increasing emission of greenhouse gas as the direct cause of climate change and ocean acidification has an intimate relation with the social choice to use fossil fuels in capitalism. It is possible to make a different choice by using renewable energy, for example. In short, there are certain things that humans can consciously modify and others that they cannot. The natural planetary boundaries must be first recognized, and a sustainable society needs to accommodate itself to these limits.[20] Thus, Malm maintains that the 'analytical distinction' between the social and the natural is '*the indispensable premise for any solution to such a combined problem*' (Malm 2018: 61; emphasis in original). Even though the critique of the Anthropocene narrative based on its Eurocentrism and productivism is totally valid, the response should not be monism. Methodological or analytical dualism is indispensable in order to critically investigate the capitalist way of organizing production and constituting various unjust hierarchies.

A just transition to a more sustainable production is also inevitably an anthropocentric project because it involves human beings aiming to overcome what they have created by themselves: 'Ecological concerns are not problems derived internally, originating from ecosystems themselves, but are produced externally, by social drivers. For example, the oceans are not polluting themselves; *humans are doing it*' (Longo, Clausen and Clark 2015: x; emphasis in original). Thus, only humans can consciously act to repair the rift. Marx demanded this in arguing for another way of conducting human metabolism with nature by freely associated producers in order to abolish private labour and wage labour.

Throughout this process, non-anthropocentric concerns are essential to problematize the current ecological crisis and abandon the instrumental attitude towards non-human nature, but they are also only accessible to us based on *our* current understanding of the world and of non-human beings and are inevitably conditioned by human interests and perspectives. In this sense, they inescapably remain 'anthropocentric' (Hailwood 2015: 20), but it is not necessary to fall into human exceptionalism.[21] Kate Soper criticizes the hypocrisy of post-humanist monism because post-humanism is actually anthropocentric and thus self-subverting:

> Posthumanist theory, however, is produced exclusively by and for human beings and it seeks a response through their particular capacities for adjusting thought and behaviour in the light of argument. It thus relies for its theoretical coherence and ethical appeal on an implicit commitment to distinctively human qualities, and by extension to intentionality and conscious agency. (Soper 2020: 22–3)

Therefore, one should not be satisfied with pointing to the hybrid situation and end the analysis with a flat ontology. Rather, accepting the state of hybridity and a flat ontology is equivalent to falling for a fetishized understanding that simply accepts what is given without revealing its social factors. In fact, the idea of 'actant' that distribute agency to things is incompatible with Marx's critique of 'fetishism' (Hornborg 2016: 11). Marx actually talked about the 'agency' of the thing in his analysis of commodity in *Capital*. He argued that in capitalism the relations of things replace the relations of humans, and human agency is rather subjected to and constituted through the movement of things: social relations 'do not appear as direct social relations between persons in their work, but rather as material [*dinglich*] relations between persons and social relations between things' (*Capital* I: 166). However, the whole point of his critique of fetishism is to reveal the uniquely human agency that produces this pathological inversion of the subject and the object in the commodity-producing society. Stopping at the level of actant mystifies the specific difference of the capitalist relations and the agency of reified things by treating all the appearances of actants in the same way. By evenly redistributing agency, a flat ontology obscures the social impact of capital upon the environment as if nature's impact were as significant as the social one in the process of capital accumulation.[22] It is after all *Anthropos* that creates oppression and hierarchy and destroys the environment. What is more, this anthropocentrism also affects the vision of a post-capitalist society.

V

ELASTICITY OF CAPITAL AND ECOLOGICAL CRISIS

Despite his provocative language, Moore's theoretical framework of capitalist development and crisis is largely a repetition of the 'second contradiction of capitalism' originally suggested by James O'Connor. According to O'Connor (1998), the first contradiction of capitalism is characterized by the increasing productivity and increasing poverty of the proletariat, which ultimately leads to the economic crisis of overproduction and the destabilization of the capitalist system. The second contradiction of capitalism arises due to an 'underproduction' of nature. In contrast to earlier crisis theories of 'underconsumption' that approach the problematic from the demand side (Luxemburg [1913] 2016), 'underproduction' of nature results in a crisis on the supply side, which affects production costs. As the productive forces continue to increase under market competition, nature gets exhausted, so that the price of raw materials, energy, food and labour power increases. This underproduction of nature decreases the rate of profit, bringing about the stagnation of capital accumulation. A sudden interruption of supply and a dramatic increase in production costs can seriously harm the economy. Workers are fired and the wages stagnate. The social system is destabilized in the moment of crisis. Moore's arguments about the end of Cheap Nature and the decline in the 'ecological surplus' appears quite similar to O'Connor's views.[23]

Thus, it is helpful to go back to earlier critiques of O'Connor's theory with its theoretical limitations as a framework for grasping the ecological crisis under capitalism. As Burkett (1999: 195) argues, O'Connor's theory pivots around a *crisis of capital* in that it is a crisis of capital accumulation due to rising production costs and a corresponding decline in profitability. O'Connor underestimated Marx's concept of the 'elasticity of capital', which offers a more dynamic account of the relationship between capital and nature. Only if we neglect the astonishing elasticity of capital, does it sound plausible that the rising price of natural resources would threaten capitalism as the law of the rate of profit to fall penetrates itself. Yet Marx did not argue for an 'iron law' of capitalism's breakdown due to the falling rate of profit, but he repeatedly emphasized that two aspects of the law of the rate of profit to fall 'contain a contradiction, and this finds expression in contradictory tendencies and phenomena. The contending agencies function simultaneously in opposition to one another' (*Capital* III: 357). He was convinced that capitalism develops through this 'living contradiction' (*Grundrisse*: 421). In other words, the existence of contradiction drives further technological progress and modifications in the production and circulation processes.

While O'Connor tends to underestimate the elasticity of capital, Moore's 'co-production' of society and nature can be regarded as an attempt to go further than O'Connor by rejecting the existence of static natural limits and by more clearly emphasizing the elasticity of nature as the source of the astonishing vitality of capital. In fact, Moore repeatedly maintains that there are no objective natural limits to capital, but that they are co-produced in the web of life. His theory of underproduction of nature attempts to avoid both Malthusianism and the social constructivism of nature.

Marx also argued that capital harnesses various elastic characteristics of the world for the sake of producing greater flexibility:

> The natural materials which are exploited productively (and which do not form an element of the capital's value), i.e. soil, sea, mineral ores, forests, etc. may be more or less severely exploited, in extent and intensity, by greater exertion of the same amount of labour-power, without an increase in the money capital advanced. (*Capital* II: 432)[24]

With the aid of both science and technology, capital constantly appropriates new raw materials and energies to increase productivity without proportionally increasing the costs of production. In addition, capital utilizes nature's elasticity to generate externalities and temporally and spatially shift the negative consequences of the social costs from the centres to the peripheries.

Nevertheless, the elasticity of capital inevitably has objective limits. Once these natural limits are surpassed, elasticity is lost entirely all of a sudden, just like an overstretched spring, so it no longer delivers capital's desired results. This dependence on natural elasticity then turns out to be problematic for the accumulation of capital. The quality of natural power degrades when its material characteristics continue to be ignored, and this can be accompanied even by the decrease in the *quantity* of products as well. The difficulty increases in the course of capitalist development because the concentration of capital – as a response to the falling rate of profit in order to increase the mass of profit – requires a larger volume of raw and auxiliary materials to keep production running. Difficulties increase as natural productivity may fail to catch up with industry's rising productivity. There is

> a contrary movement in these different spheres so that the productivity of labour rises in one place while, it falls in another. We need only consider the influence of the seasons, for example, on which the greater part of the raw materials depends, as well as the exhaustion of forests and coal and iron mines, etc. (*Capital* III: 369)

The elasticity of natural power may be able to cover such an increase of demand for a certain period, but it triggers serious degradation and exhaustion of the natural conditions of production over the long term. This inevitably constrains capital accumulation while it also accelerates capital's further intervention into nature. This is how capital and nature are 'co-produced' and Moore seems to more properly grasp this dynamic logic of capitalist development than O'Connor.

Nonetheless, Moore's prediction for the future is as apocalyptic as Engels's 'revenge of nature': the degradation of the natural environment generates a crisis for capital *one day* due to the end of Cheap Nature. However, considering the enormous elasticity of capital, it remains unclear whether capitalism or the Earth will collapse first. There is no compelling reason to believe that capitalism will collapse under rising production costs and degrading natural conditions of production. This is unlikely, as capital can profit even from natural degradation by finding new opportunities for investment in such disasters too (Burkett 2006: 136). As Naomi Klein (2007) has documented, this possibility is clearly visible in what neoliberal 'disaster capitalism' has done in the last decades. Capital continues to profit from current ecological crises by inventing new business opportunities such as fracking, geo-engineering, genetically modified organisms (GMOs), carbon trading and natural disaster insurance. Incessantly attempting to shift the rift, capitalism can keep going beyond these natural limits and accumulate more wealth. In contrast, the current level of civilization cannot sustain itself beyond a certain point *precisely due to objective natural limits*. As far as the logic of capital's accumulation is being estranged from human life and the sustainability of the ecosystem, the capitalist system might continue to exist, even if all the planetary boundaries are exceeded, but many parts of the earth will be unsuitable for civilization.

In short, there is simply no empirical evidence that the pressure on profit rates due to the increasing costs of circulating capital will bring about an 'epochal crisis' any time soon. For example, it is necessary to realize net zero carbon emissions by 2050 to keep global warming within 1.5°C by 2100. When this line is crossed, various effects might combine, thereby reinforcing their destructive impact on a global scale, especially upon those who live in the Global South. However, capitalist societies in the Global North will not necessarily collapse. This brief example suffices to show an enormous difference between the material conditions for capital accumulation and the maintenance of the liveable ecospheres.[25] Since Moore's concept of 'epochal crisis' mainly deals with the crisis of capital accumulation, it tends to marginalize ecological crisis as such.

Moore's weakness arising from this marginalization of ecological crisis manifests in his vision of a transition to the future society. Since he analyses today's general crisis mainly from the perspective of capital, his vision of emancipation contains some tension with Marx's humanism. According to Marx's theory of metabolic rift, the ecological crisis significantly undermines the possibility of free 'sustainable human development' (Burkett 2005). He warned that capitalist production 'destroys at the same time the physical health of the urban worker, and the intellectual life of the rural worker'. Humanism calls for the practical necessity of establishing a more sustainable form of production beyond capitalism before the latter collapses due to underproduction of nature. In this sense, Marx problematized the ecological crisis not from the standpoint of capital, but rather from the perspective of free and sustainable human development, which monism cannot do well as it undermines the position of humanity. In fact, Moore confronts the difficulty with Marx's vision of establishing a future society by consciously changing the form of human labour, that is transcending private labour and wage labour. Instead, Moore aims to overcome capitalism with the aid of nature as 'actant' – its exhaustion, turbulence and the rising price of natural resources and energy. This is a revolt of the 'biotariat'.

As discussed in the previous section, Marx's anthropocentrism does not automatically erase the non-identity of nature. An adequate treatment of ecological crisis requires that we recognize the non-identity of nature. Its recognition remains 'anthropocentric' in that its non-identity can only be defined in relation to identity, that is, in relation *to us*. This is not pernicious as the critics of the Anthropocene narrative fear, however. Rather, this kind of anthropocentrism is necessary in order to talk about the ecological crisis at all in a meaningful manner. Bacteria and insects may continue to live even after climate breakdown leads to the extinction of human species. However, if their existence prohibits us from talking about the ecological crisis from a human perspective, that basically negates the existence of the ecological crisis. Without anthropocentrism, it would actually be almost impossible to speak of the ecological crisis because it exists mainly *for humans*.

VI
GOOD ANTHROPOCENE?

There is no compelling reason to assume that capital will stop its intervention into nature in the face of the crisis of capital accumulation. For example, Bruno Latour argues in his article 'Love Your Monsters' that the crime of Dr Frankenstein is not that he created a monster but that he abandoned it due to fear. Latour continues:

> It is not the case that we have failed to care for Creation, but that we have failed to care for our technological creations. We confuse the monster for its creator and blame our sins against Nature upon our creations. But our sin is not that we created technologies but that we failed to love and care for them. (Latour 2011: 22)

Latour prohibits the rejection of modern technologies and productivity all of a sudden due to fear in the context of the hybrid situation. Rather, the way to go is to push this hybridization even further and to create 'intimacy with new natures' (Latour 2011: 22). Latour's attitude is *hypermodern*. His monism is exemplary in its ignorance of the 'primacy of the object' and 'the non-identity of nature', which reinforces the Promethean project of domination over nature with a strong instrumentalist attitude. This notorious example suffices to show that monism does not automatically provide a superior view of the world compared to dualism if it denies the non-identity between humans and nature as well as the latter's preponderance.

Latour's article was published in a journal edited by the US-based think tank, Breakthrough Institute, where he was a senior fellow. Although Latour denies that he fully agrees with the general agenda of the think tank (Latour 2014: 240), their affinity is visible. According to their view, the world has always been turbulent and so environmentalists are too romantic and even reactionary in attempting to protect pristine nature in a state of equilibrium that never existed and will never exist. Thus, *The Ecomodernist Manifesto* – to which Latour is a contributor – claims that further intervention in nature through 'increasing social, economic, and technological power' is a condition for the democratic 'good Anthropocene' (Breakthrough Institute 2015). It is not clear at all how the idea of 'democratic control' could be compatible with capital-intensive gigantic technologies such as geo-engineering, carbon capture and storage (CCS) and nuclear fusion.[26] In any case, if technological and economic development alone were sufficient to overcome the ecological crisis by fully remaking the earth, capitalism could be salvaged. Leigh Phillips (2015), an advocate of ecomodernism, boldly declares that 'there is no metabolic rift'.

What does ecomodernism have to do with Moore? Moore does not endorse such an idea, but he refers to Ted Nordhaus and Michael Schellenberger, the founders of the Breakthrough Institute, as powerful critics of the dualist conception dominant in Marxism:

> A radical and emancipatory alternative does not deny the degradation of nature. Far from it! But a politics of nature premised on degradation rather than work renders the radical vision vulnerable to a powerful critique. This says, in effect, that pristine nature has never really existed; that we are living through another of many eras of environmental change that can be resolved through technological innovation (Lynas 2011; Shellenberger and Nordhaus 2011). The counterargument for the Capitalocene – an ugly word for an ugly system – understands the degradation of nature as a specific expression of capitalism's organization of work. (Moore 2016: 111)

Later, Moore tacitly modified a similar passage to add that these arguments are 'rubbish' (Moore 2017a: 78),[27] but he still believes that monist ecomodernists are better than those who endorse the dualist concept of metabolic rift.

One may object that a reference to the Breakthrough Institute does not immediately mean support for its ecomodernist vision. That might be true, but this situation is similar to Harvey's reference to Greg Easterbrook. This is the risk of monism. Foster correctly emphasizes the danger of hybridism in the face of the global ecological crisis:

> In the face of the very real bifurcation of the world in the Anthropocene by capitalism's alienated social-metabolic reproduction, to focus on the truisms that in the end the world is all one, and that human production inevitably creates new hybrid forms of human-nature linkages (as if this in itself transcends natural processes and laws), is to downplay the real depths of the crisis in which the world is now placed. (Foster 2016: 407)

Moore criticized the 'fetishization of natural limits' in Engels's idea of nature's revenge, but this rejection prompts him to endorse the idea of making natural limits more elastic, although it is not comprehensible how his prediction of the end of Cheap Nature and his technological optimism can coexist consistently in Moore's theory. As a result, Moore can only vaguely anticipate the collapse of capitalism due to the end of Cheap Nature *one day* when capital's technologies cannot open up new frontiers and overcome the tendency of a falling ecological surplus.

After all, it is certainly necessary to intervene and modify the natural world in order to tackle today's climate change. Recognition of the non-identity of nature is key, lest one falls into the illusion of absolute control over the entire eco-system. It requires humans to live with the irreducible otherness of nature. Nature resists their instrumentalist purposes as long as it has its own purposiveness that eludes human's full grasp.[28] From the perspective of the 'identity of identity and non-identity' in Lukács's sense, methodological dualism turns out to be indispensable to any critical theory of nature in the Anthropocene.[29] Unfortunately, the current revival of post-capitalist discourses is heading in the opposite direction and endorses technological progress. This situation is ironic because the late Marx came to question the emancipatory character of the capitalist development of productive forces.

NOTES

1   The inability of such an approach to analyse the social system means that the solution to ecological crisis becomes a primitivist one of going back to nature or even returning to the Pleistocene in order to regain closeness to it. Or worse, the extinction of humans becomes a topic of philosophical investigation in the Anthropocene.

2   In fact, although most of the excessive burden upon the global environment is due to the economic activities of people living in the Global North, its economic development model is generally assumed to be self-evident. That is why economic growth and technological innovation continue to be regarded as the only solution to the multi-stranded crises in the Anthropocene. This solution would be, however, hypocritical because those who are responsible for these crises now propose solutions to them and praise them in order to justify their conventional rule and way of life. They are part of the problem, not the solution.

3   More recently, however, Malm (2018) seems to distance himself from his earlier usage of the 'Capitalocene'. This is presumably because Jason W. Moore (2015) propagates the same concept, but Malm is highly critical of Moore's monist understanding of the current ecological crisis.

4   McKibben's argument was also problematic due to his conflation of touching nature with the end of nature. Here it is possible to discern his Cartesian dualism.

5   Adorno, however, did not develop his theory of negative dialectic in terms of ecology. Görg's project counts as a critical expansion of original attempts made by the first generation of the Frankfurt School. One reason for this is that Adorno did not pay attention to Marx's concept of metabolism as a foundation of the ecological critique of capitalism. Likewise, Alfred Schmidt ([1971] 2014) did not elaborate on the ecological critique despite his lengthy treatment of Marx's concept of nature and rather characterizes Marx as a technological determinist. I do not necessarily agree with Cassegård's defence of Adorno's and Schmidt's interest in nature in an ecological sense (Cassegård 2017), but I am certainly sympathetic to Cassegård's insistence on the non-identity of nature as the foundation of a 'critical theory of nature'. Cassegård (2021) also supports my understanding of Marx's dialectics of 'form' and 'matter'.

6   This is true for Marx as it defined the role of labour as the 'mediating' activity of the metabolism between humans and nature. 'Mediation' implies that Marx was aware that nature cannot be erased and that it retains its independence no matter how labour seems to be able to manipulate the external nature.

7   Harvey (2011: 94) adds: 'Because capital has successfully done this in the past does not necessarily mean, of course, that it is destined to do so in perpetuity.' But taken together with his previous remark about Foster, it is questionable how much he really believes this. Only in 2019 did Harvey finally admit the seriousness of ecological crisis as an epochal crisis without attributing it to apocalypticism, but this is almost too late. Listen to his podcast 'The Plastic Industry and CO_2 Emission and Climate Change'.

8   This fear of Malthusianism is influential in the Marxian tradition. Even the young Marx fell into a productivist view that negates the existence of natural limits (Saito 2017).

9   Marx also emphasized that the modification of nature cannot be arbitrary. Labour alone cannot produce natural substances, and its power is limited; it can only modify their shapes according to various purposes. He wrote that labour provides 'natural substance' with '*external form*' (*Grundrisse*: 360; emphasis in original). For example, the form of a desk that labour provides to the 'natural substance' of wood remains 'external' to the original substance because it does not follow the 'immanent law of reproduction'. Although the immanent law maintains the wood in its specific form of a tree, the new form of a desk cannot reproduce its substance in the same way, so that it now starts to get exposed to the natural force of decomposition. In order to protect the product of labour from the power of natural metabolism, a purposeful regulation of metabolism through productive consumption is required, which nonetheless cannot fully overcome the force of nature.

10   Moore might respond that he only used the term 'actant' once, and his view is not identical with Latour's 'flat ontology'. He might add that his theory is *not* monism because he also employed the term 'monism' only once and also uses 'soft dualism' in *Capitalism in the Web of Life* (Moore 2015: 13, 85). Yet it does not really matter how many times he used these terms. After all, he fails to explain

how his view differs from Latour's flat ontology and other kinds of monism and what his ontology actually is after his determined rejection of Cartesian dualism. Actually, if he really accepts 'soft dualism', there is no significant difference between his world-ecology and the metabolic rift school.

11   'All of these de- and un-valued forms of work are, however, outside the value form (the commodity). They do not directly produce value. And yet – it is a very big and yet – value as abstract labor cannot be produced except through unpaid work/energy' (Moore 2015: 65). Others are much more explicit about the value produced by extra-human agencies, suggesting 'the value theory of nature' (Yaşın 2017: 397), but this simply reverts to physiocracy.

12   This move is not surprising in that it is more or less consistent with his earlier criticism of environmentalism that naively presupposes the harmonious totality of nature (Žižek 2008: 444). Furthermore, this leads Žižek (2020b) to criticize my understanding of nature as well as of abstract labour. Žižek – he is by no means alone – claims that abstract labour is historically specific to capitalism. However, this argument conflates value and abstract labour. Value is purely social and specific to capitalism, but abstract labour is an abstraction of one aspect of human labour, which exists as long as humans labour. According to Marx's methodology, there is nothing wrong with separating the transhistorical dimension of abstract labour from its socially specific function in valorization under capitalism.

13   Certainly, the popularity of monism is understandable, considering their common interest in overcoming Cartesian dualism of Society and Nature. However, Bonneuil and Fressoz also recognize Marx's contribution in his analysis of 'the metabolic rupture between Earth and society that capitalism had produced' (Bonneuil and Fressoz 2016: 176) and often draw upon Foster's analysis of the metabolic rift. In other words, they think it is their contribution to Marxian ecology to expand the metabolic rift approach in the context of 'world-ecologies' that deal with the unequal exchange of value and ecological flows without really questioning whether such a synthesis is really possible.

14   In fact, the term 'world-ecology' stems also from Wallerstein (1974: 44).

15   The ecofeminist tradition is also quite essential for understanding the long history of marginalization of reproductive labour from Marxist discourse. However, it is noteworthy that Silvia Federici (2004), a leading Marxist feminist, does not adopt the monist standpoint. Monism is not necessary even if we recognize the exclusion of various kinds of work from 'productive' labour.

16   Žižek (2020b) also argues that my approach is anti-Hegelian. My critique of Western Marxism strengthens this impression. However, the methodology of *Form* and *Stoff* is an inheritance from Hegel's *Wesenslogik*.

17   Marx claimed that labour cannot be realized without nature's assistance (*Capital* I: 134). In this sense, the entire world is certainly 'co-produced' in the labour process. Purely seen in terms of the circulation of matter and energy, there is no distinction among various kinds of metabolism conducted by humans,

non-human animals and non-living beings. Even if labour is a uniquely human activity, metabolism with the surrounding environment is also conducted by bees and beavers, while non-living inorganic matter is also exposed to natural processes of metabolism such as decay and oxidization. Marx's materialist view is a *monistic* one which encompasses the universal metabolism of nature. This simple explication alone should suffice to negate the accusation of Cartesian dualism directed against Marx and Foster.

18 Castree (2002: 138) recognizes this point when he criticizes ANT. It is a pity that in attempting to defend Harvey and Smith he undermines his own view.

19 The category of 'labour' does not play any noticeable part in Moore's reconceptualization of 'metabolic rift' into 'metabolic shift' within a 'singular metabolism of human-in-nature' (Moore 2015: 83). His monism undermines the importance of labour power as a specific category in value production. It is true that the contribution of natural forces gives the appearance that nature produces value too, because it cheapens the cost of production, but by attributing the role of 'unpaid work' for that reason, Moore obscures the concept of value and the historical specificity of value-producing private labour. His expression that nature also 'works' is consistent with his tendency to attribute agency to nature next to humans. Yet Marx never said that nature 'works' because such a standpoint would be a retreat to physiocracy. He criticized Adam Smith's residual physiocracy in his treatment of agriculture in *Capital*. Smith wrote in *Wealth of Nations*: 'In agriculture, too, nature labours along with man; and though her labour costs no expense, its produce has its value, as well as that of the most expensive workmen' (A. Smith 1937: 344). In Smith's view, 'labouring cattle' produce value too. This is strikingly similar to Moore's view of 'nature's work' and the 'ecological surplus' as value-producing elements. By accepting the appearance of production, value becomes a transhistorical and non-anthropocentric category. Consequently, he cannot explain *why* labour produces value only in capitalism and why the category of value becomes a universal and objective one in capitalism.

20 The same applies even for the advocators of further technocratic intervention in nature. It is first necessary to recognize the current Earth system to decide in how and at what scale geo-engineering should be introduced. This also presupposes the unity-in-separation. It is up to humans to decide whether further intervention beyond natural limits should be carried out or should be refrained from for the sake of respecting certain boundaries.

21 Moore argues that such a view 'remain[s] captive to the logic of human exceptionalism' (Moore 2015: 77), but this need not be the case. The point is simply that it is not possible for humans to obtain a non-human perspective.

22 Again, this does not deny that capital is dependent on and conditioned by material conditions.

23 Strangely enough, Moore refers to O'Connor only once in *Capitalism in the Web of Life* in an irrelevant context.

24 Changes occur in various ways, depending on how capital takes advantage of the material characteristics of each component. For example, labour power is also elastic in that it can be further exploited both intensively and extensively for the sake of increasing the rate of profit. Instead of hiring new workers in the case of a sudden increase in demand, current workers are made to work longer hours even without additional wages. Workers can be used with greater intensity too. The content of their activities is not fixed but elastic in that they can perform various tasks in accordance with constantly changing market demands.

25 Another possibility that Moore does not discuss is accumulation of capital through green technologies. Solar power in particular is an ideal source of Cheap Nature by reducing marginal costs to zero (Rifkin 2014). This issue will be partly discussed in the next chapter.

26 The problem of technology and post-capitalism will be discussed in the next chapter.

27 Moore copies and pastes this passage in another article only to add the last sentence: 'A politics of nature premised on degradation rather than work renders the radical vision vulnerable to a powerful critique. That critique says, in effect, that pristine nature has never really existed; that we are living through another of many eras of environmental change that can be resolved through technological innovation. Of course such arguments are rubbish' (Moore 2017a: 78).

28 The danger of monism is discernible even among environmentalists. While the practice of 'caring' based upon 'interspecies communication' for the sake of 'multispecies ecojustice' would be worth attempting through a post-Cartesian rationality, monist concepts such as 'forestzenship' (Barca 2020: 58), 'biotariat' (Moore 2019) and 'hybrid labour' (Battistoni 2017: 5) also risk erasing the non-identity of nature. They rather remind us of the danger of 'either equating the *domestication* of nonhuman nature with "caring" for it, or of reading human values into nonhuman nature' (Hailwood 2015: 151).

29 There is a need for pluralism (Malm 2018), but for the purpose of the current investigation, responding to the criticism of dualism, it suffices to reject the monist standpoint.

5

The Revival of Utopian Socialism and the Productive Forces of Capital

Traditionally, Marxists are sympathetic to technological progress. They often proclaim that only the further development of productive forces prepares the material conditions for the post-capitalist mode of production. While the late Herbert Marcuse (1992) came to explicitly emphasize the environmentally destructive aspects of capitalist production, even he was optimistic about the possibility of technological advancement as the major force for human emancipation beyond scarcity and poverty through the famous dialectics of quantity and quality. He suggested that the biological foundation

> would have the chance of turning quantitative *technical progress* into qualitatively different ways of life – precisely because it would be a revolution occurring at a high level of material and intellectual development, one which would enable man to conquer scarcity and poverty. If this idea of a radical transformation is to be more than idle speculation, it must have an objective foundation in the production process of advanced industrial society, in its technical capabilities and their use. For freedom indeed depends largely on technical progress, on the advancement of science. (Marcuse 1969: 19)

Unfortunately, the Promethean dream of realizing freedom through technical progress has not been realised. Or, to put it in terms of the dialectic, the dialectical transformation of quantity to quality happens only in such a way that technical 'progress' comes to exert an uncontrollable destructive power over the planet.

Despite its history of failure, Promethean ideas are again coming back to have a great influence within political ecology. In fact, ecomodernist ideas become hegemonic as the ecological crisis deepens. Now the development and application of gigantic technologies and science seems to be the only solution that is fast enough and on a sufficient scale to tackle the serious threat of climate breakdown. The new advocates of Prometheanism argue that environmentalists, by contrast, are too naïve in calling for slowing down and scaling down to live in harmony with nature. Environmental Prometheanism is 'a lesser evil' (Symons 2019: 52).

Contemporary Marxism is also responding to this situation. For example, Alberto Toscano (2011) insists upon reviving the 'Promethean' ideals of the left in order to envision a post-capitalist world. The Promethean spirit is also reflected in Aaron Bastani's vision of 'luxury communism': 'Our ambitions must be Promethean because our technology is already making us gods – so we might as well get good at it' (Bastani 2019: 189). Supporters of this ideal are often categorized as 'left accelerationists', and they are 'late-capitalist utopians' (Benanav 2020: 11).[1] This optimistic turn within Marxism, after decades of pessimism brought about by the collapse of actually existing socialism, is characterized by the open endorsement of the exponential growth of new technologies, such as full automation with the aid of artificial intelligence (AI) and robotics as well as the sharing economy through ICT and IoT. While these new technologies cause social anxiety about mass unemployment caused by competition with machines, utopian socialists boldly maintain that they open up new possibilities to establish a 'postcapitalist world without work' (Srnicek and Williams 2016).

Environmentalists might immediately dismiss such technocratic arguments as irrational. They reinforce the impression that Marxism is incapable of learning from its past mistakes. Nevertheless, I welcome new attempts to go beyond the long-lasting 'capitalist realism'. Marx valued 'utopian socialists' such as Robert Owen and Henri de Saint-Simon more highly than 'bourgeois socialists' like Pierre-Joseph Proudhon who accepted the market and wage-labour as the basis of socialism. That was because these utopians enriched the radical imaginary for an alternative post-capitalist society instead of idealizing and naturalizing particular elements of the existing society. Similarly, late-capitalist utopians provide powerful inspiration for emancipatory post-capitalist potentials. These political imaginaries are in dire need in the moment, when the legitimacy of capitalist system is increasingly in question due to the long depression, severe austerity, growing economic inequality, as well as the catastrophic degradation of natural environment.

Admitting the practical contributions of late capitalist utopians, this chapter critically examines their Promethean claims in close relation to Marx's own project, with a particular focus on his ecological critique of capitalism. The key question is why, in *Capital*, Marx abandoned some of the central ideas he elaborated in the 1850s that are nonetheless passionately endorsed by the left accelerationists. In other words, their theoretical framework is one-sidedly dependent on Marx's concept of the 'general intellect' explained in the section known as the 'Fragment on Machines' in the *Grundrisse* written in 1857/8. Marx no longer endorsed these views in *Capital*. Tracing what happened to Marx during those ten years, this chapter demonstrates that Marx became much more critical with regard to the emancipatory potentialities of the development of productive forces under capitalism. The key concept that characterizes this decisive shift in Marx's conception of history is that of 'productive forces of capital'. Furthermore, this concept is closely tied to two other important concepts: 'cooperation' and 'real subsumption of labour under capital'. Only by correctly grasping these three concepts *together* is it possible to set up criteria for adequately dealing with the dual – or 'dialectical' – aspects of incessant technological development under the capitalist mode of production. While Marx clearly continued to believe that technological development under capitalism provides the necessary material conditions for a leap to socialism, his dialectical method came to more emphatically emphasize the negative and destructive side of new technologies. His critique of technology is more important than ever in the context of the Promethean revival in the Anthropocene, but it also reveals to Marxism a wholly new horizon for a post-capitalist society.

In order to clarify this point, this chapter starts with an overview of why recent forms of Prometheanism treat new technologies as an opportunity to transcend capitalism (I). As left accelerationists admit, their view is grounded upon Marx's *Grundrisse* (II). While the *Grundrisse* was written in the late 1850s, the next section introduces Marx's concepts of 'productive force of capital' and 'real subsumption' elaborated in the 1860s in order to relativize some of the key arguments made in the *Grundrisse*. These new concepts indicate that Marx in the 1860s had consciously abandoned the productivist idea of history that was remnant in the *Grundrisse* (III). This theoretical development is of great significance for reconstructing the non-Promethean Marx. This shift is reflected in Marx's discussion on 'cooperation' in *Capital*, which is non-existent in the *Grundrisse*. Consequently, he was compelled to cast doubt on the progressive character of the development of productive forces. These three concepts, however, create some tension with his earlier view of historical materialism (IV). Since contemporary utopian socialists miss Marx's theoretical change in the 1860s, they inevitably retreat to his Prometheanism of the 1850s. One limitations of this is the one-sided focus on a *political* struggle that pivots around electoral politics without challenging the economic structure and consumerist ideas that continue to constrain our political imaginary (V).

I
FULL AUTOMATION AS AN OPPORTUNITY FOR POST-CAPITALISM

In the face of the recent development of AI, robotics, biogenetic and nanotechnology, there is growing anxiety about massive technological unemployment and growing economic inequality. Frey and Osborne (2017) predict that most work can be replaced by machines in the next decades, and there is no guarantee that even high-level professional jobs such as bankers, tax accountants and journalists will be free from this danger.[2] The underlying problem today is that, in contrast to the industrial revolution, in which the surplus population was absorbed from rural areas into a large number of factories in the city, the new industries created in the third industrial revolution do not create new jobs but rather accelerate deindustrialization in the developed countries. Combined with the global outsourcing and off-shoring of factory production, digitalization intensifies the competition among workers more than ever as it allows workers all over the world to participate in the same job market. The vast number of 'relative surplus population' is discernible in increasingly precarious jobs with casual working hours and stagnant wages. Martin Ford predicts that although the development of technology is generally regarded as the key factor for economic growth, the extreme concentration of wealth by a few privileged digital-haves will lead to 'techno-feudalism' (Ford 2015: 210). From the standpoint of the ruling class, information technology also enables the monitoring of every single activity, and big data collected through such monitoring can be used to intervene in social behaviours and desires (Zuboff 2019). In contrast to the prognosis that the development of information technology would open up a more free and democratic space, 'big data-enabled, IT-backed authoritarianism' seems to point to a 'path towards an entirely new, potentially totalitarian future'. This is a 'new digital Leninism' (Heilmann 2016)[3]

However, for some Marxists, the prognosis of digital feudalism is too pessimistic. Instead of slowing technological and scientific progress out of fear of dystopia, they even argue for accelerating it further in the name of human emancipation. In a manner that reminds me of Latour's call to 'love your monster', they also attempt to envision a post-capitalist alternative by 'reintegrating human labour into the machine' (Noys 2014: 12). They see roughly three emancipatory tendencies in contemporary capitalism.

1. Full Automation and a World without Work

Mass unemployment due to automation is certainly not desirable for workers. Even if full automation could produce massive cheap goods and services, modern wage-labourers would not be able to attain the means of subsistence if they could not sell their labour power due to harsh competition with machines and other precarious workers. Their existence is fundamentally dependent upon the wage, so workers are compelled to accept even low-paid jobs with long hours lest they starve to death.[4] However, seen from a different perspective, the threat of mass unemployment signifies the irrationality of the current economic system. If the threat of mass unemployment is emerging and wages are cut, that is *precisely because* the current level of productivity is already sufficiently high to satisfy human needs without making everyone work so long. Notwithstanding, productivity must become ever higher in capitalist production as capitalists under market competition are forced to constantly introduce new technologies, further deepening the contradiction. Capitalism cannot shorten work hours – labour is the only source of value and the rate of profit falls further due to the mechanization of capital's dependence on the production of absolute surplus-value – while the high rate of unemployment cannot be tolerated either. This dilemma shows that capitalism cannot use its high social productivity for the sake of human well-being.

Once the obsolete work ethic of capitalism is overcome, however, higher productivity can be utilized to minimize or even eliminate drudgery and to simultaneously increase the amount of wealth and free time for everyone. Accelerationists thus insist that workers should not be afraid of the threat of robots but endorse full automation: 'Full automation is a utopian demand that aims to reduce necessary labour as much as possible' (Srnicek and Williams 2016: 114). Full automation prepares the conditions whereby a great number of social needs can be satisfied with a small amount of labour and natural resources. John M. Keynes ([1930] 1971) once predicted that by 2030, work time will be reduced to 15 hours a week, so the real economic problem for the human society would be how to spend the leisure time. His prediction has certainly not come true but this is not because he was totally wrong but because capitalism persists. A post-work society could be realized immediately with a leap to a post-capitalist society.

2. Zero Marginal Cost and the Society of Abundance

Today's challenge to capitalism does not come from full automation alone. Jeremy Rifkin in his *Zero Marginal Cost Society* (2014) explicates the destructive impacts of the 'third industrial revolution' upon the current market system. According to him, information technology brings about revolutionary transformations in the entire production process because it can produce goods and service as 'free, instant and perfect' copies. Music and newspaper are Rifkin's primary examples. When they are digitalized, the production costs for an extra unit will be reduced almost to zero once the music is recorded or the texts written. This is in clear contrast to the previous method of production, which incurred an additional cost for producing every unit of CD and newspaper. Rifkin bluntly predicts that the marginal cost will be tendentially reduced to zero in various branches of production thanks to new information technologies supported by 3D printers and renewable energies.

The zero marginal cost society is characterized by an ever-greater abundance of free wealth. Expressed in Marxian terms, information technology destroys the market system by decoupling use-value from value. Perfect digital copies are free *precisely because* they are instantly produced and thus require no expenditure of human labour. Information technology exponentially increases the amount of use-value – 'Moore's law' – so that the output of labour no longer corresponds to the labour inputs. If goods and services are produced and distributed at zero marginal cost, the price mechanism breaks down according to the labour theory of value. Material and immaterial wealth is rapidly expanding, while its value is constantly decreasing. This is a great threat to capitalism. As Paul Mason (2015: 142) argues, 'a world of free stuff cannot be capitalist'.

Similarly, Rifkin highlights the incompatibility of capitalism and the newly emerging collaborative economy, which will bring about the 'demise' of capitalism:

> The slow demise of the capitalist system and the rise of a Collaborative Commons in which economic welfare is measured less by the accumulation of market capital and more by the aggregation of social capital. The steady decline of GDP in the coming years and decades is going to be increasingly attributable to the changeover to a vibrant new economic paradigm that measures economic value in totally new ways. (Rifkin 2014: 20)

Combined with full automation, renewable energy, cellular agriculture and asteroid mining, the third industrial revolution will overcome scarcity of labour, energy, food and resource, and their abundance will make the system of value obsolete. Aaron Bastani boldly declares this post-scarcity society as 'fully automated luxury communism':

> So as information, labour, energy and resources become permanently cheaper – and work and the limits of the old world are left behind – it turns out we don't just satisfy all of our needs, but dissolve any boundary between the useful and the beautiful. Communism is luxurious – or it isn't communism. (Bastani 2019: 56)

3. Network Effects and the Crisis of Private Property

As Rifkin's discussion of a zero marginal cost society indicates, immaterial production based on knowledge plays a central role in the age of information technology. Already in the early 1990s Peter Drucker pointed out that 'knowledge is now fast becoming the most important factor of production' (Drucker 1993: 8). He believed that free and autonomous collaboration assisted by information technology would destroy the managerial hierarchy in the labour process and replace it with a more horizontal and democratic form of production. This democratic production is threatening to capital because the knowledge economy is 'potentially free' (Gorz 2010: 53). Knowledge and information are common goods to be shared widely, so they are by nature incompatible with exclusive and monopolized possession. In fact, they create 'positive externalities' that emerge out of a network effect of connected individuals. The more interaction and communication develop through the network, the greater the positive externalities that can increase the productive forces. In this sense, the knowledge economy as the main driver of the third industrial revolution is essentially democratic, horizontal and communal.

Yet it is precisely this communal character of knowledge that poses a problem for capitalism. Private property is indispensable for capital accumulation. However, such a monopoly inevitably lessens the utility of immaterial goods because it weakens the positive network effect of collaborative commons created through social cooperation. There is also a problem of legitimacy too. When goods and services are essentially produced through social cooperation, it is not clear to whom they should belong, and it is questionable whether a product whose nature is inherently social should be patented and monopolized by a few. With the expansion of the social network, the system of private property is increasingly under challenge. Rifkin (2014) optimistically foresees the future of 'collaborative economy' through the exponential growth of positive network effects that would ultimately blow away the system of the private property. Of course, if the system of private property collapses, so does capitalism. Capital's countertendency to the network effects lies in constructing a monopolized digital platform and knowledge from which rent can be extracted by artificially creating scarcity and exclusivity of information (Srnicek 2016). However, the dilemma for capital never disappears. Such rent-seeking by means of monopoly inevitably hinders further development of the collaborative economy as a source of profits. Furthermore, the costs of protecting the monopoly become very high because there is a constant risk that a free network emerges, which makes the entire business no longer profitable (Hardt and Negri 2005).

Summing up these three tendencies towards post-capitalism, Mason maintains that a new form of post-capitalist society is emerging today:

The main contradiction today is between the possibility of free abundant goods and information and a system of monopolies, banks, and governments trying to keep things private, scarce and commercial. Everything comes down to the struggle between the network and the hierarchy, between old forms of society moulded around capitalism and new forms of society that prefigure what comes next. (Mason 2015: xix)

The future, in this account, looks 'clear' and 'bright' (Mason 2019), but is it true?[5]

II
THE *GRUNDRISSE* AND THE 'GENERAL INTELLECT'

Although Keynes and Drucker provide important inspiration for today's utopian visions of post-capitalism, it is without doubt Marx who unified the three aspects outlined in the last section for a project of post-capitalism. The *Grundrisse*, or more precisely, the section known in English as the 'Fragment on Machines', plays a central role here.[6]

First, Marx in the 'Fragment on Machines' argued based upon his labour theory of value that there is a serious dilemma of capitalist production. Capitalists under market competition incessantly introduce new machines and increase the productive forces in order to acquire extra surplus value. However, this process of mechanization inevitably expels workers from the labour process unless the scale of production expands more rapidly than the rate of increase in productivity. This accelerated expansion of production cannot last forever anyway, because social needs are inevitably finite, so capitalist development tendentially leads to the diminution of workers employed in the labour process: 'Capital here – quite unintentionally – reduces human labour, expenditure of energy, to a minimum' (*Grundrisse*: 701). Thus, increasing investment in fixed capital is accompanied by the diminution of the value produced by workers, while material wealth increases thanks to the increase of social productive forces under large-scale industrial production. As production becomes more and more independent from the actual expenditure of human labour and the meaning of labour for the production of social wealth declines, value ceases to be a measure of material wealth: 'But to the degree that large industry develops, the creation of real wealth comes to depend less on labour time and on the amount of labour employed than on the power of the agencies set in motion during labour time' (*Grundrisse*: 701). In the end, the gap between value and real material wealth increases to the point where the measure of value becomes 'anachronistic' (Postone 1996: 197).

Seen from a different perspective, this rapid development of productive forces significantly reduces 'necessary labour time'. Marx predicted a future of increasing 'free time' that is available for non-compulsory activities:[7]

> The saving of labour time [is] equal to an increase of free time, i.e. time for the full development of the individual, which in turn reacts back upon the productive power of labour as itself the greatest productive power.... Free time – which is both idle time and time for higher activity – has naturally transformed its possessor into a different subject, and he then enters into the direct production process as this different subject. This process is then both discipline, as regards the human being in the process of becoming; and, at the same time, practice, experimental science, materially creative and objectifying science, as regards the human being who has become, in whose head exists the accumulated knowledge of society. (*Grundrisse*: 711)

One can easily deduce from this argument the legitimation for Srnicek and Williams's claim that full automation realizes the emancipation from work as well as the full development of the individual in a post-work society.

Furthermore, in this quoted passage Marx emphasizes that the increase of free time is closely related to the social character of 'accumulated knowledge of society' by arguing that social networks based on the combination and interconnection of individuals becomes 'giant social forces' in the form of the objectified human knowledge in fixed capital. Here Marx introduced the famous concept of the 'general intellect' in order to highlight that the condition of production is increasingly dependent upon the social force mediated by autonomous social collaboration and communication: 'The development of fixed capital indicates to what degree general social knowledge has become a direct force of production, and to what degree, hence, the conditions of the process of social life itself have come under the control of the general intellect and been transformed in accordance with it' (*Grundrisse*: 706). The power of the general intellect comes from the positive network effect of free individuals. Capital cannot fully manipulate the enormous social power of the collaborative economy because the imposition of strict control and regulation for the sake of valorization undermines this social power. At the same time, further development of social collaboration and free knowledge destabilizes the market mechanism and the system of private property.

Marx even proclaimed that further increase of the new productive forces blows away the barriers set up by capital and establishes a post-capitalist society:

> On the one side, then, it calls to life all the powers of science and of nature, as of social combination and of social intercourse, in order to

make the creation of wealth independent (relatively) of the labour time employed on it. On the other side, it wants to use labour time as the measuring rod for the giant social forces thereby created, and to confine them within the limits required to maintain the already created value as value. Forces of production and social relations – two different sides of the development of the social individual – appear to capital as mere means, and are merely means for it to produce on its limited foundation. In fact, however, they are the material conditions to blow this foundation sky-high. (*Grundrisse*: 706)

Once the collaborative economy fully liberates the general intellect beyond capitalism, increasing free time and free goods will realize the all-round development of the individual. The utopian socialists thus seem to be convincingly arguing that Marx was a 'fully automated luxury communist' (Bastani 2019) – at least in the *Grundrisse*.

III
SUBSUMPTION OF LABOUR AND THE PRODUCTIVE FORCES OF CAPITAL

Although today's automation utopians appeal to the *Grundrisse*, one needs to be a little more cautious before generalizing their claims about the post-scarcity economy as embodying Marx's definitive vision of a post-capitalist society. Marx never published the *Grundrisse* during his lifetime. As the first systematic attempt of his political economy, it was theoretically premature in various ways. While it is certainly true that the *Grundrisse* contains highly original ideas that cannot be found in Marx's later economic works (Negri 1992), one should not forget that Marx abandoned some of his earlier key ideas when writing *Capital*. For example, Marx never again used the term 'general intellect' in his later writings,[8] which poses the question of whether there was a shift in his conception of capitalist development in the beginning of the 1860s. In fact, Marx introduced a series of new ideas in the 1860s. One of them was the distinction between 'formal' and 'real subsumption' in another unpublished manuscript, the *Economic Manuscripts of 1861–63*.

The distinction between 'formal' and 'real' is representative of Marx's own methodological dualism. As seen in his theory of metabolism, Marx's discussion begins with distinguishing the material side of labour process and its 'economic form determination' (*Formbestimmung*) as the valorization process in analysing their 'unity-in-separation' in actual capitalist production. In other words, the transhistorical material process of the labour process attains a uniquely capitalist function as the 'valorization process' for capital.[9] According to Marx's methodology, formal subsumption simply denotes the economic form determination as the 'valorization process' to the 'labour process'. That is, it introduces the capitalist relations of production between capital and wage-labour, while there are not yet substantial changes in the material aspects of the labour process. In this sense, the relationships between 'form' (*Form*) and 'matter' (*Stoff*) remain external to each other at this level, so the mode of production peculiar to capitalism is not yet established with formal subsumption alone. However, capital does not stop there. Marx rather asked 'to what extent the character of the labour process is itself changed by its subsumption under capital' (*MECW* 30: 64). In fact, *Form* and *Stoff* become increasingly intertwined and entangled in the course of capitalist development as capital thoroughly transforms and reorganizes the labour process. This takes place through what Marx called 'real subsumption'. It is through this 'real subsumption' that the material aspect of the labour process becomes 'adequate' to the capitalist mode of production.

The *Economic Manuscripts of 1861–63* define 'formal subsumption' in the following way:

> Historically, in fact, at the start of its formation, we see capital take under its control (subsume under itself) not only the labour process in general but the specific actual labour processes as *it finds them available* in the existing technology, and in the form in which they have developed on the basis of non-capitalist relations of production. It finds in existence the actual production process – the particular mode of production – and at the beginning it only subsumes it *formally*, without making any changes in its specific technological character. (*MECW* 30: 92; emphasis added)

The formal subsumption of labour under capital does not affect the character of the actual labour process but simply takes what it 'finds available' as it is and introduces new relations of production. In other words, the capitalist relations of production dissolve the older ones based on craftsmanship and guilds, and replace them with the new social relations of capital and wage-labour without changing the technological composition of production. Now capital supervises the workers and imposes command over them. Marx wrote that formal subsumption 'consists in the worker's subjection as worker to the supervision and therefore to the command of capital or the capitalist' (*MECW* 30: 93). This command of capital aims at 'the most effective, most exact organisation of the actual labour process, which depends on the will, the hard work etc., of the worker' for the sake of increase of the value of capital (*MECW* 30: 94).

Certainly, there already emerges a significant change in the labour process as a result of the formal subsumption of labour under capital. The duration and continuity of labour increases because the primary aim of the production becomes the production of surplus value instead of concrete use-values for the sake of satisfying human needs.[10] This change significantly degrades the physical and mental conditions of workers. Nevertheless, since the form determination of the production process as the capitalist relation of production between capital and wage-labour does not modify the organization of productive forces, only the production of 'absolute surplus value' is possible through the extension of the working day. In this sense, formal subsumption alone cannot create a system of production adequate to the capitalist mode of production.

In contrast, Marx wrote about the 'real subsumption of labour under capital' in *Results of the Immediate Process of Production* in the following manner:

> With the real subsumption of labour under capital a complete (and constantly repeated) revolution takes place in the mode of production, in the productivity of the workers and in the relations between workers and capitalists.... On the one hand, *capitalist production* now establishes itself as a mode of production *sui generis* and brings into being a new mode of material production. On the other hand, the latter itself forms the basis for the development of capitalist relations whose adequate form, therefore, presupposes a definite stage in the evolution of the productive forces of labour. (*Capital* I: 1035)

Simply gathering a number of workers in one factory is not enough for real subsumption, even if there exist cooperation and division of labour. That remains the level of formal subsumption. Real subsumption needs to push forward *with capital's own initiative* an efficient way of production that 'give[s] the very mode of production a new shape and thus first create[s] the mode of production peculiar to it' (*MECW* 30: 92). Instead of accepting as they are the conditions of labour that capital finds available, it actively creates qualitatively new productive forces and a *uniquely* capitalist way of production *sui generis*. By modifying the entire labour process not only through the application of science and technology but also through the social organization of labour – the way the workers work – capital overcomes the external relationship between *Form* and *Stoff* that can still be seen in formal subsumption.

One may immediately think about machinery and industrial production as the capitalist relations that are unique to capitalist production, but such a view narrows the whole discussion of the real subsumption to technological changes. Although large-scale industry surely realizes the specifically capitalist from of production and maximizes the productive forces of capital, Marx emphasized that the analysis of 'cooperation' 'both historically and *conceptually*' provides the theoretical foundation for the real subsumption (*Capital* I: 439;

emphasis added). He also added that cooperation is the 'fundamental form of the capitalist mode of production' (*Capital* I: 454). Cooperation is the first step in organizing the entire labour process from the standpoint of capital, which brings about 'real alteration of the mode of production itself' (*MECW* 30: 263). As Marx wrote:

> [Cooperation] is the first stage at which the subsumption of labour under capital no longer appears as a merely formal subsumption but changes the mode of production itself, so that the *capitalist* mode of production is a specific mode of production…. With cooperation a specific distinction already enters the picture. The work takes place under conditions in which the independent labour of the individual cannot be carried on – and indeed these conditions appear as a relation dominating the individual, as a band with which capital fetters the individual workers. (*MECW* 30: 262)

Cooperation 'changes the mode of production' and begins to create the 'specific' mode of production. By contrast to the formal subsumption, the real subsumption changes both the technological composition *and* the social relations of production. In fact, capital organizes cooperation in the labour process in such a way that individual workers can no longer conduct their tasks alone and autonomously, but are subjugated to the command of capital.

Harry Braverman describes this process as the 'separation of conception from execution' (Braverman 1998: 79) and he analyses it as an effective way of subjugating workers to the supervision and command of capital. Just as an orchestra requires a conductor, cooperation always requires coordination and adjustment regardless of the relations of production. That is to say, it is a transhistorical requirement. However, under capitalism this direction function is integrated as one of the 'functions of capital' and 'acquires its own special characteristics' (*Capital* I: 449). Consequently, capitalist command develops 'into a requirement for carrying on the labour process itself, into a real condition of production' (*Capital* I: 448). This command becomes indispensable for workers to successfully carry out their labour, but now this function is fundamentally driven by the effective valorization of capital, so its alien and dominating character appears 'purely despotic' to the workers (*Capital* I: 450).

The fact that workers can conduct labour only under the despotic rule of capital means that they are not simply deprived of the objective means of production. Rather, workers also lose the *subjective* conditions of performing their labour, that is, the power of 'conception'. It is this tendency inherent to cooperation that strengthens with the implementation of a 'division of labour' and of 'machinery'. Workers increasingly lose their knowledge, skills and insight into the entire labour process because it is organized by capital. Skilled workers are replaced by unskilled ones as capital analyses, divides and recombines the labour process that now consisting of simple, repetitive, calculable and mechanic tasks. Since capital entirely reorganizes the labour process independently of workers' experience and knowledge, workers have to passively follow commands from above. The results of this process are clearly discernible in that today's workers could not assemble automobiles or computers even if they had access to the means of production because they lack the knowledge of how each part functions in the final product. That is how workers become 'subjectlos' and confront the objective means of production without the ability to realize their own labour. In this way, the real subsumption greatly increases workers' dependence upon capital, while the objective conditions for realizing workers' capacity increasingly appear as 'an *alien power*, as an *independent power*'.

Insofar as capital as objectified labour – means of production – employs living labour, the 'relation of subject and object is inverted' in the labour process (*MECW* 30: 113). Marx also called this inversion of the subject and the object 'a personification of the thing and a reification of the person' (*MECW* 34: 123). Since labour is 'embodied' in capital, the role of the worker is reduced to a mere bearer of the reified thing, that is, the means of preserving and valorizing capital next to the machines (*Versachlichung der Person*), and the reified thing attains the appearance of the subjectivity that controls as an alien power the behaviour and the will of the person (*Personification der Sache*). As the reified power of capital penetrates the labour process, the increase of social productive forces emerges only through capital's initiative. Precisely due to this process, workers' autonomy and independence are fatally undermined, and they become much more easily tamed and disciplined under the regime of capital. Exposed to competition for jobs, workers passively follow the strict orders and commands of capital.

Since the conditions of carrying out labour are monopolized by capital, and since the increase of productive forces is possible *only* under capital's initiative and responsibility, the new productive forces of workers' social labour does not appear as their own productive forces but as the 'productive forces of capital': 'To the extent that the worker creates wealth, living labour becomes a power of capital; similarly, all development of the productive forces of labour is development of the productive forces of capital' (*MECW* 30: 112). Summing up, Marx wrote that

> the *social conditions* of labour, which emerge from the *social productive power* of labour and are posited by labour itself, appear most emphatically as forces not only alien to the worker, belonging to *capital*, but also

directed in the interests of the capitalist in a hostile and overwhelming fashion against the individual worker. (*MECW* 34: 29–30)

Cooperation under capital brings about new productive forces that individual workers cannot exert, but it is capital that appropriates the fruits of cooperation as a free gift: 'The socially productive power of labour develops as a free gift to capital.... [It] appears as a power which capital possesses by its nature – a productive power inherent in capital' (*Capital* I: 451).

Since the development of productive forces under capitalism only increases the alien power of capital by depriving workers of their subjective skills, knowledge and insights, it does not automatically open up the possibility of a clear bright future. Notwithstanding, contemporary utopian socialists focus solely on the *Grundrisse*, so they tend to marginalize Marx's critique of productive forces. They too narrowly understand the concept of 'productive forces' as if they were equivalent to 'productivity' defined as the ratio of input and output.[11] The concept of 'productive forces of capital' indicates that Marx's concept of productive forces is actually broader. It also has to do with what humans can produce and how they do so. In other words, it includes human productive capacities such as skill, knowledge and strength as well as natural conditions (Cohen [1978] 2000: 55). These capacities especially have to do with workers' autonomy, freedom and independence, which are essential for overcoming alienation of labour. In this sense, the concept of productive forces is both quantitative *and* qualitative.[12] The quantitative increase in productivity through full automation, for example, can be accompanied by the qualitative degradation of working conditions as well as of the natural environment, hindering the full development of the individual. For Marx, that does not necessarily count as the real development of 'productive forces'.

To sum up, Marx in the 1860s came to emphasize that the increase in the productivity of capital is accompanied by a uniquely capitalist way of organizing the material aspect of the production process. According to this understanding, the establishment of the 'capitalist mode of production' is founded upon transformations in both the 'formal' and 'material' aspects of production. That is, capitalist production is based upon the economic 'relations of production' mediated by wage-labour relations as well as the 'productive forces' that emerge from a specifically capitalist way of organizing the labour process. This dual aspect of the mode of production is consistent with Marx's method of separating and unifying the *purely social* and the *material* in order to analyse how metabolism between humans and nature is transformed and reorganized under capitalistically constituted social relations. Through his discussion of real subsumption, Marx finally attained an understanding of the 'mode of production' that was adequate to his own methodological dualism.

However, this new insight created a tension with his earlier view of 'historical materialism' formulated in the Preface to his *Critique of Political Economy*.

IV
CAPITALIST MODE OF PRODUCTION AND HISTORICAL MATERIALISM

Although there were important theoretical developments in Marx's *Capital* and other economic manuscripts in the 1860s compared with the *Grundrisse*, one should not overemphasize their discontinuity. In fact, Marx's concept of the 'productive force of capital' already appears in the *Grundrisse*. He wrote, for example:

> As the infinite urge to wealth, it strives consistently towards infinite increase of the productive forces of labour and calls them into being. But on the other hand, every increase in the productive force of labour ... is an increase in the productive force of capital and, from the present standpoint, is a productive force of labour only in so far as it is a productive force of capital. (*Grundrisse*: 341)

Marx also wrote about the productive forces of capital in relation to cooperation and division of labour:

> Like all productive powers of labour, i.e. those which determine the degree of its intensity and hence of its extensive realization, the association of the workers – the cooperation and division of labour as fundamental conditions of the productivity of labour – appears as the productive power of capital. (*Grundrisse*: 585)

From these passages, one might even think that there is no decisive change in Marx's argument, but that is not the case.[13]

In this context, it is worth referring to the analysis conducted by Japanese Marxist scholar Sadao Ohno (1983: 295),[14] because he maintains that Marx's conceptualization of the 'mode of production' in the *Grundrisse* was still insufficient. According to Ohno, Marx's discussion in the 1850s did not sufficiently include the material side of production, although he had paid attention to the social and formal aspects that consists of the social relations of capital and wage-labour. This insufficiency, Ohno argues, has to do with the fact that Marx's concept of 'cooperation' was not yet established as the elementary category of capitalist production in the *Grundrisse*.[15] In the *Grundrisse*, Marx wrote about the mode of production without mentioning cooperation: 'Productive capital, or the mode of production corresponding to capital, can be present *in only two forms*: manufacture and largescale industry' (*Grundrisse*: 585; emphasis added). It was only *after* the 1860s that Marx paid sufficient attention to the concept of 'cooperation', which also contributed in deepening his understanding of the 'mode of production' (Ohno 1983: 296).

What is the mode of production? Generally speaking the 'mode of production' is understood as consisting of 'relations of production' and 'productive forces'. Yet, following Marx's methodological dualism, one should rather say that the 'mode of production' is conditioned both socially and materially. On the one hand, the social aspects express its formal economic side, which is determined by 'relations of production' founded on the social relations of capital and wage-labour. In this aspect, the capitalist mode of production is fundamentally characterized by 'commodity production' as well as by 'production of surplus value'. The capitalist mode of production presupposes social relations in which workers are exploited by capitalists, and this relationship must be constantly reproduced in the process of capital accumulation. On the other hand, the 'relations of production' also contain material aspects as a way of organizing the metabolism between humans and nature, which consists of cooperation, division of labour and large-scale industry.

Marx's notebook to be published in the *MEGA* IV/17 confirms this point.[16] In February 1859 when Marx took up the task of continuing writing chapter 3 of *Critique of Political Economy*, he made excerpts from various books on political economy. Marx took notes from works by Richard Jones and Edmund Potter, and their arguments prompted him to focus on the category of 'cooperation' as a foundation of capitalist production. For example, Marx made an excerpt from the following paragraph in Potter's annotation to Scrope's *Political Economy* (1833):

> The principle here referred to is usually called the *division of labour*. The phrase is objectionable, since the fundamental idea is that of *concert* and *cooperation*, not of *division*. The term of division applies only to the process; this being subdivided into several operations, and these being distributed or parcelled out among a number of operatives. It is thus a *combination of labourers* effected through a *subdivision of processes*. (IISG Sig. B 91a: 109; emphasis in original)[17]

Here Marx recognized the difference between 'division of labour' and 'cooperation' and to the latter's unique role in capitalism. One can also discern this shift in his excerpts in the same notebook from Jones's *Textbook of Lectures on the Political Economy of Nations* (1852), where he documented the following passage about cooperation in the Oriental state that made possible giant construction projects such as the Pyramids and the Great Wall:

The number of the labourers, and the concentration of their efforts sufficed. We see mighty coral reefs rising from the depths of the ocean into islands and firm land, yet each individual depositor is puny, weak and contemptible. The non-agricultural labourers of an Asiatic monarchy have little but their individual bodily exertions to bring to the task; but *their number is their strength*, and the power of directing theses masses gave rise to the palaces and temples, the pyramids and the armies of gigantic statues, of which the remains astonish and perplex us. It is that *confinement of the revenues which feed them, to one or a few hands, which make such undertakings possible.* (IISG Sig. B 91a: 152; emphasis in original)

The point is that while cooperation, as the most basic form of social labour, is transhistorical, capitalism utilizes it in a unique manner. Both Potter and Jones helped Marx to comprehend both the transhistorical and the historical dimensions of cooperation.

Ohno argues that Marx's new insight into cooperation is reflected in the new plan for his project of political economy that was written after the publication of *Critique of Political Economy* in spring/summer 1859 (Ohno and Satake 1984: 22). In contrast to the *Grundrisse*, Marx for the first time included the category of 'cooperation' in his plan as part of the analysis of the production of relative surplus value. Marx wrote in the *Draft Plan of the Chapter on Capital*:

3) Relative surplus value

   a) Cooperation of masses

   b) Division of labour

   c) Machinery   (*MECW* 29: 511)

This clearly indicates that Marx came to assign cooperation as the elementary form of capitalist production in relation to the real subsumption of capital. This change is important for the current investigation. If the role of the material aspect of the mode of production was still ambivalent in the *Grundrisse* – which also means that his methodological dualism of *Form* and *Stoff* was not yet clearly established – it is understandable that his analysis of 'real subsumption' as well as of the 'productive forces of capital' was also missing. When he successfully integrated the material transformation and reorganization of the labour process into his theory of the real subsumption, Marx was able to develop his analysis of the capitalist mode of production in a way that is consistent with his methodological dualism.

This is not a minor point. Although Marx's theory of 'cooperation' in *Capital* is often neglected, one should not underestimate its importance. It implies a decisive break with the traditional view of historical materialism.

According to the traditional view based on the Preface to *A Contribution*, two elements, the 'productive forces' and the 'relations of production', are directly connected to each other, forming the 'mode of production'.[18] Marx himself expressed their relationship in stating that 'relations of production correspond [*entsprechen*] to a given stage in the development of their material forces of production' (*MECW* 29: 263).[19] This statement is basically consistent with what Marx and Engels wrote in *The German Ideology*.[20] However, in the preface to the first edition of *Capital* in 1867, Marx modified his formulation, writing 'the capitalist mode of production, and the relations of production ... that correspond [*entsprechen*] to it' (*Capital* I: 90). This change looks very subtle, but Marx must have carefully formulated the beginning of *Capital*, volume I. In fact, this change reflects the important shift in Marx's view of history related to real subsumption and cooperation.

In accordance with the traditional view of historical materialism, Marx in the preface to *A Contribution* continued to argue:

> At a certain stage of development, the material productive forces of society come into conflict with the existing relations of production or – this merely expresses the same thing in legal terms – with the property relations within the framework of which they have operated hitherto. From forms of development of the productive forces these relations turn into their fetters. Then begins an era of social revolution. The changes in the economic foundation lead sooner or later to the transformation of the whole immense superstructure. (*MECW* 29: 263)

Accordingly, in the traditional conception of historical materialism, the increase of productive forces is the independent variable and the driving force of historical progress; after they reach a certain point, the contradiction between the productive forces and the relations of production explodes to transform the latter, leading to the formation of another mode of production. As G. A. Cohen (2000: 135) succinctly puts it in his defence of historical materialism, 'changes in productive forces brings about changes in production relations'. Consequently, there emerged a common assumption that the increase of productive forces is a necessary and sufficient conditions for a post-capitalist society. Such an assumption easily results in a productivist view of historical progress that treats the productive forces as the main driver of history and aims to unlock them from their capitalist fetters. The traditional view fetishizes the productive forces developed under capitalism, regarding them as if they were neutral forces that can be taken over by the proletariat and utilized for establishing a socialist society. What is missing here is an analysis of the real material transformation of the labour process under capitalist relations of production that 'corresponds to' the capitalist mode of production.

The same problem appears in the *Grundrisse*. It is precisely in the section 'Fragment on Machines' where Marx actually referred to the concept of 'productive forces of capital'. Nevertheless, his insufficient attention to the material aspect of the labour process cannot avoid a productivist tone. As discussed earlier, he believed that new technologies 'blow this foundation -high'. It is no coincidence that Marx talked positively about the conquest of nature by science and technology in the same context:

> In the production process of large-scale industry, by contrast, just as the conquest of the forces of nature by the social intellect is the precondition of the productive power of the means of labour as developed into the automatic process, on one side, so, on the other, is *the labour of the individual in its direct presence posited as suspended individual, i.e. as social, labour. Thus the other basis of this mode of production falls away.* (*Grundrisse*: 709; emphasis in original)

Here one can find the basic logical structure of historical materialism fuelled by the development of productive forces. Combined with the idea of the anachronism of value thanks to increasing material wealth, the *Grundrisse* comes close to the breakdown theory of capitalism (Heinrich 2012: 176).[21] It is difficult to deny Marx's latent Promethean idea of the domination of nature in the *Grundrisse*, which is incompatible with environmentalism.[22]

However, Marx's Prometheanism should not be overgeneralized (Löwy 2017: 11). In the 1860s, when he consciously distanced himself from his earlier technocratic productivism, Marx was compelled to rethink his optimistic view of history and to reflect more seriously upon its negative implications. This self-critical reflection took place as he investigated the material aspect of the production process unique to capitalist production, especially how material world – human and non-human – is reorganized by capital's initiative in favour of its own accumulation. This is because the increase of productive forces subordinate workers to command of capital more effectively. If so, 'relations of production' and 'productive forces' cannot be simply separated as assumed in the traditional view of historical materialism. The development of productive forces of capital is dependent upon the thorough reorganization of human metabolism with nature in the form of cooperation, division of labour and machinery. In this sense, the 'mode of production' expresses a particular social arrangement of the material elements of production. That is why in the preface to *Capital*, Marx set himself the task of examining 'the capitalist mode of production, and the relations of production ... that correspond to it' instead of treating 'productive forces' as an independent variable as was the case in the preface to *A Contribution*.

This change concerning the 'mode of production' might be discounted as a minor philological quibble, but its theoretical significance should *not* be underestimated because it has to do with the transformation of Marx's vision of post-capitalism. When the development of productive forces is not purely formal and quantitative, but is deeply rooted into the transformation and reorganization of the labour process, one can no longer assume that a socialist revolution could simply replace the relations of production with other ones after reaching a certain level of productive forces. Since the 'productive forces of capital' that emerge through the real subsumption are materialized and crystalized in the capitalist mode of production, they disappear together with the capitalist mode of production. In this sense, we need to radically reverse the traditional historical materialist view about the actual relationship between productive forces and relations of production: '*Relations of production determine productive forces*' (Tairako 1991: 60; emphasis in original).

This is how the establishment of the concepts of 'productive forces of capital' and 'real subsumption' compelled Marx to abandon his earlier formulation of historical materialism in the preface to *A Contribution*. Since both aspects of *Form* and *Stoff* are closely entangled with each other due to the real subsumption of the labour process[23] it is not possible to change one without simultaneously changing the other. This complexity would not occur if the productive forces of capital were simply dependent upon machines. They could be utilized in socialism as before. However, the productive forces developed under capitalism are tightly connected to the uniquely capitalist way of organizing the collaborative, cooperative and other social aspects of labour.[24] If so, the transcendence of the capitalist mode of production must be a much more radical and thoroughgoing one than the mere abolition of private property and exploitation through the re-appropriation of the means of production by the working class. It requires the radical reorganization of the relations of production for the sake of freedom and autonomy among associated producers, so that the productive forces of capital disappear. Otherwise, despotic and ecologically destructive forms of production will continue in post-capitalist society. Yet when the productive forces of capital disappear, the productive forces of social labour are diminished as well.

The concept of 'real subsumption' thus marks a radical shift in Marx's evaluation of the progressive character of capitalism. In *Capital*, he was no longer able to endorse the progressive character of capitalism. André Gorz recognized this point when he wrote:

> In other words, the development of productive forces within the framework of capitalism will never lead to the gate of Communism, since the technologies, the relations of production and the nature of the products exclude not just the durable, equitable satisfaction of needs but also the stabilization of social production at a level commonly accepted as *sufficient*. (Gorz 2018: 110–11)

Mészáros argued similarly, pointing to the necessity of rejecting the *false identification* of commendable productive development, idealized as unquestionably desirable *"growth"* in general, with the *fetishistic absolute* of increasingly more destructive *capital-expansion'* (Mészáros 2012: 257; emphasis in original).

More concretely, there are four reasons for the incompatibility of capitalist cooperation and socialist cooperation. First, productive forces of capital cannot be properly transferred to post-capitalism because they are created in order to subjugate and control workers. Since the socialist organization of the labour process must be much more democratic and egalitarian, it is likely that the system of production developed under capitalism can no longer be effectively conducted in a future society without the command and supervision of capital. It is hard to imagine how the same order of things could be utilized under democratic control by freely associated producers. Rather, once capital's initiative and responsibility is dismantled, 'productive forces of capital' disappear together with their alien character. However, if the productive forces developed under the capitalist mode of production do *not* provide a material foundation for post-capitalism, this undermines the general thesis of historical materialism that presupposes that the 'transition from the capitalist to the socialist mode of production demands the scrupulous preservation of capitalist technics' (Venable 1945: 95). On the contrary, the abolition of the despotic regime of capital may even require the *downscaling* of production.[25]

Second, capitalist technologies are not suitable to the socialist requirement of reunifying 'conception' and 'execution' in the labour process.[26] As Braverman (1998) argued, this separation constitutes the condition of relation of production that is *peculiar* to the capitalist mode of production. Correspondingly, knowledge and technology developed under capitalism serve to realize the despotic domination of capital over workers, weakening their independence and autonomy in the production process through standardization and simplification of tasks. André Gorz distinguishes two types of technology here: 'open technologies' and 'locking technologies'. According to Gorz, open technologies are ones that 'promote communication, cooperation and interaction' on a wide scale. In contrast, locking technologies under capitalism are those that 'enslave the user' and 'monopolize the supply of a product or service' (Gorz 2018: 8–9).[27] Capitalism tends to develop locking technologies. Democratic control under socialism demands that they be replaced with open technologies in order to establish wholly different relations of production. While left accelerationism presupposes the harmonious incorporation of capitalist technologies into socialist production, many of the locking technologies need to be abandoned for the purpose of more egalitarian and autonomous production. In other words, the development of open technologies must start from scratch in many cases.[28]

Third, there is the problem of sustainability. Marx repeatedly warned that the capitalist development of productive forces undermines and even destroys the universal metabolism of nature. As long as the capitalist mode of production is driven by the logic of valorization, its reorganization of the material aspects of the labour process degrades the material conditions of general production. This is why Marx argued that capitalist increase of productive forces is tied to 'a progress in the art, not only of robbing the worker, but of robbing the soil' (*Capital* I: 638). Accordingly, Marx demanded in volume III of *Capital* that a future society must 'govern the human metabolism with nature in a rational way' (*Capital* III: 959). It is clear that the development of productive forces of capital do not prepare the conditions for such a sustainable regulation of the metabolism with nature. In other words, even if the 'fetter' of the development of productive forces is overcome through the transcendence of the capitalist mode of production, capitalist technologies remain unsustainable and destructive and cannot be employed in socialism.

Finally, the problems of these locking and destructive technologies cannot be overcome simply by transferring ownership from capitalists' hands to state (or communal) ownership. In this sense, the widespread identification of socialism with state-ownership – and capitalism with private ownership – is insufficient for Marx. If only formal subsumption had taken place, it would be possible to abolish the system of exploitation and to make a transition to socialism relatively easily. However, when the 'productive forces of capital' must be transformed into 'productive forces of social labour', the transfer of ownership alone does not solve the problem. If the separation of 'conception' and 'execution' continues, a bureaucratic class would rule general social production instead of capitalist class, so the alienated condition of the working class would basically remain the same. Environmental destruction would also continue under bureaucratic rule. In other words, the real subsumption poses a difficult problem of free 'socialist management', for which the traditional view of historical materialism does not provide any clue (Tairako 1991).

Obviously enough, these four problems are not easy to solve, as the disastrous past failures of really existing socialism have demonstrated. Today's (eco)socialism cannot simply utilize the productive forces of capital as the basis for a future society. If so, post-capitalism can no longer be theoretically founded upon the *Grundrisse*. Marx had serious trouble in solving the inherent problems in his earlier formulation of historical materialism. What is more, Marx was not able to provide a definitive answer to these problems even in *Capital*, so we need to go beyond it. Notwithstanding, it is precisely these presuppositions of traditional Marxism that have resurfaced among contemporary utopians due to their one-sided focus on the *Grundrisse*.

V
ELECTORALISM AND TECHNOLOGY AS IDEOLOGY

Despite these theoretical difficulties, automation utopians assume that technologies growing out of capitalism can provide the foundation for a post-capitalist society and realize universal human emancipation. Compared to Marx's treatment of 'productive forces of capital', their claim is closer to the view that Engels put forward in *Socialism: Utopian and Scientific*:

> ... now modern industry, in its more complete development, comes into collision with the bounds within which the capitalistic mode of production holds it confined. The new productive forces have already outgrown the capitalistic mode of using them. And this conflict between productive forces and modes of production ... exists, in fact, objectively, outside us, independently of the will and actions even of the men that have brought it on. Modern Socialism is nothing but the reflex, in thought, of this conflict in fact. (*MECW* 24: 307)

In addition to points clarified in Chapter 2, this is yet another important theoretical difference between Marx and Engels that emerged in the 1860s. In fact, Engels's view expressed in this passage continues to treat the development of productive forces as an independent variable. Engels did not fully comprehend the importance of Marx's theory of real subsumption and productive forces of capital. He thus continued to argue:

> Thus, the products now produced socially were not appropriated by those who had actually set in motion the means of production and actually produced the commodities, but by the capitalists. The means of production, and production itself, had become in essence socialized.... The greater the mastery obtained by the new mode of production over all important fields of production and in all manufacturing countries ... the more clearly was brought out the incompatibility of socialized production with capitalistic appropriation. (*MECW* 29: 309–10)

It sounds as if once the private property of the means of production is abolished, workers could simply take over capitalist production and transform it into a socialist one because production is already 'in essence socialized' under capitalism. Reducing the problem of capitalism to private property, Engels avoided the difficult questions concerning the new social management of productive forces under socialism. Engels's view became commonplace for traditional Marxism, and it is repeated even today in the seemingly radical theories that highlight the revolutionary potentialities of new information technologies and robotics.

Contemporary utopians only consider the efficiency and the abundance of goods and services without sufficiently taking into account the qualitative and material side of production, that is, the autonomy and independence of workers and the sustainability of the natural environment. Their vision of an economy of abundance based on market-driven innovations ends up reinforcing the real subsumption under capital and easily turns into the means of further expropriation from nature and surveillance over workers. Since alienation of work cannot be overcome in this way, fully automated post-capitalism propagates an alternative hope that everyone keeps driving electronic SUVs, changing smartphones every two years and eating cultured meat hamburgers. Such a vision of the luxury future obviously sounds attractive to many people in the Global North because ecological modernization assures them that they do not need to change anything about their extravagant lifestyle. This kind of abundant future appeals to the satisfaction of people's immediate desires without challenging the current imperial mode of living in the Global North. The problem is, however, that such a vision accepts too uncritically existing value-standards and consumerist ideals. It ends up reproducing the social relations marked by oppression, inequality and exploitation that are inherent to capitalism.

Paradoxically, hidden under the optimistic tone of this technocratic vision is actually a pessimistic 'capitalist realism' that holds that there is no strong class struggle to challenge the existing social relations and to fundamentally detach from the capitalist mode of living. People are deprived of the power to transform the system, and this is why technology must play a central role to fill the void left by agency. In fact, this transformation can be implemented without strong social movements, and its promise of a comfortable life appear attractive. Such a productivist vision of post-capitalism ends up endorsing capitalist value-standards under the guise of a grandiose emancipatory project for infinite production and consumption. It gives up the revolutionary subjectivity of the working class and accepts the reified agency of machines as the subject of history. However, such a post-capitalist project is compelling only when it demonstrates how the productive forces of capital can be transformed into productive forces of social labour that truly enable the 'full development of the individual'.

Since the automation utopians avoid the problem of production, they focus on the sphere of 'politics', which pivots around the idea of 'left populism' (Mouffe 2018). Utopian socialists claim that they are not technological determinists by emphasizing the importance of constructing a new 'political subjectivity' for a social change, especially through electoral politics.[29] Bastani openly argues for 'electoralism' as a way of transforming society to 'fully automated luxury communism': 'FALC, embedded within a luxury populism, must engage in a mainstream, electoral politics' (Bastani 2019: 195).[30] Bastani's assumption here is that ecomodernist technologies can be utilized for the sake of socialist transformation once their ownership is transferred to the state, but this assumption is ungrounded.

In this context, Ellen Meiksins Wood's critique of post-Marxism applies to Bastani's electoralism too (E. Wood 1986: 114–15). According to Wood, the theoretical apparatus of left populism is determined by 'the logic of electoral politics': 'The new "true" socialism is intended not as a strategy for transforming society but as a programme for creating a parliamentary majority.' Such a political programme presumes an ideological view of the 'neutrality' and 'universality' of the liberal democratic state. This view, however, by failing to transform the sphere of social production, misses the limitation of democracy itself. In other words, politics alone is not able to change society because the extension of democracy to the economic realm will face an insurmountable limit when it comes to challenging and undermining the power of capital. This is why a socialist strategy cannot simply focus on the autonomy of the political but needs to transform the sphere of social production: 'At least, the full development of liberal democracy means that the further extension of popular power requires not simply the perfection of existing political institutions but a radical transformation of social arrangements in general, in ways that are as yet unknown' (E. Wood 1986: 150). Technological acceleration alone does not provide a way of overcoming the barrier imposed by capital. It is too narrow to count as the radical change in social arrangements that are required for establishing a post-capitalist society. It even risks turning into a means of reinforcing the despotic power of capital over society.

In fact, it is not clear how the productive forces of capital can be transformed into democratic power in the process of accelerating them. It is more likely that this will only further exacerbate the separation between 'conception' and 'execution'. Without social struggles, the model of constructing counter-hegemony based on technological development is likely to become a project of imposing social transformation 'from above'. Intellectuals, technocrats and politicians come up with the ideas for realizing policies as they are supposed to know better in terms of how to effectively manage and mitigate the ecological and economic crisis. They will monopolize the power of decision-making about which technologies to use and how to use them. Although scientific knowledge is undoubtedly indispensable, centralized and gigantic locking technologies, by their very nature, do not lend themselves to democratic control because they require top-down policies and management.[31] Even the mitigation of the ecological crisis becomes a means of subordinating individuals to undemocratic and technocratic command from above. This is why Gorz warned that a project of Promethean modernism would end in the 'negation of both politics and modernity' (Gorz 2018: 48). This risk cannot be underestimated after the failure of the avant-garde socialist model in the 20th century.[32]

In addition, the novelty of new technologies can obscure the real problem that it is precisely the continuation of business as usual that is irrational. Technology functions as an ideology that mystifies this irrationality. In other words, technology suppresses and eliminates the possibilities of imagining a completely different lifestyle and a safe and just society in the face of the economic and ecological crisis. Crisis is supposed to be a catalyst for critical self-reflection on our irrational behaviour and for envisioning a different future that is more democratic, egalitarian and sustainable. However, locking technologies deprive us of the imaginaries and creativities needed to go beyond capitalism. The ideology of technology is one of the reasons for the poverty of imagination that pervades contemporary capitalism. Automation utopia is one manifestation of this problem.

Despite disagreeing with them, this chapter devoted many pages to the automation utopians because they, at least, have shown that 'abundance' and 'luxury' are dangerous for capitalism. They correctly grasp that the price mechanism of the market is based on scarcity, and abundance seriously disturbs this mechanism, opening up the possibility of a post-scarcity economy. Abundance is also important to envision an attractive post-capitalist future as an anti-thesis to neoliberal austerity. In order to radically challenge capitalist consumerism and productivism in the age of global ecological crisis, Marxist theory, however, needs to redefine 'abundance' because its traditional usage is incompatible with objective ecological limits. As the theoretical limitations of automation utopians show, Marx's *Grundrisse* cannot fulfil this task due to its remnant Prometheanism, so it is necessary to look elsewhere. Fortunately, Marx came to critically reflect upon this problem of his own historical materialism and attempted to reformulate his vision of post-capitalism after the 1860s. Marx's serious attempt continued throughout the 1870s and 1880s. Instead of going back to works such as the *Grundrisse* and *A Contribution* that predate *Capital*, it is thus more fertile to examine Marx's writings *after* 1868 in order to envision a post-capitalist and post-scarcity future in the Anthropocene that is radically different from 'fully automated luxury communism'.

Notes

1   In this chapter, I also use the term 'utopian socialism' instead of 'left accelerationism' because the figures mentioned here do not necessarily categorize themselves as 'accelerationists'. Christian Fuchs (2016) uses the term 'utopian socialism 2.0' in order to characterize Paul Mason's vision of post-capitalism. Obviously, there are various theoretical differences among the contemporary utopian socialists, and there are aspects that contribute to the utopian post-capitalist vision of this book discussed in Chapters 6 and 7.

2   For a compelling critique of the exaggerated threat of full automation from a Marxist perspective, see Benanav (2020). In this sense, left accelerationism does not have a solid empirical foundation. Benanav also shows some sympathy for its utopian vision for post-capitalism, while proposing another vision of the post-scarcity society that is compatible with my own view discussed in the next two chapters.

3   This vague image of 'Leninism' has actually nothing to do with Lenin's ideas. It is more adequate to call it 'digital Stalinism'.

4   They also desperately look for a job and accept low-paid and precarious jobs lest they suffer from the stigma of unemployment in order to live up to capitalism's work ethic. A strong work ethic is precisely what makes modern wage-labourers 'more productive' than premodern slaves and bondsmen. In fact, Marx argued that while slaves 'work only under external compulsion', 'the free worker can only satisfy the requirements of his existence to the extent that he sells his labour; hence is forced into this by his own interest, not by external compulsion' (*MECW* 30: 198). Modern workers sell their labour power based on their free will for the sake of satisfying their own needs, which makes them more industrious and responsible to the command of capital. They accept the logic of self-responsibility after 'freely' signing the contract with capitalists as their equal partners.

5   Incidentally, it is not clear how Mason's passionate celebration of information technology in Postcapitalism (2015) can be compatible with his straightforward defence of humanism in *Clear Bright Future* (2019).

6   The popularity of this manuscript is not new, as it has been a key text for Italian Marxists such as Antonio Negri, Mario Tronti and Paolo Virno. The contemporary utopian socialists update this tradition in a form that is adequate to the age of information technology.

7   Marx was aware that what counts as 'necessary' for the reproduction of labour power changes with the development of productive forces. He wrote in the *Grundrisse* that

> what previously appeared as a luxury is now necessary, and that so-called luxury needs appear e.g. as a necessity for the most naturally necessary and down-to-earth industry of all. This pulling-away of the natural ground from the foundations of every industry, and this transfer of its conditions of production outside itself, into a general context – hence the transformation of what was previously superfluous into what is necessary, as a historically created necessity – is the tendency of capital. (*Grundrisse*: 527–8)

8   Matteo Pasquinelli (2019) traces Marx's concept of 'general intellect' as originating from William Thompson's *An Inquiry into the Principles of the Distribution of Wealth* (1824). Furthermore, he argues that this concept was replaced by *Gesamtarbeiter* in *Capital*. This is possible, but considering the fact that his view of capitalist development significantly changed between the

Grundrisse and *Capital*, it is not merely a choice of different words with the same meaning.

9 G. A. Cohen ([1978] 2000: 104) as well as Cassegård (2021: 5) adequately grasp this method as Marx's unique conception central to his critique of political economy.

10 In the *Economic Manuscripts of 1861–63*, Marx also incorporates the intensification of labour into the production of absolute surplus value, while in *Capital* Marx discusses the issue in relation to relative surplus value. In my view, this change is adequate. This modification reflects Marx's awareness that the intensification of labour is only possible based upon the real subsumption of labour.

11 Obviously, Marx used the term in the sense of productivity too. For example, he wrote:

> But [labour time required for the production] changes with every variation in the productivity of labour. This is determined by a wide range of circumstances; it is determined amongst other things by the workers' average degree of skill, the level of development of science and its technological application, the social organization of the process of production, the extent and effectiveness of the means of production, and the conditions found in the natural environment. For example, the same quantity of labour is present in eight bushels of corn in favourable seasons and in only four bushels in unfavourable seasons. (*Capital* I: 130)

12 In this sense, one can define the 'productive forces' as the ability of humans to consciously regulate their metabolism with nature.

13 One may also point to Marx's following remark in the *Grundrisse*:

> The simplest form, a form independent of the division of labour, is that capital employs different hand weavers, spinners etc. who live independently and are dispersed over the land. (This form still exists alongside industry.) Here, then, the mode of production is not yet determined by capital, but rather found on hand by it. (*Grundrisse*: 586)

Based on these remarks, one could argue that Marx had utilized the concept of 'productive forces of capital' and distinguished 'real' and 'formal' subsumption already in the *Grundrisse*. Yet that underestimates Marx's theoretical development after the *Grundrisse*. It does not suffice to simply point out the appearance of the term because it is possible that the same term has a different degree of importance and a different role for Marx.

14 Raya Dunayevskaya (1973: 80) argued that Marx's break with theory initially took place in his decision to include the lengthy chapter on the working day in volume I of *Capital* to highlight the importance of the struggle for shortening the working day. However, this is not necessarily convincing because Marx always planned to write such a chapter, and her claim leads our focus on the production of absolute surplus value instead of relative surplus value. As Marx came to pay more attention to the actual organization of the labour process, a decisive shift occurred in his theory of cooperation.

15   Obviously, Marx used the concept of 'cooperation' in the *Grundrisse*, and he did so even in *The Poverty of Philosophy*. This does not contradict the claims made in this chapter. Cooperation obviously has a transhistorical dimension. The point is that Marx did not clearly treat cooperation as the elementary form of capitalist production until the early 1860s.

16   This notebook was not available to Ohno, although my argument here basically follows his ideas. The volume *MEGA* IV/17 that contains this notebook is currently being edited by the Japanese team, including myself. Marx's original notebooks are available online: https://search.iisg.amsterdam/Record/ARCH00860/ArchiveContentList#A072e534c62 (accessed 7 September 2022).

17   This passage is later utilized by Marx in his *Economic Manuscripts of 1861–63*. See *MEGA* II/3: 251. See the List of Abbreviations for the reference to Marx's archival materials.

18   This traditional view is not a misinterpretation of Marx's text. It is a correct interpretation of the preface, but it misses the later development of Marx's own view.

19   The translation is modified following the German original text.

20   There Marx and Engels wrote: 'The form of intercourse [that is, relations of production] determined by the existing productive forces at all previous historical stages, and in its turn determining these, is civil society' (*MECW* 5: 50; emphasis added). They continue to argue: 'In the development of productive forces there comes a stage when productive forces and means of intercourse are brought into being which, under the existing relations, only cause mischief, and are no longer productive but destructive forces' (*MECW* 5: 52). Here Marx and Engels expressed the view that productive forces determine the historical stage of human society and endorsed the possibility that once the 'fetter' is got rid of, the development of productive forces can continue in a socialist society. The problem is that Marx and Engels did not acknowledge the possibility that socialism does *not* automatically make productive forces sustainable but that their development continues to become 'destructive forces'.

21   See the *Grundrisse* (705):

> As soon as labour in the direct form has ceased to be the great well-spring of wealth, labour time ceases and must cease to be its measure, and hence exchange value [must cease to be the measure] of use value. The *surplus labour of the mass* has ceased to be the condition for the development of general wealth, just as the *non-labour of the few*, for the development of the general powers of the human head. With that, production based on exchange value breaks down.

22   This problem is also related to Marx's notorious Eurocentric endorsement of the 'great civilising influence of capital' (see Löwy 2019). This problem will be discussed in the next chapter.

23   Tairako (2017) calls this penetration of the economic form to the material aspect of things 'thingification' (*Verdinglichung*), distinguishing it from 'reification' (*Versachlichung*). He follows Marx's own usage of these two concepts.

24   While Marx did not directly mention it in this context, the capitalist mode of production is also accompanied by particular flows of natural resources and energy with the aid of science and technology. This needs to change in the course of deconstructing the productive forces of capital.

25   Obviously enough, this was not a possibility for traditional Marxists. The remaining option then becomes the bureaucratic control of social production after the disappearance of productive forces of capital, which led to the failure of this Soviet path. The central topic of the next two chapters is the need to downscale and slowdown production in order not to repeat the same failure.

26   Another problem of productivism is that the increase of quantitative production can be maximized with technologies that end up subjugating human subjectivity and strengthening the inversion between the subject and the object. This is because the criterion of abundance alone does not tell what kind of technology post-capitalism should actively employ. In fact, the analysis of the real subsumption showed how the autonomy of workers is undermined under the despotic regime of capital precisely for the sake of increasing productivity by reorganizing the entire labour process. Ecosocialism needs to develop counter-technologies which aim to endow workers with the autonomous ability to regulate and coordinate the labour process even after the capitalist function of supervision and command disappears. Otherwise, it risks the concentration of power in the hands of the few: people may be equal but unfree. The deprivation of autonomy can take place outside the domination of capital. State ownership can be introduced simply for the sake of realizing equality, which has resulted in brutal conformism. For example, in the context of the development of information technology celebrated by utopian socialists, algorithms can significantly increase productivity by effectively adjusting and directing social cooperation. However, when algorithm functions based on big data are utilized without the control and knowledge of workers, they will be controlled by the commands of the algorithm. These commands are totally alien to the workers because they do not know how this algorithm is working on them. If you are a taxi driver, you have a certain set of knowledge based on your experience as a driver. You know, for example, which road to choose in order to get more customers or to avoid crowded roads at a certain hour. This is what provides you with a degree of autonomy in work. But, when the GPS in taxis starts to collect data related to drivers' actions, the company can analyse the big data – how they drive and which roads they use, and so on. Then, the platformers can monopolize the knowledge of the taxi drivers. Based on algorithms formulated through big data, companies can introduce a new computer system that orders each driver which way to go. Capital can replace those old taxi drivers with autonomous knowledge with anyone with a driver's licence without any previous experience who simply follows the directions shown on their smartphone display. This is a new form of real subsumption as the separation of 'conception' and 'execution' in the age of information technology. Braverman's insight remains valid under digital capitalism.

27 Nuclear power and geo-engineering are prime examples of 'locking technology'. They make it impossible to democratically control the ecological system. Rather, the political decision of the developed countries will decide on irreversible interventions in the climate and ocean system, eliminating the possibility of regaining autonomous ways of organizing the metabolic interaction between humans and nature in the future.

28 Gorz does not negate the possibility of open technologies in capitalism. His optimistic view of the Internet as an open technology, however, appears naïve today in the face of the formation of 'surveillance capitalism' (Zuboff 2019).

29 What Srnicek and Williams (2016: 15) call 'folk politics' is characterized by the small-scale and horizontal assembly, based on the model of direct democracy. The 'assembly' aims at the immediate and temporal achievement of civil justice. According to them, folk politics typically gives up challenging worldwide issues and the global economic system and instead aims at 'prefigurative politics' that takes place at a face-to-face local level. Apparently, this scaling down of political ambition is the result of the failure of Soviet socialism and the corresponding formation of neoliberal common sense. Srnicek and Williams argue that local movements such as local food movements and Occupy Wall Street lack any efficacy because the issues that they are trying to solve are deeply rooted in the global capitalist system and the planetary ecological system. What is direly needed, Srnicek and Williams argue, is a universal project for progress and emancipation as a counter-hegemonic project. The problem is, however, the full automation that they advocate for undermines such subjectivity.

30 While accelerationism is a communist version of electoralism, ecomodernism presents a 'social democratic' version of electoralism that advocates state regulation and intervention in the capitalist market. Thus, Jonathan Symons (2019: 12) also argues for the importance of 'state-driven innovation' because the state is 'the only actor with the capacity and social mandate to take on such a role'. There is no reason to deny the central importance of the state in the process of mitigating the climate crisis, but ecomodernism is not the only way to utilize state power. I have no intention of defending 'folk politics' here either. Nevertheless, a one-sided focus on technologies often mystifies the irrational and exploitative character of the current system. Folk politics at least challenges the current mode of living in the Global North in search of a more solidaristic mode of living with those people in the Global South (Brand and Wissen 2021).

31 Such political decisions will likely reinforce the existing asymmetry of power. As noted earlier, if geo-engineering is introduced in such a manner, it is justified in the name of stewardship of the earth and aims to manage the entire ecological system at the cost of enslaving people – especially in the Global South through the metabolic shift – to heteronomous regulation by technologies. That is incompatible with climate justice.

32 Similarly to Srnicek and Williams's critique of 'folk politics', Andreas Malm (2020) argues for 'ecological Leninism'. While his intention is fully understandable, Leninism does not solve the problem of productive forces of capital either.

PART III

TOWARDS DEGROWTH COMMUNISM

6

Marx as a Degrowth Communist

The *MEGA* and the Great Transformation after 1868

Through discussions in previous chapters, various productivist approaches characteristic of Marxism turned out to be inadequate to formulate a response to the economic and ecological crises of the Anthropocene. Technocratic visions, despite their bold claims of emancipation, reproduce the non-democratic and consumerist relations of domination and subjugation that exist under capitalism. Furthermore, capitalist development does not guarantee the transcendence of the contradictory character of the capitalist mode of production because 'productive forces of capital' as an art of robbery severely deform the human metabolic relationship with nature, without providing a material foundation for the future society. This is not a new problem. In the 1860s Marx became increasingly aware of this problem while writing *Capital*, but due to the persistent understanding of the philosophical foundations of Marx's historical materialism as the unilateral progress of universal human history driven by the development of productive forces, his vision of revolution tended to be reduced to a Promethean one, as if the maximal acceleration of the existing tendencies of capitalism could ultimately realize a final leap to communism.

Marx's own remarks reinforce this impression. Even in the well-known passage from the preface to *A Contribution* in 1859, Marx famously wrote, for example: 'No social formation is ever destroyed before all the productive forces for which it is sufficient have been developed, and new superior relations of production never replace older ones before the material conditions for their existence have matured within the framework of the old society' (*MECW* 29: 263). This kind of assumption can easily be read as productivist, but such an interpretation is untenable today because the acceleration of productive forces will sooner or later make most of the planet inhabitable before the collapse of capitalism.

It is understandable that environmentalists often show disdain for Marxism. In fact, historical materialism is unpopular today. This is a pity considering their shared interest in criticizing capital's insatiable desire for accumulation, though from different perspectives. Admitting the inadequacy and flaws of Promethean Marxism, this chapter attempts to finally resolve the tension between Red and Green. By revisiting Marx's own texts, I re-examine whether a path exists to reconcile the long antagonism between Green and Red and to build a new Front Populaire in defence of the planet in the Anthropocene. Such a re-investigation is worth conducting because the ongoing project of publishing the complete works of Marx and Engels, *Marx-Engels-Gesamtausgabe* (*MEGA*), has made possible a more nuanced reconstruction of Marx's thinking process. His notebooks published in the fourth section of the *MEGA* are of great use for the current investigation. Although these notebooks were mostly treated as 'mere' excerpts even by serious Marxist scholars, together with his letters and manuscripts they contain ideas and insights that were not fully integrated into his published writings.[1] Because Marx barely published after volume I of *Capital* (1867) and its volumes II and III remained unfinished, his notebooks are valuable documents that shed light on unknown aspects of his unfinished project of political economy.

In short, the *MEGA* is not just for biographers who want more detailed information about Marx's and Engels's life. Rather, it has important *theoretical* implications. Combined with Marx's economic manuscripts published in its second section, the *MEGA* sets up the conditions for a new critical investigation of Marx's critique of capitalism. In fact, there have been novel attempts to reconstruct the late Marx based on the *MEGA* in recent years (K. Anderson 2010; Heinrich 2013; Vollgraf 2016; Jones 2016; Saito 2017; Musto 2020). They reveal that Marx quite intensively studied two fields after the publication of *Capital*: natural science and pre-capitalist or non-Western societies. Based on the new materials published in the *MEGA*, Kevin Anderson (2010) demonstrates Marx's departure from his earlier Eurocentric and linear view of historical progress, while Carl-Erich Vollgraf (2016) argues that Marx's passionate engagement with natural science indicates his serious concern about environmental destruction under capitalism (I).

However, no matter how important these recent discoveries of Marx as a 'non-ethnocentric' and 'ecological' thinker may be for Marxist scholars who wish to save him from various accusations directed against him, they are not sufficient to demonstrate why *non-Marxists* still need to care about Marx's interest in ecology today. In order to demonstrate why non-Marxists should still care about Marx, Marxian scholars need to offer something more positive here. This chapter goes further than previous literature by concretely depicting the late Marx's vision of post-capitalist society after he abandoned Eurocentrism and Prometheanism in the 1870s. In finally discarding both ethnocentrism and productivism, Marx abandoned his earlier scheme of historical materialism. It was not an easy task for him. His worldview was in crisis. In this sense, Marx's intensive research in his last years was a desperate attempt to reconstruct and reformulate his materialist conception of history from an entirely new perspective, resulting in a radically different conception of the alternative society (II).

Famously enough, Marx's serious engagement with non-Western society after 1868 made him recognize the revolutionary potentialities of non-Western societies based on communal landed property. This shift is clearly discernible in his famous letter to Vera Zasulich and his call for an immediate Russian Revolution bypassing the capitalist stage in Russia. Previous studies paid attention to the letter to Zasulich and its drafts (Wada 1975; Shanin 1984; J. White 2019), but their description of Marx as a non-Eurocentric thinker alone sounded 'romantic' as long as the high evaluation of Russian communes is tied to the understanding that the old Marx, giving up hope of a revolution in Western Europe, strongly sympathized with revolutionary movements in Russia. Obviously enough, romanticism does not offer any convincing reason why it is useful to go back to the late Marx today (III).

To demonstrate the contemporary relevance of Marx's theory, it is necessary to elaborate on his positive vision of the post-capitalist society. The revolutionary potentiality of Russia, about which he learned through his intellectual communication with Russian authors such as Nikolay Chernyshevsky and Maxim Kovalevsky, not only inspired him to rethink the Russian path to communism but also enriched his view of communist society *in Western Europe*. However, previous studies failed to sufficiently examine this point precisely because they did not pay attention to Marx's interest in ecology after 1868. In short, Marx's final vision of an alternative society can be developed only based upon a full synthesis of Marx's engagement with political economy, ecology and pre-capitalist societies in the last 15 years of his life. By carefully investigating the reason why he had to study pre-capitalist societies *and* natural sciences at the same time, a new and surprising possibility of interpreting Marx's letter to Zasulich emerges: Marx ultimately became a *degrowth communist* (IV).

I
THE *MEGA* AND THE LATE MARX

Recent discussions on the late Marx based on the *MEGA* offer unique insights compared with previous interpretations. According to a stereotypical account of Marx's theory of revolution, economic inequality increases under capitalism because workers' surplus labour is appropriated by capitalists. Capitalists, driven by market competition, aim to increase productive forces by introducing novel machines and produce a greater number of commodities than ever. However, workers who are severely exploited cannot afford to consume all of the new commodities. *Capital* continues to expand the market to find new demand. However, 'new markets were not limitless and the more exploitation was pursued the greater was the likelihood that what seemed like overproduction would actually happen' (Lamb 2015: 48). Overproduction results in a sudden fall in commodity prices, bankruptcy and mass employment, which degrades the living conditions of the working class even more. Ultimately, the proletariat, developing class consciousness as a universal revolutionary class, unites and stands up against the capitalists; 'the expropriators are expropriated'.

One might say that this description very roughly summarizes the basic logic of *The Communist Manifesto* of 1848. The *Manifesto* seethed with revolutionary optimism, and its tone reflects Marx's and Engels's conviction that capitalism would soon be transcended through a socialist revolution triggered by a severe economic crisis. Since the further development of capitalism prepares the way for an ever-greater economic crisis, it is probable that Marx thought it necessary to accelerate capitalism's development despite the negative side-effects of such a crisis, including economic inequality and the further degradation workers' living conditions. However, the revolution of 1848 failed, and capitalism was revived thereafter. That was also the case after the economic crises in 1857 and 1866. After all, economic crises alone have never brought about the breakdown of capitalism. An economic crisis is actually an integral part of capitalist development as it annihilates value to prepare new conditions for a next industrial cycle (Kliman 2011). Repeatedly confronted with the stubbornness of capitalism, Marx gradually corrected his optimistic view about the inevitability of a socialist revolution. Thus, no matter how accessible and encouraging the story told in *The Communist Manifesto* might be, it does not necessarily reflect Marx's definitive vision (Sasaki 2021). In this sense, we must surely deal with his magnum opus, *Capital*, but the point is that even that is not sufficient because *Capital* remains essentially an unfinished work. One needs to go *beyond* it in order to comprehend Marx's final vision of post-capitalist society.

However, traditional Marxism was often satisfied with Marx's theory of surplus value and exploitation in *Capital*, volume I. This served as 'proof' of the illegitimate domination of the bourgeoisie and the legitimacy of proletarian revolution. His theory of crisis in volumes II and III were likewise understood as a 'proof' of the inevitability of capitalism's collapse. *Capital* was celebrated as a socialist 'bible' to ground both the legitimacy and the necessity of socialism, but such a reading is not compelling today and the failure of traditional Marxism is not necessarily a negative thing to lament. The end of the Cold War also opened up new possibilities for rereading Marx. What characterizes this 'new reading of Marx' (*neue Marx-Lektüre*) compared with traditional Marxism is an honest acknowledgement of the incompleteness of his system of political economy. Scholars started to investigate his economic manuscripts, letters, and even notebooks more carefully (Dellheim and Otto Wolf 2018). They demonstrate that although volumes II and III of *Capital* were not completed during Marx's lifetime, his critique of capitalism did deepen after the publication of volume I. However, the unfinished character of Marx's critique of political economy has been underestimated in the past because it became invisible in Engels's edition of *Capital*. Engels, editing Marx's manuscripts after his death, strove to establish 'Marxism' as a doctrine to mobilize the working class. He tended to overemphasize the systematic character of *Capital* so that it could provide a universal 'worldview' for the working class.

As a consequence, Marx's thinking processes are sometimes obscured in Engels's edition. This is unfortunate because it is precisely those passages in the original manuscript for volume III, where Marx had most difficulties and planned to come back later to rework them, that had to be modified by Engels for the sake of improving the readability of Marx's text *as a book*. These passages are usually hard to read as Marx struggled to formulate his new ideas in writing. They are often accompanied by redundant repetitions, vague formulations and grammatical errors. Marx often used the mark 'L' in the manuscripts to denote where he started over his argument. Or, when he felt the need to come back later to elaborate more, he highlighted those passages in the notebooks by drawing lines in the margins.[2] However, all these traces of struggle were 'cleaned up' by Engels.[3] Of course, thanks to Engels's enormous efforts, *Capital* in three volumes became available in a form that is accessible to a broad audience (if not easily comprehensible to the working class). This enabled 'Marxism' as a doctrine of 'scientific socialism' to exert an enormous political influence throughout the 20th century. While Engels's achievement is undeniable, it is also true that the new theoretical horizon that looms in Marx's economic manuscripts became rather invisible given the impression

Engels's edition gives that the three volumes of *Capital* are more or less complete in their current form. Consequently, Marxists often assumed that Marx's research after 1867 has little meaning because it hardly contributed to volumes II and III of *Capital*. This is also reflected in the widespread view that the late Marx lost his intellectual capacity due to illness. Isaiah Berlin provides a typical example when he concludes that the late Marx 'was less capable of the active campaigns of his youth and middle years; overwork and a life of poverty had finally undermined his strength; he was tired, and often ill, and began to be preoccupied by health' (Berlin [1948] 2013: 252–3).

However, as the *MEGA* publishes the economic manuscripts of *Capital* in its second section, as well as relevant notebooks in the fourth section, it becomes clear that despite his worsening health, Marx quite passionately studied new materials and wrote various manuscripts for the sake of completing *Capital*. As an attempt to refine and revise his system of political economy even after 1868, Marx conducted a lot of calculations of the profit rate related to the law of profit rate to fall (*MEGA* II/4.3; *MEGA* II/14; Akashi 2021). He also tried to reconsider the theory of crisis in the face of the panic of 1866 (*MEGA* IV/19; Graßmann 2022) as well as the theory of ground rent (*MEGA* IV/18). Looking at the economic manuscripts, Michael Heinrich (2013: 167) even argues that due to the rise and increasing influence of the United States, as well as Russia, which volume I of *Capital* barely took into account, especially with regard to joint stock companies and the impact of railway construction, Marx was no longer certain whether England could be treated as a model of capitalism as an ideal type. Heinrich believes that this new economic situation compelled Marx to consider a reconstruction of the logical structure of *Capital* almost from scratch. Likewise, Carl-Erich Vollgraf concludes his analysis of Marx's notebooks on natural science by claiming that Marx came to recognize the 'value-producing' contribution of nature in the production process and realized that he must abandon the labour theory of value (Vollgraf 2016: 129). Heinrich and Vollgraf maintain that due to the enormous scale of such a theoretical reconsideration, Marx's unfinished project became *unfinishable*.

While Heinrich's and Vollgraf's statements exaggerate the theoretical and personal crisis Marx and his project faced after 1868 – he never explicitly admitted what they claim to be the case – their investigation of the *MEGA*, focusing on the neglected aspects of the late Marx, correctly points to the necessity for a thorough re-examination of his critique of political economy. Nevertheless, these discussions on the *MEGA* remain largely unknown outside Germany and Japan. As a result, even those scholars, who do not naively take *The Communist Manifesto* as Marx's definitive view, often fail to recognize the endpoint of his intellectual journey, especially with regard to his vision of post-capitalism. This chapter aims at revealing what the late Marx actually envisioned as an alternative to capitalism in a way that opens up new debates with contemporary currents of political economy and political ecology in the Anthropocene.

II
DECONSTRUCTING HISTORICAL MATERIALISM

As discussed in the previous chapter, Marx underwent a significant theoretical shift after he brought his attention to bear on the problem of 'productive forces of capital' in his analysis of the 'real subsumption' in the *Economic Manuscripts of 1861–63*. This shift made him thoroughly rethink his previous assumption about the progressive character of capitalism. He realized that productive forces do not automatically prepare the material foundation for new post-capitalist society but rather exacerbate the robbery of nature. However, due to the neglect of the concept of 'productive forces of capital', there remains a common misunderstanding that Marx continued to naively presume a 'progressive view of history' comparable to a natural law: 'Marx adopted Hegel's view that history was ... a development, which, like the growth of a plant, proceeded ineluctably according to its own laws' (Perry 2015: 343). Marx, like Hegel, becomes a passionate defender of linear progress in human history driven by the dialectical development of productive forces, which should dialectically bring about human emancipation despite its initially destructive impacts upon communities and the natural environment.

No wonder then that Marx's 'historical materialism' is repeatedly criticized for its economic determinism (Popper 1967). Economic determinism has two main characteristics: 'productivism' and 'Eurocentrism'. Productivism is characterized by an optimistic endorsement of capitalist modernization because technological and scientific inventions and innovations introduced under market competition lead to the elimination of poverty and shorter working hours. The affluent life that was hitherto limited to a small number of the ruling class becomes available to the working class. Since the development of productive forces counts as the main driver of historical progress, the acceleration of capitalist development becomes the *most efficient* path towards human emancipation.

Such a productivist vision simultaneously presupposes a linear progress of history. It regards the Western capitalist countries with higher productive forces as located on a higher stage of history compared to non-Western and non-capitalist countries. It follows that other non-capitalist countries *must* follow the same European path of capitalist industrialization in order to establish socialism. This kind of uncritical presupposition of the superiority of

Western Europe as it imposes its own history upon other parts of the world makes Marx's thought 'Eurocentric' (Avineri 1969: 29).

Needless to say, both productivism and Eurocentrism are untenable today. Some of these criticisms of Marx are justifiable. *The Communist Manifesto* contains passages where his and Engels's ethnocentric productivism is discernible in their writing about 'the subjugation of nature to man' and the 'barbarian and semi-barbarian countries':

> The bourgeoisie has subjected the country to the rule of the towns. It has created enormous cities, has greatly increased the urban population as compared with the rural, and has thus rescued a considerable part of the population from the idiocy of rural life. Just as it has made the country dependent on the towns, so it has made barbarian and semi-barbarian countries dependent on the civilised ones, nations of peasants on nations of bourgeois, the East on the West. (*MECW* 6: 488)

Marx and Engels continued to argue:

> The bourgeoisie, during its rule of scarce one hundred years, has created more massive and more colossal productive forces than have all preceding generations together. Subjection of Nature's forces to man, machinery, application of chemistry to industry and agriculture, steam-navigation, railways, electric telegraphs, clearing of whole continents for cultivation, canalisation of rivers, whole populations conjured out of the ground – what earlier century had even a presentiment that such productive forces slumbered in the lap of social labour? (*MECW* 6: 489)

Fascinated by new technologies, Marx praised the development of the productive forces under capitalism and hoped that the subjugation of nature would civilize the entire world and realize human emancipation. As far as these statements are concerned, it is fair to say that Marx was both Promethean (Löwy 1998) and Eurocentric (Carver 1983: 80).[4]

However, what Marx said in the *Manifesto* should not be overgeneralized because he later critically reflected upon both of these problematic assumptions. As I have pointed out throughout this book, the existence of Marx's ecology is undeniable today as seen in recent robust discussions that employ his concept of metabolic rift. Although some ecosocialists caution that the role of Liebig's *Agricultural Chemistry* in Marxian ecology should not be overemphasized because it is based on outdated science of the 19th century (Engel-Di Mauro 2014), Marx's ecological investigation of natural science did not end with Liebig. Marx was well aware that Liebig's work alone did *not* provide sufficient scientific ground for a critique of ecological degradation under capitalism. After 1868, Marx thus intensified his study of the natural sciences, including those who explicitly *criticized* Liebig's treatment of soil exhaustion and chemical fertilizer. The scope of Marx's research documented in his notebooks is astonishing, and his notebooks cover topics in geology, chemistry, mineralogy, and botany. These notebooks document that his ecological critique of capitalism went beyond Liebig's critique of robbery agriculture, covering new topics such as excessive deforestation, cruel treatment of livestock, squandering of fossil fuels and species extinction (Saito 2017).

As already mentioned in Chapter 2, Marx eagerly read the work of the German agronomist Carl Fraas in 1868, who was a harsh critic of Liebig's exaggerated claim that soil exhaustion was the cause of decay in civilizations. Instead, Fraas (1847) in *Klima und Pflanzenwelt* warned that excessive deforestation was a real threat to modern European civilization because it would change the local climate. Rising temperatures and dryness would have negative impacts on indigenous plants as well as agriculture, ultimately leading to the collapse of ancient civilizations. He was concerned that the development of logging and transportation technologies under capitalism would allow the felling of trees previously inaccessible or unprofitable, accelerating the tempo and scale of deforestation (*MEGA* IV/18: 621).[5] This marks a decisive expansion in Marx's ecological understanding.

Marx also knew about William Stanley Jevons. Jevons's warning about the exhaustion of the British coal caused heated controversy in the British Parliament at the time. Marx, who was carefully following various newspapers and magazines, came to learn of the debate and acquired a copy of Jevons's *The Coal Question*. In a notebook made in 1869, which was recently published in *MEGA* IV/19, Marx actually read Jevons's treatment of the coal question.[6] As documented in Marx's notebook, Jevons warned about the 'probable exhaustion' of coal reserves 'in 100 years'.[7] He predicted that Britain would be at a disadvantage in the international competition with the United States because 'their coal is often better in quality and incomparably more accessible than ours'. Marx recognized that while '*great economy in the use of coal* [has been] already introduced', the consumption of coal kept increasing because of its cheap price. This constitutes 'the Jevons Paradox'.

In the same notebook of 1869, he went on to cover other ecological topics too. Marx, for example, read articles published in the *Economist* on the rinderpest epidemic in Great Britain between 1865 and 1867. At the time, meat consumption was growing, and the fattening of domestic animals for meat and profit intensified. As he noted from the *Economist* dated 10 February 1866:

Year by year the amount of meat consumed in the country augments. Following shows how rapidly the trade is augmenting:

Number of living animals imported in the 11 months ended November 30			
	1863	1864	1865
Oxen, bulls and cows	89,518	141,778	196,030
Calves	36,930	44,678	48,926
Sheep and lambs	380,259	412,469	763,084
Swine and hogs	24,311	68,777	117,766

(*MEGA* IV/19)

Marx documented the following passage about the relationship between 'cattle plague' and a modern system of breeding obsessed with fattening of cows:

> Mr. Cousmaker said: 'too much importance could not be attached to the system of breeding … they ought to combine the breeding of stocks with its fattening: fattening.' 'He had himself escaped the cattle plague, although violently raging in his neighbourhood. In August and September they had lost in his parish 270 head of cattle. One of the causes of this escape was that he had not for years bought stock. He bred at one end and fattened on the other, and he never bought or sold, except to the butcher, beyond buying about once every 2 years a yearling bull, for the sake of change of breed....' (*MEGA* IV/19)

Marx already studied Léonce de Lavergne and Wilhelm Hamm in 1864 on how modern livestock farming increases the vulnerability of animals to disease because these animals are kept inactive in a closed space for the sake of speedier maturity with excessive fat. Marx's comments are quite critical of such 'improvements' and sympathetic to animal welfare. Responding to Léonce de Lavergne's enthusiastic reports about the 'system of selection' developed by English breeder Robert Bakewell, Marx wrote in his notebook: 'Characterized by precocity, in entirety sickliness, want of bones, a lot of development of fat and flesh etc. All these are artificial products. Disgusting!' (*MEGA* IV/18: 234).[8] In the notebooks of 1868, cattle plague provided Marx with another more horrifying manifestation of the metabolic rift created by industrial meat production. It does not end with the sacrifice of individual animal welfare, but the spread of viruses that created pandemics in the entire country at that time.[9]

Furthermore, Marx clearly recognized the multi-faceted development of the ecological problem. On the one hand, the rearing of a great number of cattle is also tied to soil exhaustion:

> There is a very large area of grassland, which is in a very impoverished condition. The land is grazed year after year; young cattle are reared, and dairy produce sold; but nothing is returned to the soil. It will not be long before the Irish farmer experiences that this system will end in the total exhaustion of the land. (*MEGA* IV/19)

Instead of returning to the soil, soil nutrients contained in the food consumed by the working class in the large cities was digested and then flowed into the river through water closets as sewage. This was tied to the degradation of living conditions in the city:

> 'We learn', say the Commissioners, 'with something approaching to dismay, that one manufacturer alone employs from 1 to 2 tons of oxalic acid in bleaching straw plaits, but are somewhat reassured upon consideration that the poisonous character of this substance is entirely destroyed by admixture with the carbonate and sulphate of lime contained in the water of the river.' Then, the river is polluted by sheep washing, and, as the preparation for dipping sheep contains arsenic, another noxious ingredient is added to the new witches' cauldron. But, besides these directly poisonous substances, the river receives the sewage of Hatfield, Hertford, Ware, Enfield, Barnet, and Tottenham. (*MEGA* IV/19)

The foulness of waterways was a serious issue at the time, and every town blamed the town upriver. Sewage in the River Thames is known to have been the cause of the cholera outbreak of the 1830s, which persisted for over 20 years. A similar problem occurred even in the 1860s. Although based on articles in the *Economist*, Marx's notebook of 1868 documents how he came to deal with the ecological complex around modern food production consisting of water pollution, soil exhaustion and pandemic disease. This insight marks a clear advancement compared to his earlier reception of Liebig in 1864 that focused solely on the problem of soil exhaustion.

The research objective that is discernible from Marx's late notebooks is very different from his earlier optimistic view. Abandoning his celebration of the increasing productive forces under capitalism, he came to recognize that the sustainable development of the productive forces is not possible under capitalism because it only reinforces intensive and extensive squandering and robbery of human and nature for the sake of short-term profit and endless capital accumulation, creating more complicated and extensive ecological issues. The reparation of the metabolic rift necessitates a different economic system, and this is the fundamental insight of Marx's 'ecosocialism' in the 1860s.

Marx's endorsement of 'ecosocialism' in the 1860s certainly counts as a significant modification of his earlier view. Yet this theoretical shift is only the beginning of a more profound change. Marx's decisive break with productivism shook his larger worldview called 'historical materialism'. Abandoning productivism, Marx must have recognized that higher productive forces by themselves no longer automatically guarantee Western capitalism a higher historical status compared with non-Western and non-capitalist societies. It is not clear at all whether the development of destructive technologies counts as 'development' towards free and sustainable human development. In fact, in *Capital* Marx characterized the power of capital to expropriate from nature as 'robbery' (*Raub*). When Marx jettisoned productivism as the essential component of his view of human history, he was also compelled to reconsider his biased Eurocentrism, which is the other side of the same coin. Furthermore, if he ultimately discarded both productivism and Eurocentrism, Marx must have completely parted ways with 'historical materialism' as it has traditionally been understood. In this case everything would have to start over again. It is easy to imagine that this was a painful task for the old Marx, but he did not give up his project as is demonstrated by his research on the world history and non-Western/pre-capitalist societies.

Before reconstructing what happened to Marx's vision of post-capitalism after he consciously discarded historical materialism, it is useful to briefly sketch the problem of Marx's Eurocentrism. The most famous criticism was raised by Edward Said, who characterized Marx as a typical 'Orientalist' that treats the non-Europeans as barbaric and inferior in order to legitimize Western domination over them. Said wrote about Marx's comments on British colonialism in India published in the *New York Daily Tribune* in 1853:

> In article after article he returned with increasing conviction to the idea that even in destroying Asia, Britain was making possible there a real social revolution.... Marx's economic analyses are perfectly fitted thus to a standard Orientalist undertaking, even though Marx's humanity, his sympathy for the misery of people, are clearly engaged. Yet in the end it is the Romantic Orientalist vision that wins out, as Marx's theoretical socio-economic views become submerged in this classically standard image. (Said 1979: 153–4)

Indeed, Marx wrote in one of those articles titled 'The British Rule India':

> England, it is true, in causing a social revolution in Hindostan, was actuated only by the vilest interests, and was stupid in her manner

of enforcing them. But that is not the question. The question is, can mankind fulfil its destiny without a fundamental revolution in the social state of Asia? If not, whatever may have been the crimes of England she was the unconscious tool of history in bringing about that revolution. (*MECW* 12: 132)

Certainly, Marx acknowledged the brutality of British colonialism in India at that time, but his tone is somewhat ambivalent. He maintained that British colonialism 'has to fulfil a double mission' that is not only 'destructive' towards Indian villages but also 'regenerating' for Asian society by introducing new technologies brought about by Western capitalism, such as railways, steam engines and irrigation systems. Marx emphasized the progressive role of British colonialism in terms of the dissolution of communal landed property and its replacement with private land ownership as well as of the caste system through modern industrialization. This is because he assumed that Indian village communes were stagnant and lacked all communication with the outside world and failed to take note of technological development and commodity production in precolonial India. He thus argued in another article 'The Future Results of British Rule in India' that Asian societies are static and passive by themselves, even claiming that 'Indian society has no history at all' (*MECW* 12: 217). For Marx, the 'unchanging nature of non-European society is thus a drag on the progress of history and a serious threat to socialism' (Avineri 1969: 21) This is why, Marx argued, Indians needed compulsion from without through the imperialist intervention of European societies. It seems that Marx accepted the sufferings of the Indian people as a necessary evil for the general progress of humankind towards socialist emancipation. Said's critique of Orientalism sounds appropriate here.

However, before too hastily accepting these accusations of Eurocentrism, it is worth pointing to a number of rebuttals of them (Ghosh 1984; Pradella 2016). One can respond to Said's criticism by arguing that already in the late 1850s, Marx more emphatically expressed his anti-colonialist and abolitionist position and acknowledged the agency of the Indian people (Jani 2002: 94). For example, Marx wrote about the Revolt of 1857 against British colonialism in India, asking readers 'whether a people are not justified in attempting to expel the foreign conquerors who have so abused their subjects' (*MECW* 15: 341). This was not a one-off remark. Whether it was Indian colonialism, the Polish Uprising, the American Civil War, or the Irish question, Marx always stood on the side of the oppressed and more clearly denounced the brutality of imperialism and slavery under capitalism (K. Anderson 2010).

This does not necessarily mean that he fully distanced himself from Eurocentrism. Actually, abolitionist remarks can be found already in the 1840s

184 | *Marx in the Anthropocene*

when he wrote in *The Poverty of Philosophy* that 'direct slavery is just as much the pivot of bourgeois industry as machinery, credits, etc' (*MECW* 6: 167).[10] In other words, it is possible that Marx, despite his hatred of and anger towards British imperialism, still believed in the passive and static character of non-Western societies. This can be characterized as a trait of Orientalism.

In fact, it is likely that Marx ultimately accepted colonial rule from the perspective of the progress of human history as a whole. Even though he started to pay attention to the destructive character of capitalist development of productive forces in the beginning of the 1860s, similar 'Orientalist' remarks can still be found in the 1860s. For example, in the *Economic Manuscripts of 1861–63*, Marx criticized Jean Charles Léonard de Sismondi by arguing:

> To oppose the welfare of the individual to this end, as Sismondi does, is to assert that the development of the species must be arrested in order to safeguard the welfare of the individual, so that, for instance, no war may be waged in which at all events some individuals perish. Sismondi is only right as against the economists who conceal or deny this contradiction. Apart from the barrenness of such edifying reflections, they reveal a failure to understand the fact that, although at first the development of the capacities of the human species takes place at the cost of the majority of human individuals and whole human classes, in the end it breaks through this contradiction and coincides with the development of the individual; the *higher development of individuality is thus only achieved by a historical process during which individuals are sacrificed....* (*MECW* 31: 347–8; emphasis added)

Increase the productive forces, even if individuals are sacrificed! Market and capitalism all over the world for human emancipation! It is as if Marx were an ideologue of neoliberal globalization.

Furthermore, it is not obvious whether Marx really abandoned his Eurocentrism even in volume I of *Capital*, where he continued to talk about the stationary character of Asian societies: 'This simplicity supplies the key to the riddle of *the unchangeability of Asiatic societies*' (*Capital* I: 479; emphasis added). In the 1850s, this passivity and steadiness were exactly the reasons Marx pointed to the need for European intervention in Asia from without. Non-Western societies remained deprived of historical agency, despite their essential contribution to the affluence of Western capitalism by supplying labour power and natural resources.

In addition, Marx notoriously wrote in the preface to the first edition of *Capital*: 'The country that is more developed industrially only shows, to the less developed, the image of its own future' (*Capital* I: 91). Such a unilateral view of historical development counts as another trait of his Eurocentrism, because it uncritically projects the trajectory of European history onto the rest of the world. Such a violent universalization of the particular justified colonialism. This kind of Eurocentric framework easily falls into a reductionist analysis of non-Western societies from the hegemonizing perspective of European capitalism, marginalizing the specificities of local social relations. Thus, Marx's emphasis on the universalizing tendency of capitalist development shows 'ambivalences' (Chakrabarty 2000: 65) without paying sufficient attention to what resists the universal logic of capital. It is necessary, so Dipesh Chakrabarty argues, to thoroughly reconstruct Marx's view of history in a way that does not erase contingencies and discontinuities in particular cases. They cannot be explained using the universal law of capitalist development but have essential impacts upon the history of both European and non-European countries in the process of capital's globalization.

Chakrabarty concludes that 'Marx does not himself think through this problem' (Chakrabarty 2000: 67), but that is not necessarily the case.[11] By the latter half of the 1860s at the latest, Marx reflected much more critically upon the destructive character of Western intrusion into non-Western societies and the limits to the universalization of capital. Instead of emphasizing the 'double mission', Marx problematized the asymmetrical subjugation of peripheral regions into the capitalist world system, which prevents them from achieving the promised modernization process. This shift in his tone in the 1860s needs to be understood in relation to the new concept of 'productive forces of capital', with which he reconsidered the progressive character of capitalism in general. As a result, similarly to the sphere of ecology, a decisive shift occurred after 1868 in terms of his treatment of non-Western societies. This revision becomes apparent in his alliance with people in Ireland against English colonial rule. In his letter to Engels dated 10 December 1869, Marx wrote:

> For a long time, I believed it would be possible to overthrow the Irish regime by English working class ascendancy. I always took this viewpoint in the *New York Tribune*. Deeper study has now convinced me of the opposite. The English working class will never accomplish anything before it has got rid of Ireland. The lever must be applied in Ireland. This is why the Irish question is so important for the social movement in general. (*MECW* 43: 398; emphasis added)

In this letter, Marx clearly admitted that he changed his earlier view from the 1850s, arguing that colonized Ireland plays a rather leading and *active* role in the fight against English capitalism and imperialism without ascribing a progressive role to England in pushing forward history in another region. This marks his first explicit break from the logic of Eurocentrism. Although Ireland is located within Western Europe, underlying this break was the fact that Marx had started intensively studying not only natural sciences but also non-Western and pre-capitalist societies *immediately after* the publication of volume I of *Capital*.

It is not unreasonable to suspect that Marx's theoretical transformations regarding of Prometheanism and ethnocentrism occurred at the same time. This dual shift is a reflection of Marx's parting way with historical materialism. One should recall that in the same letter dated March 1868, in which Marx found a 'socialist tendency' in Fraas's work, he also found the same socialist tendency in Maurer's work (see Chapter 2). At that time, he was simultaneously reading Fraas's ecological investigation and Maurer's historical analysis of Teutonic communes. These two research topics – natural science and pre-capitalist/non-Western societies – are closely related in the late Marx.

Marx was interested in Teutonic communes and their sustainability, and he started to spend more time studying various non-Western and pre-capitalist societies with a particular focus on non-capitalist agriculture and systems of landed property. After 1868 Marx read books on ancient Rome, India, Algeria, Latin America, the Iroquois in North America and Russian agrarian communes. The change of his view is clearly documented, especially with regard to Russia.

Even in the late 1860s, Marx did not hide his dismissiveness not only of Tsarist Russia but of Russian revolutionaries like Mikhail Bakunin. In the first edition of *Capital*, volume I, Marx mocked the Russian populist and Slavophile, Alexander Ivanovich Herzen, together with August von Haxthausen, a German historian who wrote extensively on Russian peasant communes and land reform:[12]

> If on the continent of Europe the influence of capitalist production continues to develop as it has done up till now, enervating the human race by overwork, the division of labour, subordination to machines, the maiming of women and children, making life wretched, etc., hand in hand with competition in the size of national armies, national debts, taxes, sophisticated warfare etc., then the rejuvenation of Europe by the knout and the obligatory infusion of Kalmyk blood so earnestly prophesied by the half-Russian and full Muscovite Herzen may become inevitable. (This belletrist, incidentally, has noted that he made his discoveries on 'Russian' communism, not in Russia, but in the work of the Prussian Privy Councilor Haxthausen.) (*MEGA* II/5: 625)[13]

Here Marx did not recognize the revolutionary potentiality of Russian communes at all, dismissing Herzen's romantic optimism. At the time, agrarian communes called 'mir' or *obshchina* still existed in Russia, and there was also a group called the 'Narodoniks', who aimed for a socialist revolution against Tsarism based on these agrarian communes. Among those Russian populists,

Haxthausen's work had the most decisive impact. Nevertheless, Marx also wrote in his letter to Engels dated 7 November 1868: 'The whole business [in the Russian communal system], down to the smallest detail, is absolutely identical with the primaeval Germanic communal system.... The whole shit is breaking down' (*MECW* 43: 154). Despite his intensive engagement with Maurer in March 1868, Marx at the time did not believe that primitive communism existing in the Russian communal system – Haxthausen ([1847–52] 1972) often compared the Germanic and Russian communes[14] – could persist any longer, let alone function as a place of resistance to capitalist invasion from the West.

Marx's attitude towards Russia gradually changed, however, through his contact with the Russian populist revolutionary movement. They not only wished to translate *Capital* into Russian but also supplied him with recommendations about writings on Russia. Prompted by them, Marx even started to learn Russian in November 1869, in order to get access to direct information about Russian society. He affirmatively read Nikolay Chernyshevsky's *Outlines of Political Economy According to Mill* in summer 1870. Chernyshevsky was one of the main figures in the Narodoniks who defended the significance of *obshchina* for a Russian revolution as well as Haxthausen's work. Marx was quite impressed by Chernyshevsky's works, even attempting to translate his political testament, *Letters without an Address* into German (IISG Sign. B112: 131–52). Another indication of Chernyshevsky's influence upon Marx is that the dismissive passage on Herzen and Haxthausen disappeared in the second edition published in 1873. He instead praised Chernyshevsky's *Outlines* in the postface to the second edition: '... an event already illuminated in a masterly manner by the great Russian scholar and critic N. Chernyshevsky' (*Capital* I: 98). This modification implies that his attitude towards Russia somewhat shifted already between 1868 and 1872 (J. White 2019: 12), even if he was not yet fully convinced of the revolutionary potentialities of Russian society.

Marx also integrated the result of his new findings into the French edition of *Capital*. He emphasized the importance of this new French edition in his letter to Danielson dated 15 November 1878 about the second edition of the Russian translation of *Capital*, suggesting that 'the translator always compare carefully the second German edition with the French one, since the latter contains many important changes and additions' (*MECW* 45: 343). In the French edition of *Capital* (1872–5), Marx, for example, added a sentence in the chapter on 'primitive accumulation', in which he explicitly restricted the scope of his analysis to Western Europe:

> At the core of the capitalist system, therefore, lies the complete separation of the producer from the means of production ... the basis of this whole development is the expropriation of the agricultural producer. To date this has not been accomplished in a radical fashion anywhere except in England.... But *all the other countries of Western Europe* are undergoing the same process. (*MEGA* II/7: 634; emphasis added)[15]

Considering his remark in the letter, it is clear that Marx quite consciously modified this passage as a result of his engagement with non-Western societies.

In the same letter dated 15 November 1878, written shortly after Maxim Kovalevsky's visit to Marx in London, Marx wrote about the disputes on *Capital* in Russia:

> Of the polemics of Tschischerin and other people against me, I have seen nothing, save what you sent me in 1877 (one article of Sieber, and the other, I think, of Michailoff, both in the *Fatherlandish Annals*, in reply to that queer would-be Encyclopedist – Mr Joukowsky). Prof. Kowalewskiy, who is here, told me that there had been a rather lively polemics on the *Capital*. (*MECW* 45: 343–4)

The Russian translation of *Capital* was published in March 1872, and it was quite successful, selling 3,000 copies within a year. While Kovalevsky apparently exaggerated the scale of the polemics in Russia, the dispute that Marx referred to in this letter was initiated by a Russian Narodnik, Nikolay K. Mikhailovsky. It concerned whether socialism could be established in Russia without going through the stage of capitalism. This makes one passage in the preface to the first edition of *Capital* problematic: 'The country that is more developed industrially only shows, to the less developed, the image of its own future' (*Capital* I: 91). The central question was whether this description would apply to Russia.

Although he had written a positive review of *Capital* in 1872 and continued to cherish its importance, Mikhailovsky later expressed doubts about the applicability of Marx's historico-philosophical theory to Russia. In an article titled 'Karl Marx before the Tribunal of Mr Zhukovsky' published in the *Otechestvenniye Zapiski* in November 1877, Mikhalovsky, while defending the general theoretical validity of *Capital* from Zhukovsky, doubted that Russia needed to go through the process of capitalist development in order to achieve the socialization of labour. Referring to Marx's dismissal of Herzen in the first edition of *Capital*, he problematized this dismissive attitude towards the desperate attempt of Russians to save their suffering peasants from the catastrophic consequences of Tsarist government policies as well as of the capitalist invasion of Russia. The polemic continued when Nikolai Sieber, a passionate defender of Marx's *Capital*, replied to Mikhalovsky in the same journal, where he maintained that Marx's description of history is universally applicable, and Russia is no exception (J. White 2019: 33).

In summary, Marx himself already confronted criticism for falsely imposing a Eurocentric 'universal' law on non-Western societies in the form of these Russian critiques. Similar criticisms would be repeated many times in the 20th century. Marx attempted to respond to Mikhalovsky in November 1878.[16] In this letter to the editorial board of the *Otechestvenniye Zapiski*, Marx explicitly denied that his rejection of Herzen's Pan-Slavism immediately meant the negation of a uniquely Russian path to socialism. In order to ground his claim that Mikhalovsky misrepresents the logical structure of *Capital*, he drew upon his own treatment of Chernyshevsky in the postface to the second edition of *Capital* as well as the modified passage in the French edition, which limits the scope of his discussion of the primitive accumulation to Western Europe (*MECW* 24: 199). Marx continued to complain that Mikhalovsky had distorted his own view:

> It is absolutely necessary for him to metamorphose my historical sketch of the genesis of capitalism in *Western Europe* into a historico-philosophical theory of general development, imposed by fate on all peoples, whatever the historical circumstances in which they are placed, in order to eventually attain this economic formation which, with a tremendous leap of the productive forces of social labour, assures the most integral development of every individual producer. (*MECW* 24: 200; emphasis added)

Marx insisted upon the importance of studying particular the historical context of each society instead of taking a homogenizing approach within a pre-given schema of private and communal property system based on the European experience of the transition from feudalism to capitalism: 'Thus events strikingly analogous, but occurring in different historical milieu, led to quite disparate results.' The dissolution of communal landed property, for example, brings about different consequences depending on the historical and social context.

In this way, Marx maintained that his view was actually close to Mikhalovsky's own. However, it is unfair to take recourse to the second edition of *Capital* to justify Marx's 'true' intentions because such a view is not discernible in the first edition upon which the Russian translation was based. Mikhalovsky did not misunderstand *Capital*. On the contrary, it was Marx who changed his view after 1868 (Wada 1975: 110). In any case, Marx in the draft letter expressed his own tentative conclusion in the following manner: 'I have arrived at this result: if Russia continues along the path it has followed since 1861, it will miss the finest chance that history has ever offered to a nation, only to undergo all the fatal vicissitudes of the capitalist system' (*MECW* 24: 199). In Western Europe, the process of capitalist formation was accompanied by the transformation of peasants into proletarians, but this is not inevitable in other regions. As long as there existed no mass proletariat, Russia would not necessarily follow the same law of capitalist development. There was still a chance to avoid it, so Marx advocated for an immediate uprising in Russia.

This letter was never actually sent, and Engels found it in 1883 after his death. Marx was probably aware of the weakness of his critique of Mikhalovsky, and he was also afraid that his critique of Mikhalovsky would work negatively for the Russian populists as well as create tension with Sieber, who was a passionate supporter of his views in Russia. However, Marx was destined to return to this question in the 1880s.

III
THE LAST MARX AND HIS NEW IDEA OF COMMUNISM

Between 1879 and 1881, Marx engaged in the study of non-Western societies and polemics on the Russian revolution, which is documented in his so-called *Ethnological Notebooks*. In September 1879, Marx read Maxim Kovalevsky's *Common Landownership: The Causes, Course and Consequences of Its Decline* (1879), a large part of which is dedicated to the analysis of Indian society. In the following years, in addition to Lewis H. Morgan's *Ancient Society*, he also read *Java, or How to Manage a Colony* (1861) by James Money; The Aryan Village in India and Ceylon (1880) by John Phear; and *Lectures on the Early History of Institutions* (1875) by the historian Henry Maine. Reading these books, Marx studied how non-Europeans regulated property rights over many years until their colonization by Europeans.

For example, Marx carefully followed Kovalevsky's description about the persistent vitality of rural communes in India. According to Kovalevsky, this is explained by the fact that the 'characteristic of Indians consists of the solidity of their communal bond' (Harstick 1977: 37–8). Although systematic extermination and robbery weakened the rural communes in many places, he maintained that 'they did not completely disappear'. In the notebook, Marx highlighted the 'survival of the rural communes on a large scale'.[17] Kovalevsky distinguished 'natural causes' and 'human causes' in the process of their dissolution. If these communes would have declined anyway in the long run, communal property can be regarded as a historically transitory form, but Kovalevsky paid special attention to the human causes of their decline under British colonial rule. Marx summarized in his own words the negative impact of British colonialism upon communes in India, criticizing Kovalevsky's teacher Henry Maine because he marginalized the active role of English colonialism during the dissolution of Indian rural communes:

> The English Indian officials, and the publicists supported upon these, as *Sir H. Maine, etc.*, describe the decline of common property in the Punjab as the mere result, – in spite of the loving English treatment of the archaic form, – of economic progress, whereas they themselves are the *chief bearers* (active) of the same – to their own danger (p. 184). (Krader 1975: 394)

In this passage, Marx modified his original expression to make an even more emphatic criticism of Maine's defence of the dissolution of rural communes in India than did Kovalevsky (Wada 1975: 145). Their dissolution was not inevitable in the course of 'natural' development, and Marx was interested in the possibility of active resistance by Indian communes when they collided with the British invasion, creating a 'danger' for British rule in India. He would later repeat this point in his letter to Zasulich too in relation to Russia.

Reading various books on non-capitalist societies, Marx reflected upon the flaws in his earlier homogenizing approach and paid attention to particularities and differences among non-Western societies and their historical changes instead of simply subsuming them under the single European category of a 'feudal' or 'Asiatic' mode of production. This is visible from the fact that he explicitly criticized those European historians who imposed a Eurocentric conception of history as if its categories were universally applicable to non-European regions. For example, Marx called John Phear a 'donkey' (*Esel*) in characterizing 'the constitution of the villages' in India as 'feudal' (Krader 1974: 256).[18] Marx's comment here differs radically from his earlier statements made in the 'British Rule in India' where he had applied the Orientalist framework to India's static and passive society and was happy to let it dissolve in the name of economic progress.[19] He no longer praised the superiority of European societies or justified their colonial intervention in Asia in the name of historical progress. Kolja Lindner (2010: 34) thus concludes that 'Marx breaks with Eurocentric conception of development' in *The Ethnological Notebooks*. Kevin Anderson (2010: 237) similarly argues that the late Marx had 'created a multilinear and non-reductionist theory of history, to have analyzed the complexities and differences of non-Western societies, and to have refused to bind himself into a single model of development or revolution'. Although Marx did not elaborate on this topic in detail in his published writings, one can still discern the process by which he was 'provincializing Europe' (Chakrabarty 2010).

If Marx really reduced the entire world to the universal law of capitalist development due to his economic determinism and historicism, it would be incomprehensible why Marx had to spend so much time conducting research on non-Western and pre-capitalist societies. Rather, he explicitly acknowledged that the existence of the universal law of capitalism does not negate particularities and contingencies and refused to subsume them within a historico-philosophical theory of general development: 'By studying each of these evolutions on its own, and then comparing them, one will easily discover the key to the phenomenon, but it will never be arrived at by employing the all-purpose formula of a general historico-philosophical theory whose supreme virtue consists in being supra-historical' (*MECW* 24: 201). The real world is full of contingencies and particularities, and they cannot necessarily be analysed adequately using European categories. However, Marx's point is that universal economic categories such as 'commodity', 'money' and 'capital' objectively exist in any capitalist society regardless of our consciousness and of the historical particularities of each region. These 'economic forms' are universal as long as the capitalist mode of production exists, no matter where you are and what cultural and geographical background you have. Marx's methodological dualism is discernible here too in his abstraction of 'economic forms' from the concrete material reality of the world. Without such a universal theoretical framework, scientific investigation falls into a relativist and empiricist understanding of reality that consists of isolated particular facts and lacks the ability to reveal the historical dynamics of the capitalist development.

Of course, Marx's investigation did not stop there. He also analysed how these economic forms are intertwined with particular realities through the mediation of labour. This analysis inevitably requires paying careful attention to the differences and specificities of each society with various contingencies and discontinuities. Marx thus attempted to carefully study each society in order to discern how the contradictions between the universal law of capitalist development and its particular constellation creates not only degradation of the conditions of sustainable human metabolic interaction with nature but also a possible rupture with the capitalist system in the course of its global expansion. This kind of analysis is, however, only possible *after* the general social dynamics of capitalist development are correctly grasped, and it actually lies outside of the proper task of his critique of political economy. Although this analysis lies outside the scope of *Capital*, it does not mean that this issue is of secondary importance for Marx.

After his intensive engagement with Kovalevsky, in 1881 Marx was suddenly and unexpectedly compelled to come back to the issue of historical materialism upon receiving a request from the Russian revolutionary

Vera Zasulich. Intrigued by the polemics in Russia, Zasulich in her letter dated 16 February 1881 asked Marx directly about his real intention, so that she could publish his opinion in Russia:

> You would be doing us a very great favour if you were to set forth Your ideas on the possible fate of our rural commune, and on the theory that it is historically necessary for every country in the world to pass through all the phases of capitalist production. (Shanin 1983: 99)

It is in the letter and its drafts that one can discern how Marx's view changed in the 14 years since the publication of volume I of *Capital*. Marx's rejection of a Eurocentric view of history is clearly visible and his new vision of post-capitalist society begins to emerge.

The actual reply sent to Zasulich is quite short. This is partly because Marx was supporting the populist group People's Will in Russia, who were in opposition to Zasulich's Black Repartition. Marx knew that sending a letter to Zasulich would not profit People's Will. He simply repeated the same point he had made in his letter to *Otechestvenniye Zapiski* that the 'historical inevitability' of the law of capitalist development in *Capital* is expressly limited to the countries of Western Europe' (Shanin 1983: 100). Nevertheless, he actually wrote three drafts to answer Zasulich's question. This indicates that the question Zasulich posed was quite striking to him. This is not surprising because her question, coming from Eastern Europe, hit the problematic point in volume I of *Capital*. Zasulich asked whether such a Eurocentric view of history was really Marx's own. He thus used this opportunity to formulate his ideas based on what he had acquired through his intensive engagement with Russian and other non-capitalist countries.

In the Second Draft,[20] Marx quoted from the French edition and repeated the same point he had made in his draft letter to Mikhalovsky:

> '[o]nly in England has it (the expropriation of the agricultural producer) been accomplished in a radical manner.... All the other countries of Western Europe are following the same course' (loc. cit.). Thus [in writing these lines] I expressly restricted [the development in question] this 'historical inevitability' to 'the countries of Western Europe'. (Shanin 1983: 100)

In this draft, however, he did not refer to the possibility of a Russian revolution. Instead, he concluded: 'What threatens the life of the Russian commune is neither a historical inevitability nor a theory; it is state oppression, and exploitation by capitalist intruders whom the state has made powerful at the peasants' expense' (Shanin 1983: 104–5). However, the shift in his view of Russian society is obvious when he pointed to 'the economic *superiority* of communal property' (Shanin 1983: 104; emphasis added). This is because communal property functions as the basis of co-operative and associated labour, which was, however, being rapidly destroyed by the capitalist intrusion into Russia.

In the First Draft Marx again made the same point that Russia has 'an element of superiority over countries still enslaved by the capitalist regime' (Shanin 1983: 106). Compared to the Second Draft, what is striking is his more detailed discussion of the Russian agrarian communes as 'an archaic form'.[21] Marx cautioned that the term 'archaic' ought not have a negative connotation, stating that one 'should not, then, be too frightened by the word "archaic"' (Shanin 1983: 107). Referring to Georg L. Maurer, Marx also distinguished between 'archaic commune' and 'commune of the secondary formation' among the Germanic tribes. He argued that one of the key differences between these two types of communes was that while archaic communes carry out collective production and distributes its products directly among members, the newer (secondary) commune maintained collective property of land but allocated and distributed it among members, so that its members individually appropriated their fruits. Due to this 'dualism' of collectivism and individualism, the 'commune of the secondary formation' is at risk of decay, but the dissolution of an excessively strong communal bond also created the possibility of 'a development of individuality' (Shanin 1983: 109). According to Marx, it depends on each 'historical context' whether individualism will overwhelm collectivism and lead to the disintegration of communes, or collective regulation will remain in the process of socialization of labour, opening up a socialist path.

In Marx's opinion, the historical context was favourable for the Russian agricultural communes: 'Russia is the only European country in which the "agricultural commune" has maintained itself on a national scale up to the present day' (Shanin 1983: 110). Acknowledging that the 'commune perished in the midst of never-ending foreign and intestine warfare' in Western Europe (Shanin 1983: 107), he pointed out that the historical circumstances surrounding Russian communes in the late 19th century were quite different and unique. Unlike in India, they existed together with Western capitalism without being subjugated to its colonial rule. Furthermore, although the isolation of the communes as a 'localised microcosm' was a source of weakness, the positive fruits of the capitalist development of technologies and means of communication and transportation in the West could help overcome such isolation and enable collective labour. Marx thus maintained that there was no need to let Russia's remaining rural communes and their communal properties perish under the tidal waves of capitalist modernization and globalization that would then engulf the entire planet. The vitality of the rural communes in Russia could provide a basis for resistance against ruthless and limitless capitalist expansion. Marx affirmed Russia's potential for a communist transition without going through the historical stage of capitalism: 'The *contemporaneity* of Western [capitalist] production, which dominates the world market, enables Russia to build into the commune all the positive achievements of the capitalist system, without having to pass under its harsh tribute' (Shanin 1983: 110).

Marx did not demand the preservation of the pre-capitalist condition of the rural commune as it was but rather advocated for the development of the communes 'on their present foundations' by actively absorbing the positive outcomes of Western capitalism. Only then could they utilize this encounter with the West as a chance to establish communism in Russia. However, the remaining time was limited as the decay of the *mir* was already happening. Marx thus argued for an immediate Russian revolution: 'If the revolution takes place in time, if it concentrates all its forces to ensure the unfettered rise of the rural commune, the latter will soon develop as a regenerating element of Russian society and an element of superiority over the countries enslaved by the capitalist regime' (Shanin 1983: 116–17).

Marx's view of history changed by 1881 in that he explicitly acknowledged the power of Russian rural communes to make their own history by leaping to socialism based on existing communal property without going through the destructive process of capitalist modernization. Marx discovered the possibility of a Russian Revolution by focusing on the active elements of resistance to capitalist expansion in non-Western societies. His conclusion in the unsent letter was not an arbitrary one. In fact, Marx together with Engels expressed the same view in the preface to the second Russian edition of *The Communist Manifesto*:

> Can the Russian *obshchina*, a form, albeit heavily eroded, of the primeval communal ownership of the land, pass directly into the higher, communist form of communal ownership? Or must it first go through the same process of dissolution that marks the West's historical development? Today there is only one possible answer: If the Russian revolution becomes the signal for a proletarian revolution in the West, so that the two complement each other, then Russia's peasant communal landownership may serve as the point of departure for a communist development. (Shanin 1983: 139)

This statement is not mere lip service to their Russian readers. On the contrary, without this explicit clarification in the new preface, the publication of *The Communist Manifesto* in Russian would make people wonder even more whether Marx naively held a Eurocentric view of history. Thus, Marx and Engels cautioned that the Russian communes could not only avoid going through the capitalist stage but even demanded that they *initiate* communist development by sending 'the signal for a proletarian revolution in the West'. They recognized the active agency of Russian society as the driving motor of history.[22]

There is no need to limit this argument to Russia. The same logic can be applied to other agrarian communes existing in those areas that Marx intensively studied at that time in Asia, Africa and Latin America. Marx viewed Asian communes as agricultural rural communes of the most recent type that survived destruction through war and invasion (Shanin 1983: 108).[23] Unlike the 1850s when he still praised the 'double mission', Marx in the Third Draft much more explicitly denounced British 'vandalism' in India (Shanin 1983: 118) and its destruction of indigenous agriculture: 'The English themselves made such attempts in the East Indies; they only managed to spoil indigenous agriculture and to swell the number and intensity of famines' (Shanin 1983: 121). This has to do with his recognition with the 'element of superiority' that was being destroyed under colonial rule. Various archaic communes that remained all over the world had the same potential power, though of course to different degrees. Marx came to advocate that they could and should *actively* resist capitalism and that they possessed collective *agency* to establish socialism as a new stage of human history. In other words, they were no longer a passive object of history without their own agency to resist capitalism and create a new society. Given this transformation in the thought of the late Marx, Said was not justified in denouncing Marx as a typical 'Orientalist'.

IV
THE TRANSFORMATION OF MARX'S VISION
OF COMMUNISM

However, this is not the end of the story. The last section details what can be regarded as today's shared understanding of the late Marx, at least among Marxian scholars, thanks to Haruki Wada (1975), Kevin Anderson (2010), and Kolja Lindner (2010). Nevertheless, some scholars reject these attempts at reinterpreting the late Marx's thought to demonstrate his theoretical relevancy to contemporary capitalism. In his recent biography, published on the bicentenary of Marx's birth, the British historian Gareth Stedman Jones (2016: 569), like Anderson and Lindner, points to a 'remarkable change' in the late Marx. His overall evaluation of this shift is, however, a negative one, confining the validity of Marx's argument to the 19th century.

Stedman Jones is worth referring to in the current analysis because he is one of the few who pay attention to the key year of 1868, when Marx encountered the work of Georg Ludwig von Maurer. However, Stedman Jones is dismissive of both Maurer and of Marx's reception of his work. His intention in discussing Maurer's work becomes apparent in the concluding part of his biography, which refers to Fustel de Coulanges's refutation of Maurer in his *Origin of Property in Land* (1889). In Stedman Jones's opinion, Coulanges successfully repudiated Maurer's romantic and nationalistic idealization of the Teutonic tribes, but even before that, it was almost 'outmoded by the time of Marx's death', Stedman Jones argues, because it was not based on empirical research but mainly on 'classical or biblical' speculation – Maurer's work is based on Caesar's *Gallic Wars* and Tacitus's *Germania* – that conflates historical fact and fiction (Jones 2016: 592).[24] Marx's attraction to Maurer and to Henry L. Morgan implies that Marx's youthful 'romanticism', which according to Jones was stronger when the young Marx dreamt of becoming a poet, underwent a revival as the tide of revolution receded in the West in the 1870s, especially after the bloody defeat of the Paris Commune. He concludes that Marx's 'romantic' conclusions are not acceptable today because his interest in the agricultural rural communes reflects 'a nineteenth-century phantasm' (Jones 2016: 568). In short, Marx's analysis of non-Western and pre-capitalist societies is nothing but a nostalgic and Orientalist fiction that fetishizes the Other.

A question arises here. Is it just the nostalgic 'romanticism' of an older person to search for revolutionary possibilities in non-Western society? This kind of criticism is nothing new. As seen earlier, many scholars have argued that the old Marx lost his intellectual capacity and revolutionary hope in the West due to his severe illness: 'But there is little to show for the last decade of his life. It is a period of decline and of increasing ill-health and incapacity' (Carr 1934: 279). This is why Eric Hobsbawm (2011: 162–3) felt compelled to highlight the danger of such a reactionary characterization of the late Marx: 'The view that the older Marx lost some of the revolutionary ardour of the younger, is always popular among critics who wish to abandon the revolutionary practice of Marxism while retaining a fondness for his theory.' Confining Marx to the theory and history of the 19th century without any practical implication for today's world is a safe way to treat him within academic discourse.

Stedman Jones's claim about Marx's retreat to romanticism only makes sense if the late Marx did erroneously idealize the Russian commune. This is clearly not the case. First, his study of Russian society was based upon various studies *by Russians* that contain more empirical analysis than Maurer's, and he was aware that these communes, often accompanied by poverty and unfreedom, were rapidly decaying in the face of capitalist intrusion.[25] Second, when the real contradictions become more manifest in the peripheries of capitalism, there is nothing wrong with researching the possibility of a social revolution in Russia seriously, paying attention to its specificities. Finally, even before weakening of a revolutionary hope in Western societies after the collapse of the Paris Commune, Marx in 1868 emphasized that the revolution in England could only occur when the Irish people were liberated. Since he clearly emphasized at that time that revolutionary movements in the capitalist centre alone are not sufficient to overthrow capitalism, his engagement with non-Western societies in the 1870s and 1880s cannot simply be explained by his disappointment at the harsh reality in Western Europe and by his illness.

However, it is not adequate to respond to Stedman Jones's criticism by arguing that Marx shifted from a unilateral view to a multilinear view of history, as Kevin Anderson (2010) does. Stedman Jones does not necessarily deny this point. Rather, he dismisses this move as a form of romanticism. In addition, the claim that the late Marx significantly changed his attitude towards the possibility of Russian revolution is also not very new, as Haruki Wada (1975) and Teodor Shanin (1983) already pointed it out several decades ago. Furthermore, Marx had already studied various non-Western societies in the late 1850s and subsequently strengthened his anti-colonial and abolitionist position (Ghosh 1984). Considering these facts, Anderson underestimates Marx's intellectual ability in concluding that his final theoretical standpoint after more than 20 years is the acquisition of a non-Eurocentric and multilateral view of history. Unfortunately, this underestimation is one reason why Stedman Jones's critique appears compelling because it strengthens the impression that Marx did not achieve much after 1868. In order to refute Stedman Jones, one needs to demonstrate the late Marx's theoretical relevance to today's world. For that purpose, it does not suffice to show that Marx abandoned his earlier unilinear view of history because hardly anyone adopts such a reductionistic view today. In a word, it is necessary to show that the new theoretical scope indicated in his letter to Zasulich is larger than both Stedman Jones and Anderson assume. In fact, once this new scope is properly grasped, Stedman Jones's critique of Marx's romanticism appears trivial because the price he had to pay for his interpretation is higher: by dismissing the revolutionary character of the late Marx's theoretical engagement after 1868 altogether, Stedman Jones fails to recognize Marx's final vision of post-capitalism.

Furthermore, even if Anderson determinedly rejects the old dogma of Marxism, it is undeniable that his entire polemics pivot around a Eurocentric/ linear vs postcolonial/multilinear view of history. In a sense, they are still confined by the very traditional paradigm of historical materialism. That narrows the scope of the discussion. To put it bluntly, Marx's primary interest was *not* to establish the law of history. In other words, Marx's main theoretical task in engagement with pre-capitalist and non-Western societies was *not* to test the applicability of his law. The idea of historical materialism as an 'iron law' was strengthened by later Marxists after his death. By abandoning the paradigm of historical materialism today, one can reinvestigate what was really at stake for Marx's project in the 1880s. This requires to challenge both Eurocentrism *and* productivism.

If the conclusion of Anderson's path-breaking investigation of Marx's notebooks appears somewhat predictable, and if Stedman Jones's response ends up repeating the stereotypical criticism of Marx, it is because they only deal with *one* aspect of Marx's historical materialism, that is 'Eurocentrism', neglecting the other, that is 'productivism'.[26] The need remains for a more integral approach.

This is a decisive point. Only by looking at the problems of *both* Eurocentrism and productivism does a completely new interpretation of the late Marx become compelling. That is, not that the paths to communism became plural but that *Marx's idea of communism itself* significantly changed in the 1880s as a result of his conscious reflection upon earlier theoretical flaws and the one-sidedness of historical materialism. The transcendence of capitalism and the establishment of communism was apparently the main theoretical and practical task throughout Marx's life, but this problem has never been discussed in the previous literature in relation to his letter to Zasulich. Actually, Marx in 1881 utilized this opportunity to formulate his vision of non-class society based on what he had learned through his intensive study of rural communes.[27]

The possibility that Marx's idea of communism transformed in his late years is hinted at by the substantial delay in publishing volumes II and III of *Capital*. Even though Engels strongly desired their completion as soon as possible, Marx conducted his research in natural science and pre-capitalist societies. The riddle remained for a long time why Marx spent so much time on these topics instead of finishing *Capital*. Indeed, it looks as if Marx, under pressure and with worsening health, wanted to escape from the painful job of writing *Capital*. For example, Ludo Cuyvers (2020: 33) commented on Marx's 'erratic' interest rather negatively: 'Marx's perfectionism, combined with a wide and seemingly erratic interest in knowledge – which also explains his studies in the 1870s of Russian, mathematics, geology, ethnography, etc. – most likely contributed much to *Capital* being left unfinished.' However, such an explanation is not compelling as long as Cuyvers does not investigate the actual content of these notebooks. In contrast, I argue that Marx did not completely lose his intellectual capacities and passion despite his serious health condition, and he strove to learn new things *in order to complete Capital*.[28]

The hint for solving this riddle is Marx's theory of metabolism as the central pillar of his political economy. In other words, his intensive engagement with ecology and pre-capitalist/non-Western societies was indispensable in order to deepen his theory of metabolism. Marx attempted to comprehend the different ways of organizing metabolism between humans and nature in non-Western and pre-capitalist rural communes as the source of their vitality. From the perspective of Marx's theory of metabolism, it is not sufficient to deal with his research in non-Western and pre-capitalist societies in terms of communal property, agriculture and labour. One should note that agriculture was the main field of Marx's ecological theory of metabolic rift. In other words, what is at stake in his research on non-Western societies is not merely the dissolution of communal property through colonial rule. It has ecological implications. In fact, with his growing interest in ecology, Marx came to see the plunder of the natural environment as a manifestation of the central contradiction of capitalism. He consciously reflected on the irrationality of the development of the productive forces of capital, which strengthens the robbery praxis and deepens the metabolic rift on a global scale. Marx also studied radically different ways of social organization of metabolic interaction between humans and nature in precapitalist and non-Western societies from an ecological perspective.

It is through the mediation of this concept that these two research fields prove to be closely connected to each other. Here one also needs to recall why the late Marx started studying pre-capitalist and non-Western societies: he was prompted to deal with Maurer's analysis of the Teutonic communes after reading Carl Fraas's ecological work in the beginning of 1868. Fraas's discussion on Teutonic 'mark association' (*Markgenossenschaft*) and its sustainable agriculture draws upon Maurer's analysis. In other words, *the issues of ecology and pre-capitalist societies are connected from the very beginning.* While Marx's ecological interest certainly existed before reading Fraas, his work expanded its scope, so that Marx not only found a 'socialist tendency' in his critique of excessive deforestation but also came to pay more attention to the concrete ways of metabolic interaction in pre-capitalist societies from an ecological perspective.[29] He now recognized that cooperative production and corresponding communal property in those societies are related to more sustainable form of human metabolic interaction with their environment. In fact, Marx found the same 'socialist tendency' in Maurer's *Einleitung*, referring to radical 'egalitarianism' in the Teutonic communes:

> The second reaction is to look beyond the Middle Ages into the primitive age of each nation, and that corresponds to the socialist tendency, although these learned men have no idea that the two have any connection. They are therefore surprised to find what is newest in

what is oldest – even equalitarians, to a degree which would have made Proudhon shudder. (*MECW* 42: 557)

By characterizing both Maurer and Fraas with the same 'socialist tendency', Marx implied a connection between sustainability and social equality. But how are they related?

According to Maurer, 'mark association' is a transitory period from nomadic to agricultural life.[30] In contrast to Justus Möser, who insisted upon the existence of private property as the basis of the *Mark*, Maurer emphasized the fundamentally communal character of the Germanic form of property, as Marx documented in his notebook:

> Individual yards without any cooperative ties ... did not originally exist at all. *Family and tribal cooperatives* rather already existed before the permanent settlements, *they already settled as such*, and did not only come into being since their settlement. (*MEGA* IV/18: 544; emphasis in original)

Teutonic tribes treated the land as communal property, so land did not belong to any single individual. They carefully arranged the regular allocation of the land so that its fruits were equally distributed without the concentration of wealth in the hands of the few.

> Only that part of the field that could be cultivated was divided, and at first only as much as was needed to feed the members. All other land not capable of cultivation or not necessary for cultivation remained in an undivided community. This included first of all the *forests, pastures, heaths, moors, etc.* (p. 84) Also in Gaul and the other conquered provinces only the already cultivated and tilled land was subjected to division. In contrast, many *fields* and *forests* (silva indivisa, silva communis) etc. remained there in undivided community. p. 87. (*MEGA* IV/18: 554; emphasis in original)

Marx carefully traced passages of Maurer's *Einleitung* in which he explained not only that mark associations secured common pasture for grazing but also that they introduced a lottery in the process of allocating land among members:

> In all these communities, the mark village with all the gardens, fields, meadows, pastures and forests was in the undivided community of the cooperative members, as already at the time of Caesar. The individual received his share of the common mark, as far as it was distributed, for a number of years, but only for cultivation and use. The share of each in the gardens, fields and meadows was allotted to him and was called the whole share. After the expiration of the years designated for special use, all shares reverted to the community and were then remeasured and again distributed to the individuals. The pastures were used jointly and

the community's needs and taxes were met from the yield of the forests, but what remained was distributed among all the members in proportion to the lots assigned to them. (6, 7). (*MEGA* IV/18: 545)

This was an effective way to prevent the formation of relationships of domination and subjugation among its members due to the concentration of wealth. This communal treatment of lands marks a clear contrast to *Latifundium*, the system of large landed property worked with slave labour in ancient Rome, although Maurer also traced how under the influence of the Roman law this lottery system was gradually replaced by the system of private property (Maurer 1865: 98).

At the same time, since land did not belong to anyone, the commune also prevented particular individuals from arbitrary usage of land as well as sales of its products, guaranteeing the sustainability of social production. Maurer wrote about the closed character of *Markgenossenschaft* in those passages in *Geschichte der Dorfverfassung* to which Fraas referred to in his *Ackerbaukrisen und ihre Heilmittel*:

> The export of wood from the village commons and sale outside the commons was forbidden in free communities as well as in manorial communities... For the same reason, houses, barns, warehouses and other buildings were not allowed to be sold from the village commons.... The same prohibition applies to the export of manure or dung, straw, hay and other fodder, then brooms and other products of the village.... The same also applies to the sale of fish and crabs caught in the village.... In the same way, the fruits and animals raised in the village should be consumed as much as possible in the village itself or the products should at least be processed there. Therefore, the pigs fattened in the village should not be sold outside it.... For the same reason, the crops and wines grown in the village should also be ground, baked, eaten and drunk in the village itself, which then led to socage rights in many villages. (Maurer 1865: 313–16)[31]

Being familiar with Justus von Liebig, one immediately realizes that such a strong system of communal regulation over lands guaranteed the circulation of soil nutrients, which realized sustainable agriculture by securing the 'law of replenishment'. Fraas (1866: 209) thus concluded, based on Maurer's analysis, that 'the first Teutonic village formation already always followed the law of the necessity of increasing soil power' instead of robbery of the soil. In this way, Maurer and Fraas agreed that communal regulation was indeed founded upon both sustainability *and* social equity. These two aspects were closely linked in Marx's notebook in March 1868. Underlying them was the radically different metabolic relation between humans and nature within the Teutonic commune compared to the capitalist mode of production.

Marx's characterization of Fraas and Maurer with the same 'socialist tendency' indicates the central importance of 'social equity' and 'sustainability' in his socialist project. This insight is essential to understanding the late Marx. Certainly, Marx was well aware that pre-capitalist communes were more egalitarian than modern society before reading Fraas and Maurer. He characterized communal primitive societies even as 'indigenous communism' (*Capital* III: 970), but he did not sufficiently take its ecological dimension into account and often dismissed its exclusionary and steady character. His re-evaluation of 'indigenous communism' after 1868 is related to his deepening ecological awareness, a tendency that continued until his reception of Morgan's 'communism in living' in 1880–1.[32]

Marx wrote to Engels in the same letter dated on March 1868 about his surprise at finding 'what is newest in what is oldest' (*MECW* 42: 557). For Stedman Jones, this simply represents a further manifestation of his romanticism. However, this statement was made in March 1868. Why had Marx suddenly become 'romantic' only a few months after the publication of volume I of *Capital*? He must have been quite passionate about the possibility of a socialist revolution with the publication of his masterpiece. Paying attention to the interconnectedness of sustainability and social equality, the story looks quite different. It becomes clear why Marx started to simultaneously study pre-capitalist societies and natural sciences after 1868. With this in mind, one can imagine that Marx must have been surprised again to 'find what is newest in what is oldest' when he studied Russian agricultural communes in the 1870s. In fact, Marx reread Maurer's *Einleitung* together with two other books by him in 1876.[33]

In the Third Draft of his letter to Zasulich, Marx refers to Maurer again when he repeated the same point about the perpetual character of the Germanic communes that he had made in the letter of March 1868:

> More importantly, however, we find the clear imprint of this 'agrarian commune' so clearly traced on the new commune which emerged from it that Maurer was able to reconstruct the former while working to decipher the latter. The new commune – in which cultivable land is privately owned by the producers, while the forests, pastures, waste ground, etc., still remain communal property – was introduced by the Germans to all the countries they conquered. Thanks to certain features borrowed from its prototype, it became the only focus of popular life and liberty throughout the Middle Ages. (Shanin 1983: 118–19)

The '*natural vitality*' (Shanin 1983: 118) of the agrarian communes was so strong that while other communes collapsed and disappeared due to war and invasion, these agrarian communes survived for a long time as the 'new commune' in Germany at Marx's time.[34] In Russia, the 'agrarian commune' existed more solidly, so it could be utilized as the foundation for a socialist revolution.

However, one should note that this is only one part of the story. Marx was interested in how non-Western viability could be utilized in Western Europe for the purpose of leaping to a post-capitalist society. It is not an exaggeration to say that the main purpose of his long engagement with the rural communes and natural sciences is not the revolutionary potentiality of those non-Western communes but rather *their meaning for Western Europe*. Since Zasulich suddenly asked him, he was compelled to 'descend from pure theory to Russian reality' (Shanin 1983: 112), writing directly about the path of the Russian Revolution in his letter. Yet Marx was originally studying pre-capitalist and non-Western societies because their 'natural vitality' was inspiring even for the sake of envisioning a post-capitalist society in Western Europe. This might sound contradictory, but in order to comprehend this point, one needs to analyse Marx's letter to Zasulich from an ecological perspective.

As discussed earlier, Marx was forced to critically reconsider his earlier theoretical scheme in the 1860s due to the ecological degradation brought about by capitalist development. Metabolic rift is nothing but a manifestation of the degradation of 'natural vitality' through the capitalist destruction of communal production and property. In this sense, class formation and environmental degradation have the same root cause. This made Marx doubt whether Western Europe, with its 'higher' productive forces, was in fact superior to non-Western and pre-capitalist societies. His use of the expression 'economic superiority' in the letter in relation to pre-capitalist communes, confirms this doubt. For example, even though the productive forces of mark association are much lower than Western capitalist societies, they are 'superior' in that they had a much more conscious regulation of their metabolic interaction with nature, simultaneously securing social equality and soil fertility. This was the source of their long-lasting natural vitality. Since productive forces of capital do not provide the foundation for a post-capitalist society, Marx was prompted to argue that Western societies need to learn different ways of organizing metabolism from these agrarian communes. This attitude marks an absolute departure from his earlier Eurocentrism.

Through this learning process, Marx's analysis of Western capitalism and his vision of post-capitalist society changed significantly over time. One can detect a hint of this theoretical modification in his letter to Zasulich, when Marx pointed to the 'crisis' of capitalism in Western Europe:

> Today, [capitalism] faces a social system which, both in Western Europe and the United States, is in conflict with science, with the popular masses,

and with the very productive forces that it generates – in short, in a crisis. (Shanin 1983: 106)

It is noteworthy that Marx discussed the crisis of capitalism not just in relation to working-class movements but also to 'science' and 'productive forces'. Marxism–Leninism almost naturally read the meaning of this crisis in a productivist fashion to mean that the further development of science and technology would ultimately blow capitalism sky high and terminate the crisis of capitalism. However, when considering Marx's ecology in *Capital*, such a productivist reading of the passage is no longer compelling.

If one reads this passage in the letter from the perspective of Marx as a *critic* of productivism, its meaning becomes the opposite one. Capitalism finds itself in the middle of perpetual crises because it is exposed to harsh criticisms from 'science' that capitalism has become an obstacle to the sustainable development of productive forces. For example, Liebig and Fraas maintained that, under capitalism, new technologies would only reinforce robbery of nature. Its unsustainable character is far from the 'rational' application of modern science in Liebig's and Fraas's sense. These ecological scientists questioned the legitimacy of capitalism as a progressive social system. In other words, they unveiled the failure of the modern Promethean project to subjugate and manipulate nature. In contrast, when natural science is brought into the service of such a capitalist purpose, it inevitably turns out to be 'exploitative' and 'wasteful'.

As Marx argued in volume III of *Capital*, the earth is a common property, and this irrational treatment of the earth is unacceptable: 'The entire spirit of capitalist production, which is oriented towards the most immediate monetary profit – stands in contradiction to agriculture, which has to concern itself with the whole gamut of permanent conditions of life required by the chain of human generations' (*Capital* III: 754). The capitalist system of private property, including the private ownership of land, legitimizes the arbitrary usage of what belongs to private individuals. Furthermore, the damage caused by the selfish misbehaviour of atomized individuals would spill over to the whole society in a disproportionate manner. By contrast, Marx demanded that 'the associated producers, govern the human metabolism with nature in a rational way' (*Capital* III: 959). This is also exactly what Liebig and Fraas demanded, which amplified the crisis of capitalism.

How does this crisis end? Marx continued to argue in the First Draft that the crisis of capitalism 'will end through its own elimination, *through the return of modern societies to a higher form of an "archaic" type of collective ownership and production*' (Shanin 1983: 107; emphasis added). Here again, 'what is newest is what is the oldest'. Marx did not argue that communism would be established after pushing capitalist development as far as possible. Surprisingly, he now claimed that Western Europe needed to 'return' to pre-capitalist society. Is this romanticism? The real question becomes what exactly Western Europe needs to integrate from non-Western societies so that they can 'return' to a higher form of an archaic type.

We are finally approaching the theoretical core of the late Marx. As seen earlier, after Marx speculated about the interrelation of 'sustainability' and 'social equality' in the 1870s, he took Zasulich's question as an opportunity to formulate a new form of rational regulation of human metabolism with nature in Western Europe and the United State. In doing so, he amended his presupposition about the superiority of Western societies for ecological reasons. Now he insisted that Western societies revive the superior elements of archaic communes in the process of establishing communism. In other words, what is important is not the pluralization of the historical course and the provincialization of Europe but that Marx significantly modified his vision of communism as such.

The expression of returning to a 'higher form' is influenced by Henry L. Morgan's *Ancient Society*.[35] Morgan argued that the main aim of modern Western society has become a 'mere property career'. He also argued for returning to the democratic communal life at a higher scale in order to rehabilitate liberty, equality and fraternity in 'a higher form'. Marx noted the following passage:

> The time will come, nevertheless, *when* human intelligence *will rise to the mastery over property*…. A *mere property career is not the final destiny* of mankind. The *time which has passed away since civilisation* began is but a fragment (and very small) of the past duration of man's existence; and *but a fragment of the ages yet to come. <u>The dissolution of society bids fair to become the termination of a career of which property is the end and aim; because such a career contains the elements of self-destruction</u>*…. It (a higher plan of society) *will be a revival, in a higher form, of the liberty, equality and fraternity of the ancient gentes.* (Krader 1974: 139; emphasis in original)

Although Morgan did not elaborate in detail what this higher form of society should look like, he repeatedly used the term 'communism in living' in opposition to a capitalist society, especially focusing on the sindiasmic family of the Iroquois.[36] It is noteworthy that Marx was adding comments in brackets on their similarity with Russian rural communes:

> *Communism in living* seems to have originated *in the necessities of the consanguine family*, to have been continued in the punaluan, and transmitted to the *syndyasmian* under the American aborigines, with whom it remained a practice down to the epoch of their discovery –

(and the *South Slavonians*? and even *Russians* to a certain degree?) (Krader 1974: 115; emphasis in original)

Marx repeated the same point by inserting comments in brackets again, indicating that he was influenced by Haxthausen's analysis of the abolition of serfdom in Russia in 1861:

> *forming a communal household [like South Slavonians and. in some degree: Russian peasants* before and after serf emancipation] in which the *principle of communism in living was practised.* This fact proves *that the family was too feeble an organisation* to face alone the hardships of life. (Krader 1974: 116; emphasis in original)

Compelled by the hardship of the natural environment, Russians had to rely on mutual aid instead of Darwinian natural selection based on *bellum omnium contra omnes*, a view that Peter Kropotkin put forward later.

Through the communal regulation of lands and property, communism in living basically repeated the same cycle of production every year. That is, its long-lasting traditional way of production realized a *stationary and circular economy without economic growth*, which Marx once dismissed as the regressive steadiness of primitive societies without history. This principle of steady-state economy in agrarian communes is radically different from capitalism that pursues endless capital accumulation and economic growth. Marx was aware of this point as he noted Caesar's description of the Teutonic communes in Morgan's *Ancient Society*:

> For agriculture they have no zeal, and the greater part of their food consists of milk, cheese, and flesh. No man has a definite quantity of land or estate of his own: the magistrates and chiefs every year assign to tribes and clans that have assembled together as much land and in such place as seems good to them, and compel the tenants after a year to pass on elsewhere. They adduce many reasons for that practice – the fear that they may be tempted by continuous association to substitute agriculture for their warrior zeal; that they may become zealous for the acquisition of broad territories, and so the more powerful may drive the lower sort from their holdings; that they may build with greater care to avoid the extremes of cold and heat; that some passion for money may arise to be the parent of parties and of quarrels. It is their aim to keep common people in contentment, when each man sees that his own wealth is equal to that of the most powerful.[37] (Krader 1974: 413)

Communal regulation and restriction were necessary for people to reproduce themselves, and the development of productive forces was quite slow as technologies remained 'persistent', as Marx noted: 'The arts by which savages maintain their lives are remarkably persistent' (Krader 1974: 143). Nevertheless, the low and stationary level of productive forces was not because they were 'barbaric' and 'ignorant' of science. Even if they had possibilities of increasing productive forces or working for longer hours, these communities *intentionally* avoided doing so. In this way, they consciously prevented the concentration of power which generates the relationship of domination and subjugation (Clastres 1989).

Marx's call for returning to the archaic type in the letter to Zasulich is not a careless and arbitrary one. By the 1880s Marx recognized that the persistent stability of communes without economic growth is the underlying foundation for realizing sustainable and egalitarian metabolic interaction between humans and nature. This marks a clear contrast to Marx's previous negative comments on the stationary state and invariability of the Asian communes in the 1850s and even in volume I of *Capital*. This is how these two seemingly irrelevant research fields of natural science and communes prove tightly interwoven in Marx's abandonment of his earlier historical materialism. After 14 years of research, he concluded that sustainability and equality based on a steady-state economy is the source of power to resist capitalism, and it would be no wonder should Russian communes skip the capitalist stage to arrive at communism. It is also this kind of sustainability and equality of the steady-state economy that Western societies consciously need to 'return' as a higher form of the archaic type as a solution to the crisis of capitalism. In short, Marx's last vision of post-capitalism is *degrowth communism*.

Marx's call for a 'return' to non-capitalist society demands that any serious attempt at overcoming capitalism in Western society needs to learn from non-Western societies and integrate the new principle of a steady-state economy. Marx's rejection of productivism is *not* identical with the romantic advocation of a 'return to the countryside'. In fact, he repeatedly added that the Russian communes would have to assimilate the positive fruits of capitalist development. The critique of productive forces of capital is not equivalent to a rejection of all technologies. Western Europe must not abandon all of its own previous development, and it is the combination of the fruits of capitalist development and the principle of steady-state economy in non-Western societies that would allow Western societies to leap communism as a higher stage of the archaic communes. This revival of communism in living as degrowth communism is utterly different from the productivist approach of traditional Marxism in the 20th century, but it is consistent with Marx's recognition that the further development of 'productive forces of capital' does not lead to the establishment of a post-capitalist society.

The idea of degrowth communism is opposite to the young Marx's Prometheanism and nor is it quite identical with the standpoint of 'ecosocialism' that he put forward in *Capital* through his reception of Liebig's critique of robbery agriculture. Ecosocialism does not exclude the possibility of pursuing further sustainable economic growth once *capitalist* production is overcome, but degrowth communism maintains that growth is not sustainable nor desirable even in socialism. Accordingly, degrowth communism is also different from Engels's vision of post-capitalism. Engels believed that once capitalism was transcended, ecosocialism would fully emancipate productive forces for the sake of the working class: socialism realizes 'constantly accelerated development of the productive forces, and ... a practically *unlimited increase* of production itself' (*MECW* 25: 269; emphasis added). By contrast, in 1881 Marx distanced himself from the endorsement of endless growth, and pointed to the need for social equality and sustainability based on the principle of 'communism in living'. This great transformation is comparable to a *coupure épistémologique* in the Althusserian sense (Althusser 2005).

Only after Marx completely abandoned productivism and Eurocentrism was he able to fully integrate the principle of a steady-state economy as the foundation of the future society. The degrowth communism that Marx was hinting at in the last stage of his life was not an arbitrary interpretation, considering his passionate endorsement of the Narodiniks. In addition, the idea of 'endless growth' belongs to the 20th century under the hegemony of GDP growth as if there were not substantial limits to human economic activities (Schmelzer 2017). In the 19th century, the impossibility of endless growth was rather keenly felt beneath the optimistic tone about future technological progress. For example, Ricardo and Malthus were aware of the insurmountable natural limits in his discussion on the law of diminishing returns. More famously, John Stuart Mill (1849: 326) argued for the 'impossibility of ultimately avoiding the stationary state' due to the falling rate of profit in advanced capitalism.[38] Furthermore, anarchist communists such as Peter Kropotkin and Eliseé Reclus, together with ecosocialists such as William Morris, also envisioned a future society that is not based upon endless material consumption (Ross 2015: 104).[39] In this sense, Marx's high evaluation of the Paris Commune as well as of rural communes in non-Western societies is not exceptional.[40]

However, it is this possibility of Marx as a degrowth communist that even Engels was unable to recognize despite their close collaboration. State socialism in the Soviet as well as social democracy in Western Europe in the 20th century also dismissed such communal forms of regulating social production and reproduction. Instead, both aimed at modernization and economic growth. As a result, Marx's view of history was reduced to a linear and productivist one – ironically quite similar to the capitalist goal of endless GDP growth, marginalizing environmental issues and suppressing other emancipatory imaginaries.[41] Many still believe that Marxism and degrowth are incompatible (Schwartzman 1996). Marxists stick to the belief in the need for further growth in order to improve the living conditions of the working class. Even those ecological Marxists who clearly distance themselves from such a naïve vision of abundance are hesitant to accept the idea of degrowth, as Michael Löwy (2020) writes: 'Since these and similar measures of draconian austerity risk being quite unpopular, some of them … play with the idea of a sort of "ecological dictatorship".[42]

However, it was John Bellamy Foster, referring to Lewis Mumford's 'basic communism', who pointed to the need for the transition of high-income countries to a steady-state economy in order to avoid ecological breakdown:

> Therefore, society, particularly in rich countries, must move towards a steady-state economy, which requires a shift to an economy without net capital formation, one that stays within the solar budget. Development, particularly in the rich economies, must assume a new form: qualitative, collective, and cultural – emphasizing sustainable human development in harmony with Marx's original view of socialism. (Foster 2015: 9)

Nevertheless, Foster, who usually passionately defends the consistency of Marx's ecology, does not make it clear whether a steady-state economy is compatible with Marx's own view of post-capitalism. By comprehending the theoretical potentialities of the late Marx there emerges a new path to enrich a Marxist vision of an alternative to capitalism. The final chapter attempts to push Marx's unfinished critique of capitalism beyond *Capital* by revisiting it from the perspective of degrowth communism in order to envision a post-scarcity economy in the Anthropocene.

NOTES

1   Engels's notebooks are just a few volumes in the *MEGA* while Marx's 200 notebooks occupy a large part of its fourth section. Marx's financial difficulties are not the only reason he had to visit the British Museum to gather materials necessary for writing *Capital*. The young Marx had already acquired the habit of studying new materials by taking notes.

2   These marks and lines are deleted in Engels's edition as well as in the recent English translation of the manuscript (Marx 2015).

3   Another reason for this cleaning up was that Engels used the text dictated by Eisengarten in order to edit Marx's manuscript.

4   Foster (1998: 171) puts forward another interpretation of these passages that is more sympathetic to Marx and Engels. While Foster treats Marx as a consistent ecologist since the 1840s, I argue that Marx became an ecologist only in the 1860s.

5 Fraas is hardly known today, but his strong influence is discernible in the work of George Perkins Marsh's *Man and Nature* (1864), a work that contributed to launching the modern conservation movement in the USA.

6 The fourth section of the *MEGA* is now published online. The notebook 'London. 1868' that contains excerpts from Jevons's book can be found here: https://megadigital.bbaw.de/exzerpte/detail.xql?id=M0004847&sec=1 (accessed 7 September 2022).

7 Emphasizing the importance of cheap coal for British capitalism, Jevons referred to Liebig: 'Civilisation, says Baron Liebig, is *the economy of power*, and our power is coal' (Jevons 1865: 105; emphasis in original).

8 Joel Kovel (2001: 80) doubts that Marx recognized the intrinsic value of nature. According to Kovel, Marx treated nature merely as humanity's instrument, but this kind of criticism can be refuted by remarks recorded in Marx's notebooks. Kovel instead endorses an aesthetic intuition of nature's value, as suggested by Jakob Böhme, which marks a retreat into idealism and romanticism. This is a typical tendency within environmentalism, as exemplified by deep ecology (Næss 1973), when it attempts to go beyond anthropocentrism.

9 In the manuscript for volume II of *Capital*, Marx also came up with another example from stock farming about the constant pressure to shorten the time required for rearing, quoting from William Walter Good's *Political, Agricultural and Commercial Fallacies* (1866). There exists a biological limit to the shortening of production time, which leads to the premature slaughter of animals (*Capital* II: 313). Marx referred to Robert Bakewell's attempt to shorten the time for rearing through his careful breeding 'system of selection', lamenting the growing sickliness of animals raised for profit (*MEGA* IV/18: 232).

10 Thierry Drapeau (2017) argues that Marx already took an anti-colonial and abolitionist position to be an essential component of anti-capitalism in 1853, after he was inspired by Ernest Jones's denunciation of British imperialism and his argument about the need for the working class to support resistance movements against British rule abroad. Influenced by Jones, Marx, Drapeau argues, condemned British rule in India as an example of 'the inherent barbarism of bourgeois civilization' in his famous article 'The Future Results of British Rule in India'. However, Drapeau does not give a convincing account of the passage from Marx already quoted about the progressive character of British imperialism. Furthermore, Engels argued even more explicitly in his speech on Poland in 1847 that 'a nation cannot become free and at the same time continue to oppress other nations' (*MECW* 6: 389). If Marx were so dramatically influenced by Richard Jones in the beginning of the 1850s through their collaboration, Engels must have had a much stronger influence upon Marx's view of anti-colonialism already in the 1840s.

11 As discussed here, I disagree, although it is true that Marx did not elaborate on these points in published writings. At the same time, I agree with his discussion on Marx's history consisting of 'History 1' and 'History 2'. Such a conception constitutes his methodological core as discussed here.

12   Marx's evaluation of Haxthausen was also quite negative. He wrote in 1858 that 'we shall have proof of the full extent to which the worthy Privy Councilor Haxthausen has allowed himself to be hoodwinked by the [Russian] "authorities" and by the peasants those authorities have trained' (*MECW* 40: 346).

13   This English translation is taken from J. White (2019: 8).

14   Haxthausen assumed that Russian communes differ from Germanic ones, but he emphasized the similarities of the two types of communes throughout his analysis.

15   This modification is not reflected in the standard English translations.

16   It is generally assumed that Marx's letter to the *Otechestvenniye Zapiski* editorial board was written in November 1877 soon after the publication of Mikhalovsky's article. But the expression in the letter to Danielson dated 15 November 1878, 'the other, I think, of Michailoff', indicates that Marx was not really familiar with Mikhalovsky's claims until then.

17   These passages are not available in English translation of the excerpts published in Krader (1975).

18   Marx distanced himself from Kovalevsky in this point as the latter also applied 'feudalism in the West European sense of the term' to India. Marx pointed out that Kovalevsky misses that fact that 'serfdom', the essential component of feudalism, does not exist in India (Krader 1975: 383).

19   Hans-Peter Harstick thus wrote: 'Im ganzen plädiert Marx für eine differenzierte Betrachtung der asiatischen und europäischen Geschichte und zielt seine Argumentation gegen eine zu starke Generalisierung des Feudalismusbegriffs und überhaupt gegen die simple Übertragung von am Modell Westeuropas entwickelten Strukturbegriffen auf indische oder asiatische Verhältnisse' (Harstick 1977: 13).

20   Here I follow Hinada (1975) who argued that the order of writing these three drafts was actually Second, First, and Third.

21   Once Marx argued that 'the Asiatic or Indian property forms everywhere mark the beginning' (*MECW* 42: 547), but he corrected his view here.

22   Wada (1975: 206) highlighted the difference between Marx and Engels. Marx was more passionate about the possibility of a Russian revolution than Engels. Engels wrote in 1875 that

> the possibility undeniably exists of raising this form of society to a higher one ... without it being necessary for the Russian peasants to go through the intermediate stage of bourgeois small holdings. This, however, can only happen if, before the complete break-up of communal ownership, a proletarian revolution is successfully carried out in Western Europe, creating for the Russian peasant the preconditions requisite for such a transition, particularly the material things he needs. (*MECW* 24: 48)

But in the Russian edition of the *Manifesto* the initiative lies in Russia, although the Russian preface was written by Engels. Wada finds evidence for Marx's intervention here. Marx and Engels clearly shared the view that Russia could follow the non-Western path to socialism at that time, but Engels emphasized the need for a Western proletarian revolution as a condition for the success of Russian revolution. After Marx's death, Engels also judged that the time for a Russian revolution based on the agricultural communes had already passed.

23 Marx wrote: 'The "rural commune" may also be found in Asia, among the Afghans, etc. But it everywhere appears as the most recent type – the last word, so to speak, in the archaic formation of societies' (Shanin 1984: 119).

24 This is not entirely the case. Marx was greatly inspired by Maksim M. Kovalevsky, and he is of a younger generation than Maurer and Morgan, and Kovalevsky did not solely focus on 'outdated' philological study. Stedman Jones intentionally marginalizes the importance of Marx's extensive notebook on Kovalevsky, only mentioning his work in a short single paragraph. This is unfair. In addition, as Kolja Lindner (2010: 36) argues, Marx's conceptual approach 'has not lost all relevance', even if some of his analysis of the Russian rural communes is based on erroneous information. For example, with regard to the section titled 'Forms Which Precede Capitalist Production' in the *Grundrisse*, its description has also been criticized for its inaccurate historical assumptions about Asian, Roman and Germanic societies. Once the theoretical aim become clear, it is not necessary to abandon Marx's insight due to some errors in terms of historical facts. As Ellen M. Wood has argued:

> Marx was indeed seriously wrong in his historical observations, for reasons having less to do with his own shortcomings than with the existing state of historical scholarship at the time of his writing the *Grundrisse*; but the edifice he constructed on the foundation of this faulty knowledge reveals the power, not the weakness, of historical materialism as he conceived it, which pushed him beyond the limitations of existing scholarship. (E. Wood 2008: 79)

However, the late Marx went further. Marx was not studying these regions simply to recognize the specificity of capitalism but also to comprehend the revolutionary vitality of these non-Western communes, which compelled him to rethink the revolutionary path in the West as well.

25 In the bibliographic list made in 1881, Marx listed 115 books that he found important. In Marx's bookshelves, there were 67 books in Russian.

26 Not only Anderson and Stedman Jones, but also Kolja Lindner (2010) and Marcello Musto (2020) do not pay attention to Marx's treatment of ecological issues in their discussion of his engagement with non-Western societies. As a result, they all tend to reduce the theoretical importance of Marx's notebooks to a tool for replying to questions and criticisms posed by post-colonial studies.

27 In this sense, unlike Stedman Jones's assumption, Marx's recognition of the vitality of Russian communes as a place of resistance against capital is by no means equal to 'idealizing' communal society. In fact, in his letter to Zasulich, Marx did not call for a return in the Western countries to rural agrarian communes nor uncritically endorse their rural life. Marx was always concerned about the exclusive, patriarchal and conservative characteristics of traditional

communes. As far as I know, only Masami Fukutomi (1970: 172) insists that the actual content of the letter to Zasulich has to do with Marx's formulation of post-capitalist society in Western Europe. However, he did not elaborate on this in detail.

28 As indicated earlier, Marx wrote the manuscripts for volume II of *Capital*, which are now available in *MEGA* II/4.3 and II/11. Marx prepared eight manuscripts for volume II of *Capital* and the last one was written in the first half of 1881, using the same paper as his letter to Zasulich. In terms of the content, Marx in the eighth manuscript largely solved the remaining problems of volume II, especially with regard to the reproduction scheme (*MEGA* II/11). Stedman Jones (2016) does not refer to this manuscript either, in order to give impression that Marx in the 1880s had already completely lost his intellectual capacity and fell into romantic nostalgy.

29 Notably, Liebig also discussed pre-capitalist society in his critique of robbery praxis (Liebig 1862), but Marx did not pay attention to it and did not make excerpts on these relevant sections in 1864, which indicates the expansion of his interest after 1868 (Saito 2017).

30 Marx later made excerpts from Maurer twice in the 1870s. This indicates how important Maurer was for him. Although unpublished, it would be necessary to investigate these later notebooks to trace the shifts in Marx's interests in more detail.

31 Marx also read Maurer's *Geschichte der Dorfverfassung* in 1876. It would be necessary to examine these excerpts in order to more concretely discuss Marx's interest in Maurer's work.

32 As Tomonaga Tairako (2016) points out, there is also a change in Marx's conception of property in the Teutonic communes after having read Maurer's book compared with the *Grundrisse*. Such a shift needs to be reexamined from an ecological perspective.

33 These excerpts will be published in *MEGA* IV/24.

34 Maurer insisted that some aspects of these agrarian communes remained even into the 19th century:

> Folgt aus dem zu Cäsars Zeiten bei allen Germanen, insbes. auch den Sueven 25 geltenden jährlichen Wechsel des Besitzes u. den jedes Jahr neuerdings wieder vorgenommenen Anweisungen v. Grund u. Boden (Cäsar IV, I, VI, 22.), noch zu Tacitus Zeit (Germ. c. 26. arva (das Ackerland) per annos mutant\wechseln sie jährlich, et superest ager (u. Gemeindeland bleibt übrig, d.h. eine gemeine, unvertheilte Mark.)), in Deutschland hier 30 u. da bis auf unsre Tage fortgedauert. (*MEGA* IV/18: 544)

35 According to Andrzej Walicki (1969: 189), Marx's letter to Zasulich also follows Chernyshevsky's. The 'reasoning of Marx bears much resemblance to Nikolay Chernyshevsky's *Critique of Philosophical Prejudices against the Communal*

Ownership of the Land'. This is another important source of his inspiration, which Wada (1975) summarizes.

36   In this context, Haxthausen also compared the Russian agrarian commune with existing communism in his *Zustand*. It was Chernyshevsky who strongly influenced Marx to pay attention to Haxthausen through his review of the book and of the revolutionary potentials of Russian communes in the 1870s.

37   As Caesar argued in the following paragraph, even the existence of wasted lands was intentional because it was meant to show the power of a commune to other people:

> It is the greatest glory to the several states to have as wide deserts as possible around them, their frontiers having been laid waste. They consider this the real evidence of their prowess, that their neighbors shall be driven out of their lands and abandon them, and that no one dare settle near them; at the same time they think that they shall be on that account the more secure, because they have removed the apprehension of a sudden incursion.

38   Marx was highly critical of Mill, and he never discussed Mill's 'stationary state'. The comparison here is simply meant to indicate that the idea of a steady-state economy was not entirely alien to classical political economy. Chernyshevsky's *Outlines of Political Economy According to Mill* does not deal with Mill's discussion of the steady-state economy either, so it is unlikely that Marx's engagement with the book in 1870 contributed to changing his view of Mill's prediction about the future of capitalism.

39   One thing that Ross (2015: 77) highlights and this book cannot analyse in detail with regard to the post-capitalist imaginary is Marx's encounter with the Paris Commune, which was 'enormously generative' for his thinking. It is necessary to examine more carefully how his experience altered his frame of perception and opened up a new field of the possible. Ross argues furthermore that Marx's attraction to the Russian *obshchina* was because he found there the traces of the primary communism observed in the Paris Commune.

40   Kristin Ross (2015: 104) proposes the concept of 'anarchist communism', which is quite similar to what I call degrowth communism in this book.

41   As Ross (2015: 78) points out, Marx added in the second German edition of *The Communist Manifesto* published in 1872 that 'the working class cannot simply lay hold of the ready-made state machinery and wield it for their own purpose' (*MECW* 23: 175). This remark indicates that his experience of the Commune prompted him to rethink his earlier strategy of state centralization.

42   One exception is the open endorsement of degrowth and Marxian economics by Max Koch (2019), but he simply uses Marx's critique of endless capital accumulation as an inspiration for his degrowth theories without asking whether degrowth is compatible with Marx's own view.

7

The Abundance of Wealth in Degrowth Communism*

In the 'Paralipomena' (or side notes) to *On the Concept of History*, Walter Benjamin (2003: 393) once criticized the Marxist conception of labour for its characteristic 'exploitation of nature'. In an attempt to overcome the Promethean vision of revolution, Benjamin famously wrote:

> Marx says that revolutions are the locomotive of world history. But perhaps it is quite otherwise. Perhaps revolutions are an attempt by passengers on this train – namely, the human race – to activate the emergency brake. (Benjamin 2003: 402)

The metaphor of the 'emergency brake' is more important than ever today. In the face of ecological disasters, environmentalism starts to demand radical systemic change by ending limitless economic growth in order to terminate the ceaseless exploitation of humanity and the robbery of nature. In short, today's emergency brake implies a call for degrowth.[1]

Marxism has been, however, unable to adequately respond to this call for degrowth. Even those eco-Marxists who are critical of productivism are reluctant to accept the idea of degrowth, which they believe is politically unattractive and ineffective. Instead, they stick to the possibility of further sustainable growth under socialism, once the anarchy of market competition under capitalism is transcended (Vergara-Camus 2019). Thus, even after the idea of ecosocialism has softened the long-lasting antagonism between

---

*A part of this chapter draws on material from 'Primitive Accumulation as the Cause of Economic and Ecological Disaster', in *Rethinking Alternatives with Marx*, ed. Marcello Musto (New York: Palgrave, 2021), 93–112. Published with permission. The content is significantly modified, enlarged and updated for the current book.

Green and Red, there remains a significant tension between ecosocialism and degrowth. The situation is changing, however. One of the most important advocates of degrowth, Serge Latouche (2019: 65), has accepted the idea of ecosocialism as a basis for degrowth, advocating the need 'to propose forms of politics in a way that is coherent with the objectives of the ecosocialist project for the next era'. Considering the fact that degrowth is often conceived as the third path alternative to both capitalism and socialism,[2] there has been a remarkable shift in recent years among the proponents of degrowth in a clearly *anti-capitalist* direction. This opens up a space for new dialogues with Marxists, who have been critical of degrowth's ambiguity in terms of its compatibility with the market economy. It is worth investigating further whether 'socialism without growth' (Kallis 2017) and 'ecosocialist degrowth' (Löwy et al. 2022) are compatible with Marx's own vision of post-capitalism.

Based on Marx's last idea of 'degrowth communism' as discovered in the previous chapter, this chapter attempts to fully sublate the long-lasting antagonism between Red and Green and create a new space for reviving Marx's theoretical legacy in the Anthropocene. Since Marx was not able to elaborate on degrowth communism, it is necessary to revisit the unfinished project of *Capital* *retrospectively*, from the perspective of degrowth communism, to update its contents. This is an attempt to go beyond *Capital* in order to concretize his final vision of post-capitalism. The key for such a reconstruction is the 'negation of the negation', discussed in one of the most famous passages in volume I of *Capital*. This is a passage to which Marx paid careful attention, demonstrated by the fact that he modified the passage between the second and the third edition of *Capital*.

This chapter starts with Marx's theory of 'primitive accumulation' as the first negation of a radical transformation of human metabolic interaction with nature. While previous literature on primitive accumulation tends to focus on its destructive impact on human life, Marx's theory of metabolism deals with its negative effects on nature too. By fully appreciating the theoretical scope of Marx's discussion of primitive accumulation of capital, one can more concretely envision from an ecological perspective the second negation as the re-establishment of the original unity of humans and nature on a higher scale (I). Marx's theory of primitive accumulation also shows that capitalism is ultimately a social system that constantly increases *scarcity* rather than creating an abundance of wealth through its incessant increase of productive forces. In order to understand this paradoxical point, one needs to revisit his concept of 'wealth' in the opening passage of volume I of *Capital*. The very beginning of Marx's critique of political economy reveals the problems of the narrow conception of wealth in capitalist categories that reduce various dimensions of reality to a simple logic of value and thus destroys the richness of society and nature (II). Marx argued that this narrow capitalist conception of wealth inevitably turns out to be incompatible with the material conditions for a sustainable development of human metabolism with nature. Through this critique of the category of capitalist wealth, the Marxian understanding of 'abundance' will be reconfigured in a non-consumerist and non-productivist way. This reconceptualization and reinvention of wealth allows us to reconsider various passages related to abundance and wealth in an utterly new and more consistent manner. This includes Marx's discussion of the abundance of 'common wealth' (*genossenschaftlicher Reichtum*) in the *Critique of the Gotha Programme*. Although it is elaborated in the most famous description of communism in Marx's writings, ecosocialists often suppressed this well-known passage precisely because the passage looks Promethean. However, by correctly understanding the 'paradox of wealth', it is possible to interpret the passage in a non-productivist manner (III). Such a new interpretation ultimately solves the fundamental problem that Marx did not answer in *Capital*, namely, how to repair the 'irreparable rift' in humanity's metabolic interaction with their environment in a post-capitalist society. Degrowth communism as a post-scarcity future without economic growth aims to reduce the 'realm of necessity' and expand the 'realm of freedom' without necessarily increasing productive forces (IV).

I
PRIMITIVE ACCUMULATION AS THE CAUSE OF ECONOMIC AND ECOLOGICAL DISASTER

Marx maintained that the typical example of the historical process of 'primitive accumulation' of capital as the precondition for capitalist development can be found in the 'enclosure' movement in England. In contrast to Adam Smith's narrative about the formation of the capitalist economy having been initiated by industrious capitalists who saved money and carefully invested it to increase it, Marx argued that primitive accumulation of capital was a violent and bloody process of separation forcefully 'divorcing the producer from the means of production' (*Capital* I: 875). As David Harvey (2005: 149) succinctly summarizes, primitive accumulation 'entailed taking land, say, enclosing it, and expelling a resident population to create a landless proletariat, and then releasing the land into the privatised mainstream of capital accumulation'. After losing means of production and subsistence under the monopoly of lands by the few, peasants were turned into precarious wage-labourers for whom selling their own labour power was their only means to acquire money necessary for living. This process of primitive expropriation continues even today as it 'not only maintains this separation, but reproduces it on a constantly extending scale' (*Capital* I: 874), increasing the misery of the working class.

While it is important to highlight the destructive impact of this violent process upon direct producers and how it worsened their living conditions, one needs to recall that Marx defined 'labour' as a conscious mediating activity of the incessant metabolism between humans and nature.[3] From this perspective, primitive accumulation as the separation of the original unity of the producers from their objective conditions of production encompasses great transformations in the life of workers *and* in their relationship with nature.[4] In fact, Marx, in the *Grundrisse*, highlighted the formation of a historically peculiar chasm between humans and nature due to primitive accumulation of capital. He wrote:

> It is not the *unity* of living and active humanity with the natural, inorganic conditions of their metabolic exchange [*Stoffwechsel*] with nature, and hence their appropriation of nature, which requires explanation or is the result of a historic process, but rather the separation between these inorganic conditions of human existence and this active existence, a *separation* which is completely posited only in the relation of wage labor and capital. (*Grundrisse*: 489)

In pre-capitalist societies, as Marx noted, humans retained their 'unity' with nature. Certainly, slaves and serfs were dominated and exploited by the master and the lord. They were unfree and even treated like things. In other words, they were reduced to a part in the objective conditions of production and reproduction next to cattle. However, this way of existence, in spite of an apparent lack of freedom, also prevented the formation of a chasm in their metabolism with nature. As the master does not let cattle starve to death, the satisfaction of the basic needs of slaves and serfs was more or less guaranteed in precapitalist societies. In short, the reduction of their existence to a part of inorganic nature like cattle ironically realized what Marx called 'original unity between the worker and the condition of labourer' (*MECW* 33: 340).

The dissolution of this original unity is a precondition for the commodification of labour power in order to realize full-scale commodity production. Only when the overwhelming majority of means of subsistence become commodities are they forced to sell their labour as commodities.[5] What underlies this historical process is the 'separation' in the metabolism between humans and nature that is unique to modern capitalist society.[6] As a result of this alienation from nature, labour as the mediation of human interactions with nature came to be carried out in a totally differently manner – now the entire production process is thoroughly reorganized for the purpose of maximal capital valorization – so that the expenditure of human labour and human metabolic exchanges with nature also begin to take on an utterly different form. This transformation exerts a powerful influence not only on the economic but also on the ecological sphere. Due to the mediation of labour, different organizations of social labour and the corresponding reorganization of the metabolism between humans and nature in capitalism do harm to *all* kinds of wealth. Samir Amin (2018: 85) puts it thus: 'Marx concludes his radical critique in *Capital* with the affirmation that capitalist accumulation is founded on the destruction of the bases of all wealth: human beings and their natural environment.' Stefania Barca also points to the close interrelationship between the degradation of living conditions and that of the natural environment through primitive accumulation: 'From a historical-materialist perspective, the working class, or proletariat, and metabolic rift originate from a unique, global process of violent separation of people from their means of subsistence, which also disrupts the biosphere. The ecological crisis is thus a direct consequence of class making' (Barca 2020: 42).

In arguing for re-establishing the 'original unity' in the future society beyond this alienating separation from nature under capitalism, Marx was consistent with his theory of metabolism: 'The original unity can be re-established only on the material foundation which capital creates and by means of the revolutions which, in the process of this creation, the working class and the whole society undergo' (*MECW* 33: 340). In addition, his remark on the 'negation of the negation' in volume I of *Capital* logically corresponds to this reconstitution of the 'original unity' as a process of overcoming the antagonistic separation in the metabolic exchange between humans and nature. However, to clarify what needs to be re-established in communism, it is first necessary to grasp more carefully what had to be destroyed in the formation of capitalism through the dissolution of the 'original unity' between humans and nature. To put it bluntly, it is the 'wealth' of society and nature that is severely impoverished under capitalism. It may sound paradoxical to claim that capitalism destroys wealth despite the magnificent increase in productive forces it generates. Indeed, our society is filled with an excess of commodities. However, this poverty in plenty constitutes the 'paradox of wealth' (Foster and Clark 2020: 152).

II
Marx's Concept of 'Wealth' and the True Beginning of *Capital*

To understand this paradox, it is first necessary to adequately comprehend the Marxian category of 'wealth'. Here, the beginning of *Capital*, volume I, functions as a useful reference point. Although written in a logical manner that starts with the analysis of the 'commodity', the description at the beginning of *Capital* presupposes the historical process of primitive accumulation of capital.

With this historical presupposition in mind, one notices that the opening passage already hints at the fundamental contradiction of capitalism created by the historical chasm in the metabolic exchange between humans and nature. Marx began his discussion of the commodity by writing:

> The wealth of societies in which the capitalist mode of production prevails appears as an 'immense collection of commodities'; the individual commodity appears as its elementary form. Our investigation therefore begins with the analysis of the commodity. (*Capital* I: 125)

It is certainly true that *Capital* starts with the 'analysis of the commodity', but John Holloway demands that we pay attention to its true beginning. The subject of the first sentence, which is not the 'commodity' but the 'wealth' (*Reichtum*) of societies (Holloway 2015: 5). The verb is also important: the wealth of societies 'appears' (*erscheint*) as an 'immense collection of commodities' in capitalism. The verb 'appear' implies that wealth and commodities 'are' (being = *Wesen*) actually not identical, and in fact, the majority of wealth in non-capitalist societies does not 'appear' as commodities as long as non-capitalist wealth is produced, distributed and consumed without the mediation of market exchange. Only under certain social relations does the wealth of societies 'appear' as the commodity, or in Marxian terminology, the product of labour receives a 'commodity form'. Distinguishing *Wesen* and *Erscheinung*, Marx proceeded in a manner that is true to his own method of analytical dualism of *Stoff* and *Form* from the very beginning of *Capital*. According to this view, 'wealth' is the material aspect of the product of labour, while 'commodity' appears as its economic form determination.

The non-identity between wealth and commodity contains a fundamental tension, although they appear identical in capitalism. Karl Polanyi ([1944] 2001) once warned that 'land', 'labour' and 'money' are 'fictitious commodities' that must not be completely commodified and subjected to the dictates of the market. Otherwise, says Polanyi, social reproduction will be seriously threatened because they do not properly function under the logic of commodity exchange. These three categories can be considered typical forms of 'wealth' that are incompatible with full commodification under capitalism. Yet Marx's concept of 'wealth' is even broader than Polanyi's and includes other kinds of products of labour. His intention might be difficult to grasp at first because the contemporary image of 'wealth' is often reduced to its capitalist form so that being wealthy (*reich*) usually signifies having a lot of money and real estate. However, wealth does not have to be understood this way. As Holloway (2015: 5) argues, the German term *Reichtum* can be translated to mean 'richness' because *reich* means 'rich'. Of course, 'being rich' can mean the possession of a large sum of monetary wealth. Yet it also has broader connotations, such as richness in taste and smell, experience of life and nature. Thus, its noun *Reichtum* can be understood as a broader category of richness than monetary wealth, once it is possible to remove the capitalist constraint imposed upon it.

This is not an arbitrary claim. Marx wrote in the *Grundrisse* about the vast possibilities of non-capitalist wealth, saying:

> In fact, however, when the limited bourgeois form is stripped away, what is wealth other than the universality of individual needs, capacities, pleasures, productive forces etc., created through universal exchange? The full development of human mastery over the forces of nature, those of so-called nature as well as of humanity's own nature? The absolute working out of his creative potentialities, with no presupposition other than the previous historic development, which makes this totality of development, i.e. the development of all human powers as such the end in itself, not as measured on a predetermined yardstick? ... In bourgeois economics – and in the epoch of production to which it corresponds – this complete working-out of the human content appears as a complete emptying-out, this universal objectification as total alienation, and the tearing-down of all limited, one-sided aims as sacrifice of the human end-in-itself to an entirely external end. (*Grundrisse*: 488)

Marx considered the richness of culture, skills, free time and knowledge as the wealth of societies. In other words, the wealth or richness of societies cannot be measured by an ever-greater quantity of commodities produced and their monetary expressions, but rather by the full and constant development and realization of the potentialities of human beings. The full and all-round development of human capacities and creative potentialities is, however, heavily constrained under capitalism because they are always measured on a 'predetermined yardstick', namely, how much use they can be for profit-making. Capitalist production sacrifices social wealth under 'total alienation' and the 'complete emptying-out' of human activities by imposing 'an entirely external end' upon producers solely for the sake of capital valorization. Marx problematized this tendency of capital as the *impoverishment of social wealth* under the accumulation of an 'immense collection of commodities'. Against this tendency, he maintained that the full realization of human creative potentialities requires stripping away the 'bourgeois form' of wealth as commodity.

The wealth of society is not limited to social wealth. Marx also used the expression 'natural wealth' (*natürlicher Reichtum*) to designate the natural and material conditions of production and reproduction. For example, he wrote in volume I of *Capital*:

External natural conditions can be divided from the economic point of view into two great classes, namely (1) natural wealth in the means of subsistence, i.e. a fruitful soil, waters teeming with fish, etc., and (2) natural wealth in the instruments of labour, such as waterfalls, navigable rivers, wood, metal, coal, etc. (*Capital* I: 535)

The richness of nature in the form of land, water, and forests is obviously indispensable for human flourishing as means of subsistence and production as well as for a healthy life. The abundance and quality of natural wealth provided by the earth surely counts as the fundamental 'wealth' of all societies: 'The earth is the reservoir, from whose bowels the use-values are to be torn' (*MECW* 31: 465). This statement is consistent with Marx's recognition of the essential contribution of nature to the production process: 'Labour is not the source of all wealth. Nature is just as much the source of use values (and it is surely of such that material wealth consists!) as labour' (*MECW* 24: 81).

However, out of the commodification of social and natural wealth, there arises an increasing tension between 'wealth' and 'commodity' because commodities focus one-sidedly on the value of the labour product and marginalize that which does not possess value because the 'predetermined yardstick' does not properly function for them. This tension is visible in terms of nature. On the one hand, natural forces are thoroughly exploited by capital as 'free gifts': 'Natural elements which go into production as agents without costing anything, whatever role they might play in production, do not go in as components of capital, but rather as a free natural power of capital' (*Capital* III: 879). Nature enters the labour process and aids in the production of commodities together with workers but does not enter the valorization process as it is not a product of labour. Nature is free, and capital seeks to utilize its power as much as possible. Capital's treatment of nature strengthens the destruction and squandering of the richness of nature in favour of capital's incessant valorization. Nevertheless, nature remains the material 'bearer' of wealth as well as value. Wealth is often something that capital does not create by itself (capital creates neither knowledge and culture nor land and water), and wealth has its own characteristics and dynamics that are independent of and incompatible with capital's aims. Consequently, as use-value is subordinated to exchange value under the logic of capital's valorization that is blind to its own material substance, the contradiction manifests as metabolic rift.

On the other hand, nature is increasingly commodified because wild nature is worthless when left as it is. Its commodification, however, occurs by dissolving the abundance of social and natural wealth. Enclosure dissolved the commons, commodifying lands and expelling the people living on them. Nature was devastated after the expulsion from the land of peasants who had taken care of it. Capitalist farmers sought only short-term profit without taking good care of the soil. Quoting various reports, Marx in volume I of *Capital*, especially in the French edition, also pointed to the fact that the most fertile lands in Scotland were totally laid waste after the enclosure. These lands were actually intentionally left wasted for the sake of a more profitable usage:

> Immense tracts of land, much of which is described in the statistical account of Scotland as having a pasturage in richness and extent of very superior description, are thus shut out from all cultivation and improvement, and are solely devoted to the sport of a few persons for a very brief period of the year. (*Capital* I: 894)

Apparently, this transformation of land usage had an immense impact on the daily life of people in the countryside, as seen in the general impoverishment of people's living conditions through the second enclosure in the 18th century. While the agricultural revolution based on the Norfolk four-course system significantly increased the production of wheat, peasants lost access to common lands and forests, where they used to raise pigs with acorns, collect mushrooms, woods and fruits, and catch birds. Living in the countryside, they also had access to the river to catch fish and for fresh water. Now driven into the city, they almost completely lost access to such natural wealth and could consume much less meat. Even if they remained in the countryside, their previous daily activities in the commons were now criminalized as acts of trespass and theft. Furthermore, enclosure concentrated lands in the hands of fewer capitalist farmers. As they hired peasants only during the busy season and fired them thereafter, the farming villages disappeared, and the small vegetable gardens maintained by the villagers ceased to provide fresh vegetables for their dinner tables. As it was no longer clear by whom and how the vegetables sold in the market were grown – they might, for example, be smeared with excreta of cattle and poultry – they became inedible without cooking, and fresh salads disappeared from the menu.

In addition, all family members had to work in the factories to make a living in the city. The loss of access to the commons significantly increased the financial burden on households because now they had to buy their means of subsistence from the market. They began working in factories from an early age, so children were not able to attend school. They could not acquire basic cooking skills at home or during the festivals and ceremonies of the farming villages, where they were served free and luxurious meals. Even if they acquired and maintained some cooking skills, working-class families in the city were no longer able to buy expensive meat and other ingredients but only the cheap potatoes that were sold on the street. Consequently, the traditional English recipes based on ingredients available to the rural villages became useless for working-class families living in the large cities.

Finally, English food culture was destroyed by adulteration. Marx documented this custom in volume I of *Capital*, explaining the adulteration of bread with alum, soap, pearl ash and chalk based on Arthur Hill Hassall's work *Adulterations Detected*. Adulteration was quite widespread as a way of reducing production costs and of providing cheap food for the poor working class: the worker 'had to eat daily in his bread a certain quantity of human perspiration mixed with the discharge of abscesses, cobwebs, dead cockroaches and putrid German yeast, not to mention alum, sand and other agreeable mineral ingredients' (*Capital* I: 359). The problem was not limited to bread. Hassall reported various adulterations in milk, butter, vegetables, and beer (Hassall 1861). These foods were apparently unhealthy and unsafe, but since they were cheap, the poor working class had to depend on them in order to fill their hungry stomachs.

In short, culture, skills and knowledge were impoverished, the financial burden for working-class families increased, and the quality of natural wealth was sacrificed as the world became increasingly commodified. From the perspective of capital, the same situation looks very different, however. Paradoxically, this is how capitalism took off, emancipating the full potentialities of productive forces, as workers became more and more dependent on commodities in the market.

This tension between wealth and the commodity is what underlies 'Lauderdale's paradox' (Daly 1998: 22). James Maitland, the eighth Earl of Lauderdale pointed to an inverse relationship between 'public wealth' and 'private riches'. Namely, if one increases, the other decreases. According to Lauderdale, this is a paradox that Adam Smith overlooked in believing that the 'wealth of nations' is an aggregate sum of 'private riches'. He demonstrated this point by introducing the third concept of 'public wealth'.

Lauderdale defined 'public wealth' as consisting 'of all that man desires, as useful or delightful to him'. In contrast, 'private riches' has an additional character, in that it comprises 'all that man desires as useful or delightful to him; which exists in a degree of scarcity' (Lauderdale 1819: 57–8). The difference between the two concepts is 'scarcity'. Expressed in Marxian terms, 'public wealth' possesses 'use-value', but not 'value' because it exists abundantly in nature and is available to everyone that wishes to use it in order to satisfy their needs. Public wealth includes the air, common lands, forests, and river water. 'Public wealth', however, can be turned into 'private riches' when it becomes scarce. Lauderdale argued that scarcity does not necessarily arise from the exhaustion of natural resources. It is often *intentionally created* by constructing gates and by forcefully expelling people from the land. In other words, land, water and food are artificially made scarce so that they can function to augment the 'private riches' of their owners expressed in monetary terms (as well as the wealth of nation that comprises the sum total of individual riches). The obvious problem here is, as Lauderdale argued, that the increase in private riches is inevitably accompanied by the augmentation of scarcity in a society, that is, the decrease in the free and abundant common public wealth for the majority of the people. As seen in the primitive accumulation of capital, common lands and forests were gated and became inaccessible and scarce for peasants, which increased the misery of the masses and the devastation of the natural environment, while this process of creating artificial scarcity amplified private riches of the few.

While there obviously exists 'natural' scarcity of arable lands and available water independently of humans, scarcity under capitalism is different. It is a 'social' one. This social scarcity is also an 'artificial' one because the richness of social and natural wealth was originally abundant in the sense that they did not possess value and were accessible to members of the community. Scarcity must be *created* by thoroughly destroying the commons, even if this brings about a disastrous situation for the many in an economic and ecological sense. Lauderdale provided cases where edible products were intentionally thrown away and arable lands were deliberately wasted, so that market supply could be limited in order to keep commodity prices high. Herein manifests the fundamental tension between wealth and the commodity, and this is the 'paradox of wealth' that marks the historical peculiarity of the capitalist system (Foster and Clark 2009).

It is in this sense of the term that the opposition of 'abundance' and 'scarcity' needs to be discussed. No matter how much capitalism increases the productive forces, this paradox of wealth does not disappear but is rather intensified due to the constant creation of artificial scarcity. At the same time, it is not necessary to maximize productive forces in order to overcome this kind of scarcity. A post-scarcity society could be founded upon the reconstruction of the abundance of the commons found in pre-capitalist societies on a higher scale, through the transcendence of artificial scarcity. Marx's degrowth communism aims to repair the 'irreparable' metabolic rift and to rehabilitate the non-consumerist 'abundance' of the social and natural wealth beyond the Lauderdale paradox through the 'negation of the negation'.

III

THE NEGATION OF THE NEGATION AND THE ABUNDANCE IN COMMUNISM

Primitive accumulation of capital, as the first negation, dismantles individual property as founded on the labour of its proprietor. In contrast, communism aims at the 'negation of the negation', through which the 'expropriators are expropriated' and the original unity of humanity and nature is re-established. Marx wrote in the famous passage that appeared in volume I of *Capital*:

> But capitalist production begets, with the inexorability of a natural process, its own negation. This is the negation of the negation. It does not re-establish private property, but it does indeed establish individual property on the basis of the achievements of the capitalist era: namely co-operation and the possession in common of the land and the means of production produced by labor itself. (*Capital* I: 929)

Interestingly, this passage was modified in the third edition based on Marx's comments in his own copy of the second edition of *Capital*. He modified this passage in the 1880s shortly before his death. In the second edition, he still wrote:

> It is the negation of negation. This re-establishes individual property, but on the basis of the acquisitions of the capitalist era, i.e., on co-operation of free workers and their possession in common of the land and of the means of production produced by labour. (*MEGA* II/6: 683)

Marx modified this passage in the third edition in order to more explicitly distinguish between 'private property' and 'individual property'. What does this change imply?

In the *Civil War in France* published in 1871, Marx came back to this problem of individual property in communism with the same logic in his mind, as is seen clearly in the expression 'the expropriation of the expropriators':

> ... the Commune intended to abolish that class-property which makes the labour of the many the wealth of the few. It aimed at the expropriation of the expropriators. It wanted to make individual property a truth by transforming the means of production, land and capital, now chiefly the means of enslaving and exploiting labour, into mere instruments of free and associated labour.... If co-operative production [*genossenschaftliche Produktion*] is not to remain a sham and a snare; if it is to supersede the Capitalist system; if united co-operative societies are to regulate national production upon a common plan, thus taking it under their own control, and putting an end to the constant anarchy and periodical convulsions which are the fatality of Capitalist production – what else, gentlemen, would it be but Communism, 'possible' Communism? (*MECW* 22: 335)

The Paris Commune was an attempt to 'make individual property a truth' through the negation of the negation. As explained in the second half of the quoted passage, 'co-operative production' aims to regulate social production through common planning and communal control of the means of production. In this way, it allocates individual shares among members through democratic and communal management. This is how 'individual property' is rehabilitated. In a sense, individual property is equivalent to 'co-operative' (*genossenschaftlich*) property. For Marx, this is 'possible Communism'. Here he seems to have established the concept of 'individual property' as clearly distinguished from 'private property', which led to the modification of the relevant expression in the third edition of *Capital*.[7]

Yet the Paris Commune was not the only reason for this modification. Considering the fact that he modified the relevant passage on post-capitalist society in the 1880s for the third edition of *Capital*, it needs to be examined in relation to his view on the rural communes elaborated in his letter to Zasulich. Marx wrote as follows in his letter to Zasulich when he returned to this topic:

> The peoples among which it reached its highest peak in Europe and [the United States of] America seek only to break its chains by replacing capitalist with co-operative production [*la production coopérative*], and capitalist property with a higher form of the archaic type of property, that is, communist property. (Shanin 1984: 102)

Here again, Marx argues that developed capitalist societies need to return to a 'higher form of the archaic type' after transcending the system of private property in capitalism. In a sense, he went further here than in the *Civil War in France*. What Marx demanded in the *Civil War in France* as the 'united co-operative societies' is now specified in that they should be realized through the principles of a steady-state economy imminent to the archaic commune. 'Communist property' is not just based on 'co-operative' (*genossenschaftliche*) production, but also seeks to revive a communal form of property in Mauer's sense of 'mark cooperative' (*Markgenossenschaft*). As discussed in the previous chapter, the archaic commune was characterized by the 'dualism' of collectivism and individualism. This dualism needs to be rehabilitated in Western Europe not by going back to isolated small-scale production in rural communes but by transforming the large-scale production developed under capitalism into co-operative production. Private property is turned into individual property, but its content can be better expressed as 'co-operative' (*genossenschaftliche*) property as the higher form of the archaic type. Indeed, this understanding will prove decisive in interpreting the term 'communal wealth' (*genossenschaftlicher Reichtum*), which appears in Marx's famous description of communism in the *Critique of the Gotha Programme*.

There is another important term worth paying attention to in the passage on the 'negation of the negation' in *Capital*. The term 'land' used in the quote above is *Erde* in German. It also means 'earth'. In fact, Marx used this expression to designate natural resources other than land too. Marx argued that the earth (natural resources) must be controlled 'in common', meaning that it must be used cautiously, so as to care for the interests of future generations. Marx wrote in volume III of *Capital*, in which the term *Erde* is translated as 'earth', saying:

> From the standpoint of a higher socioeconomic formation, the private property of particular individuals in the earth will appear just as absurd as the private property of one man in other men. Even an entire society, a nation, or all simultaneously existing societies taken together, are not the owners of the earth. They are simply its possessors, its beneficiaries, and have to bequeath it in an improved state to succeeding generations, as *boni patres familias*. (*Capital* III: 911)

The earth is what the current generation succeeded from the previous one, and they are obliged to pass it on to the next generation without destroying it. This, however, is what capitalism cannot fulfil due to its one-sided focus on the endless augmentation of private riches. By contrast, the perspective of sustainability is essential for enriching social and natural wealth, especially because capitalism is a system of profit-making, private property and anarchic competition. Against the logic of commodification by capital, communism seeks the *commonification* of wealth. However, this statement must not be understood as the full realization of human desire to enjoy the world's riches without any constraint. Marx was well aware that the availability of natural wealth is inevitably limited and cannot be arbitrarily utilized for satisfying unlimited human desires. This is why the 'negation of the negation' transcends artificial scarcity, but not scarcity as such.

This ecosocialist insight must be contrasted with the popularized vision of socialist society where material abundance is supposed to become almost infinite, so that the working class can enjoy the same luxurious life without natural limits. In *Self-Ownership, Freedom and Equality*, G. A. Cohen describes abundance under communism in this manner. According to Cohen's left-wing libertarian interpretation, Marx's vision of an equal society is still trapped in 'certain radical bourgeois values' (Cohen 1995: 116). He held 'a conviction that industrial progress brings society to a condition of such fluent abundance that it is possible to supply what everyone needs for a richly fulfilling life' (Cohen 1995: 10). Infinite material abundance is the condition of material equality for all, but such a productivist negation of natural limits in the future society is absolutely incompatible with the planetary boundaries that exist independently of human will. Thus, Cohen concludes that it is no longer possible to 'sustain Marx's extravagant, pre-green, materialist optimism', and it is necessary to 'abandon the vision of abundance' (Cohen 1995: 10).

Cohen is surely right in emphasizing the need to reject the extravagant and productivist vision of social and economic equality in socialism. Yet this rejection does not require abandoning the 'vision of abundance' in Marx's critique of capitalism. In fact, Marx's critique of political economy would be inconsistent and mediocre if he so naively endorsed 'bourgeois values'. In order to avoid this confusion, one needs to understand the category of 'scarcity' as an inherently socio-historical category. According to Marx, scarcity has two aspects, social and natural. Natural scarcity cannot be entirely overcome, no matter how much technology may advance. By contrast, social scarcity increases in capitalism in the face of unlimited capital expansion. Everything is by definition scarce in capitalism: *'capital always is* – and, this cannot be stressed strongly enough, it *always must remain,* as a matter of inner systemic determination – insuperably *scarce,* even when under certain conditions it is contradictorily *overproduced'* (Mészáros 2012: 304; emphasis in original). The more capital develops for the sake of overcoming self-imposed scarcity, the more destructive the entire system becomes, but the abundance it generates can never eliminate the artificial scarcity created by capital itself. This is the fundamental paradox of wealth in capitalism.

Cohen assumes that Marx envisioned the abundance of a post-capitalist society based on that of capitalist society, that is, the abundance of 'private riches' for all beyond natural scarcity. If this were the case, Marx's claim would be inconsistent with his demand in the *Grundrisse* for the 'stripping away' of the bourgeois form of wealth. It is much more consistent to assume that what needs to be overcome in a post-capitalist society is not scarcity as such but the 'objective conditions of socially specific *capital-accumulating scarcity'* (Mészáros 2012: 269; emphasis in original). Nevertheless, there is a certain ambivalence in the *Grundrisse* too, where Marx explicitly stated that the 'full development of human *mastery over the forces of nature,* those of so-called nature as well as of humanity's own nature' (*Grundrisse*: 488; emphasis added). Such a statement can be easily presented as strong proof of Marx's naïve endorsement of bourgeois values, especially because he also praised the 'great civilising influence of capital' (*Grundrisse*: 409).[8]

However, as discussed in previous chapters, Marx's treatment of nature became more nuanced in the 1860s. With this ecosocialist understanding of *Capital* in mind, it is worth revisiting Cohen's critique of Marx's concept of abundance. As evidence of Marx's productivist vision of abundance, Cohen refers to the famous passage in his *Critique of the Gotha Programme,* where he wrote about the future communist society:

> In a higher phase of communist society, after the enslaving subordination
> of the individual to the division of labour, and thereby also the antithesis
> between mental and physical labour, has vanished; after labour has
> become not only a means of life but life's prime want; after the
> productive forces have also increased with the all-round development
> of the individual, and *all the springs of common/co-operative/communal*

wealth [genossenschaftlicher Reichtum] flow more abundantly – only then can the narrow horizon of bourgeois right be crossed in its entirety and society inscribe on its banners: From each according to his abilities, to each according to his needs! (*MECW* 24: 87; emphasis added)

Cohen is not alone here. Herman Daly (1991: 196) similarly argued that for Marx, the 'materialistic determinist, economic growth is crucial in order to provide the overwhelming material abundance that is the objective condition for the emergence of the new socialist man. Environmental limits on growth would contradict "historical necessity"'. In fact, this passage from the *Critique of the Gotha Programme* appears to be identical with Marx's naïve endorsement of infinite wealth thanks to the development of productive forces and the continuation of the absolute domination over nature in the *Grundrisse*. It is no coincidence that ecosocialists such as Foster and Burkett do not refer to this famous passage, although this is one of the rare cases where Marx directly discussed the future society.

However, considering the ecosocialist background to Marx's *Capital*, it would be inconsistent to read this passage as a celebration of productivist domination over nature to achieve an abundance of wealth in the future society. In addition, Cohen's attribution of left-wing libertarianism and its principle of self-ownership to Marx fails to explain why the latter thought this abundance of wealth in communism could overcome 'the narrow horizon of bourgeois right'.[9] When Marx demanded that the metabolic exchange between humans and nature should be regulated more rationally by freely associated producers free from the pressure of capital accumulation, he did so precisely because he was aware of the fact that the universal metabolism of nature consists of various biophysical processes that cannot be socially transcended even in socialism. The persistent existence of natural scarcity demands a more conscious regulation of social and natural wealth, even in a post-capitalist society.

Thus, it is not compelling to argue that Marx's conception of 'abundance' demanded the satisfaction of all unlimited desires.[10] It is also possible to imagine a different kind of abundance of wealth, that is, one founded upon the abundance of *common wealth*. Here one needs to recall the 'Lauderdale paradox'; the capitalist process of creating artificial scarcity. Transcendence of the artificial scarcity of private riches as the negation of the negation requires the re-establishment of the abundance of common wealth, which is available to everyone without the mediation of monetary exchange. The point is that this rehabilitation of communal abundance does not have to negate natural scarcity.

It is noteworthy that Marx in this passage referred to the *genossenschaftlicher Reichtum* as the form of post-capitalist abundance flowing from its springs. He used this expression only once, but its significance cannot be overestimated. This expression needs to be contrasted with the opening sentence of his *Critique of Political Economy* (1859). Like *Capital*, the *Critique of Political Economy* starts with an analysis of the commodity, where Marx wrote: 'The bourgeois wealth [*der bürgerliche Reichtum*], at first sight, presents itself as an immense accumulation of commodities, its unit being a single commodity' (*MECW* 29: 269). Here Marx designated the commodity as the 'bourgeois wealth' that can be contrasted with the post-capitalist wealth, i.e., 'common wealth' (*der genossenschaftliche Reichtum*) that does not appear as commodity. Common wealth is democratically managed by the associated producers and produced according to their abilities as well as distributed according to their needs. This is exactly how 'individual property' is rehabilitated based on 'co-operative [*genossenschaftliche*] production' as discussed in the *Civil War in France*. Although Marx did not believe that it would be possible to produce infinite amounts of wealth without any natural limit, he was convinced that once capitalism is overcome there would be sufficient to feed everyone. In other words, abundance is not a technological threshold, but a social relationship. This insight is fundamental to the abundance of common wealth to be re-established beyond the artificial scarcity of 'bourgeois wealth'.

Kristin Ross calls this kind of abundance of common wealth as 'communal luxury' by demanding the 'end of the scarcity capitalism produces through waste, hoarding, and privatization' (Ross 2015: 127). Similarly, Jason Hickel (2019) names it 'radical abundance' because this form of abundance inherent to common wealth is *radically* different from the bourgeois form of material wealth that is inevitably based on ever-increasing productivity and endless mass consumption of commodities. 'Communal luxury' and 'radical abundance' are not equivalent to the unlimited access to abundant private properties in a consumerist fashion; otherwise communist society would simply preserve the bourgeois form of private riches, contributing to the further degradation of the natural environment. Since primitive accumulation created 'artificial scarcity', the 'negation of the negation' reverses the order of the Lauderdale paradox with the aim of recovering the 'radical abundance' of common wealth, making it equally accessible to everyone at the cost of private riches. In other words, the abundance of common wealth is about sharing and cooperating by distributing both wealth and burdens more equally and justly among members of the society. Only by recognizing this point can 'the narrow horizon of bourgeois right be crossed in its entirety'.

The point is that unlike the left accelerationists discussed in Chapter 5 who place their hope for a post-scarcity society in unprecedented technological breakthroughs, Marx and other theorists of post-scarcity such as Thomas More,

Étienne Cabet and Peter Kropotkin did not advocate the full-automation of production for the sake of the abolition of labour or emancipation from labour (Benanav 2020: 83). In this sense, Marx's remark about the development of productive forces in the *Critique of the Gotha Programme* is not equivalent to the 'mere' increase of productivity because productive forces are both quantitative and qualitative. For example, in a higher phase of communism, the productive forces of capital based on 'the enslaving subordination of the individual to the division of labour' as well as 'the antithesis between mental and physical labour' – the separation of 'conception' and 'execution' – vanishes, so that labour becomes 'life's prime want' as it becomes more attractive as an opportunity for 'all-round development of the individual'. This reorganization of the labour process may decrease productivity by abolishing the excessive division of labour and making labour more democratic and attractive, but it nonetheless counts as the 'development' of productive forces of social labour because it ensures the free and autonomous activity of individual workers.

Based upon this understanding, the famous declaration 'From each according to his abilities, to each according to his needs!' can be interpreted in a non-productivist manner too. Marx envisioned a society in which natural and social differences of abilities and talents among individuals do not appear as social and economic inequality but as individual uniqueness because they can be compensated and supplemented by each other. What one person cannot do well – something that will always remain despite all-round development – can be done by others, and you can help others with what you are good at. What everyone is not willing to do – unpleasant and boring work cannot be fully eradicated – can be shared by everyone more fairly. In this sense, communism does not impose conformity and uniformity upon everyone for the sake of equality, but it is about social organization and institutionalization that aims to demolish the capitalist tie between differences in abilities and skill and economic inequality, as well as the imposition of unpleasant work on a particular social group.

This alternative interpretation of the *Critique of the Gotha Programme* from the perspective of degrowth communism makes the meaning of the 'negation of the negation' clear: de-enclosing and expanding the commons for the sake of the many. Marx used the term 'genossenschaftlich' in order to signify the future associated mode of production – in this case one can simply translate it as 'co-operative', but its meaning gradually shifts into the archaic type of *Markgenossenschaften* – thus the term *genossenschaftlich* also signifies 'communal'. It is the rehabilitation of communal wealth in a higher form without going back to the isolated small-scale production of precapitalist communes. Rather, it presupposes socialized production under capitalism, but with social planning and regulation to hinder infinite economic growth and to decrease output in those branches that drive extravagant consumption. Instead, the expansion of communal wealth through basic services and public spending will enable people to satisfy their basic needs without constantly seeking after a higher level of income by working longer hours and being promoted. In contrast, it lessens the pressure for endless competition and expands the possibility of free choice outside the market.

In this way, it is possible to revisit Marx's famous discussion in volume III of *Capital* with regard to the distinction between the realms of 'freedom' and 'necessity':

> This realm of natural necessity expands with his development, because his needs do too; but the productive forces to satisfy these expand at the same time. Freedom, in this sphere, can consist only in this, that socialized man, the associated producers, govern the human metabolism with nature in a rational way, bringing it under their collective control instead of being dominated by it as a blind power; accomplishing it with the least expenditure of energy and in conditions most worthy and appropriate for their human nature. But this always remains a realm of necessity. The true realm of freedom, the development of human powers as an end in itself, begins beyond it, though it can only flourish with this realm of necessity as its basis. The reduction of the working day is the basic prerequisite. (*Capital* III: 959)

Like the passage in the *Critique of the Gotha Programme*, this has often been celebrated as an endorsement by Marx of the unlimited growth of productive forces through full-automation and a provocation for absolute domination over nature so that the realm of freedom can expand by reducing the working day.

Again, such an interpretation is incompatible with the ecosocialist character of Marx's *Capital*. From the perspective of radical abundance and degrowth communism, the expansion of the 'realm of freedom' need not solely depend on ever-increasing productive forces. Rather, once the artificial scarcity of capitalism is overcome, people, now free from the constant pressure to earn money thanks to the expanding common wealth, would have an attractive choice to work less without worrying about the degradation of their quality of life. Jason Hickel (2019: 66) nails down this point: 'Liberated from the pressures of artificial scarcity, the compulsion for people to compete for ever-increasing productivity would wither away. We would not have to feed our time and energy into the juggernaut of ever-increasing production, consumption and ecological destruction.' Without the market competition and endless pressure for capital accumulation, freely associated labour and cooperative production could possibly reduce the working day to just three–six hours. Only then will people have sufficient time for non-consumerist activities such as leisure, exercise, study and love. In other words, it is possible to reduce the realm of necessity not by increasing the productive forces, but by rehabilitating communal luxury, which allows people to live more stably without the pressure of being subjugated to the wage-labour system.

Degrowth communism produces less not only to increase free time but also to simultaneously lessen the burden on the natural environment. Certainly, the shortening of the working day is a precondition for the expansion of the realm of freedom, but the fairer (re)distribution of income and resources can also shorten the working day without the increase of productive forces. In addition, by cutting down unnecessary production in branches such as advertisement, marketing, consulting and finance, it would also be possible to eliminate unnecessary labour and reduce excessive production as well as consumption. Emancipated from the constant exposure to advertisement, planned obsolescence and ceaseless market competition, there would emerge more room to autonomously 'self-limit' production and consumption (Kallis 2020). When Marx argued that humans can organize their metabolic interaction with the environment in a conscious manner, it means that they can consciously reflect upon their social needs and limit them if necessary. This act of self-limitation contributes to a conscious downscaling of the current 'realm of necessity' which is actually full of *unnecessary* things and activities from the perspective of well-being and sustainability. They are only 'necessary' for capital accumulation and economic growth and not for the 'all-round development of the individual'. Since capital drives us towards endless consumption, especially in the face of 'the *total absence* of identifiable *self-limiting* targets of productive pursuit admissible from the standpoint of capital's mode of social metabolic reproduction' (Mészáros 2012: 257; emphasis in original), self-limitation has a truly revolutionary potential.

At the same time, as Kate Soper (2020) argues, even if the current way of life became fully sustainable thanks to unprecedented technological development, it would nonetheless not be a desirable world that could fully realize human potentialities and a good life. This is because of its constant pressure to engage in competitive work and consumption and its tendency to impoverish other opportunities for satisfying experiences and a more meaningful life outside the market. Post-capitalism needs to invent wholly different value-standards and social behaviours, and a new sense of sufficiency and well-being needs to replace the widespread aspiration to become upper-middle class. Soper's call for 'alternative hedonism' in a post-growth society, however, does not mean austerity and poverty because it simultaneously aims to enrich various non-commercial activities that are not necessarily reflected in the gross domestic product (GDP). People will have different wants. Instead of wanting destructive, extravagant and wasteful products, people will desire healthier, more solidaristic and democratic ways of living. In this way, *degrowth communism expands the 'realm of freedom' without depending on an increase in productivity and even by downscaling production.* This is how the 'negation of the negation' reconstructs the radical abundance of 'common wealth' and increases the chances for free and sustainable human development without repeating the failures of really existing socialism in the 20th century.

IV
COMMON LABOUR AS A WAY OF REPAIRING THE METABOLIC RIFT

Marx's idea of degrowth communism is founded upon the radical abundance of communal wealth (*genossenschaftlicher Reichtum*). It does not require unlimited growth because the abundance of common wealth can be multiplied by abolishing the artificial scarcity of the commodity and money and by sharing social and natural wealth with others. This offers an important insight for reconstructing how Marx after 1868 strove to find a way of repairing the metabolic rift, which he characterized as 'irreparable' in volume III of *Capital*. Carl-Erich Vollgraf judges that Marx's language here is haunted by an 'apocalyptic metaphor' that leaves no space for the future optimism and that he would not have used the same expression in the final manuscript if he were able to complete volume III (Vollgraf 2016: 130). Vollgraf's concern arises from the fact that, when reading *Capital*, volume III, one cannot find Marx's explanation about how 'the freely associated producers' would be able to 'govern the human metabolism with nature in a rational way, bringing it under their collective control instead of being dominated by it as a blind power'. Marx's silence here signifies the incomplete character of *Capital*.

Under a productivist reading, the subsequent remark about 'accomplishing [the regulation of human metabolism with nature] with the least expenditure of energy' 'instead of being dominated by it as a blind power' is understood as the manipulation of natural phenomena through intensive and extensive usage of technologies. Of course, the rational regulation of natural law is essential for the sake of successfully carrying out labour. However, one should also recall that human metabolism with nature came to be dominated by a 'blind power' not only due to a lack of natural scientific knowledge but due to the reified social relations that exist under capitalism. For Marx, this is the main reason labour in capitalism cannot be carried out 'in conditions most worthy and appropriate for their human nature' even given today's level of technology. Alien social power of capital is so strong that the recognition of natural law alone does not allow humans to regulate their metabolism with the environment in a 'rational' (that is, sustainable) manner and leads to the waste of so much energy and resources for the sake of infinite capital accumulation. Seen from this perspective, the human metabolism with nature under capitalism turns out to be irrational because it is far from satisfying social needs 'with the least expenditure of energy'. This is why as long as the dominance of this blind power of reified things persists, the metabolic rift will be 'irreparable'.

However, the question remains as to why the conscious regulation of means of production and subsistence under socialism would realize a more rational metabolic exchange with nature. This point is not necessarily clear in *Capital*, and the sustainability of socialism cannot be taken for granted. In fact, if a socialist society continues to raise its productive forces in order to satisfy all kinds of human needs, it would be a catastrophe for the environment. A more equal society is not automatically more sustainable. While the earth has biophysical constrains, social demands are potentially limitless. Marx thus came to admit that the principles of a steady-state economy need to be rehabilitated in Western society. In this context, it is worth revisiting *Capital* retrospectively from the standpoint of degrowth communism in order to envision a more sustainable future.[11] There are at least five reasons that communism increases the chance of repairing the metabolic rift compared with capitalist production.

First, the aim of social production shifts from profit to use-values. Capitalist production continues to expand, endlessly seeking after the maximization of profits. Capital is concerned about use-values only insofar as they are required for selling products. Due to this marginalization of use-values, products that are not essential for social reproduction or that are destructive of humans and the environment – for example, SUVs, fast fashion and industrial meat – are mass produced, as long as they sell well. At the same time, goods and service that do not make a profit are under-produced, no matter how essential they are. Marx's point is that by abolishing the law of value, it becomes possible to shift the focus of social production to the production of higher use-values and their quality would be freed from the constant pressure of infinite economic growth. It is true that in some sectors production must *improve* (not *grow*) because some essential sectors are currently *under*developed in capitalism. This improvement requires reallocating money and resources to provide better education, care work, art, sports and public transportation. These sectors, however, do not aim for unlimited growth, and in this sense they are already realizing a stationary economy today – a university that grows at the rate of 3 per cent per year would be absurd. The qualitative improvement of education, for example, cannot be measured using GDP.

Looked at from a different angle, these sectors are not fit to increase productivity.[12] Much essential work cannot be fully automated but remains labour intensive. Consequently, it is often treated as 'unproductive' compared with other industrial sectors that become more and more capital intensive through mechanization. Unlike the industrial sectors whose production can double and triple with the introduction of new machines, the productivity of care work such as nursing and teaching cannot increase in the same manner. In many cases, these caring sectors cannot increase productivity without sacrificing use-value and increasing the risk of incidents and maltreatment. There are thus innate limits to the increase of productive forces imposed by the nature of care work, this creates the problem known as 'Baumol's cost disease'. The more society shifts towards essential work that produces basic use-value, the slower the entire economy is likely to become.

Second, Marx stated in *Capital* that the 'reduction of the working day is the basic prerequisite' for the realm of freedom. However, no matter how much capitalism develops productive forces, work hours did not decline during the 20th and 21st centuries. On the contrary, the increasing number of precarious and low-paid jobs compels people to work longer hours. Mass production for the sake of capital valorization also increases non-essential jobs such as advertising, marketing, finance and consulting. Marx wrote about such unnecessary jobs that inevitably increase with capitalist development:

> The capitalist mode of production, while it enforces economy in each individual business, also begets, by its anarchic system of competition, the most outrageous squandering of labour-power and of the social means of production, not to mention the creation of a vast number of functions at present indispensable, but in themselves superfluous. (*Capital* I: 667)

By reducing the production of non-essential goods that are produced simply for the sake of profit-making, it is possible to significantly reduce unnecessary labour. In other words, this reduction of 'the realm of necessity' and the corresponding expansion of the 'realm of freedom' can occur by eliminating unnecessary labour and sharing the remaining work among everyone.

The paradox of capitalist production is that 'necessary labour time' that corresponds to the reproduction of the labour power of individual workers is actually spent on producing an enormous collection of unnecessary products. In other words, from the social and ecological standpoint, a large part of necessary labour is already *unnecessary* labour. This manifests in the widespread phenomena of 'bullshit jobs' (Graeber 2018), that is, jobs that even workers themselves know are meaninglessness for society. Even if these meaningless jobs are eliminated in socialism, this does not negatively affect the prosperity of society and the well-being of its members because they were meaningless and unproductive of use-values from the beginning. Well-being can even improve because spending a large part of one's life upon meaningless jobs is harmful for mental health and these jobs also create meaningless products such as excessive advertisements, intimidation lawsuits, and high-frequency trading. Furthermore, this kind of meaningless labour consumes a lot of energy and resources as well as the support of care workers. The elimination of bullshit jobs would not only reduce social labour time but also immediately reduce environmental impacts without waiting for unrealistic technological advancements in the future.

Certainly, surplus labour and surplus products will remain necessary to some extent to safeguard against unexpected natural disasters, wars and famines.[13] However, once the aim of social production is emancipated from the pressure of infinite capital accumulation, there is no need to produce an enormous and even wasteful amount of surplus products. The elimination of excessive surplus products is fully compatible with Marx's insight into the steady-state economy. This counts as 'the basic prerequisite' for the realm of freedom to truly bloom in a post-scarcity economy. In fact, utopians of the post-scarcity economy typically assume 15–25 hours work per week, but this does not necessarily require full-automation of the labour process (Benanav 2020). On the contrary, it is possible to realise such a post-work society by sharing essential work among all the members of society. However, this way of reducing work hours is incompatible with the principle of profit-making and economic growth.

Third, degrowth communism transforms the remaining realm of necessity in order to increase workers' autonomy and make the content of work more attractive. This transformation of work is essential because the realm of necessity inevitably remains in a post-revolutionary society. One need not be pessimistic about the transhistorical necessity of labour. As seen above, Marx argued for abolishing 'the enslaving subordination of the individual to the division of labour, and thereby also the antithesis between mental and physical labour', placing a high value on 'the all-round development of the individual' through labour.[14] Labour becomes 'life's prime want' (*MECW* 24: 87). Here Marx adopted a 'more optimistic view' of emancipatory labour (Klagge 1986: 776).

Through the real subsumption of labour under capital, cooperation and the division of labour reinforce domination and discipline over workers. The increase of productive forces under capitalism accelerates due to market competition only to establish the 'despotism of capital' (*Capital* I: 793). In this context, the first step for degrowth communism is to abolish the excessive division of labour that turns workers into a partial existence not capable of autonomously collaborating with others to produce an entire product. Marx's strategy for modifying work, when understood in a non-productivist manner, differs decisively from the emancipation of humans from labour through full automation.[15] In his opinion, the problem of capitalist production is that labour lost its content due to the boring repetition of simple tasks without any skill or autonomy, while full automation can strengthen this tendency without making labour 'life's prime want'. In order to end this alienation of work, Marx argued for abolishing 'the enslaving subordination of the individual to the division of labour'. De-division of labour and the expulsion of those machines that deprive workers of their autonomy and independence in the labour process slows down the economy and creates more attractive work as the basis of individual self-realization.[16]

Although Marx focused on the need to secure 'attractive work, the individual's self-realization' (*Grundrisse*: 611), this does not mean that labour becomes 'play' even in a post-capitalist society, as Charles Fourier once advocated. Indeed, Marx cautioned that this 'in no way means that it becomes mere fun, mere amusement, as Fourier, with *grisette*-like naivete, conceives it'. He continued to argue that

> ... really free working, e.g. composing, is at the same time precisely the most damned seriousness, the most intense exertion. The work of material production can achieve this character only (1) when its social character is posited, (2) when it is of a scientific and at the same time general character. (*Grundrisse*: 611–12)

Marx acknowledged that certain kinds of labour continue to exist in post-capitalism and cause suffering and pain as they are boring and tiresome. These kinds of work need to be reduced with the aid of new technologies. Alternatively, a just society needs to fairly allocate dirty or unpleasant tasks through work rotations instead of imposing them on those with less power.[17] If excessive division of labour is replaced by fairer rotation of work and equal distribution of collaborative work, this protection of the 'general character' of labour is likely to slow the production process, but this is welcome in degrowth communism.

Fourth, the abolition of market competition for profits in degrowth communism also deaccelerates the economy:

> in the absence of market compulsions, it is more likely that the realm of necessity would change slowly, by adapting innovations from the realm of freedom. The practical implementation of those innovations might take a long time, since the rush to implement changes in process would no longer be enforced by market competition, but instead would need to

be decided through coordination among various committees. (Benanav 2020: 92)

In this vein, Aaron Benanav also recognizes that there will be 'no built-in growth trajectory' in such a post-capitalist system.[18]

Finally, what Marx demanded as the abolition of the 'antithesis between mental and physical labour' in the *Critique of the Gotha Programme* is of great significance. This transcendence of the antithesis should not be confused with the de-division between material labour and immaterial labour. Marx's usage of mental and physical labour rather corresponds to Harry Braverman's concepts of 'conception' and 'execution' respectively (Braverman 1998). The problem of the despotism of capital lies in the total deprivation of workers' subjective power of 'conception', so that they are subordinated to the command of capital that decides what, how and how much they produce independently of their will and desires. As a result of the real subsumption, workers simply execute according to the imperative and command of capital. By contrast, the reunification of conception and execution requires establishing substantive equality in the production process among producers beyond their formal equality within market exchange. Marx wrote about communal production from this perspective:

> The communal character of production would make the product into a communal, general product from the outset. The exchange which originally takes place in production – which *would not be an exchange of exchange values but of activities*, – determined by *communal needs and communal purposes* – would from the outset include the participation of the individuals in the communal world of products. (*Grundrisse*: 171; emphasis in original)

The key here is the active participation of workers in deciding what, how and how much they produce. This democratic production is the direct antithesis of the 'despotic' character of capitalist production. Associated producers more actively participate in the decision-making process without the imposition of the will of the few. Hierarchal control is incompatible with Marx's vision of providing more autonomy to the associated producers, but without hierarchy, it takes more time to mediate between different opinions and reach a consensus. Since the increase of productive forces under capitalism relies upon the undemocratic and top-down character of the production process with the concentration of power in the hands of the few, democratic decision-making in the workplace inevitably slows down the entire process of production. The USSR was not able to accept this and imposed bureaucratic control upon social production. Through collective decision-making processes, workers have more room to reflect upon the necessity of their products, egalitarian relations of class, gender and race, and environmental impacts. Thus, Giorgos Kallis (2017: 12) concludes: 'Genuine democratic socialism cannot grow at the pace of capitalism, which sidelines and destroys what slows it down.'

Taking into account these five transformations that Marx demanded as conditions of socialism, one may wonder how they could be achieved without degrowth. They also help explain why degrowth communism is more likely to repair the metabolic rift than capitalism. Furthermore, economic growth does not become green simply because it occurs in socialism. As long as economic growth is founded upon the biophysical process of production and consumption, growth is not sustainable after a certain point *in any society*. In other words, Marx's ecosocialism needs to be specified as a degrowth one, and this is the conclusion that Marx arrived at after seriously studying natural sciences and pre-capitalist societies after 1868.

It should be clear by now that socialism promotes a social transition to a degrowth economy. The regulation of capital's reckless attempt to valorize itself creates a greater chance of reducing the working day and thus the environmental impact. More autonomy for workers who are free from the market competition also gives them opportunities to reflect on the meaning of work and consumption. Social planning is indispensable to banning excessive and dirty production and to staying within planetary boundaries while satisfying basic social needs. These transformations reinforce the possibility of slowing down and scaling down the economy in order to create a more sustainable and egalitarian economy. Although it was never recognized during the 20th century, Marx's idea of degrowth communism is more important than ever today because it increases the chance of human survival in the Anthropocene.

NOTES

1   The COVID-19 pandemic has also demonstrated the possibility of pulling an emergency brake on economic activities for the sake of protecting human lives. The obvious problem was that it created serious disturbances under an economic system that presupposes constant economic growth.

2   Latouche (2006) used to characterize degrowth in this way. In addition, Herman E. Daly (1992) is far from endorsing Marx's socialism as discussed below. The shift in tone can be also found in Tim Jackson (2021), although he is far from endorsing socialism or communism.

3   Harvey (2004) expands Marx's concept of primitive accumulation to an analysis of neoliberalism as 'accumulation by dispossession'. While Harvey focuses on the political project of taking wealth from the working class for the capitalist class, the problem of nature remains largely absent (see Chapter 4).

4   This is Marx's consistent standpoint since the *Economic and Philosophical Manuscripts* of 1844 (see Saito 2017).

5   The 'unprotected' (*vogelfrei*) proletariat did not automatically become diligent workers. It took a long time to subjugate them to the command of capital with punishment and discipline. In this sense, primitive accumulation is not a one-time process but must be repeated. Yet, once the regime of capital is firmly established, the situation looks quite favourable for it. Since their objective existence was basically secured, slaves and serfs worked only out of fear under direct personal domination, while workers in capitalist society work 'freely', which make them more productive in spite of the absence of such an external threat of physical violence:

> In comparison with that of the slave, this work is more productive, because more intensive and more continuous, for the slave only works under the impulse of external fear, but not for his own existence, which does not belong to him; the free worker, in contrast, is driven on by his own WANTS. The consciousness of free self-determination – of freedom – makes the latter a much better worker than the former, and similarly the feeling of RESPONSIBILITY. (*MECW* 34: 98–9; emphasis in original)

6   The contrast of wage labour with slavery should not eliminate the similarity between them. Marx used the expression 'wage slavery' to highlight this point. In one passage, he even argues that the system of wage-labour is nothing but 'veiled slavery':

> While the cotton industry introduced child-slavery into England, in the United States it gave the impulse for the transformation of the earlier, more or less patriarchal slavery into a system of commercial exploitation. In fact the veiled slavery of the wage labourers in Europe needed the unqualified slavery of the New World as its pedestal. (*Capital* I: 925)

7   Marx did not fully distinguish between private property and individual property in the second edition of *Capital* as individual property appears in chapter 25 in an utterly different sense (*MEGA* II/6: 685). In the French edition of 1875, Marx thus corrected that to 'private property' (*MEGA* II/7: 682). Engels did not reflect this modification in the third German edition. This implies that Engels was not as sensitive as Marx about the difference between these concepts.

8   Whereas John Bellamy Foster (2008: 96) highlighted the existence of Marx's ecological critique of capitalism in the *Grundrisse*, it is not necessarily clear in my opinion whether Marx was fully ecologically conscious at that time. It is relatively easy to find productivist statements in the *Grundrisse*.

9   The characterization of 'left-wing libertarianism' is also incompatible with Marx's intensive engagement with precapitalist communes after 1868.

10   It is helpful to recall that Ernest Mandel (1992: 206) defined 'abundance' as 'saturation of demand'. He continues to argue that 'a large number of goods already fall into this category in the richer countries – not only for millionaires but for the mass of the population'. Abundance already exists, but it cannot be felt as such under capitalism.

11   The abolition of the reified power of capital alone does not guarantee the realization of sustainable production because production is a material process, and burning fossil fuel means the same for the climate whether that happens in capitalism or socialism. The point is that non-capitalist society expands the room for more conscious control of production and consumption once freed from the endless competition and endless accumulation of capital.

12   This is the main reason why these sectors inevitably remain underdeveloped in capitalism and are characterized by low wages and long working hours.

13   Thus, Marx highlighted that surplus labour and surplus products always existed in any society. However, only under capitalism are they extended almost infinitely.

14   'Labour' needs to include reproductive labour. It should not be reduced to the capitalist category of wage labour.

15   The position put forward here is different from the abolition of abstract labour (Postone 1996). Considering its material character, abstract labour is not peculiar to the capitalist mode of production, and it cannot be abolished, although value can be transcended with private labour. Both concrete labour and abstract labour remain in the post-capitalist society, but the persistence of abstract labour does not result in domination by real abstraction because value is no longer the organizing principle of social reproduction.

16   Thus, the slowing down of the economy in favour of the autonomy of everyone in the production process poses a limitation to shortening of work hours. This makes it all the more important to transform the content of labour into an attractive one. At the same time, it does not exclude the possibility of introducing new technologies that will allow everyone to work more freely and autonomously.

17   Another way of allocating work is a different way of renumeration. In capitalism, high-skilled labour is often characterized by high income, which creates economic inequality. In degrowth communism these jobs will be renumerated with shorter working hours, and not with a higher salary.

18   One should add that this course of trajectory is not inevitable in a degrowth economy. One can imagine that freely associated producers can come up with more innovative and original ideas once freed from the constant pressure of profit-making. For example, researchers in academic institutions are not driven by profit-making, but their motivation comes from intellectual curiosity and joy, leading to some epoch-making discoveries.

Conclusion

Joseph Schumpeter (1951: 293) once said, 'Capitalism is a process, a stationary capitalism would be a contradictio in adjecto.' Degrowth is incompatible with capitalism, and it is essentially an anti-capitalist project. However, there has been little intellectual dialogue between degrowth and Marxism in the past mainly because of the latter's alleged Prometheanism. This needs to change, and, fortunately, it has already started to change with advocacy for an 'ecosocialist degrowth' (Löwy et al. 2022). This situation reflects the theoretical and practical progress of political ecology in the last two decades.

Today, the existence of Marx's ecology has become undeniable thanks to recent robust attempts by Marxian scholars to critically comprehend the historical dynamics of capital accumulation and its contradictions from an ecological perspective, especially by those ecosocialists who employ the concept of 'metabolic rift'. This concept opened up a space of critical engagements with other traditions of environmentalism and political ecology, including degrowth. In this context, the recent renaissance of degrowth theory provides a great opportunity to re-examine and update Marx's vision of a post-scarcity economy. Also inspired by new findings from the *MEGA*, this book attempted to decisively liberate Marxism from productivist 'socialism' by reinterpreting the late Marx as a 'degrowth communist'.

The positive elaboration of Marx's vision of post-capitalist society in this book is also an attempt to respond to those who doubt the fruitfulness of investigating Marx's ecology in his notebooks. It is true that the existence of Marx's ecology alone does not necessarily mean that his insights are useful today nor justify the need to engage with his political economy. Thus, critics express concerns about whether Marx's ecology can be applied to the contemporary world because the economic and ecological situation in the 21st century is wholly different from his time, and the level of scientific knowledge is incomparable. Others object that such a 'greening' of Marx's critique of capitalism is a mere imposition of 'our' concerns upon Marx's text, distorting and neglecting the deep flaws and limitations in Marx's theory. Due to the 'obsolescence' of Marx's theory, critics even conclude that 'Marxism has become so theoretically marginal that hopes for an "ecological Marx" are now best regarded as illusory' (Boggs 2020: 83).

Indeed, Marx was not always consistent but ambivalent in a number of points. This ought not to be a surprise. His ideas were inevitably limited by his own personal experiences as well as the social and economic structure and dominant value-standards and norms of Western Europe in the 19th century. One can thus find productivist and Eurocentric remarks in his writings and criticize them, but it would be reductionistic to reject his entire theoretical contribution because of some isolated remarks without sufficiently considering their historical, theoretical and political contexts and Marx's intentions. This reductionism is especially problematic because Marx often reflected upon his earlier flawed assumptions and developed more sophisticated views. As I discussed throughout the book, he clearly corrected his own earlier productivist and Eurocentric positions after the 1860s. By carefully tracing Marx's theoretical development during his life, it is possible to avoid infertile polemics based on either dogmatically defending the correctness of Marx's theory or blindly denying its usefulness by overgeneralizing the immature views of the young Marx. While the former attitude is obviously inadequate, the latter rejection is unfortunate because Marx is clearly one of the few theorists to have developed a systematic critique of the capitalist system. By negating his intellectual legacy too hastily, it becomes increasingly hard to criticize capitalism, especially when endless capital accumulation is the obvious cause of today's environmental crisis. This reproduces and reinforces 'capitalist realism'.

One should note that digging into unpublished writings of Karl Marx through the *MEGA* is *not* yet another attempt to deify his omnipotent worldview that perfectly predicted the environmental catastrophe in the Anthropocene. At the same time, my extensive investigation of Marx's notebooks in my earlier work, *Karl Marx's Ecosocialism: Capital, Nature and the Unfinished Critique of Political Economy*, did not aim to save Marx by demonstrating the 'mere' fact that he was interested in ecological issues. Such a philological quibble would only be relevant to Marxian scholars who wish to defend Marx's *Capital* as a bible. The discussion in the current book should once again make it clear that Marx's project of political economy essentially remains unfinished, and *Capital* did not explain everything.[1]

Even if Marx's ecological project cannot be directly applied to today's situation in the Anthropocene, his notebooks offer useful hints that enable us to speculate how Marx would have developed his critique further if he were able to integrate recent scientific findings into his critique of political economy. This is the task that today's Marxists are expected to fulfil because *it offers a wholly new vision of post-capitalism* after the collapse of the USSR. In this sense, *Karl Marx's Ecosocialism* was a preparation for *going beyond Capital* in order to open up new dialogues with other currents of environmentalism in the Anthropocene and to more concretely envision a post-capitalist future. Yet, going beyond *Capital* is not equivalent to denying it. Marx's ecological critique of capitalism in *Capital* provides an indispensable methodological foundation for a critical understanding of capitalist ecological destruction. With this methodology, more recent scientific discoveries on the Earth system, soil and marine ecology, and climate change can be used to supplement Marx's ecosocialist critique of capitalism. This will substantiate the idea of degrowth communism further.

Unfortunately, Marx did not elaborate on the idea of degrowth communism. Until his death, he was struggling with various theoretical inconsistencies and limitations, especially those having to do with the development of productive forces. After all, he was not able to fully correct and expand his earlier arguments in volumes II and III of *Capital* in the 1870s, which sometimes leaves the impression that he remained a productivist and Eurocentric thinker. That negative impression multiplied after his death partly because even Engels, the founder of Marxism, was not able to fully understand what Marx was seeking beyond *Capital*. This is not meant to negate Engels's great achievements in the history of Marxism. Without Engels's reassembling of Marx's theory, the enormous success of Marxism in the 20th century would have been impossible.

Nonetheless, the reason for Engels's success largely owes to his 'simplification' of Marx's theory in addition to his own sharp analyses of concrete social and political events. Engels recognized that the extensive scope of Marx's project went far beyond the short-sighted interests of the working class, which would make the wide reception of Marx's theory among workers difficult. The essence of Engels's theoretical endeavour is thus not a simple 'deformation' of Marx's theory based on an insufficient understanding, but rather an intentional 'reconstruction' of its key elements in a way that was adjustable to and compatible with socialist and workers' movements in his time. 'Marxism' for Engels provided a comprehensive intellectual orientation for the working class as a counter-ideology against the main capitalist ideology of modernization. In this attempt, however, Engels ended up overemphasizing some aspects of Marx's theory, such as 'rationalism', 'positivism', 'progressive view of history', 'productivism' and 'Eurocentrism'.

Insofar as the secret of Engels's success was based on his uncritical appraisal of the modernization process, 'Marxism' was not able to provide the theoretical scope necessary to truly go beyond modern capitalist society. As Immanuel Wallerstein (1979) pointed out, Marxism in the 'centres' of the capitalist world-system turned into social democracy that demands reforms of the capitalist economy and representative democracy. In the 'semi-peripheries' and 'peripheries' where socialist revolutions succeeded, Wallerstein argued, Marxism functioned as an ideology that legitimized industrialization and modernization in the form of un-democratic 'state capitalism'.[2] As a result, the 'actually existing socialist countries' remained trapped within the global capitalist system of sovereign states.

It is in this sense that Engels's theoretical intervention – more or less legitimately – came to be regarded as responsible for the political dogmatization of 'Marxism' as well as for 'deformation' of Marx's theory. Although Engels shared many views with Marx, there were theoretical differences between them. This is not surprising as they were two different people after all. Engels's philosophical project was not quite compatible with Marx's late theoretical endeavours. This is why distinguishing Marx and Engels is an indispensable condition for going beyond *Capital*.

As discussed in this volume, it is worth revisiting Georg Lukács in this context as he criticized Engels already in the 1920s and contributed to the formation of Western Marxism. Even though his critique of Engels caused grave misunderstandings due to his careless formulation and ended up being criticized for inconsistencies and ambivalences by other Marxists, Lukács, unlike the later Western Marxists, integrated Marx's concept of 'metabolism'. He successfully developed a Marxian methodology to thematize the tense relationship between humans and nature under capitalism. Lukács's 'methodological dualism' – not 'ontological dualism' – elaborated in *Tailism and the Dialectic*, is loyal to Marx's own method of political economy. His Hegelian concept of the 'identity of identity and non-identity' also makes an essential contribution to critically comprehending the historical dynamics of capital accumulation and its limits even in the Anthropocene.

Marx's dualist methodology is of great significance in the Anthropocene as it opens up an alternative to the recent popular discourse on post-Cartesian ontology between humans and nature. Various forms of dualism are certainly inadequate to respond to the multi-stranded crisis of the Anthropocene, a crisis characterized by the entanglement of the natural and the social. However, flat ontologies or other forms of monism are not the only alternatives to Cartesian dualism. Since the analytical distinction between society and nature does not necessarily mean Cartesian dualism, many monist critiques of the Cartesian dualism often attributed to Marxism are strawmen in that they exclude the possibilities of more productive 'dualist' approaches a priori. Jason W. Moore employs such a strawman argument against the metabolic rift approach, but Marx's methodological dualism is founded upon his unique conception of 'material' (*Stoff*) and 'form' (*Form*), which is essential to grasp the historical particularity of capitalist production and its contradiction with the material conditions for sustainable production. The social and the natural are deeply intertwined in reality, and pristine nature does not exist anymore, but it is nonetheless necessary to distinguish between the social and the natural *analytically*.

While Alf Hornborg and Andreas Malm have already defended the validity of such analytical dualism against Bruno Latour and Moore, the current book also aims to go further by demonstrating that Marx's methodological dualism has theoretical consequences for his vision of post-capitalism.[3] In contrast to the recent revival of post-capitalism based on the *Grundrisse*, which is still haunted by productivist attitudes under the name of the stewardship of the earth, Marx actually changed his understanding of productive forces of capital in the beginning of the 1860s in a manner that is consistent with his methodological dualism. By paying attention to the intertwined character of form and matter, the late Marx became aware of the likelihood that the annihilation of productive forces of capital will result in the decrease of social productivity for the sake of more autonomous and sustainable production in democratic socialism. This awareness represents a clear contrast to the left accelerationism based on full automation, and it offers a wholly new vision of post-capitalism. For Marx in the 1870s, a post-scarcity society need not be grounded upon technocratic development of productive forces. The abundance of 'common/communal wealth' (*der genossenschaftliche Reichtum*) that appears in his *Critique of the Gotha Programme* enables to integrate degrowth into a Marxian vision of post-capitalist society, although such a possibility was completely neglected for such a long time. In this vein, I revisited *Capital* in the final chapter in order to truly go beyond it by explicating why Marx's vision of degrowth communism can increase the chance of establishing a more equal and sustainable society beyond capital's regime of infinite economic growth at the cost of our invaluable planet.

Admitting the current political unpopularity of 'degrowth communism', the term intends to highlight differences not only from the increasingly popular vision of green capitalism but also from technocratic ecosocialism. Ecosocialism, like green capitalism, can be growth driven, but it will not be sustainable. Degrowth communism as a variant of ecosocialism aims for a post-scarcity society without economic growth. It aims to rehabilitate the abundance of common wealth against the artificial scarcity created by capital. If so, Marxism needs to be thoroughly reinterpreted from this standpoint of 'ecosocialist degrowth' without negating Marx's theory of value, reification, class and socialism. This bold renewal of Marx's post-capitalism after the collapse of the USSR is indispensable in order to enrich dialogues with non-Marxian environmentalism and to envision the possibility of human survival in the Anthropocene. Whether the political project of degrowth communism will inevitably remain 'illusory' will be judged by history.

NOTES

1   The impression that Marx's ecology depends excessively on the outdated science of the 19th century is the result of a one-sided focus on his reception of Justus von Liebig in *Capital*. However, it is not necessary to absolutize Liebig's critique of the robbery system of agriculture. Marx corrected his overvaluation of Liebig's critique of robbery agriculture in the second edition of *Capital* (Saito 2017).

2   The same point was recently put forward by Branko Milanović (2019) about China. In this sense, what he discusses as 'political capitalism' is nothing new to Marxism.

3   Now Hornborg (2020) also argues for degrowth, but his vision of a post-capitalist future remains abstract. Malm (2021) remains silent with regard to this point.

References

Adamiak, Richard. 1974. 'Marx, Engels and Dühring'. *Journal of the History of Ideas* 35 (1): 98–112.

Adorno, Theodor W. [1966] 1990. *Negative Dialectics*. London: Routledge.

———. 1974. *Philosophische Terminologie zur Einleitung*. Vol. 2. Frankfurt am Main: Suhrkamp.

Akashi, Hideto. 2016. 'The Elasticity of Capital and Ecological Crisis'. *Marx-Engels-Jahrbuch* 2015/16 (1): 45–58.

———. 2021. 'Rate of Profit, Cost Price and Turnover of Capital: An Examination of the Manuscript for *Capital* in MEGA II/4.3'. *Marxism 21* 18 (3): 140–76.

Althusser, Louis. 2001. *Lenin and Philosophy and Other Essays*. New York: Monthly Review Press.

———. 2005. *For Marx*. London: Verso.

Amin, Samir. 2018. *Modern Imperialism, Monopoly Finance Capital and Marx's Law of Value*. New York: Monthly Review Press.

Anderson, Kevin B. 2010. *Marx at the Margins: On Nationalism, Ethnicity and Non-Western Societies*. Chicago: Chicago University Press.

Anderson, Perry. 1976. *Considerations on Western Marxism*. London: NLB.

Anguélov, Stéfan. 1980. 'Reflection and Practice'. In *Contemporary East European Marxism*, edited by Edward D'Angelo, David H. DeGrood, Pasquale N. Russo and William W. Stein, 1:125–34. Amsterdam: B. R. Grüner Publishing Co.

Arato, Andrew, and Paul Breines. 1979. *The Young Lukács and the Origins of Western Marxism*. London: Pluto Press.

Arboleda, Martin. 2020. *Planetary Mine Territories of Extraction under Late Capitalism*. London: Verso.

Aronoff, Kate, Alyssa Battistoni, Daniel Aldana Cohen and Thea Riofrancos. 2019. *A Planet to Win: Why We Need a Green New Deal*. London: Verso.

Avineri, Shlomo. 1969. *Karl Marx on Colonialism and Modernization: His Despatches and Other Writings on China, India, Mexico, the Middle East and North Africa*. New York: Anchor Books.

———. 1970. *The Social and Political Thought of Karl Marx*. Cambridge: Cambridge University Press.

Badiou, Alain. 2008. 'Live Badiou: Interview with Alain Badiou'. In *Alain Badiou: Live Theory*, edited by Oliver Feltham, 136–9. London: Continuum.

Ball, Terence. 1979. 'Marx and Darwin: A Reconsideration'. *Political Theory* 7 (4): 469–83.

Barca, Stephania. 2020. *Forces of Reproduction: Notes for a Counter-Hegemonic Anthropocene*. Oxford: Oxford University Press.

Bastani, Aaron. 2019. *Fully Automated Luxury Communism: A Manifesto*. London: Verso.

Battistoni, Alyssa. 2017. 'Bringing in the Work of Nature: From Natural Capital to Hybrid Labor'. *Political Theory* 45 (1): 5–31.

Beck, Ulrich. 1992. *Risk Society: Towards a New Modernity*. London: Sage.

Benanav, Aaron. 2020. *Automation and the Future of Work*. London: Verso.

Benjamin, Walter. 2003. *Selected Writings: 1938–1940*. Cambridge, MA: The Belknap Press of Harvard University Press.

Benton, Ted. 1989. 'Marxism and Natural Limits: An Ecological Critique and Reconstruction'. *New Left Review* I/178 (November/December): 51–86.

Berlin, Isaiah. [1948] 2013. *Karl Marx*. Princeton: Princeton University Press.

Blackledge, Paul. 2020. 'Engels vs Marx? Two Hundred Years of Frederick Engels'. *Monthly Review* 72 (1): 21–39.

Boggs, Carl. 2020. 'Was Karl Marx an Ecosocialist?'. *Fast Capitalism* 17 (2): 67–94.

Bonneuil, Christoph, and Jean-Baptiste Fressoz. 2016. *The Shock of The Anthropocene: The Earth, History and Us*. London: Verso.

Boyd, William, W. Scott Prudham and Rachel A. Schurman. 2001. 'Industrial Dynamics and the Problem of Nature'. *Society and Natural Resources* 14 (7): 555–70.

Brand, Ulrich, and Markus Wissen. 2021. *Imperial Mode of Living*. London: Verso.

Brassier, Ray. 2014. 'Prometheanism and Its Critics'. In *#Accelerate: The Accelerationist Reader*, edited by Robin Mackay and Armen Avanessian, 467–87. Falmouth: Urbanomic.

Braverman, Harry. 1998. *Labour and Monopoly Capital: The Degradation of Work in the Twentieth Century*. 25th anniversary edition. New York: Monthly Review Press.

Breakthrough Institute. 2015. *The Ecomodernist Manifesto*. http://www.ecomodernism. org/. Accessed 7 September 2022.

Brock, William H. 1997. *Justus von Liebig: The Chemical Gatekeeper*. Cambridge: Cambridge University Press.

Brownhill, Leigh, Salvatore Engel-Di Mauro, Terran Giacomini, Ana Isla, Michael Löwy and Terisa E. Turner, eds. 2022. *The Routledge Handbook of Ecosocialism*. London: Routledge.

Buck-Morss, Susan. 1977. *The Origin of Negative Dialectics: Theodor W. Adorno, Walter Benjamin and the Frankfurt Institute*. New York: The Free Press.

Burkett, Paul. 1999. *Marx and Nature: A Red and Green Perspective*. New York: Palgrave.

———. [2001] 2013. 'Lukács on Science: A New Act in the Tragedy'. *Historical Materialism* 21 (3): 3–15.

———. 2005. 'Marx's Vision of Sustainable Human Development'. *Monthly Review* 57 (5): 34–62.

———. 2006. *Marxism and Ecological Economics: Toward a Red and Green Political Economy*. Leiden: Brill.

Carr, E. H. 1934. *Karl Marx: A Study in Fanaticism*. New York: J. M. Dent & Sons.

Carver, Terrell. 1983. *Marx and Engels: The Intellectual Relationship*. Brighton: Wheatsheaf.

Cassegård, Carl. 2017. 'Eco-Marxism and the Critical Theory of Nature: Two Perspectives on Ecology and Dialectics'. *Distinktion* 18 (3): 314–32.

———. 2021. *Toward a Critical Theory of Nature: Capital, Ecology and Dialectics*. New York: Bloomsbury.

Castree, Noel. 2001. 'Socializing Nature: Theory, Practice and Politics'. In *Social Nature: Theory, Practice and Politics*, edited by Noel Castree and Bruce Braun, 1–21. Malden, MA: Blackwell Publishers.

———. 2002. 'False Antitheses? Marxism, Nature and Actor–Networks'. *Antipode* 34 (1): 111–46.

———. 2005. *Nature*. London: Routledge.

———. 2013. *Making Sense of Nature*. London: Routledge.

Césaire, Aimé. [1955] 2000. *Discourse on Colonialism*. New York: Monthly Review Press.

Chakrabarty, Dipesh. 2009. 'The Climate of History: Four Theses'. *Critical Inquiry* 35 (2): 197–222.

———. 2010. *Provincializing Europe: Postcolonial Thought and Historical Difference*. Princeton: Princeton University Press.

Clark, Brett. 2002. 'The Indigenous Environmental Movement in the United States: Transcending Borders in Struggles against Mining, Manufacturing and the Capitalist State'. *Organization and Environment* 15 (4): 410–42.

Clark, Brett, and John Bellamy Foster. 2009. 'Ecological Imperialism and the Global Metabolic Rift: Unequal Exchange and the Guano/Nitrates Trade'. *International Journal of Comparative Sociology* 50 (3–4): 311–34.

———. 2010. 'The Dialectic of Social and Ecological Metabolism: Marx, Mészáros and the Absolute Limits of Capital'. *Socialism and Democracy* 24 (2): 124–38.

Clark, Brett, and Richard York. 2005. 'Carbon Metabolism: Global Capitalism, Climate Change and the Biospheric Rift'. *Theory and Society* 34 (4): 391–428.

———. 2008. 'Rifts and Shifts: Getting to the Root of Environmental Crisis'. *Monthly Review* 60 (6): 13–24.

Clark, John. 1984. *The Anarchist Moment Reflections on Culture, Nature and Power*. Montréal: Black Rose Books.

Clastres, Pierre. 1989. *Society against the State: Essays in Political Anthropology*. New York: Zone Books.

Cohen, G. A. [1978] 2000. *Karl Marx's Theory of History: A Defence*. Princeton: Princeton University Press.

———. 1995. *Self-Ownership, Freedom and Equality*. Cambridge: Cambridge University Press.

Colletti, Lucio. 1973. *Marxism and Hegel*. London: NLB.

Commoner, Barry. 1971. *The Closing Circle*. New York: Knopf.

Congdon, Lee. 2007. 'Apotheosizing the Party: Lukács's "Chvostismus und Dialektik"'. *Studies in East European Thought* 59 (4): 281–92.

Cook, Deborah. 2011. *Adorno on Nature*. London: Routledge.

Crutzen, Paul J. 2006. 'Albedo Enhancement by Stratospheric Sulfur Injections'. *Climate Change* 77 (July): 211–19.

Crutzen, Paul J., and Eugene F. Stoermer. 2000. 'The "Anthropocene"'. *Global Change Newsletter* 41 (May): 17.

Cushman, Gregory T. 2013. *Guano and the Opening of the Pacific World*. Cambridge: Cambridge University Press.

Cuyvers, Ludo. 2020. 'Why Did Marx's Capital Remain Unfinished? On Some Old and New Arguments'. *Science and Society* 84 (1): 13–41.

Daly, Herman E. 1991. *Steady-State Economics: Second Edition with New Essays*. Washington, DC: Island Press.

———. 1998. 'The Return of Lauderdale's Paradox'. *Ecological Economics* 25 (1): 21–3.

Deborin, Abram. 1924. 'Lukács und seine Kritik des Marxismus'. *Arbeiler-Literatur*, no. 10, 615–40.

Dellheim, Judith, and Frieder Otto Wolf, eds. 2018. *The Unfinished System of Karl Marx: Critically Reading Capital as a Challenge for Our Time*. New York: Palgrave.

Deutscher, Isaac. 1967. *The Unfinished Revolution: Russia 1917–1967*. London: Oxford University Press.

Drapeau, Thierry. 2017. '"Look at Our Colonial Struggles": Ernest Jones and the Anti-colonialist Challenge to Marx's Conception of History'. *Critical Sociology* 45 (7–8): 1195–208.

Drucker, Peter. 1993. *Post-capitalist Society*. New York: HaperBusiness.

Dunayevskaya, Raya. 1973. *Philosophy and Revolution: From Hegel to Sartre and from Marx to Mao*. New York: Columbia University Press.

Ehrlich, Paul R., and Anne H. Ehrlich. 1990. *The Population Explosion*. New York: Simon & Schuster.

Engel-Di Mauro, Salvatore. 2014. *Ecology, Soils and the Left: An Ecosocial Approach*. New York: Palgrave.

Extinction Rebellion. 2019. *This Is Not a Drill: An Extinction Rebellion Handbook*. London: Penguin.

Federici, Silvia. 2004. *Caliban and the Witch: Women, the Body and Primitive Accumulation*. New York: Autonomedia.

Feenberg, Andrew. 1981. *Lukács, Marx and the Sources of Critical Theory*. Totowa, NJ: Rowman and Littlefield.

———. 2015. 'Fracchia and Burkett on Tailism and the Dialectic'. *Historical Materialism* 23 (2): 228–38.

———. 2017. 'Why Students of the Frankfurt School Will Have to Read Lukács'. *The Palgrave Handbook of Critical Theory*, edited by Michael J. Thompson, 109–33. New York: Palgrave.

Ferkiss, Victor. 1993. *Nature, Technology and Society: Cultural Roots of the Current Environmental Crisis*. New York: New York University Press.

Ferraris, Maurizio. 2014. *Manifesto of New Realism*. Albany: SUNY Press.

Fischer-Kowalski, Marina. 1997. 'Society's Metabolism'. In *International Handbook of Environmental Sociology*, edited by Michael R. Redclift and Graham Woodgate, 119–37. Northampton: Edward Elgar.

Fisher, Mark. 2009. *Capitalist Realism: Is There No Alternative?* Winchester, UK: Zero Books.

Ford, Martin. 2015. *Rise of the Robots: Technology and the Threat of a Jobless Future.* New York: Basic Books.

Foster, John Bellamy. 1998. 'The Communist Manifesto and the Environment'. In *The Socialist Register*, edited by Leo Panitch and Colin Leys, 169–89. London: Merlin Press.

———. 2000. *Marx's Ecology: Materialism and Nature.* New York: Monthly Review Press.

———. 2008. 'Marx's *Grundrisse* and the Ecological Contradiction of Capitalism'. In *Karl Marx's Grundrisse: Foundations of the Critique of Political Economy 150 Years Later*, edited by Marcello Musto, 93–106. London: Routledge.

———. 2013. 'Marx and the Rift in the Universal Metabolism of Nature'. *Monthly Review* 65 (7): 1–19.

———. 2014. 'Paul Burkett's Marx and Nature Fifteen Years After'. *Monthly Review* 66 (7): 56–62.

———. 2015. 'Marxism and Ecology: Common Fonts of a Great Transformation'. *Monthly Review* 67 (7): 1–13.

———. 2016. 'Marxism in the Anthropocene: Dialectical Rifts on the Left'. *International Critical Thought* 6 (3): 393–421.

———. 2017. 'The Return of Engels'. *Monthly Review* 68 (10): 46–50.

———. 2020. *The Return of Nature: Socialism and Ecology.* New York: Monthly Review Press.

Foster, John Bellamy, and Ian Angus. 2016. 'In Defence of Ecological Marxism'. *Climate and Capitalism*, 6 June 2016. https://climateandcapitalism.com/2016/06/06/in-defense-of-ecological-marxism-john-bellamy-foster-responds-to-a-critic/. Accessed 7 September 2022.

Foster, John Bellamy, and Paul Burkett. 2016. *Marx and the Earth: An Anti-Critique.* Leiden: Brill.

Foster, John Bellamy, and Brett Clark. 2009. 'The Paradox of Wealth: Capitalism and Ecological Destruction'. *Monthly Review* 61 (6): 1–18.

———. 2020. *The Robbery of Nature: Capitalism and the Ecological Rift.* New York: Monthly Review Press.

Foster, John Bellamy, Hannah Holleman and Brett Clark. 2019. 'Imperialism in the Anthropocene'. *Monthly Review* 7 (3): 70–88.

Foster, John Bellamy, Richard York and Brett Clark. 2010. *The Ecological Rift: Capitalism's War on the Earth.* New York: Monthly Review Press.

Fraas, Carl. 1847. *Klima und Pflanzenwelt in der Zeit: Ein Beitrag zur Geschichte beider.* Wölfle: Landshut.

———. 1866. *Ackerbaukrisen und ihre Heilmittel.* Leipzig: Brockhaus.

Fracchia, Joseph. 2013. 'The Philosophical Leninism and Eastern "Western Marxism" of Georg Lukács'. *Historical Materialism* 21 (1): 69–93.

Fraser, Nancy. 2014. 'Beyond Marx's Hidden Abode: For an Expanded Conception of Capitalism'. *New Left Review* 86 (March/April): 55–72.

Frey, Carl Benedikt, and Michael A. Osborne. 2017. 'The Future of Employment: How Susceptible Are Jobs to Computerisation?'. *Technological Forecasting and Social Change* 114 (January): 254–80.

Fuchs, Christian. 2016. 'Henryk Grossmann 2.0: A Critique of Paul Mason's Book *PostCapitalism: A Guide to Our Future*'. *TripleC* 14 (1): 232–43.

Fukutomi, Masami. 1970. *Kyodotai Ronso to Syoyu no Genri* [Debates on communes and the principle of property]. Tokyo: Miraisha.

Fukuyama, Francis. 1992. *The End of History and the Last Man*. New York: Free Press.

Gabriel, Markus. 2019. *I Am Not a Brain: Philosophy of Mind for the 21st Century*. Cambridge, MA: Polity.

Ghosh, Suniti. 1984. 'Marx on India'. *Monthly Review* 35 (8): 39–53.

Giddens, Anthony. 1981. *Contemporary Critique of Historical Materialism*. Berkeley: University of California Press.

Goodman, David C. 1972. 'Chemistry and the Two Organic Kingdoms of Nature in the Nineteenth Century'. *Medical History* 16 (2): 113–30.

Görg, Christoph. 2011. 'Societal Relationships with Nature: A Dialectical Approach to Environmental Politics'. In *Critical Ecologies: The Frankfurt School and Contemporary Environmental Crises*, edited by Andrew Biro, 43–72. Toronto: University of Toronto Press.

Gorz, André. 1980. *Ecology as Politics*. Boston: South End Press.

———. 2010. *The Immaterial: Knowledge, Value and Capital*. Calcutta: Seagull Books.

———. 2018. *Ecologica*. Calcutta: Seagull Books.

Gouldner, Alvin W. 1980. *The Two Marxisms*. New York: Seabury Press.

Graeber, David. 2018. *Bullshit Jobs: A Theory*. New York: Simon & Schuster.

Gramsci, Antonio. 1971. *Selections from the Prison Notebooks of Antonio Gramsci*. New York: International Publishers.

Graßmann, Timm. 2022. *Der Eklat Aller Widersprüche: Marx Studien Und Theorie Der Wiederkehrenden Wirtschaftskrisen*. Berlin: De Gruyter.

Griese, Anneliese, and Gerd Pawelzig. 1995. 'Why Did Marx and Engels Concern Themselves with Natural Science?'. *Nature, Society and Thought* 8 (2): 125–37.

Gunderson, Ryan. 2011. 'The Metabolic Rifts of Livestock Agribusiness'. *Organization and Environment* 24 (4): 404–22.

Hailwood, Simon. 2015. *Alienation and Nature in Environmental Philosophy*. Cambridge: Cambridge University Press.

Haraway, Donna. 2015. 'Anthropocene, Capitalocene, Plantationocene, Chthulucene: Making Kin'. *Environmental Humanities* 6 (1): 159–65.

Hardt, Michael, and Antonio Negri. 2005. *Multitude: War and Democracy in the Age of Empire*. New York: Penguin Books.

Harvey, David. 1974. 'Population, Resources and the Ideology of Science'. *Economic Geography* 50 (3): 256–77.

———. 1990. 'Between Space and Time: Reflections on the Geographical Imagination'. *Annals of the Association of American Geographers* 80 (3): 418–34.

———. 1996. *Justice, Nature and the Geography of Difference*. Oxford: Wiley-Blackwell.

————. 1998. 'Marxism, Metaphors and Ecological Politics'. *Monthly Review* 49 (11): 17–31.

————. 2004. 'The "New" Imperialism: Accumulation by Dispossession'. In *The Socialist Register*, edited by Leo Panitch and Colin Leys, 63–87. London: Merlin Press.

————. 2005. *The New Imperialism*. Oxford: Oxford University Press.

————. 2011. 'The Enigma of Capital and the Crisis This Time'. In *Business as Usual: The Roots of the Global Financial Meltdown*, edited by Craig Calhoun and Georgi M. Derluguian, 89–112. New York: NYU Press.

Harstick, Hans-Peter, ed. 1977. *Karl Marx über Formen vorkapitalistischer Produktion: Vergleichende Studien zur Geschichte des Grundeigentums 1879–80*. Frankfurt am Main: Campus Verlag.

Hassall, Arthur Hill. 1861. *Adulterations Detected, or Plain Instructions for the Discovery of Frauds in Food and Medicine*. 2nd ed. London: Longman, Green, Longman and Roberts.

Haxthausen, August von. [1847–52] 1972. *Studies on the Interior of Russia*. Chicago: The University of Chicago Press.

Hegel, G. W. F. 1977. *Phenomenology of Spirit*. Oxford: Clarendon Press.

Heilmann, Sebastian. 2016. 'Leninism Upgraded: Xi Jinping's Authoritarian Innovations'. *China Economic Quarterly* 20 (4): 15–22.

Heinrich, Michael. 2012. *An Introduction to the Three Volumes of Karl Marx's Capital*. New York: Monthly Review Press.

————. 2013. 'Marx' Ökonomiekritik nach der MEGA Eine Zwischenbilanz nach dem Abschluss der II. Abteilung'. *Marx-Engels-Jahrbuch* 2012/13: 144–67.

————. 2016. '*Capital* after MEGA: Discontinuities, Interruptions and New Beginnings'. *Crisis and Critique* 3 (3): 92–138.

Hennig, Christoph. 2020. 'The Politics of Nature, Left and Right: Comparing the Ontologies of Georg Lukács and Bruno Latour'. In *Georg Lukács and the Possibility of Critical Social Ontology*, edited by Michael J. Thompson, 289–317. Leiden: Brill.

Hickel, Jason. 2019. 'Degrowth: A Theory of Radical Abundance'. *Real-World Economic Review* 87 (March): 54–68.

Hinada, Shizuma. 1975. 'On the Meaning in Our Time of the Drafts of Marx's Letter to Vera. Zasulich. 1881. With Textual Criticism'. *Sulavu Kenkyu* 20 (1): 69–80.

Hobsbawm, Eric. 2011. *How to Change the World Reflections on Marx and Marxism*. New Haven: Yale University Press.

Hochuli, Alex, George Hoare and Philip Cunliffe. 2021. *The End of the End of History: Politics in the Twenty-First Century*. Winchester, UK: Zero Books.

Holleman, Hannah. 2018. *Dust Bowls of Empire Imperialism, Environmental Politics and the Injustice of 'Green' Capitalism*. New Haven: Yale University Press.

Holloway, John. 2015. 'Read Capital: The First Sentence; Or, Capital Starts with Wealth, Not with the Commodity'. *Historical Materialism* 23 (3): 3–26.

Holloway, John, and Sol Picciotto. 1978. 'Introduction: Towards a Materialist Theory of the State'. In *State and Capital: A Marxist Debate*, edited by John Holloway and Sol Picciotto, 1–31. London: Edward Arnold.

Honneth, Axel. 2008. *Reification: A New Look at an Old Idea*. Oxford: Oxford University Press.

————. 2017. *The Idea of Socialism: Towards a Renewal*. Cambridge, MA: Polity Press.

Horkheimer, Max. [1947] 2005. *Eclipse of Reason*. New York: Continuum.

Horkheimer, Max, and Theodor W. Adorno. [1944] 2007. *Dialectic of Enlightenment: Philosophical Fragments*. Redwood City, CA: Stanford University Press.

Hornborg, Alf. 2012. *Global Ecology and Unequal Exchange: Fetishism in a Zero-Sum World*. London: Routledge.

————. 2015. 'The Political Ecology of the Technocene Uncovering Ecologically Unequal Exchange in the World-System'. In *The Anthropocene and the Global Environmental Crisis: Rethinking Modernity in a New Epoch*, edited by Clive Hamilton, Christophe Bonneuil and Francois Gemenne, 57–69. London: Routledge.

————. 2016. *Global Magic: Technologies of Appropriation from Ancient Rome to Wall Street*. New York: Palgrave.

————. 2020. *Nature, Society and Justice in the Anthropocene: Unravelling the Money–Energy–Technology Complex*. Cambridge: Cambridge University Press.

Hornborg, Alf, and Joan Martinez-Alier. 2016. 'Ecologically Unequal Exchange and Ecological Debt'. *Journal of Political Ecology* 23 (1): 328–33.

Illich, Ivan. 1977. 'Disabling Professions'. In *Disabling Professions*, edited by Ivan Illich, Irving Kenneth Zola, John McKnight, Johnathan Caplan and Harley Shaiken, 11–40. London: Marion Boyars.

Infranca, Antonio, and Miguel Vedda. 2020. 'Ontology and Labor in Lukács' Late Thought'. In *Georg Lukács and the Possibility of Critical Social Ontology*, edited by Michael J. Thompson, 13–27. Leiden: Brill.

Jackson, Tim. 2021. *Post Growth: Life after Capitalism*. Cambridge, MA: Polity.

Jacoby, Russell. 1983. 'Western Marxism'. In *A Dictionary of Marxist Thought*, edited by Tom Bottomore, 581–4. Oxford: Blackwell.

Jahn, Thomas und Peter Wehling. 1998. 'Gesellschaftliche Naturverhältnisse - Konturen eines theoretischen Konzepts'. In *Soziologie und Natur: Theoretische*, edited by Karl-Werner Brand, 75–93. Opladen: Leske + Budrich.

Jameson, Fredric. 2011. 'Dresden's Clocks'. *New Left Review* 71 (September/October): 141–52.

————. 2016. *An American Utopia Dual Power and the Universal Army*. Edited by Slavoj Žižek. London: Verso.

Jani, Pranav. 2002. 'Karl Marx, Eurocentrism and the 1857 Revolt in British India'. In *Marxism, Modernity and Postcolonial Studies*, edited by Crystal Bartolovich and Neil Lazarus, 81–97. Cambridge: Cambridge University Press.

Jay, Martin. 1984. *Marxism and Totality: The Adventures of a Concept from Lukács to Habermas*. Berkeley: University of California Press.

Jevons, W. Stanley. 1865. *An Inquiry Concerning the Progress of Nation, and the Probable Exhaustion of Our Coal-Mines*. London: Macmillan and Co.

Jones, Gareth Stedman. 1971. 'The Marxism of the Early Lukács: An Evaluation'. *New Left Review* 1 (70): 27–64.

————. 2016. *Karl Marx: Greatness and Illusion*. Cambridge, MA: Belknap Press.

Jordan, Zbigniew A. 1967. *The Evolution of Dialectical Materialism*. London: Macmillan.

Kallis, Giorgos. 2017. 'Socialism Without Growth'. *Capitalism Nature Socialism* 30 (2): 189–206.

———. 2020. *Limits: Why Malthus Was Wrong and Why Environmentalists Should Care*. Redwood City, CA: Stanford University Press.

Kangal, Kaan. 2020. *Friedrich Engels and the Dialectics of Nature*. New York: Palgrave.

Kapp, Karl William. [1963] 2000. *Social Costs of Business Enterprise*. Nottingham: Russell Press.

Keynes, John Maynard. [1930] 1971. 'Economic Possibilities for Our Grandchildren'. In *The Collected Writings of John Maynard Keynes*. Vol. 9, *Essays in Persuasion*, edited by Donald E. Moggridge, 321–32. London: Macmillan.

Klagge, James C. 1986. 'Marx's Realms of "Freedom" and "Necessity"'. *Canadian Journal of Philosophy* 16 (4): 769–77.

Klein, Naomi. 2007. *Shock Doctrine: The Rise of Disaster Capitalism*. New York: Picador.

———. 2014. *This Changes Everything: Capitalism vs the Climate*. New York: Simon & Schuster.

———. 2017. *No Is Not Enough: Resisting Trump's Shock Politics and Winning the World We Need*. Chicago: Haymarket Books.

———. 2019. *On Fire: The (Burning) Case for a Green New Deal*. London: Allen Lane.

———. 2020. 'Democratic Socialism for a Climate-Changed Century'. In *We Own the Future: Democratic Socialism–American Style*, edited by Kate Aronoff, Peter Dreier and Michael Kazin, 78–91. New York: The New Press.

Kliman, Andrew. 2011. *The Failure of Capitalist Production: Underlying Causes of the Great Recession*. London: Pluto Press.

Kloppenburg, Jack R., Jr. 1988. *First the Seed: The Political Economy of Plant Biotechnology, 1492–2000*. Cambridge: Cambridge University Press.

Koch, Marx. 2019. 'Growth and Degrowth in Marx's Critique of Political Economy'. *Towards a Political Economy of Degrowth*, edited by Ekaterina Chertkovskaya, Alexander Paulsson and Stefania Barca, 69–82. London: Rowman & Littlefield.

Korsch, Karl. 1966. *Marxismus und Philosophie*. Berlin: Europa Verlag.

Kovel, Joel. 2001. 'A Materialism Worthy of Nature'. *Capitalism Nature Socialism* 12 (2): 73–84.

———. 2007. *The Enemy of Nature: The End of Capitalism or the End of the World?* 2nd ed. London: Zed Books.

Kołakowski, Leszek. 1978. *Main Currents of Marxism: Its Rise, Growth and Dissolution*. Vol. 1. New York: Oxford University Press.

Krader, Lawrence. 1974. 'Introduction'. In *The Ethnological Notebooks by Karl Marx*, translated and edited by Lawence Krader. Assen, Netherlands: Van Gorcum.

———. 1975. *The Asiatic Mode of Production: Sources, Development and Critique in the Writings of Karl Marx*. Assen, Netherlands: Van Gorcum & Comp. B. V.

Laclau, Ernesto, and Chantal Mouffe. 1985. *Hegemony and Socialist Strategy*. London: Verso.

Lamb, Peter. 2015. *Marx and Engels' 'Communist Manifesto': A Reader's Guide*. New York: Bloomsbury.

Latouche, Serge. 2006. *Le pari de la décroissance*. Paris: Fayard.

———. 2019. *La décroissance*. Paris: Humensis.

Latour, Bruno. 1993. *We Have Never Been Modern*. Cambridge, MA: Harvard University Press.

———. 2004. *Politics of Nature How to Bring the Sciences into Democracy*. Cambridge, MA: Harvard University Press.

———. 2011. 'Love Your Monsters: Why We Must Care for Our Technologies as We Do Our Children'. In *Love Your Monsters: Postenvironmentalism and the Anthropocene*, edited by Ted Nordhaus and Michael Shellenberger, 16–23. Oakland: Breakthrough Institute.

———. 2014. *Facing Gaia: Eight Lectures on the New Climatic Regime*. Cambridge, MA: Polity.

Latour, Bruno, and Vincent Antonin Lépinay. 2009. *The Science of Passionate Interests: An Introduction to Gabriel Tarde's Economic Anthropology*. Cambridge, MA: Prickly Paradigm Press.

Lauderdale, James Maitland. 1819. *An Inquiry into the Nature and Origin of Public Wealth*. 2nd ed. Edinburgh: Archibald Constable & Co.

Lebowitz, Michael A. 2009. *Following Marx: Method, Critique and Crisis*. Leiden: Brill.

Levine, Norman. 1975. *The Tragic Deception: Marx contra Engels*. Oxford: Clio Books.

Lessenich, Stephan. 2018. *Neben uns die Sintflut: Wie wir auf Kosten anderer leben*. Munich: Piper Verlag.

Lichtheim, George. 1961. *Marxism: An Historical and Critical Study*. New York: Frederick A. Praeger.

Liebig, Justus von. 1859. *Familiar Letters on Chemistry*. 4th ed. Edited by John Blyth. London: Walton and Maberly.

Liedman, Sven Eric. 2017. *A World to Win: The Life and Works of Karl Marx*. London: Verso.

Lindner, Kolja. 2010. 'Marx's Eurocentrism: Postcolonial Studies and Marx Scholarship'. *Radical Philosophy* 161 (3): 27–41.

Lipietz, Alain. 2000. 'Political Ecology and the Future of Marxism'. *Capitalism Nature Socialism* 11 (1): 65–85.

Loftus, Alex. 2012. *Everyday Environmentalism: Creating an Urban Political Ecology*. Minneapolis: University of Minnesota Press.

Longo, Stefano, Rebecca Clausen and Brett Clark. 2015. *The Tragedy of the Commodity: Ocean Fisheries and the Aquaculture*. New Brunswick: Rutgers University Press.

Löwy, Michael. 1998. 'Globalization and Internationalism How Up-To-Date Is the Communist Manifesto?'. *Monthly Review* 50 (6): 16–27.

———. 2013. 'Revolutionary Dialectics against "Tailism": Lukács' Answer to the Criticisms of History and Class Consciousness'. In *Georg Lukács Reconsidered: Critical Essays in Politics, Philosophy and Aesthetics*, edited by Michael J. Thompson, 65–72. New York: Continuum.

———. 2015. *Ecosocialism: A Radical Alternative to Capitalist Catastrophe*. Chicago: Haymarket Books.

———. 2017. 'Marx, Engels and Ecology'. *Capitalism Nature Socialism* 28 (2): 10–21.

———. 2019. 'From Marx to Ecosocialism'. *New Politics*, 3 February 2019. https://newpol.org/review/from-marx-to-ecosocialism/. Accessed 7 September 2022.

———. 2020. 'Ecosocialism and/or Degrowth?'. *RISE*, 5 October 2020. https://www.letusrise.ie/rupture-articles/2wl71srdonxrbgxal9v6bv78njr2fb. Accessed 7 September 2022.

Löwy, Michael, Bengi Akbulut, Sabrina Fernandes and Giorgos Kallis. 2022. 'For an Ecosocialist Degrowth'. *Monthly Review* 73 (11): 56–8.

Lukács, Georg. 1971. *History and Class Consciousness*. London: Merlin Press.

———. 1975. *Conversations with Lukács*. Cambridge, MA: MIT Press.

———. 1984. *Prolegomena: Zur Ontologie des gesellschaftlichen Seins*. Vol. 1. Darmstadt: Luchterhand Verlag.

———. 1986. *Prolegomena. Zur Ontologie des gesellschaftlichen Seins*. Vol. 2. Darmstadt: Luchterhand Verlag.

———. 2002. *A Defence of History and Class Consciousness: Tailism and Dialectic*. London: Verso.

Luxemburg, Rosa. [1913] 2015. *The Accumulation of Capital*. In *The Complete Works of Rosa Luxemburg Volume II: Economic Writings 2*. London: Verso.

Magdoff, Fred, and Harold van Es. 2010. *Building Soils for Better Crops: Sustainable Soil Management*. College Park, MD: SARE Outreach.

Malm, Andreas. 2016. *Fossil Capital: The Rise of Steam Power and the Roots of Global Warming*. London: Verso.

———. 2018. *Progress of This Strom: Nature and Society in a Warming World*. London: Verso.

———. 2020. *Corona, Climate, Chronic Emergency: War Communism in the Twenty-First Century*. London: Verso.

———. 2021. *How to Blow Up a Pipeline: Learning to Fight in a World on Fire*. London: Verso.

Malm, Andreas, and Alf Hornborg. 2014. 'The Geology of Mankind? A Critique of the Anthropocene Narrative'. *Anthropocene Review* 1 (1): 62–9.

Mancus, Philip. 2007. 'Nitrogen Fertilizer Dependency and Its Contradiction'. *Rural Sociology* 72 (2): 269–88.

Mandel, Ernest. 1992. *Power and Money: A Marxist Theory of Bureaucracy*. London: Verso.

———. 1995. *Long Waves of Capitalist Development: A Marxist Interpretation*. London: Cambridge University Press.

Marcuse, Herbert. 1958. *Soviet Marxism: A Critical Analysis*. New York: Columbia University Press.

———. 1969. *An Essay on Liberation*. London: Allen Lane.

———. 1978. *Aesthetic Dimension*. Boston: Beacon Press.

———. 1992. 'Ecology and the Critique of Modern Society'. *Capitalism Nature Socialism* 3 (3): 29–37.

Martinez-Alier, Joan. 2002. *Environmentalism of the Poor: A Study of Ecological Conflicts and Valuation*. New York: Edward Elgar.

Marx, Karl. 1973. *Grundrisse*. London: Penguin.

———. 1976a. *Capital*. Vol. 1. London: Penguin Books.

———. 1976b. *Results of the Immediate Process of Production*. In *Capital*, Vol. 1. London: Penguin Books.

———. 1978. *Capital.* Vol. 2. London: Penguin Books.

———. 1981. *Capital.* Vol. 3. London: Penguin Books.

———. 2015. *Marx's Economic Manuscript of 1864–1865.* Leiden: Brill.

Marx, Karl, and Friedrich Engels. 1975–. *Marx-Engels-Gesamtausgabe.* Sections I–IV. Berlin: Dietz Verlag, Akademie Verlag, De Gruyter.

———. 1975–2004. *Marx Engels Collected Works.* 50 vols. New York: International Publishers.

Mason, Paul. 2015. *Postcapitalism: A Guide to Our Future.* New York: Penguin Books.

———. 2019. *Clear Bright Future: A Radical Defence of the Human Being.* New York: Allen Lane.

Maurer, Georg Ludwig von. 1865. *Die Geschichte der Dorfverfassung.* Vol. 1. Erlangen: Verlag von F. Enke.

McKibben, Bill. 1989. *The End of Nature.* New York: Random House.

———. 2007. *Deep Economy: The Wealth of Communities and the Durable Future.* New York: Henry Holt and Company.

McLellan, David. 1977. *Engels.* London: Fontana/Collin.

McMichael, Philip. 2008. 'Agro-fuels, Food Security and the Metabolic Rift'. *Kurswechsel* 23 (3): 14–22.

McNeil, J. R., and Peter Engelke. 2016. *The Great Acceleration: An Environmental History of the Anthropocene since 1945.* Cambridge, MA: Belknap Press.

Merleau-Ponty, Maurice. 1973. *Adventures of the Dialectic.* Evanston, IL: Northwestern University Press.

Mészáros, István. 1970. *Marx's Theory of Alienation.* London: Merlin Press.

———. [1972] 2014. *The Necessity of Social Control.* New York: Monthly Review Press.

———. 1986. *Philosophy, Ideology and Social Science: Essays in Negation and Affirmation.* Brighton: Wheatsheaf Books.

———. 1995. *Beyond Capital: Toward a Theory of Transition.* New York: Monthly Review Press.

———. 2012. *The Work of Sartre: Search for Freedom and the Challenge of History.* New York: Monthly Review Press.

Milanović, Branko. 2019. *Capitalism, Alone: The Future of the System That Rules the World.* Cambridge, MA: Harvard University Press.

Mill, John Stuart. 1849. *Principles of Political Economy with Some of Their Application to Social Philosophy.* 2nd ed. London: John W. Parker West Strand.

Mitchell, Timothy. 2013. *Carbon Democracy: Political Power in the Age of Oil.* London: Verso.

Miyamoto, Kenichi. 1967. *Shakai Shihon Ron.* Tokyo: Yuhikaku.

Moore, Jason W. 2000. 'Environmental Crises and the Metabolic Rift in World-Historical Perspective'. *Organization and Environment* 13 (2): 123–57.

———. 2002. 'The Crisis of Feudalism: An Environmental History'. *Organization and Environment* 15 (3): 301–22.

———. 2014. 'Toward a Singular Metabolism: Epistemic Rifts and Environment-Making in the Capitalist World-Ecology'. *New Geographies* 6 (August): 10–19.

———. 2015. *Capitalism in the Web of Life: Ecology and the Accumulation of Capital.* New York: Verso.

————. 2017a. 'Anthropocenes and the Capitalocene Alternative'. *Azimuth* 9 (1): 71–9.

————. 2017b. 'Metabolic Rift or Metabolic Shift? Dialectics, Nature and the World-Historical Method'. *Theory and Society* 46 (4): 285–318.

————. 2019. 'Capitalocene and Planetary Justice'. *Maize* 6 (July): 49–54.

Moore, Jason W., ed. 2016. *Anthropocene or Capitalocene? Nature, History and the Crisis of Capitalism*. Oakland: PM Press.

Moseley, Fred. 2015. 'Introduction'. In *Marx's Economic Manuscript of 1864 –1865*, edited by Fred Moseley, 1–44. Leiden: Brill.

Mouffe, Chantal. 2018. *For a Left Populism*. London: Verso.

Musto, Marcello. 2020. *The Last Years of Karl Marx, 1881–1883: An Intellectual Biography*. Redwood City: Stanford University Press.

Naess, Arne. 1973. 'The Shallow and the Deep, Long-Range Ecology Movement. A Summary'. *Inquiry* 16 (1): 95–100.

Napoletano, Brian M., John Bellamy Foster, Brett Clark, Pedro S. Urquijo, Michael K. McCall and Jaime Paneque-Gálvez. 2019. 'Making Space in Critical Environmental Geography for the Metabolic Rift'. *Annals of the American Association of Geographers* 109 (6): 1811–28.

Neckel, Sighard. 2021. 'Scholastic Fallacies? Questioning the Anthropocene'. *Thesis Eleven* 165 (1): 136–44.

Negri, Antonio. 1992. *Marx beyond Marx*. London: Pluto Press.

Neyrat, Frédéric. 2019. *The Unconstructable Earth: An Ecology of Separation*. New York: Fordham University Press.

Nordhaus, William D. 1991. 'To Slow or Not to Slow: The Economics of the Greenhouse Effect'. *Economic Journal* 101 (407): 920–37.

Noys, Benjamin. 2014. *Malign Velocities: Accelerationism and Capitalism*. Winchester, UK: Zero Books.

O'Connor, James. 1998. *Natural Causes: Essays in Ecological Marxism*. New York: The Guilford Press.

Ohno, Sadao. 1983. 'Marx ni okeru Shakai Kouseitai to Seisan Yoshiki' [Marx's concept of social formation and mode of production]. *Keizai* 198 (May): 290–302.

Ohno, Sadao, and Hiroaki Satake. 1984. 'Marx Inyonoto no Sakuseikatei. 1859–1861' [The making of Marx's excerpt notes between 1859–1861]. *Keizaigaku Ronso* 32 (1/2): 11–46.

O'Rourke, James J. 1974. *The Problem of Freedom in Marxist Thought: An Analysis of the Treatment of Human Freedom by Marx, Engels, Lenin and Contemporary Soviet Philosophy*. Dordrecht: Reidel.

Otani, Teinosuke. 2013. 'Das *Kapital* in Marx' Selbstverständnis'. *Marx-Engels-Jahrbuch* 2012/13: 134–43.

————. 2016. *Marx no Rishiumi Shihonron* [Marx's theory of interest-bearing capital]. Tokyo: Sakurai Shoten.

————. 2018. *A Guide to Marxian Political Economy What Kind of a Social System Is Capitalism?* New York: Springer.

Pasquinelli, Matteo. 2019. 'On the Origins of Marx's General Intellect'. *Radical Philosophy* 2 (6): 43–56.

Pepper, David. 2002. *Eco-Socialism: From Deep Ecology to Social Justice*. London: Routledge.

Perry, Marvin. 2015. *Western Civilization: Ideas, Politics and Society*. Vol. 2. Boston: Cengage Learning.

Phillips, Leigh. 2015. *Austerity Ecology and the Collapse-Porn Addicts: A Defence of Growth, Progress, Industry and Stuff.* Winchester, UK: Zero Books.

Piketty, Thomas. 2020. *Capital and Ideology*. Cambridge, MA: Harvard University Press.

———. 2021. *Time for Socialism*. New Haven: Yale University Press.

Plumwood, Val. 2002. *Environmental Culture: The Ecological Crisis of Reason*. London: Routledge.

Polanyi, Karl. [1944] 2001. *The Great Transformation: The Political and Economic Origins of Our Time*. Boston: Beacon Press.

Popper, Karl. 1967. *Open Society and Its Enemies*. Vol. 2. *The High Tide of Prophecy: Hegel, Marx and the Aftermath*. Princeton: Princeton University Press.

Postone, Moishe. 1996. *Time, Labour and the Social Domination: A Reinterpretation of Marx's Critical Theory*. Cambridge: Cambridge University Press.

Pradella, Lucia. 2016. *Globalization and the Critique of Political Economy: New Insights from Marx's Writings*. London: Routledge.

Purdy, Jedediah. 2015. *After Nature: A Politics for the Anthropocene*. Cambridge, MA: Harvard University Press.

Rancière, Jacques. 1998. *Disagreement: Politics and Philosophy*. Minneapolis: University of Minnesota Press.

Raupach, Michael R., and Josep G. Canadell. 2010. 'Carbon and the Anthropocene'. *Current Opinion in Environmental Sustainability* 2 (4): 210–18.

Rifkin, Jeremy. 2014. *The Zero Marginal Cost Society: The Internet of Things, the Collaborative Commons and the Eclipse of Capitalism*. New York: St Martin's Press.

Rojahn, Jürgen. 2002. 'The Emergence of a Theory: The Importance of Marx's Notebooks Exemplified by Those from 1844'. *Rethinking Marxism* 14 (4): 29–46.

Rosa, Hartmut, Christoph Henning and Arthur Bueno, eds. 2021. *Critical Theory and New Materialisms*. London: Routledge.

Ross, Kristin. 2015. *Communal Luxury: The Political Imaginary of the Paris Commune*. London: Verso.

Roth, Regina. 2002. 'The Author Marx and His Editor Engels: Different Views on Volume 3 of *Capital*'. *Rethinking Marxism* 14 (4): 59–72.

Royle, Camilla. 2020. 'Engels as an Ecologist'. In *Engels's Legacy in the 21st Century*, edited by Kohei Saito, 171–93. New York: Palgrave.

Rudas, Ladislaus. 1924. 'Orthodoxer Marximsus?'. *Arbeiter-Literatur*, no. 9, 493–517.

Said, Edward. 1979. *Orientalism*. New York: Vintage.

Saito, Kohei. 2017. *Karl Marx's Ecosocialism: Nature, Capital and the Unfinished Critique of Political Economy*. New York: Monthly Review Press.

———. 2018. 'Elasticity, Nature and Profit'. In *The Unfinished System of Karl Marx: Critically Reading Capital as a Challenge for our Time*, edited by Judith Dellheim and Frieder Otto Wolf, 187–217. New York: Palgrave.

Salleh, Ariel, James Goodman and S. A. Hamed Hosseini. 2015. 'From Sociological Imagination to "Ecological Imagination"'. In *Environmental Change and the*

World's Futures: Ecologies, Ontologies, Mythologies, edited by Jonathan Paul Marshall and Linda H. Connor, 96–109. London: Routledge.

Sartre, Jean-Paul. 2004. *The Transcendence of the Ego: A Sketch for a Phenomenological Description.* London: Routledge.

Sasaki, Ryuji. 2018. 'Karl Marx: Economic Manuscript of 1864–1865. Translated by Ben Fowkes. Edited and with an Introduction by Fred Moseley'. *Marx-Engels Jahrbuch* 2017 (1): 238–45.

———. 2021. *A New Introduction to Karl Marx: New Materialism, Critique of Political Economy and the Concept of Metabolism.* New York: Palgrave Macmillan.

Schmelzer, Matthias. 2017. *The Hegemony of Growth: The OECD and the Making of the Economic Growth Paradigm.* Cambridge: Cambridge University Press.

Schmidt, Alfred. [1971] 2014. *The Concept of Nature in Marx.* London: Verso.

Schneider, Mindi, and Philip McMichael. 2010. 'Deepening, and Repairing, the Metabolic Rift'. *Journal of Peasant Studies* 37 (3): 461–84.

Schumpeter, Joseph. 1951. *Essays.* Cambridge, MA: Addison-Wesley.

Schwartzman, David. 1996. 'Solar Communism'. *Science and Society* 60 (3): 307–31.

Shanin Teodor. 1984. *Late Marx and the Russian Road: Marx and the Peripheries of Capitalism.* New York: Monthly Review Press.

Shiva, Vandana. 2015. 'We Are Soil'. In *Dirt: A Love Story,* edited by B. Richardson, 173–7. Lebanon: University Press of New England.

Smith, Adam. 1937. *An Inquiry into the Nature and Causes of the Wealth of Nations.* New York: The Modern Library.

Smith, David Norman. 2002. 'Accumulation and the Clash of Cultures: Marx's Ethnology in Context'. *Rethinking Marxism* 14 (4): 73–83.

Smith, Neil. [1984] 2008. *Uneven Development.* 3rd edition. Athens: University of Georgia Press.

Soper, Kate. 1995. *What Is Nature? Culture, Politics and the Non-Human.* Oxford: Blackwell.

———. 2020. *Post-Growth Living: For an Alternative Hedonism.* London: Verso.

Srnicek, Nick. 2016. *Platform Capitalism.* Cambridge: Polity.

Srnicek, Nick, and Alex Williams. 2016. *Inventing the Future: Postcapitalism and a World Without Work.* Revised and updated ed. London: Verso.

Stanley, John L. 2002. *Mainlining Marx.* Piscataway, NJ: Transaction.

Steffen, Will, Jacques Grinevald, Paul Crutzen and John McNeill. 2011. 'The Anthropocene: Conceptual and Historical Perspective'. *Philosophical Transactions of the Royal Society* 369 (1938): 842–67.

Sweezy, Paul. 1973. 'Cars and Cities'. *Monthly Review* 24 (11): 1–18.

Symons Jonathan. 2019. *Ecomodernism: Technology, Politics and The Climate Crisis.* Cambridge, MA: Polity.

Tairako, Tomonaga. 1991. *Shakaishyugi to Gendaishakai* [Socialism and the modern world]. Tokyo: Aoki Shoten.

———. 2016. 'Marx no Maurer Kenkyu no Shatei' [The scope of Marx's study on Maurer]. In *Marx Bassuinoto kara Marx wo Yomu,* edited by Teinosuke Otani and Tomonaga Tairako, 217–57. Shakurai Shoten: Tokyo.

————. 2017. 'Versachlichung and Verdinglichung: Basic Categories of Marx's Theory of Reification and their Logical Construction'. *Hitotsubashi Journal of Social Studies* 48 (1): 1–26.

Tanuro, Daniel. 2003. *Green Capitalism: Why It Can't Work*. London: Merlin.

Therborn, Göran. 2009. *From Marxism to Post-Marxism?* London: Verso.

Thomas, Paul. 1976. 'Marx and Science'. *Political Studies* 24 (1): 1–23.

Thomas, Peter. 1998. 'Nature and Artifice in Marx'. *History of Political Thought* 9 (3): 485–503.

————. 2008. *Marx and Scientific Socialism: From Engels to Althusser*. London: Routledge.

Toscano, Alberto. 2011. 'The Prejudice against Prometheus'. *Stir Magazine*, 15 August 2011. https://stirtoaction.wordpress.com/2011/08/15/the-prejudice-against-prometheus/. Accessed 7 September 2022.

Tsuru, Shigeto. 1976. *Towards a New Political Economy*. Tokyo: Kodansha.

US Congress. 1973. *Energy Reorganization Act of 1973: Hearings, Ninety-Third Congress, First Session, on H.R. 11510*. Washington, DC: US Government Printing Office.

Venable, Vernon. 1945. *Human Nature: The Marxian View*. New York: Alfred A. Knopf.

Vergara-Camus, Leandro. 2019. 'Capitalism, Democracy and the Degrowth Horizon'. *Capitalism Nature Socialism* 30 (2): 217–33.

Vernadsky, Vladimir I. [1926] 1997. *Biosphere*. Edited by Mark A. S. McMenamin. New York: Copernicus.

Vogel, Steven. 1996. *Against Nature: The Concept of Nature in Critical Theory*. Albany: SUNY Press.

————. 2015. *Thinking Like a Mall: Philosophy after the End of Nature*. Cambridge, MA: MIT Press.

Vollgraf, Carl-Erich. 2016. 'Marx über die sukzessive Untergrabung des Stoffwechsels der Gesellschaft bei entfalteter kapitalistischer Massenproduktion'. *Beiträge zur Marx-Engels-Forschung Neue Folge* 2014/15: 106–32.

Wada, Haruki. 1975. *Marx, Engels, to Kakumei Russia* [Marx, Engels and revolutionary Russia]. Tokyo: Keiso Shobo.

Walicki, Andrzej. 1969. *The Controversy Over Capitalism: Studies in the Social Philosophy of the Russian Populists*. Oxford: Clarendon.

Wallace-Wells, David. 2019. *The Uninhabitable Earth: A Story of the Future*. London: Allen Lane.

Wallerstein, Immanuel. 1974. *The Modern World-System I: Capitalist Agriculture and the Origins of the European World-Economy in the Sixteenth Century*. New York: Academic Press.

————. 1979. *The Capitalist World Economy*. Cambridge: Cambridge University Press.

————. 1983. *Historical Capitalism*. London: Verso.

————. 1999. 'Ecology and Capitalist Costs of Production: No Exit'. In *Ecology and the World System*, edited by Walter L. Goldfrank, David Goodman and Andrew Szasz, 3–11. Westport, CT: Greenwood Press.

———. 2013. 'Structural Crisis; Or, Why Capitalists May No Longer Find Capitalism Rewarding'. In *Does Capitalism Have a Future?*, edited by Immanuel Wallerstein, Randall Collins, Michael Mann, Georgi Derluguian and Craig Calhoun, 9–36. Oxford: Oxford University Press.

Welty, Gordon. 1983. 'Marx, Engels and "Anti-Dühring"'. *Political Studies* 31 (2): 284–94.

Wendling, Amy E. 2009. *Karl Marx on Technology and Alienation*. New York: Palgrave.

Weston, Del. 2014. *The Political Economy of Global Warming: The Terminal Crisis*. London: Routledge.

White, Hylton. 2013. 'Materiality, Form and Context: Marx contra Latour'. *Victorian Studies* 55 (4): 667–82.

White, James. 2019. *Marx and Russia: The Fate of a Doctrine*. New York: Bloomsbury.

Wood, Allen. 1981. *Karl Marx*. London: Routledge and Kegan Paul.

Wood, Ellen Meiksins. 1986. *The Retreat from Class: A New 'True' Socialism*. London: Verso.

———. 1995. *Democracy against Socialism: Renewing Historical Materialism*. Cambridge: Cambridge University Press.

———. 2008. 'Historical Materialism in "Forms Which Precede Capitalist Production"'. In *Karl Marx's Grundrisse Foundations of the Critique of Political Economy 150 Years*, edited by Marcello Musto, 79–92. London: Routledge.

Yaşın, Zehra Taşdemir. 2017. 'The Adventure of Capital with Nature: From the Metabolic Rift to the Value Theory of Nature'. *Journal of Peasant Studies* 44 (2): 377–401.

Yoshida, Fumikazu. 1980. *Kankyo to gijyutu no keizaigaku: Ningen to shizen no bussitsutaishya no riron* [Economics of the environment and technology: A theory of metabolism between humans and nature]. Tokyo: Aoki Shoten.

Žižek, Slavoj. 2008. *In Defense of Lost Causes*. London: Verso.

———. 2009. 'Ecology'. In *Examined Life: Excursions with Contemporary Thinkers*, edited by Astra Taylor, 155–83. New York: The New Press.

———. 2017. *The Courage of Hopelessness: Chronicles of a Year of Acting Dangerously*. London: Allen Lane.

———. 2020a. *Pandemic! COVID-19 Shakes the World*. Cambridge: Polity.

———. 2020b. 'Where Is the Rift? Marx, Lacan, Capitalism and Ecology'. *Res Pública. Revista de Historia de las Ideas Politicas* 23 (3): 375–85.

Zuboff, Shoshana. 2019. *The Age of Surveillance Capitalism: The Fight for a Human Future at the New Frontier of Power*. New York: PublicAffairs.

Index

absolute surplus value production, 147
abstraction, 88, 97n14, 133n12, 192,
   244n15
abstract labour, 24, 121, 133n12, 244n15
abundance, 8, 140–1, 160, 162, 166n26,
   210, 216–42, 243n10, 249–50
Accumulation of Capital, The (1913), 6, 14
actant, 73, 115, 117, 125, 128, 132n10
actor–network theory (ANT), 73, 116,
   134n18
Adorno, Theodor, 44, 70n12, 99n22,
   109–10, 113, 132n5
agency, 73, 91, 110–11, 116–17, 125,
   160, 196
Agrarian Crisis and Its Solutions, 64–5
agribusiness, 31
Agricultural Chemistry (1862), 15, 24–5,
   61–2
agricultural chemistry, 4, 59
agricultural commune, 194
agriculture, 15, 24–6, 29–30, 39n3, 53,
   56, 62–3, 66, 134n19, 141,
   178–9, 186, 200, 202, 205,
   207–9
Algeria, 186
alienation, 21, 24, 40n13, 59, 80, 99n22,
   122, 150, 160, 219, 222, 240
Althusser, Louis, 6, 47, 209

Amin, Samir, 220
Ancient Society, 190, 206–7
Anderson, Kevin, 16, 172, 183, 191, 196,
   198
antagonism, 13, 31, 57–8, 71n21, 172,
   216–17
Anthropocene
   concept, 104–7
   defined, 2–3
   monist approach, 3
Anthropocentrism, 104, 114–16, 120,
   125, 128–9
Anthropos, 105
Anti-Dühring, 46, 49, 51, 58
antithesis
   between mental and physical labour,
     230, 233
   of town and country, 53, 58, 67
apocalypticism, 2, 59, 111, 132n7
appropriation, 41n22, 52, 59, 65, 107,
   156, 159, 219
archaic commune, 194
artificial intelligence (AI), 7, 137
association, 151, 200–1, 204, 207, 219,
   228
autonomy, 31, 38–9n2, 104, 149–50,
   156–7, 160–1, 166n26, 239–42,
   244n16

'Baconian-Prometheanism' belief, 58
Badiou, Alain, 43–4
Bakewell, Robert, 180
barbarian and semi-barbarian countries, 178
Barca, Stefania, 106, 116, 220
Bastani, Aaron, 141
Benanav, Aaron, 137, 163n2, 233, 239–41
Benjamin, Walter, 216
Berlin, Isaiah, 176
Beyond Capital, 14, 17–18
big data-enabled, IT-backed authoritarianism, 139
binary. *See* dualism
biodiversity, 1
biomedical implants, 31
Bonneuil, Christoph, 117
Bourgeois ideology, 78
Braverman, Harry, 148, 157, 166n26, 241
Buck-Morss, Susan, 68
Bukharin, Nikolai, 76
Burkett, Paul, 4, 13, 15, 23, 38n1, 39n4, 44, 48, 68n1, 69n2, 70n11, 74–5, 85–6, 89, 126–8, 231

Cabet, Étienne, 232–3
Caesar, 197, 201, 207, 215n37
capital and ecological crisis, 125–9
capitalist production, 25, 150, 222
capitalist realism, 3, 6, 137, 160, 246
Capitalocene, 107, 114–15, 130, 131n3
capital's countertendency, 142
carbon capture and storage (CCS), 34, 130
carbon trading, 127–8
Cartesian dualism, 89, 114
Cartesian
  non-Cartesian, 119–25
  post-Cartesian, 74, 90, 104, 118–19, 135n28, 248
Castree, Noel, 5, 7, 73, 107–11, 114–15, 134n18
Chakrabarty, Dipesh, 105, 185, 191
Cheap Nature, 118, 122, 126, 131

Chernyshevsky, Nikolay, 173, 187, 189, 214n35, 215n36
Civil War, 183
class, 7, 13, 18, 26, 77, 79–84, 96n3, 158, 170, 174, 199
climate change
  climate breakdown, 1–2, 33, 129, 137
  climate crisis, 33, 37, 41n23, 167n30
Club of Rome's report, 112
coal, 27–8, 40n17, 50, 65–6, 108, 115, 127, 179, 211n7, 223
Coal Question, The, 179
co-evolution, 59
Cohen, G. A., 150, 154, 164n9, 229–31
Colletti, Lucio, 48
colonialism, 182–3, 185, 190–1, 211n10
commodity analysis, 221
Commoner, Barry, 34
commons, 142, 202, 223–4, 226, 233
communal luxury, 232
commune of the secondary formation, 194
communism, 3, 6, 8, 162, 173, 199, 203, 208–10, 218, 226–36
Communist Manifesto, The, 2, 37, 174, 178
Communist Party of the Soviet Union (CPSU), 82
concrete labour, 24, 121, 244n15
constructivism, 79, 84, 90–1, 93, 104, 107, 109, 120, 126
consumption, 1, 26, 50, 53, 123, 132n9, 160, 179, 209, 232–5, 242, 244n11
contradiction, 2, 6, 15, 17, 25–6, 29, 31, 34, 36–7, 41n19, 48, 94–5, 98n19, 104, 117, 120, 125–6, 140
cooperation, 20, 31, 87, 138, 142, 147–55, 157, 164n14, 165n15, 166n26, 227, 239
Coulanges, Fustel de, 197
crisis
  ecological, 1, 2, 5, 8, 13–38, 48, 60, 70n12
  economic, 46, 104, 161, 174

Critique of the Gotha Programme, 8, 218, 228, 230–1, 233–4, 241, 249
cruel treatment of livestock, 179
Crutzen, Paul, 106
Cuyvers, Ludo, 199

Daly, Herman, 231
Daniels, Roland, 50
'Darwinist before Darwin', 63–4
Darwin, 62–4, 66–7, 70–1*n*16, 97–8*n*15
Deborin, Abram, 82–4
deforestation, 28, 62–3, 67, 123, 179, 200
degrowth, 6, 8, 171–210, 216–50
de Lavergne, Léonce, 180
democracy, 1, 3–4, 161, 167*n*29, 209, 248
de Saint-Simon, Henri, 137
determinism, 15, 38–9*n*2, 47, 69–70*n*10, 115, 177, 192
Deutscher, Isaak, 17, 21
dialectical materialism, 47
Dialectic of Enlightenment, 113
Dialectics of Nature, 46, 49, 55–7, 62–3, 69*n*6
dialectics
    of nature, 45–7, 49, 51, 54–5, 57–8, 61, 67, 70*n*12, 71*n*20, 75–6, 83–5, 87–8
    division of labour, 25–6, 31, 45, 48–9, 51, 58, 68, 87, 97–8*n*15, 121–2, 147–8, 151–2, 155, 164*n*13, 186, 230, 233, 239, 240
domination and revenge, 58–61
Drucker, Peter, 142–3
dualism
    dichotomy, 54, 67
Dühring, Eugen, 45–6, 69*n*3

Easterbrook, Greg, 130
ecofacism, 106
ecomodernism, 99*n*24, 130, 167*n*30
Ecomodernist Manifesto, The, 130
Economic and Philosophical Manuscripts of 1844, 68, 69*n*4, 243*n*4
economic determinism, 177

economic growth, 8, 27, 34, 106, 131*n*2, 139, 207–9, 216, 218, 231, 233–5, 237, 239, 242, 249
Economic Manuscripts of 1861–3, 145–7, 184
Economist, 179, 181, 184
ecosocialism, 3–4, 6, 14–17, 182, 208–9, 216–17, 242, 249
Ehrich, Anne H., 112
Ehrich, Paul R., 112
elasticity, 33, 59, 125–9
electoralism and technology, 159–62
emancipation, 2, 5, 14, 17, 128, 137, 139, 144, 159, 167*n*29, 171, 177–8, 183–4, 207, 233, 240
end of human history, 1
Engels, Frederick, 5–8, 44–55, 61–70, 83–5, 114–20
entropy, 50, 70*n*11, 113
environmental destruction, 158
environmentalism, 3, 13, 18, 43, 104, 111–12, 133*n*12, 155, 211*n*8, 216, 245
epistemic rift, 74
'epochal crisis' concept, 128
equality, 9*n*3, 166*n*26, 201, 203–4, 206, 208–9, 229, 233, 241
Ethnological Notebooks, 190–1
Eurocentrism, 124, 173, 177–8, 182–5, 198–9, 204, 209, 247–8
excessive deforestation, 179
exhaustion, 4, 20, 24–6, 28, 30–3, 36, 53, 127–8, 179, 184, 225
exploitation, 18, 29, 31, 33, 36, 46, 97*n*14, 105, 108, 118, 156, 158, 160, 174–5, 193, 216, 243*n*6
externalization, 35–7, 41*n*22
Extinction Rebellion, 2
extractivism, 33

false identification, 157
fertilizer, 30–2, 71*n*22, 179
fetishism, 105
feudalism, 139, 189, 212*n*18

Feuerbach, Ludwig, 70n12, 79–80, 122
Fisher, Mark, 3
forces of reproduction, 106
Ford, Martin, 139
form determination, 53–4, 56, 145–7, 221
Fossil Capital (2016), 27
fossil fuel, 1, 4, 27–8, 33–4, 50, 108, 123, 127, 179, 244n11
Foster, John Bellamy, 3, 15, 23, 33, 44, 86, 110–11, 114, 120, 210, 243n8
Fraas, Carl, 62–7, 179, 200–5, 211n5
fracking, 127
'Fragment on Machines', 138, 155
Fraser, Nancy, 15
freedom, 55, 60–1, 65, 67, 136, 150, 156, 218–19, 234–6, 238–40, 243n5
free time, 140, 144–5, 222, 235
Fressoz, Jean-Baptiste, 117
Fukuyama, Francis, 1
full automation, 140

gender, 15, 89, 105, 107, 118, 241–2
general intellect, 138, 144–5, 163n8
genetically modified organisms (GMOs), 31, 127
geo-constructivism, 104
geo-engineering, 106, 113, 127–8, 130, 134n20, 167n27, 167n31
geology, 4, 16, 50, 57, 59, 65–6, 107, 179, 199
Germanic. *See* Teutonic
German Ideology, The, 40n12, 57, 67, 79–80, 154
globalization, 1, 13, 43, 184–5, 194
Global North/Global South, 31–3, 35, 37, 41n23, 105, 113, 118, 128, 131n2, 160, 167n30
global warming. *See* climate change
Görg, Christoph, 109, 132n5
Gorz, André, 156–7
Gramsci, Antonio, 76
Great Acceleration, 1
gross domestic product (GDP), 235

Guano War (1865–6), 32–3
György, Lukács, 5, 47, 74

Haber-Bosch process, 30, 33
Hamm, Wilhelm, 180
Haraway, Dana, 107
Harvey, David, 28, 43, 103–4, 110–14, 130, 132n7, 134n8, 218, 242n3
Hassall, Arthur Hill, 225
Haxthausen, August von, 186–7, 207, 212n12, 215n36
Hegel, 47–9, 54, 61, 75, 83, 91, 93, 96n2, 98n19, 99n22, 120, 133n16, 177, 248
Heinrich, Michael, 45–6, 52, 69n3, 155, 172, 176
Herzen, Alexander Ivanovich, 186–9
Hickel, Jason, 232, 234
historical materialism, 2, 14, 45, 47–8, 90, 95, 138, 151, 153–8, 162, 171–3, 177, 182, 186, 192–3, 198–9, 208, 213n24
History and Class Consciousness, 47, 74
    ahistoricity, 77
    Bourgeois ideology, 78
    contemplative attitude, 77, 79
    immediacy, 77
    Marx's dialectical method, 75
    natural science and social analysis, 76
    ontological dualism, 76
    Orthodox Marxism, 75
    simplicity, 77
    social constructs, 79
    total quantification, 77
Hobsbawm, Eric, 197
Holloway, John, 93, 98n17, 221
Honneth, Axel, 15
Horkheimer, Max, 73
Hornborg, Alf, 13, 41n22, 92, 104–5, 107, 118, 125, 149, 249, 250n3
Housing Question, The, 53
human development, 128, 182, 210, 236
humanism, 84, 117, 124, 128, 163n5
Humboldt, Alexander von, 32
hybrid, 5, 92, 116–17, 124–5, 129

idealism, 67, 83, 98*n*18, 211*n*18
ideology, 13, 34, 48, 78–80, 88, 97*n*14,
    112–13, 123, 159–62, 247–8
imperialism, 33–4, 58, 113, 183–5,
    211*n*10
India, 37, 182–3, 186, 190–1, 194, 196,
    211*n*10, 212*n*18, 212*n*21
indigenous communism, 203
industrial revolution, 7, 139–42
information technology (IT), 7, 139–42,
    163*nn*5–6, 166*n*26
innovation, 130, 131*n*2, 135*n*27, 160,
    167*n*30, 177, 240
'intellectual relationship'
    concept of 'nature', 44
    of labour
        socialist rivals, 45
Intergovernmental Panel on Climate
    Change (IPCC), 111
International Institute of Social History
    (IISG), 45
Internet of things (IoT), 7
Iroquois, 186, 206

Jahn, Thomas, 110
Jameson, Fredric, 15
Jevons, William Stanley, 28, 41*n*18, 179,
    211*nn*6–7
Johnston, James F. W., 50, 66
Jones, Richard, 152, 211*n*10
Jones, Stedman, 196–7, 199
Jukes, Joseph Beete, 50, 65–7

Keynes, John Maynard, 140, 143
Khrushchev, Nikita, 47
Klein, Naomi, 3–4, 9*n*3, 23, 34, 127
Kołakowski, Leszek, 14
Kovalevsky, Maxim, 173, 188, 190–2,
    212*n*18, 213*n*24
Kovel, Joel, 15
Kropotkin, Peter, 207, 209, 232–3

labour, defined, 19
labour power, 24, 27, 34–6, 118, 122,
    125–6, 134*n*19, 135*n*24, 140,
    163*n*4, 163*n*7, 184, 218–9, 238

Lassalle, Ferdinand, 45
late-capitalist utopians, 137
Latifundium, 202
Latouche, Serge, 217
Latour, Bruno, 3, 73–4, 107, 116–17,
    129–30, 132*n*10, 139, 249
Lauderdale Paradox, 225–6, 231–2
*Lectures on the Early History of
    Institutions* (1875), 190
left accelerationists, 137
'left apocalypticism', 59
Lessenich, Stephan, 34
Liebig, Justus von, 15, 24, 202
Liedman, Sven-Eric, 15
Limitis to Growth, 17, 38*n*1, 112
Lindner, Kolja, 191, 196, 213*n*24
locking technologies, 157
London Notebooks, 66
Löwy, Michael, 3, 15, 83, 96*n*6, 155,
    165*n*22, 178, 210, 217, 245
Lukács theory. See *History and Class
    Consciousness*; metabolism;
    ontological monism; scientific
    dualism
Luxemburg, Rosa, 5–6, 14, 34–8, 125

machine, 28, 31, 50, 106, 137–40, 143,
    147–9, 153, 155–6, 160, 174,
    178, 184, 186, 215*n*41, 238, 240
Maine, Henry, 190–1
Maitland, James, 225
Malm, Andreas, 3, 27, 92, 104–5, 107–8,
    122–4, 131*n*3, 135*n*29, 167*n*32,
    249, 250*n*3
Malthusianism, 104, 112
Malthus, Robert, 98, 111, 113, 209
Marcuse, Herbert, 70*n*12, 97*n*14, 136
Marx-Engels-Gesamtausgabe (MEGA),
    4, 6, 16–17, 45
    and late Marx, 174–7
Mason, Paul, 141, 162*n*1
materialism, 2, 14, 20, 44–9, 54, 67,
    69*n*10, 75, 77, 79, 83, 85, 90, 95
Maurer, Georg L., 64, 194

McKibben, Bill, 2, 9*n*1, 34, 73, 108,
131–2*n*4
mediation, 20–2, 25, 27–8, 40*n*13, 53–4,
56–7, 94, 132*n*6, 192, 200,
219–21, 231
Mészáros, István 5, 14, 17–23, 29, 34,
37, 40*n*10, 40*n*13, 96*n*1, 115,
156–7, 230, 235
metabolic rift, 4, 74, 119, 178, 204,
236–42, 245
abstract labour, 24
agricultural production, 32
analysis, 23
concept, 14–15
dimensions, 28
economic and ecological crisis, 29
factors of production, 24
human and non-human beings, 23
production of NH$_3$, 30
productive forces, 28
'robbery agriculture', 25
soil fertility, 30
spatial rift, 25–6
and systematic character, 23
temporal rift, 27
metabolism, 5–7, 13–42, 44–5, 52–61,
64–5, 67, 69, 70*n*12, 71*n*19, 73–
99, 103, 115, 117–24, 132*nn*5–
6, 132*n*9, 133*n*17, 134*n*19, 145,
150, 158, 200, 206
methodological dualism, 80, 124
methodology, 3, 6–7, 81, 91–2, 97*n*13,
98*n*17, 98*n*19, 104, 133*n*12,
133*n*16, 146, 247–8
Mikhailovsky, Nikolay K., 188
Mill, John Stuart, 209
mir, 186, 195
Mitchell, Timothy, 40*n*17
mode of production, 2, 15, 18, 35–7,
59–61, 71*n*22, 93, 106, 118,
121, 136, 138, 146–8, 150–9,
152–3, 155–6, 164*n*13, 166*n*24,
171, 191–2, 202, 221, 233, 238,
244*n*15
money, 18–19, 65, 93, 121–2, 126, 190,
192, 207, 218, 221, 234, 236–7

monism, 107–13, 116–19
Moore, Jason W., 5, 7, 41*n*19, 58–9, 74,
103, 114, 116, 131*n*3, 249
Moore, Samuel, 50
More, Thomas, 232–3
Morgan, Henry L., 197, 206
Morgan, Lewis H., 190
Morris, William, 209
Möser, Justus, 204

Narodoniks, 186
natural disaster insurance, 127–8
natural limits, 14, 18, 29, 56, 59–60, 104,
111–15, 126–8, 131, 132*n*8,
134*n*20, 209, 229
natural science, 4–6, 8, 15–16, 28, 38,
39*n*8, 44–54, 61, 63, 67–8,
76–8, 172–3
natural vitality, 203–4
Neckel, Sighard, 105
negation of the negation
commonification of wealth, 229
co-operative production, 227–8
expropriation of the expropriators,
227
expropriators, 227
private and individual property, 227
united co-operative societies, 228
negative emission technology, 34
Negri, Antonio, 142, 145, 163*n*6
neoliberal globalization, 13
network effects and crisis of private
property, 142–3
non-identity of nature 22, 94–5, 99*n*22,
99*n*24, 103–31, 132*n*5
non-Malthusianism, 103–4
non-Western societies, 37–8, 67–8, 173,
177, 182, 184–6, 188–91, 195,
198–200, 204, 206, 208–9,
213*n*26
Nordhaus, Ted, 130
nuclear fusion, 130

object's preponderance, 109
obshchina. See *mir*
O'Connor, James, 15, 41*n*19, 104, 125–7,
134*n*23

Ohno, Sadao, 151
ontological dualism, 74, 76, 79–80
ontological monism, 77, 79
  History and Class Consciousness, 87–8
  human metabolism, 88
  knowledge of nature, 87
  labour process, 87
  nature and social factors, 88
Ontology of Social Being, 84, 86
open technologies, 157
Orthodox Marxism, 7, 13–14, 17, 74–5
overproduction, 1, 125, 174
Owen, Robert, 137

pan-slavism, 189
Paris Commune, 197–8, 209, 215n39,
  227–8
Petty, William, 19
Phear, John, 190–1
Phillips, Leigh, 130
Piketty, Thomas, 3, 9n3
planetary boundaries, 123–4, 128, 229,
  242
Plantationocene, 107
Polanyi, Karl, 221
post-capitalism, 3–4, 6, 8, 66, 135n26,
  139–43, 156–8, 160, 162,
  162n1, 163n2, 166n26, 176,
  182, 198, 208–10, 217, 235,
  240, 247, 249
  full automation and world without
    work, 140
  network effects and crisis of private
    property, 142–3
  zero marginal cost and society of
    abundance, 140–1
posthumanist theory, 124
post-Marxism, 38–9n2, 161
Potter, Edmund, 152–3
Poverty of Philosophy, 165n15, 183–4
pre-capitalist societies, 8, 21, 64–5, 67,
  72n26, 173, 182, 185–6, 192,
  197, 199–200, 203–4, 219,
  226, 242

primitive accumulation, 26, 37, 187, 189,
  216–20, 226–7, 232, 242n3,
  243n5
primitive accumulation theory, 37, 138,
  153, 177, 185. See also negation
  of the negation
  commodification, 223
  external natural conditions, 223
  humans and nature, 219
  immense tracts of land, 224
  natural elements, 223
  original unity, 219–20
  wage-labourers, 218
Prison Notebooks, 76
private producers, 121
private property, 142
problem of sustainability, 158
production of nature, 7, 40n11, 73, 80,
  103–4, 107–15
productive forces/forces of production
  of capital, 8, 71n18, 78, 136–62,
    164n13, 166nn24–5,
    167n32, 171, 177, 185, 200,
    204, 208, 233, 249
productivism, 2, 8, 15, 43, 110, 124, 155,
  162, 166n26, 173, 177–8, 182,
  199, 205, 208–9, 216, 248
productivity, 17, 22, 28–9, 44, 48, 64–6,
  125–7, 129, 140, 143, 147,
  150–1, 164n11, 166n26, 232–4,
  236, 238, 249
profit, 21, 24–5, 27, 31, 52–3, 56, 66, 78,
  118, 121–2, 125–8, 135n24,
  140, 176, 179, 181, 193, 205,
  209, 211n9, 222–4, 229, 237–9,
  244n18
progress, 2, 8, 15, 17, 22, 25, 66, 68, 77,
  92, 110, 113, 126, 131, 136,
  139, 154, 158, 167n29, 171–2,
  177, 183–4, 191, 209, 229, 245
Prometheanism, 5, 8, 14, 43, 58, 113,
  137–8, 155, 162, 173, 186, 208,
  245

property
  communal, 189–90, 193–5, 200–1, 203
  individual, 226–8, 232, 243n7
  private, 21, 142–4, 156, 159, 201–2,
    205, 227–9, 243n7
Proudhon, Pierre-Joseph, 137, 200–1
public wealth, 225

race, 27, 59, 89, 105, 186, 216, 241–2
radical abundance, 232
rationalisation, 95
raw materials, 28–9, 38n1, 67, 118,
  125–7
realism, 3, 6, 73–96, 103, 137, 160, 246
realm of freedom, 55, 60–1, 65, 67, 218,
  234–6, 238–40
real subsumption, 146–7, 156
Reclus, Eliseé, 209
reification (reified), 55, 59, 62, 69–70n10,
  77–9, 81, 83, 88, 93–4, 96n3,
  96n5, 98–9n21, 113, 125, 149,
  160, 165n23, 236–7, 244n11
relations of production, 2, 112, 146, 148,
  150, 152, 154–7, 165n20, 171
relativism, 89
rents, 61, 142, 176
revenge, 55–6, 58–65, 73, 103, 114–15,
  127, 131
revolution, 7, 18, 27, 46–7, 83, 139–42,
  147, 154, 156, 173–5, 182–3,
  187
Riazanov, David, 16
Ricardo, David, 209
Rifkin, Jeremy, 135n25, 140–2
robbery, 5, 15, 22, 24–6, 29–30, 34, 36,
  41n23, 53, 56, 62, 118, 171,
  177, 179, 181–2, 190–200,
  202, 205, 208–9, 214n29, 216,
  250n1
romanticism, 70n12, 173, 197–8, 203,
  207, 211n8
Rome, 17, 38n1, 112, 186, 202
Ross, Kristin, 232
Rudas, Ladislaus, 82–4, 89, 97nn8–9,
  97n13

Russia, 9n2, 38, 45, 47, 69n4, 82, 96n6,
  173, 186–99, 203–4, 206–8, 212
Russian State Archive of Socio-Political
  History (RGASPI), 45
Russo-Ukrainian War, 3

Said, Edward, 182
Saint-Simon, Henri de, 137
Saltpetre War (1879–84), 33
Sartre, Jean-Paul, 47–8
scarcity, 20, 27, 38n1, 111–13, 136,
  141–2, 145, 162, 163n2, 217,
  225–6, 229–34, 239
Schellenberger, Michael, 130
Schmidt, Alfred, 48, 61, 70n12, 132n5
Schorlemmer, Carl, 50
Schumpeter, Joseph, 245
science, 5–6, 15–16, 18, 28, 34, 38, 39n7,
  44–52, 54, 59, 61, 63, 67–8,
  76–80, 85, 88–91, 93–5, 96n3,
  97n14, 98n19, 112, 123, 126–7,
  136–8
scientific dualism, 80
scientific socialism doctrine, 175
second contradiction of capitalism, 15,
  104, 125
second nature, 40n11, 79, 85
second-order mediation, 21, 27–8,
  40nn13–14, 53–4, 57
serf, 207, 219, 243n5
Shanin, Teodor, 198
Shiva, Vandana, 30
Sieber, Nikolay, 188, 190
Sismondi, Jean Charles Léonard, 184
slave, 33, 35–7, 106, 116, 118, 157,
  163n4, 183–4, 194–5, 202, 219,
  243nn5–6
Smith, Adam, 134n19, 218, 225
Smith, Neil, 7, 59, 103–4, 107, 109, 111,
  114–15
social constructivism, 79, 84, 90–1, 93,
  107–9, 120, 126
socialism, 2–4, 6, 9n3, 13–16, 18,
  22, 39n4, 46–8, 55–6, 61,
  69–70n10, 71n21, 136–67

socialist tendency, 62, 64–5, 186,
    200–1, 203
social labour, 91, 149, 153, 155–6, 158,
    160, 178, 189, 219–20, 233, 239
social metabolism theory, 14, 18–19
'societal relationship with nature'
    concept, 109–10
Soper, Kate, 20, 89–90, 119, 124, 235
spatial rift, 25–6
species extinction, 179
Srnicek, Nick, 5, 137, 140, 142, 144,
    167n29, 167n32
Stanley, John L., 60
steam engine, 27, 183
Student Manual of Geology, 65
subsumption
    formal, 31, 146–8, 158, 164n13
    real, 8, 31, 58, 71n18, 138, 145–50,
        153–4, 156, 158–60,
        164n10, 166n26, 177, 239,
        241
surplus labour, 165n21, 174, 239, 244n13
surplus product, 239, 244n13
surplus-value, 24, 140
sustainability, 9n3, 67, 128, 158, 160,
    186, 201–3, 206, 208–9, 229,
    235, 237

Tailism and the Dialectic, 74, 81–2, 84
Technocene, 107
technofascism, 106
techno-feudalism, 139
technological determinism, 15
technological shift, 30
technology, 7, 14, 18, 34, 41n23, 105–6,
    126, 135n26, 137–42, 146–7,
    155, 157, 159–62, 163nn5–6,
    166n24, 166n26, 167nn27–8,
    205, 230, 236–7
Teutonic, 186, 197, 200–2, 207, 214n32
Thunberg, Gretha, 2
time–space compression, 28
Toscano, Alberto, 137

underconsumption theory, 125
unequal exchange, 14, 33, 35–6,
    41nn22–3, 118, 133n13
Union of Soviet Socialist Republics
    (USSR), 1, 13, 15
use-value, 19, 21, 29, 93–4, 121, 141,
    147, 223, 225, 237–9
Utopian socialists, 137, 160

valorization process, 23, 93, 146
Vogel, Steven, 74, 76–7, 79–82, 84, 86,
    89–90, 92–3, 96nn3–4, 108–9
Vollgraf, Carl-Erich, 172, 176, 236

Wada, Haruki, 173, 189, 191, 196, 198,
    212n22, 214–15n35
Wallerstein, Immanuel, 248
war communism, 3
waste, 16–18, 26, 53, 65, 203, 205,
    215n37, 224, 226, 232, 235–7,
    239
wealth
    common, 8, 218, 231–2, 234, 236,
        249–50
    public, 225–6
wealth, Marx's concept, 220–6
Wehling, Peter, 110
Western Marxism, 6–7, 39n6, 43–5,
    47–9, 51, 68n1, 69n9, 74–6,
    81–2, 84, 96n2, 133n16, 248
Wood, Allen, 76
Wood, Ellen Meiksins, 4, 161
'world-ecology' theory, 104, 114–15, 118

Yeats, John, 65, 67

Zasulich, Vera, 8, 173, 191–3, 198–9,
    203–4, 206, 208, 213n27,
    214n28
zero marginal cost, 140–1
Žižek, Slavoj, 3, 43, 117

Printed in the United States
by Baker & Taylor Publisher Services